W9-BAH-242

CRIMINAL EVIDENCE

Fifth Edition

Judy Hails, J.D., LL.M.

California State University, Long Beach

THOMSON

™

WADSWORTH

Australia • Canada • Mexico • Singapore • Spain
• United Kingdom • United States

This book is dedicated to
Dr. Jan Kuzma and Mr. Lester Cushman
Who inspired me to teach

THOMSON
™
WADSWORTH

Acquisitions Editor: Jay Whitney
Assistant Editor: Jana Davis
Editorial Assistant: Jennifer Walsh
Technology Project Manager: Susan DeVanna
Marketing Manager: Terra Schultz
Marketing Assistant: Annabelle Yang
Advertising Project Manager: Stacey Purviance
Project Manager, Editorial Production:
   Matt Ballantyne

Art Director: Vernon Boes
Print Buyer: Lisa Claudeanos
Permissions Editor: Stephanie Lee
Production Service: River Enterprises, LLC
Copy Editor: Jean Privett
Cover Designer: Yvo
Cover Printer: Malloy, Inc.
Compositor: River Enterprises, LLC
Printer: Malloy, Inc.

COPYRIGHT © 2005 Wadsworth, a division of Thomson Learning, Inc. Thomson Learning™ is a trademark used herein under license.

ALL RIGHTS RESERVED. No part of this work covered by the copyright hereon may be reproduced or used in any form or by any means—graphic, electronic, or mechanical, including but not limited to photocopying, recording, taping, Web distribution, information networks, or information storage and retrieval systems—without the written permission of the publisher.

Printed in the United States of America
2 3 4 5 6 7 08 07 06 05 04

For more information about our products,
contact us at:
Thomson Learning Academic
Resource Center
1-800-423-0563
For permission to use material from this text or product, submit a request online at
http://www.thomsonrights.com.
Any additional questions about permissions can be submitted by email to
thomsonrights@thomson.com.

Thomson Wadsworth
10 Davis Drive
Belmont, CA 94002-3098
USA

Asia
Thomson Learning
5 Shenton Way #01-01
UIC Building
Singapore 068808

Australia/New Zealand
Thomson Learning
102 Dodds Street
Southbank, Victoria 3006
Australia

Canada
Nelson
1120 Birchmount Road
Toronto, Ontario M1K 5G4
Canada

Europe/Middle East/Africa
Thomson Learning
High Holborn House
50/51 Bedford Row
London WC1R 4LR
United Kingdom

Library of Congress Control Number:
2004109167

ISBN: 0-495-00138-4

CONTENTS

Chapter 3

Types of Evidence   53

Chapter 4

Direct and Circumstantial Evidence   69

Chapter 5

Witnesses   93

Chapter 6

Crime Scene Evidence, Experiments, and Models   123

Chapter 7

Documentary Evidence   149

Chapter 8

Hearsay and Its Exceptions   167

Chapter **9**

Privileged Communications   191

Chapter **10**

Developing Law of Search and Seizure   211

Chapter 11

Chapter 12

Chapter 13

Chapter 14

Chapter 15

Chapter 16

TABLE OF CASES

PREFACE

This book has been written as an introductory course in evidence primarily for criminal justice personnel. It is introductory in the sense that it is intended for students who have no legal background. It is not introductory in the sense of being superficial.

Criminal Evidence is a comprehensive evidence text. All evidentiary topics that commonly occur in criminal proceedings are included. Hearsay and privileges are thoroughly covered. Six chapters are devoted to constitutional issues that are essential to the collection of admissible evidence. United State Supreme Court decisions through May 31, 2004 are covered.

All legal texts, except those designed for use in only one state, must face the diversity that exists in the laws of the various states. The Federal Rules of Evidence provide a starting point because they are in use in the federal courts as well as in the courts of several states. *Criminal Evidence* makes frequent reference to the Federal Rules of Evidence for this reason. Codes from some of the states are also cited. The approach used in the text is to state the most common rules and definitions. Where wide variation exists among the states, students are specifically urged to consult their local laws.

Most definitions have been converted to itemized lists that are easy for the student to understand. Whenever possible, legal jargon has been avoided. Key terms are **boldfaced** throughout the chapters, as well as listed at the beginning of each chapter, in order to draw the reader's attention to the importance of these terms. All concepts have been amply illustrated with examples arising in criminal cases. Chapters are carefully subdivided into suitable teaching units.

Specifics about the Text

Chapters 1 and 2 provide a basic introduction to the American legal system. State criminal trials are placed in the larger context of the state and federal judicial systems. Variations among states and the ever-changing nature of law are explained. Chapter 2 provides a detailed explanation of the trial process and related court activities. New trends, such as allowing judges to conduct *voir dire* during jury selection and expanding the use of hearsay at preliminary hearings, are covered.

Chapter 3 defines basic concepts of evidence: relevance, direct evidence, circumstantial evidence, testimonial evidence, real evidence, stipulations, judicial notice, and presumptions.

Chapter 4 explores direct and circumstantial evidence in more depth. A wide array of situations in which circumstantial evidence can play a key role in criminal trials is discussed. A discussion of the use of the Battered Child Syndrome, Rape Trauma Syndrome, and Battered Woman Syndrome as circumstantial evidence is included.

Witnesses are covered in Chapter 5. Topics related to the handling of trial witnesses include: competence, impeachment, rehabilitation, and corroboration. The Opinion Rule is covered in depth with the role of the expert witness illustrated by examples related to sanity, ballistics, and blood matching.

Chapters 6 and 7 focus on real evidence. Preservation of evidence at the crime scene and maintaining the chain of custody are emphasized. Basic rules on the use of scientific evidence are given with background information on the scientific basis for fingerprints, blood tests, ballistic testing, and DNA matching. Documentary evidence is covered in detail. Authentication requirements are enumerated. The capabilities of forensic document examiners are discussed. The need to account for the original document is included in the section on the Best Evidence Rule.

Chapter 8 is devoted to the Hearsay Rule. Recent Supreme Court cases on the use of hearsay are covered. Over a dozen exceptions to the Hearsay Rule are discussed in detail. The use of itemized lists in place of more traditional definitions is one of the strong points of this chapter. Numerous examples that illustrate each exception make the exceptions to the Hearsay Rule easier to understand.

Privileges are covered in Chapter 9. Again, itemized lists replace definitions to assist in the learning process. Eight different privileges are covered in detail. Illustrations are included for each.

Chapters 10 through 15 are devoted to constitutional issues. The framework of the Fourth Amendment and the Exclusionary Rule are covered in Chapter 10. The numerous exceptions to the Exclusionary Rule are explained. This chapter also contains a detailed discussion of the procedures that must be followed in order to obtain a warrant.

Chapter 11 focuses on detentions. Field interviews, arrests, booking, and custodial situations are discussed. In each of these situations the grounds for detaining a subject are established, as is any right to search that accompanies the detention.

A thorough discussion of other warrantless searches is contained in Chapters 12 and 13. These chapters cite over 70 major Supreme Court cases. Topics covered in Chapter 12 include: Plain View Doctrine; Open Fields Doctrine; abandoned property; consent searches; vehicle searches (incident to arrest, probable cause, inventory, reasonable suspicion); DUI roadblocks; and administrative searches. Chapter 13 covers eavesdropping; electronic surveillance; border searches (international border, fixed checkpoints, roving checkpoints); closed containers; and employee drug testing.

Self-incrimination is covered in Chapter 14. *Miranda,* of course, is the key to this discussion. A wide variety of situations that complicate the application of *Miranda* are discussed. The right to counsel during post-arraignment interrogation is also covered.

Chapter 15 is devoted to identification procedures. All constitutional aspects of lineups, showups, and photographic lineups are discussed. This short but comprehensive chapter serves as a guide for avoiding the pitfalls of improperly handling witnesses during the identification process.

The duties of the officer once the case goes to court are covered in Chapter 16. A convenient record-keeping system is suggested to help collect all needed information. Tips are given on courtroom demeanor and dress, along with suggestions for dealing with jurors and the media.

A glossary containing over 200 terms (including all key terms) is conveniently located at the back of the book. In addition to a comprehensive index, the Table of Cases enables the reader to quickly locate the discussion and full citation for each of the over 160 United States Supreme Court cases covered in the book.

Mastery of the material presented in *Criminal Evidence* will enable a law enforcement officer to analyze the evidence collected with an eye toward building a solid case. Interaction with the prosecutor will be improved because the officer will understand what is required to admit crucial evidence. On the witness stand, the officer will be better prepared to testify because he/she has a better understanding of the strategies used to establish credibility and impeach witnesses.

Acknowledgments

The following reviewers generously provided feedback in preparation for the Fifth Edition of this text. I would like to thank:

James L. Edwards, Piedmont Technical College
Steven L. Garrett, Austin Peay State University
Alan Kraft, Seminole Community College–Criminal Justice Institute

To the Instructor

A complete Instructor's Manual is available online at http://cj.wadsworth.com/hails_crimevidence5e.

You will find lecture notes and chapter quizzes, along with rationales for each quiz answer.

About the Author

Judy Hails has taught in the criminal justice field for over 30 years. She is currently a Professor in the Department of Criminal Justice at California State University, Long Beach, where she received the Distinguished Faculty Teaching Award in 1998. She was a Visiting Assistant Professor at Illinois State University (1981–83) and an adjunct professor at John Jay College in New York City (1978–1980). From 2000 to 2002 she was also an adjunct instructor at Los Angeles Harbor College and Long Beach City College.

Dr. Hails is a former sergeant with the Los Angeles County Sheriff's Department. Her education includes: B.S. in mathematics from Loma Linda University; M.S. in criminology from CSU Long Beach; J.D. from Southwestern University School of Law; and an LL.M. in criminal justice from New York University School of Law.

She has published four well-received books, *Criminal Evidence, Criminal Procedure, Criminal Procedure: A Case Approach,* and *Criminal Law.* She has also published numerous articles in professional journals on criminal procedure, prisoners' rights, and domestic violence.

Dr. Hails is a past president of both the California Association of Administration of Justice Educators and the Western and Pacific Association of Criminal Justice Educators; she also served a three-year term as trustee for Region V of the Academy of Criminal Justice Sciences. She is an inactive member of the California State Bar.

CHAPTER 1

Introduction

Outline

Key Terms

- Beyond a reasonable doubt
- Burden of persuasion
- Burden of proof
- Case law
- Evidence
- Federal Rules of Evidence
- Harmless Error Rule
- Judicial discretion
- *Stare decisis*
- Trier of the facts
- Trier of the law

After studying this chapter, you will be able to:
- Define the term *evidence.*
- Explain who has the burden of proof in a criminal case.
- Describe the role of the judge and jury in a criminal case.
- Specify the historical changes that have occurred in the way evidence is presented at trial.
- Identify three sources of the law governing evidence.
- Discuss the relationship between federal and state rules of evidence.
- Clarify how case law can change statutory rules of evidence.
- Describe what materials are used for legal research.
- Look up a case if provided with the correct legal citation.

1-1 What Is Evidence?

We all use **evidence** every day. For example, we might look out the window to see what the weather is like and use this evidence to decide what to wear. Commercial companies collect sales statistics and use that evidence to guide their marketing strategy. Teachers give tests to see how much their students are learning and use this evidence to assign grades. Scientists conduct experiments and use the evidence to find cures for diseases.

Evidence Defined

Something that proves or disproves allegations and assertions. Evidence, in the legal sense, includes only what is introduced at trial. The testimony of witnesses, documents, and physical objects can all be evidence.

Police investigators also try to gather as much evidence as possible. If they are convinced a case has been established, they take all the information to the prosecutor. The prosecutor evaluates the evidence in order to decide if the case should be filed. Ultimately, the jury (or the judge if both sides decide to forego the jury) will hear all the evidence and decide if the defendant is guilty.

Along with other aspects of evidence, this book is interested in the process of introducing evidence at trial. You will find it helpful to understand the legal definition of evidence. *Black's Law Dictionary* (2001) gives comprehensive definitions and the Pocket Edition is a convenient size for students.

Evidence, in the legal sense, includes only what is introduced at trial. Lawyers and judges use the phrase, "introduced into evidence." Only the things that have been formally introduced at trial are evidence. Some commonly used terms, such as "inadmissible evidence," are misleading. If the object is not admissible it cannot be evidence. One side may *attempt* to admit something into evidence, but if it is not admitted it does not become evidence in the case.

A wide range of things can be used as evidence. If you go to court and watch a trial, the most obvious evidence is the testimony of the witnesses. What a person says from the witness stand while under oath is evidence. All evidence must be introduced via the testimony of a witness. For example, a physical object, such as a gun, may be introduced into evidence only after a witness has testified about it, thus providing a foundation for its admission. Such testimony might include, among other facts, the circumstances under which the gun was found. The variety of things that can be used as evidence is only limited by the facts of the case. A gun might be evidence in a murder case where the victim was shot, but a gun would not be evidence in a murder case where poison was used by an unarmed assailant.

A survey of recent murder cases reveals a vast assortment of things that could be used as evidence, such as guns, knives, scissors, lead pipes, baseball bats, blunt objects, bombs, cars, poisons, lye, acids, water, ice picks, and even pillows and knitting needles.

Many types of documents can also be evidence. Anything written or printed, pictures (whether still, movies, or videos), sound recordings, and electronic files are also considered documents when introduced into evidence. A forged check is a document; the demand note given to a bank teller during the robbery is another example of a document. Counterfeit money is considered to be documents, as well as graffiti on a wall or inscriptions on tombstones. An email message is also a document. Court records can be important documents if the prosecutor needs to prove that the defendant had a prior conviction.

Some evidence is developed just for the trial. A wide variety of tests are done in forensics laboratories to prepare cases for trial. The defendant may be fingerprinted solely for the purpose of comparing his/her prints with those found at the scene. The case may be reenacted to determine if the scenario given by a witness could possibly be true. Scale models may even be constructed for submission as evidence.

Several chapters in this book will be devoted to explaining what evidence is legally admissible in court. The mere fact that something *could* be admitted is not enough. The proper groundwork must be laid before the judge will allow the evidence to be introduced. These requirements will also be covered.

Since the U.S. Supreme Court decided *Mapp v. Ohio* in 1961, the police have also had to be concerned with how the evidence is obtained. Information and physical objects obtained in violation of the defendant's constitutional rights are generally not admissible as evidence in a case. Later chapters will deal with those problems.

1-2 Burden of Proof

It is widely said that the prosecution has the "**burden of proof**" in criminal cases. This means that the prosecution is required to produce credible evidence to prove every element of each crime charged. The proof must be "**beyond a reasonable doubt.**" This places a heavy burden on the prosecution. Our society, however, has decided that it is better to let the guilty go free than to convict innocent people.

Black's Law Dictionary (2001) gives a brief definition of proof beyond a reasonable doubt.

Beyond a Reasonable Doubt Defined
Proof "beyond a reasonable doubt" is proof that leaves you firmly convinced. In criminal cases, the accused's guilt must be established "beyond a reasonable doubt."

There have been many attempts to explain the reasonable doubt standard. Pattern Criminal Jury Instruction 1.03, as used by the U.S. Court of Appeals for the Sixth Circuit, gives a useful explanation:

> The defendant starts the trial with a clean slate, with no evidence at all against him, and the law presumes that he is innocent. The presumption of innocence stays with him unless the government presents evidence here in court that overcomes the presumption, and convinces you beyond a reasonable doubt that he is guilty.
>
> This means that the defendant has no obligation to present any evidence at all, or to prove to you in any way that he is innocent. It is up to the government to prove that he is guilty, and this burden stays on the government from start to finish. You must find the defendant not guilty unless the government convinces you beyond a reasonable doubt that he is guilty.
>
> The government must prove every element of the crime charged beyond a reasonable doubt. Proof beyond a reasonable doubt does not mean proof beyond all possible doubt. Possible doubt or doubts based purely on speculation are not reasonable doubts. A reasonable doubt is a doubt based on reason and common sense. It may arise from the evidence, the lack of evidence, or the nature of the evidence.
>
> Proof beyond a reasonable doubt means proof which is so convincing that you would not hesitate to rely and act on it in making the most

important decisions in your own lives. If you are convinced that the government has proved the defendant guilty beyond a reasonable doubt, say so by returning a guilty verdict. If you are not convinced, say so by returning a not guilty verdict.

Thus, the prosecutor is required to fully satisfy the jury that the defendant committed each crime charged. Prosecutors must look at the definition of each crime and make sure that proof has been presented on each element of every offense. Many states have pattern jury instructions for each offense that the judge will read to the jury at the end of the trial. Prosecutors frequently use these instructions to help itemize what they will be required to establish.

The defense does not have to prove that the defendant did not commit the crime. Even so, the defense attorney frequently calls witnesses. The defendant may also take the witness stand even though the Fifth Amendment gives him/her the right to refuse to do so. These acts are usually the result of a "game plan" developed by the defendant and his/her attorney. Although it is true the defense does not have to do anything, as a practical matter the defendant is more likely to be convicted if no defense evidence is presented. It is usually safer to call defense witnesses and try to convince the jury that the prosecution's evidence does not establish the case beyond a reasonable doubt. For example, the defense could try to show any or all of the following: that the prosecution's witnesses are lying; the case rests on mistaken identity; the defendant has an alibi; or the defendant is "not guilty by reason of insanity."

Another way to explain this adversarial relationship between defense and prosecution is that the prosecution has the burden of producing evidence which establishes the crime(s) beyond a reasonable doubt. The defense, on the other hand, will have the **burden of persuasion.** This means that the defense can try to persuade the jury that the prosecution has not established the defendant's guilt.

There are some special situations where the defendant does have the burden of proof. These are the so-called "affirmative defenses." Self-defense, duress, intoxication, entrapment and insanity are good examples. The defense must introduce evidence on these issues. Some states even require the defendant to prove them, usually by a preponderance of the evidence. The U.S. Supreme Court has upheld this allocation of the burden of proof as long as the defendant is not required to disprove an element of the crime. Due to the variations between the states, you should consult local laws to see who bears what burden on each affirmative defense.

In cases where the defense is attacking the constitutionality of the methods used to obtain evidence, the burden may be altered by the fact that the police obtained a warrant. Searches without a warrant are usually presumed to be unconstitutional; that is, the prosecution has the burden of proof. Search warrants are frequently treated differently. The defense has the burden of proving that the search incident to a warrant was illegal.

1-3 Role of Judge and Jury

In a jury trial the roles of judge and jury are distinct: the judge is the "**trier of the law**" and the jury is the "**trier of the facts**." If the case is heard without a jury, the judge plays both roles.

The "trier of the law" determines what laws apply to the case. This is clearly shown in the selection of jury instructions. After consultation with the attorneys for both sides, the judge selects instructions which inform the jury what the law is. Errors in selecting jury instructions may be grounds for reversal of a conviction.

Not as obvious, but equally important, is the role of the judge in deciding what evidence is admissible at trial. In some areas this is easier than others. For example, if a statement is privileged, the judge must exclude it unless there is an applicable exception to the privilege. If a confession was obtained by coercion, the judge must exclude it. Even in these examples, the judge must analyze the facts and conclude that the privilege applied to the conversation or that the tactics used to obtain the confession were coercive. This is done, of course, after each side has had a chance to argue what ruling should be made. The judge may have the benefit of reviewing written briefs, submitted by both sides, giving legal points and authorities relevant to the decision. Judges are also allowed to do legal research or have their law clerks check the legal basis for the decision.

Perhaps the hardest decisions are those where the judge must rule on specific questions the attorneys want to ask the witnesses. While some questions are obviously permitted and others are not, there is a gray area in between. The judge must try to apply the law to these situations and make a ruling. This is referred to as "**judicial discretion**." The judge has the legal right to decide if the questions should be allowed and must rule on numerous objections by the lawyers during each trial. Higher courts will uphold the trial judge's rulings unless there is an obvious abuse of discretion.

A good example of this use of discretion is the right to ask questions to test the witness's memory. The Sixth Amendment gives criminal defendants the right to cross-examine their accusers. Obviously, this includes the right to try to show the jury that the witness has a bad memory. On the other hand, it is unrealistic to expect a witness to recall every minute detail of an event which may have happened six months or a year ago. Additionally, excessive questioning wastes time and may confuse the jury. At some point, the judge will rule that no more questions on this issue will be allowed.

Questions which attempt to introduce evidence which has only slight value to the case are also involved here. The side wishing to introduce the evidence will probably argue that the evidence is very important. The opposing side will tell the judge that the information is useless. The judge must use discretion and decide if there is a valid reason for introducing the evidence.

Other rules of evidence call for similar determinations by the judge. For example, evidence that is too prejudicial or photographs that are too graphic are inadmissible. The individual judge is left to decide where the line is to be drawn between what is acceptable and what is too prejudicial—what is merely a realistic depiction and what is too graphic or gruesome.

The jury is the "trier of the facts." This means that the jury reviews the evidence presented, decides which evidence to believe, and applies the legal instructions the judge gave to the facts. If two witnesses have given conflicting testimony, the jury must decide whom to believe. The jury decides how much weight to give to the testimony of each witness and which witnesses are telling the truth.

This function of determining the truthfulness of the witnesses is particularly important. Our legal system gives jurors almost total responsibility for determining the credibility of witnesses. Very few cases successfully argue credibility of a witness as grounds for reversal.

1-4 History and Development of Rules of Evidence

The rules of evidence were designed to control both the judge and the jury. They were also intended to make the trial more businesslike and efficient. The evolutionary process that resulted in our present rules of evidence is a reflection of both English and American history.

In the Middle Ages, glaring abuses of the trial process, such as the Star Chamber and the Inquisition, developed. Strangely enough, the Star Chamber was originally developed to cure abuses by the royalty. At their height, both the Star Chamber and the Inquisition became obsessed with forcing the suspect to confess. The noble ideal that a person could not be convicted solely on the allegations of others dissolved into a nightmare of torture chambers designed to force the suspect to confess.

The earliest forms of juries differed greatly from our current jury. At one time, jurors were selected based on their knowledge of the case. Unlike our present system where jurors are not supposed to have an opinion about the case prior to the trial, early jurors were only selected if they had personal knowledge of the facts. Busybodies made excellent jurors. Juries were also given the right to conduct their own investigations into the cases.

During the sixteenth century the rule developed that anyone having a personal interest in the case was disqualified from testifying. This was based on a belief that someone with an interest in the case would more likely be biased and untruthful. In addition to disqualifying people with a financial interest in the outcome of the lawsuit, this rule prevented the parties to the case from testifying. The spouses of parties were also disqualified as witnesses. Connecticut was the first state in the United States to abolish this rule, but that did not happen until the 1840s. Some states retained the rule until after the Civil War.

Old transcripts indicate that trials were much less formal between 1776 and 1830 than they are today. Hearsay was freely admitted, witnesses were allowed to give long narrative answers, and opposing attorneys broke in to cross-examine whenever they wished. Many of our present rules of evidence were developed to correct problems posed by these unruly trials.

As with many reforms, the rules that emerged were found to be too rigid. Exceptions to the rules were developed to make the new rules work better. The numerous exceptions to the Hearsay Rule are good examples of this process. From time to time, legal reformers have attempted to replace old rules with more modern ones. Some prestigious national organizations, such as the American Law Institute and the National Conference of Commissioners on Uniform State Laws, have solicited input from the leading scholars in the field and attempted to draft model laws.

Unfortunately, our federal system of government makes system-wide reform nearly impossible. Except where the U.S. Constitution is controlling, each state is free to enact its own rules of evidence and other laws. Somewhere in the legislative process the model codes are frequently altered or amended. Therefore, in evidence, as in many areas of the law, each state's law is unique.

1-5 Sources of Evidence Law

Evidence law reflects both historical evolution and the strengths and weaknesses of our federal system of government. Both statutory law and case law have definite impacts; federal law and state law interact.

1-5a United States Constitution

As you learned in high school, the United States Constitution is the supreme law of the land. But there is very little in the Constitution that has a direct bearing on evidence. Several provisions of the Bill of Rights, however, do restrict the actions of government in criminal prosecutions. Although early U.S. Supreme Court decisions found no connection between these protections and the admission of evidence, the mid-twentieth century saw a reversal of those rulings.

Generally speaking, nothing obtained in violation of the defendant's constitutional rights may be used at trial. Later chapters of this book will deal with how specific provisions of the Bill of Rights are currently being applied in criminal trials.

The U.S. Constitution is not static. Each year the U.S. Supreme Court rules on a variety of cases. Every one of these decisions, in some small way, interprets the Constitution, Bill of Rights, or federal laws. This process has allowed the Constitution to be a living document. The Fourth Amendment is a prime example of this process. As recently as 1948, it was believed that the amendment did not apply to the states. The rulings of the Supreme Court have so drastically altered this view that many have nearly forgotten that the Fourth Amendment has not always been applied to acts of state government.

Where there are no provisions of the Constitution or Bill of Rights involved, our federal system allows each state to enact its own rules of evidence. The common heritage of English law in most of the states has resulted in a great deal of similarity. Even so, there are many differences.

1-5b United States Supreme Court

Evidence is only one of the many topics addressed each year in the opinions of the United States Supreme Court. Two important functions of the U.S. Supreme Court should be noted: (1) the Court is the final arbiter of the meaning of the U.S. Constitution; and (2) the Court acts as supervisor of the federal court system. Rulings of the Court which interpret the

Constitution are binding on all federal and state courts. On the other hand, if the Court is acting in its supervisory capacity, the decision does not control the state courts.

When ruling on the meaning of the Constitution, the U.S. Supreme Court has the authority to overrule any court in the nation. It also has the power to overrule its own prior decisions. Gradual changes can be seen in the Court's decisions as justices retire and are replaced.

The Court is very selective about which cases it hears. It obviously does not have the time to review every case filed in the United States. The vast majority of appeals to the U.S. Supreme Court and requests for review are denied. This means the Court does not hold a hearing on the cases. It does not mean that the Court agreed with the rulings of the lower courts. Refusal to hear a case sets no legal precedent. Due to the enormous number of requests received by the Court, only a small percentage can be heard each year.

1-5c Federal Courts

The federal courts hear cases involving violations of federal statutes. A panel of three judges at a U.S. Court of Appeals can rule on the constitutionality of state and federal laws. If the U.S. Supreme Court has not made a definitive statement on a particular issue, the federal Court of Appeals decision is binding on all states within its boundaries. This may cause confusion because the 13 Courts of Appeals that exist in the United States can make rulings that conflict with each other. Ultimately the problem will be resolved by a new U.S. Supreme Court case ruling. Such a case takes precedence over the lower court decision.

1-5d Federal Rules of Evidence

The **Federal Rules of Evidence** are laws governing the admission of evidence in federal courts. They are enacted by Congress in the same manner as any other federal regulations. A comprehensive set of rules of evidence for federal courts was adopted by the U.S. Supreme Court in 1972. They were forwarded to Congress where they were duly enacted. The Federal Rules of Evidence became effective January 2, 1975. Some of the rules have been amended since then.

Enactment of the Federal Rules of Evidence was significant for several reasons. The rules represented a comprehensive set of rules designed to work together as a whole. The authors believed they incorporated the best of the old law and corrected the problems that had developed. The new rules replaced both the existing statutory and case law.

The process of developing the new Federal Rules of Evidence received a great deal of publicity within the legal profession. The drafting committee had input from nationally renowned judges, attorneys, and legislators. The final draft was viewed by many as the best evidence code ever drafted.

The new Federal Rules of Evidence immediately affected all federal courts—but the long-range impact was even greater. Many states imitated the federal rules. Some simply declared that the federal rules would be the binding law of evidence in their state. Nearly half of the states now take that approach. Additionally, many other states modeled portions of their evidence laws after the federal rules.

As with any other piece of legislation, the federal rules have been subject to court interpretation. Title 28 of the *United States Code (Annotated)* lists the decisions of all federal courts that relate to the rules. The U.S. Constitution is controlling. When interpreting this type of legislation, the courts also look at the drafting committee's comments that accompanied the legislation. If there was no comment, or the comment does not cover the question that is raised by the appeal, common law will also be considered. Due to the fact that the rules were enacted as a comprehensive package, the courts usually try to make their rulings reflect the overall purpose of the code if none of the above sources is controlling.

1-5e State Rules of Evidence

Each state has the right to enact its own evidence code. As mentioned previously, many states now follow the Federal Rules of Evidence. Some, like Arizona and California, have placed all their rules of evidence in one code. Determining the evidence law in states that follow either of these approaches is fairly easy.

Unfortunately, there are quite a number of states whose legislatures have not enacted comprehensive evidence codes. In these states, the law of evidence is spread over several codes and usually involves case law as well. For example, the law of privilege may be in the Code of Civil Procedure, but the "dying declaration" exception to the Hearsay Rule may be in the Penal Code. There may not be any specific legislation on many kinds of evidence. If a rule is needed, case law is the only place to look. This obviously complicates the task of discovering what law to apply to specific situations.

1-5f State Case Law

Each state is free, within Constitutional limits, to enact and interpret its own laws. The laws of other states are not binding, but they may influence the judge. When there is no binding case law on a point, or when one side is seeking to modify the existing law, an attorney may try to convince the judge that case law from another state is persuasive. If the judge studies the case law presented and finds the reasoning sound, he/she may apply that same logic when making a decision in the current case. While the case law of a sister state has no legal effect, it may informally affect the final outcome of the case.

1-6 Impact of Case Law

Our legal system is based on the concept that the legislature enacts laws but the courts have the right to interpret them. The courts also have the right to rule that a statute is invalid because it violates the state or federal constitution. The U.S. Supreme Court interprets the federal Constitution. Those rulings apply to the entire country. State courts can also rule that a state law violates the U.S. Constitution. These rulings will stand until the U.S. Supreme Court has ruled in a contrary manner on a similar law.

Prior cases are considered binding. This is called *stare decisis.* These earlier decisions are what we are referring to when we talk about "**case law.**" The rule of a case will continue to be in effect until it is reversed, vacated, or overruled. A higher court can change the rule by making a new ruling on the same issue. This is done by reversing the original decision or making the new rule in a later case which presents the same issue. If there is no higher court, or the higher court has not ruled on the issue, the original court can change the case law in the same manner.

One problem that arises in using case law is that there is no automatic feedback from the courts to the legislature. Even though the U.S. Supreme Court or the highest court in the state may have ruled that a code section is void, there is no way to change the code except for the legislature to pass a new law. This causes a delay in revising the codes. Sometimes the legislature does not follow through with the process and the codes retain invalid laws for years. This makes the study of case law very important.

The highest court of the state (called the Supreme Court, in most states, and not to be confused with the U.S. Supreme Court) has authority over all of the state's courts as long as its rulings do not violate the U.S. Constitution and Bill of Rights. Figure 1-1 illustrates the organization of the typical state judicial system. Below the high court are several appellate courts of equal authority. Each makes decisions which control the actions of all courts below it on the organizational chart. If a higher court has not ruled on an issue, the intermediate appellate courts may make their own rulings. These may differ from the decisions other courts of equal author-

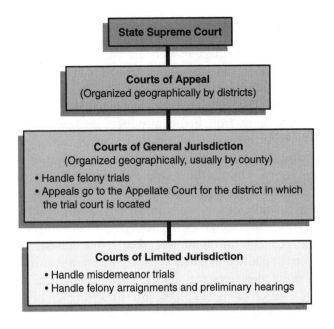

Figure 1-1
Typical State Judicial System

ity have made on the same issue. When these differences occur, the lower courts must follow the decisions of the courts immediately above them.

The following examples refer to Figure 1-1. Suppose the state has divided the Court of Appeals into two districts. The Court of Appeals for the First District held that the physician-patient privilege does not apply in criminal trials. The Court of Appeals for the Second District held that the physician-patient privilege applies in criminal matters except when the doctor was consulted to help the patient commit a crime. If defendant Doe commits a crime in a county whose trial courts must follow the precedents from the First District, the physician-patient privilege cannot be claimed. If Doe's offense was perpetrated in a county located in the Second District, the privilege can be used unless the doctor helped Doe commit a crime. These discrepancies will continue until the state's Supreme Court makes a ruling on the use of the physician-patient privilege in criminal cases or one of the District Courts changes its ruling.

Each court has the power to reverse its earlier rulings as long as it continues to follow the rulings of the higher courts, including the U.S. Supreme Court. Again using the example of the physician-patient privilege, the Second District Court of Appeals could decide that the privilege does not apply in criminal cases. This would result in both the First District and Second District having the same rule.

1-6a Review of Evidentiary Matters on Appeal

In most situations, evidentiary matters are considered on appeal only if the issue was raised in the trial court. Attorneys are expected to make objections before the evidence is introduced. This is done to make the trial more efficient—the trial judge has the chance to make a ruling and prevent inadmissible things from being introduced into evidence. Hopefully, the judge has made the correct rulings and a retrial can be avoided. It is part of our adversary system that you only have the right to exclude evidence if your attorney makes the proper objection at the right time.

Some questions regarding what evidence is admissible are decided during the trial, while others are customarily ruled on before the trial begins. Objections to specific questions asked of a witness are usually made immediately after the question is asked. If one side claims that a witness should not be allowed to testify at all, arguments are most often heard before the witness takes the stand. On the other hand, questions related to the legality of a search or attacks on the interrogation methods which produced a confession are usually settled before the trial date.

When the judge's ruling on the admissibility of evidence is challenged on appeal, the attorneys are required to submit briefs giving their legal arguments. Specific statutes and case law must be cited as authority for the court to make a ruling. The easiest example would be where one side can cite a case that is an exact match for the facts and issues of the present case. This is referred to as being "on all fours." Otherwise, each side will try to persuade the judge regarding the appropriate way to interpret the law. Analogies will be drawn from prior decisions to the current case. An attorney may also base arguments on public policy, common law, or the intent of the legislature when it enacted the law. This last rationale is more commonly seen when the court is ruling on a new law.

If the appellate court finds that the trial judge made an error, one question remains: Does the error justify reversal? Unless there is a substantial likelihood that the error was serious enough to affect the outcome of the case the "**Harmless Error Rule**" will be applied.

The Harmless Error Rule Defined

The Harmless Error Rule states that an error will not cause a case to be reversed on appeal unless the appellate court believes the error was likely to affect the outcome of the case.

In other words, would the jury have been likely to arrive at a different verdict if the judge had made the correct ruling? In many cases, the conclusion is that the error had no impact on the verdict.

1-7 How Legal Research Is Done

A variety of books are available in the law library to help you discover what the law is on any given issue. A great number of legal materials are available on the Internet. These resources take several forms. Some, like *American Jurisprudence* (Am.Jur.), are similar to encyclopedias. They are carefully indexed for ease in finding the issue. They give a summary of the law with numerous footnotes. Treatises, like *McCormick on Evidence*, more closely resemble lengthy textbooks. They frequently are on only one subject, but they carefully explain it in minute detail.

Legal digests are organized by topic. They usually give short quotes from individual cases rather than a textbook-style explanation of the law. The annotated codes also use quotations from many cases. These quotes are usually listed right after the code section that they interpret. The researcher looks for the quotes that appear to be on point and then reads the cases. Cases are then checked to verify that they are still good precedent (currently prevailing law). Special books and databases are published for this latter purpose.

Most cases can be found in two or more books. This is because the content of the opinions cannot be copyrighted. Judicial opinions are printed by the publishing company authorized by the state or federal government. They are published by other companies as well. The digests and other legal references frequently give all the places a case can be found. These are called parallel citations. Reading any one of these is sufficient because the full text of the case is given in each one.

For example, the opinions of the U.S. Supreme Court can be found in three series of books: *United States Reports* (U.S.); *United States Supreme Court Reports, Lawyers Edition* (L.Ed.); and *Supreme Court Reporter* (S.Ct.). If we wanted to look up the *Miranda* decision, we would first look up the citation: *Miranda v. Arizona*, 384 U.S. 436, 16 L.Ed. 2d 694, 86 S.Ct. 1602 (1966). We would then determine which books containing Supreme Court decisions are in our library. Law libraries frequently have all three, but other libraries may have only one. If the *United States Reports* are available, we look up the citation 384 U.S. 436: we find volume 384 and the *Miranda* case will start on page 436. We would find the same case in volume 86 of the *Supreme Court Reporter* on page 1602. The procedure for finding a case in *United States Supreme Court Reports, Lawyers Edition*, is slightly different. The Lawyers Edition started with volume one and was numbered consecutively, then a new series was started which also began with volume one and was numbered consecutively. The second set of volumes is called the "Second Series." "Second Series" is printed on the spine of the book and "2d" appears in the citation. Thus, if we look up 16 L.Ed. 2d 694 to find *Miranda,* we first find the second series of books for the *United States Supreme Court, Lawyers Edition,* then open volume 16 and look on page 694.

Cases from state courts and the lower federal courts are located in much the same way. Due to variations in publishing companies, not all cases from a state may be available from the same source. Some states have one set of publications for opinions from the highest court and another for lower appellate court cases. Some states do not publish all of the appellate court decisions. Unpublished decisions do not set precedents. Trial court opinions are not considered precedent and therefore are not usually published. Students should become familiar with how to find both the decisions of the U.S. Supreme Court and the published decisions of the courts in their state.

Computerized research materials are readily available. Penal codes and other statutes may be purchased on CD-ROM. Major publishers sell their digests, case reports, and other materials on CD-ROM. Subscriptions are available that provide frequent updates. Online services make codes, case law, and other materials for every state as well as the federal courts available. These Internet databases are updated almost daily.

One of the advantages of computerized material is the speed with which an experienced researcher can locate material. Key word searches can be used to identify every case in the file that discusses a topic or every case that discusses a particular code section or case. General terms, such as *due process* or *Fourth Amendment,* are not useful because there are thousands of cases that use these words. To use the database efficiently, the person conducting the search must know the specific words or phrases used by the courts when discussing the topic. For example, a search of United States Supreme Court cases using "vehicle search based on probable cause" would produce every case that used exactly that phrase but miss cases where the court used the phrase "car search based on probable cause." Internet search engines that combine words and phrases, such as "arrest" and "exigent circumstances" enable more efficient searches. These search engines usually make it possible to find and download relevant materials from the Internet to a disk or directly into a word processor file for use in briefs and other materials. This saves a great deal of time.

Summary

In a trial, *evidence* refers to all items which are admitted to prove any issue in the case. This includes testimony of sworn witnesses, documents, physical objects, and other items that are relevant to the case.

The prosecution bears the burden of proof in criminal cases. The jury must be convinced beyond a reasonable doubt that the defendant committed the crime(s). The defense usually has the burden of persuasion when affirmative defenses are used.

The judge is the trier of the law at trial. Selection of jury instructions is part of the duties of the trier of the law. The judge also rules on the admissibility of all items either side wants to use to prove its case. Judicial discretion is used to determine admissibility if there is no clear-cut law that applies.

The trier of the facts is the jury or, if there is no jury, the judge. The trier of the facts determines credibility of witnesses, the weight to be given to the testimony of each witness, how the facts match the definition of the crime, and if the prosecution has established the case beyond a reasonable doubt.

Rules of evidence have changed over time. While jurors were once selected on the basis of their personal knowledge of the case, we now try to have jurors who have no knowledge of the facts prior to trial. The procedures used in trial have generally become more formal. Exceptions to the rules of evidence have developed when specific rules have been shown to be too rigid.

The U.S. Supreme Court interprets the U.S. Constitution. These decisions are binding on all courts in the country. It also makes decisions that involve the Federal Rules of Evidence. These opinions are binding only on the federal courts.

Each state has the right to enact its own laws as long as those laws do not violate the U.S. Constitution. State courts interpret state laws and the state constitutions. Each state court is bound by the decisions of higher courts within the organization of its own state court system. Opinions of other states may be considered in order to decide if the appellate courts agree with their reasoning, but they do not have any direct effect on decisions in any state except the one where they were issued.

Evidentiary issues usually must be raised at the trial court in order to preserve them for appeal. When an appellate court decides that there was an error at trial, the case is normally reversed only if the error is believed to have had an impact on the verdict.

Resources for legal research are available in book form, on CD-ROM, and on the Internet. Codes and case law are available as well as digests and other tools.

Discussion Questions

1. Define the general term *evidence.*
2. Explain the term *burden of proof.*
3. Define what is meant by *beyond a reasonable doubt.*
4. Who has the burden of proof on affirmative defenses?
5. In a criminal trial, who is the trier of the law, who is the trier of the facts, and what are their respective roles?
6. List three sources of law that govern evidence.
7. What is the role of the U.S. Supreme Court in determining the rules of evidence for federal courts and for state courts?
8. Define *stare decisis* and explain how it applies.
9. Describe the role of state courts in interpreting the laws of evidence.
10. Explain how the courts determine if a decision should be reversed based on a question of admissibility of evidence.
11. Define the term *judicial discretion.*
12. Explain the Harmless Error Rule.
13. Explain the basis for a court's interpretation of a new statute.
14. What effect does the law of State "A" have on a court's decision of a case tried in State "B"?
15. Explain how to find the opinion of the U.S. Supreme Court in *Terry v. Ohio,* 392 U.S. 1, 20 L.Ed. 2d 889, 88 S.Ct. 1868 (1968).

CHAPTER 2

The Court Process

Outline

Key Terms

- Affidavit
- Arraignment
- Challenge for cause
- Charge bargaining
- Clerk's transcript
- Contemporaneous Objection Rule
- Direct appeal
- Direct examination
- Discovery
- Double jeopardy

- *Habeas corpus*
- Harmless Error Rule
- Hold the defendant to answer
- Impeachment
- Indictment
- Information
- Laying the foundation
- Leading question
- Peremptory challenges
- Plea bargaining

- Polling the jury
- Preliminary hearing
- *Prima facie* case
- Probable cause
- Rebuttal
- Rejoinder
- Reporter's transcript
- Sequestered
- Suppression hearing
- *Voir dire*

After studying this chapter, you will be able to:

- List what evidence is considered by the prosecutor when filing criminal charges.
- Identify what evidence is needed at the preliminary hearing.
- Identify the types of evidence considered by grand juries.
- Explain what information the prosecutor must give the defense during discovery.
- Describe what evidence the defense can use at suppression hearings.
- Explain how juries are selected.
- List the order of events at a criminal trial.
- Describe what law and evidence juries are allowed to consider when they decide a case.
- Explain what evidence can be considered at a sentencing hearing.
- Identify what evidence can be used for an appeal of a criminal conviction.

2-1 Introduction

The evidence that is required at various stages of any court proceeding varies according to the type of proceeding and the crime charged. In order to adequately prepare for each court appearance, it is necessary to understand what evidence will be needed at each stage of the proceeding. It must be remembered that preparation of the case begins with the officer's initial observations in the case, not when the prosecutor is doing the final preparation to take the case to court. For example, if an officer stops a car based on reasonable suspicion, the officer should make notes on all of the facts that were used to establish reasonable suspicion. If an arrest is made, the officer needs to record all facts used to establish probable cause for that arrest.

This chapter briefly discusses the different court proceedings in a criminal case, along with which evidence will be used. Issues relating to illegal search and seizure and obtaining confessions are covered in Chapters 10 through 14.

2-2 The Criminal Complaint

Criminal cases come to court from three main sources: the police, private persons ("citizen's arrests"), and grand jury **indictments.** Some states allow police officers to bring misdemeanor cases directly to court. Others have the prosecutor's office handle the filing of the first court documents for police and private persons. If an arrest warrant has been issued, it may serve in lieu of filing additional documents to charge the suspect with a crime. The grand jury procedure is somewhat different and will be outlined in a later section of this chapter.

There are several variations of the procedure for cases brought to the prosecutor by the police. If the police made the arrest based on an arrest warrant, the application for the warrant will be the first official document filed with the court. Some states require the officer to obtain an arrest warrant after the arrest if none was issued earlier. If there is no arrest warrant, the complaint will be the first document filed.

The prosecutor decides which cases should be filed and what crimes will be charged. In order to do this, he/she will need a report which clearly states the facts of the case and what information is available to the police. While the Fourth Amendment establishes **probable cause** as the standard for arrest, there is no precise standard for the prosecutor to use when filing the charges.

Some of the things the prosecutor will consider include:

1. How strong is the case against the suspect?
2. Did police conduct their investigation thoroughly?
3. Based on the facts in the police report, what crime(s) was committed?
4. Were the suspect's constitutional rights violated?
5. Are the witnesses credible?

The prosecutor does not want to file criminal charges against an innocent person. Since most prosecutor's offices are overworked, cases that do not appear to be "winnable" frequently are not filed.

The way a prosecutor handles the case at this stage varies. In the most serious cases, the prosecutor may interview witnesses prior to filing the charges. On the other hand, for misdemeanors the prosecutor may proceed after only reading the police report. Many states allow the prosecutor

---

Sample Complaint

COUNT I: John Smith is hereby charged with the violation of Section 459 of the Penal Code, burglary, in that on or about May 1, 2004, he entered a residence located at 123 Main Street, Los Angeles, CA with the intent to steal.

COUNT II: John Smith is hereby charged with the violation of Section 242 of the Penal Code, battery, in that on or about May 1, 2004, he willfully, and without consent, hit Jane Jones. Said event occurred at 123 Main Street, Los Angeles, CA.

COUNT III: John Smith is hereby charged with the violation of Section 488 of the Penal Code, petty theft, in that on or about May 1, 2004, he took merchandise valued at $124.99 without consent and without paying for it from Lucky Market located at 125 Main Street, Los Angeles, CA.

Figure 2-1
Sample Complaint

to consider information that is not given under oath or otherwise admissible in court. In some cities and counties, one officer takes all of the minor cases to the prosecutor at once, rather than having each arresting officer go to the prosecutor's office. Other areas of the country require the arresting officer to personally swear out the complaint.

The complaint must state the facts for each charge. This includes at least a description of what crime was committed, where it occurred, and when. The description of the crime must cover every element in the definition of that crime; this is frequently done by using the wording from the penal code. At a minimum, the place where the crime occurred must show that the event occurred within the court's jurisdiction. The date is needed to satisfy the statute of limitations. Figure 2-1 shows an example of a complaint.

Some states have attempted to save paperwork by allowing specially formatted police reports to substitute for complaints. The traffic ticket is probably the most common example. Some states also use the citation in lieu of an arrest for misdemeanors and do not require the drafting of a formal complaint in these cases.

If the police seek an arrest warrant prior to taking the person into custody, the formal procedures for obtaining a warrant must be followed. These include making out an **affidavit** which includes all the facts of the case. The affidavit is made under oath. Normally the prosecutor reviews the warrant application. The final decision on issuing the warrant must be made by a judge or magistrate. If the judge accepts the affidavit as sufficient, the warrant will be issued. Arrest warrants frequently use the same type of wording as complaints. Many states allow the arrest warrant to take the place of the complaint after the arrest has been made.

When a private person wants to file charges, he/she is usually required to go to the prosecutor's office and give all the information needed under oath. Some states require the prosecutor to file the charges requested by a private person; other jurisdictions give the prosecutor the right to decide if the cases should proceed. When the prosecutor files the case, the complaint is usually in the same format as the one used for cases handled by the police. The prosecutor handles the case from this point on in the same way as if the police had requested the complaint.

After the prosecutor decides what charges to file, the complaint will be typed and taken to the court clerk. The clerk's office will handle the paperwork, including scheduling the case for future court dates. Delivering the complaint to the clerk is called "filing the complaint." Once the complaint has been filed, the suspect is legally known as the defendant.

2-3 Arraignment

The **arraignment** is the defendant's first court appearance on the charge. Nationwide a variety of names are used, such as the "first appearance," "preliminary hearing," etc. To avoid confusion, it will be referred to as an arraignment in this text. It is a brief court proceeding with the following purposes:

1. Inform the defendant what charges have been filed.
2. Make sure the defendant has an attorney.
3. Set bail.
4. Enter a plea.
5. Set the next court appearance.

If the defendant does not have an attorney, the judge will try to determine if the defendant qualifies for a free, court-appointed lawyer or if the defendant wishes to represent him- or herself. This is a high priority because in many states the defendant cannot enter a plea without counsel or a formal waiver of the right to counsel.

At the arraignment, the defense may seek to dismiss the case because the complaint does not contain all the required information. This is a challenge to the wording of the complaint. Witnesses are usually not called; neither is the evidence in the case evaluated at the arraignment.

The defendant will be asked to enter a plea. Guilty and Not Guilty are the most common. If a defendant pleads *Nolo Contendere* (no contest) the criminal courts will treat the case the same as if a guilty plea was entered but civil courts may treat it differently. Other pleas, such as Not Guilty by Reason of Insanity, are frequently entered at a later time because the attorney needs more time to determine if they are appropriate.

The arraignment can also serve as a probable cause hearing. To qualify as a probable cause hearing, the arraignment must be held within 48 hours of arrest, and the judge must review sworn statements to determine if there is probable cause. This type of hearing is not required if a judge previously issued an arrest warrant for the defendant or if the defendant will not be held in custody pending trial.

2-4 Preliminary Hearing

In most states, felony cases that have not been heard by a grand jury must have a **preliminary hearing** (also called a *preliminary examination*), unless the defense waives it. Statutes rarely require preliminary hearings in cases involving only misdemeanors. As with arraignments, names of the hearing may vary from state to state.

The preliminary hearing is a "mini-trial" without a jury. The defendant is present with his/her attorney; the prosecutor represents the State. In many states the preliminary hearing is held in a lower court than the one where felony trials are conducted.

The primary purpose of the preliminary hearing is to have a judge hear the case and decide if there is enough evidence to:

1. Prove that a crime was committed.
2. Require the defendant to face trial on the charge.

In some states this is done at the arraignment instead of holding a separate hearing at a later time. In cases where an arrest warrant was not obtained, this is the first time a judge reviews the facts of the case.

Some states permit hearsay that would not otherwise be admissible at trial to be used at the preliminary hearing. For example, California allows police officers to testify to hearsay at the preliminary hearing even though the statement is not covered by an exception to the Hearsay Rule. This makes it possible to reduce the number of times the victim must appear in court.

In many cases, the preliminary hearing will also be the first time the witnesses are required to take an oath that what they are saying is true. The defense has the right to ask these witnesses questions for the purpose of showing that they have not been truthful or they are mistaken. By listening to all of the witnesses, the defense can also decide how strong a case the prosecutor has. This information may become very helpful during plea bargaining.

The defense also has the right to call witnesses. The defendant may testify in his/her own defense. It is very common for the defense to decide that it is not to its advantage to call any witnesses at this stage of the proceedings.

At the end of the preliminary hearing the judge decides if there is enough evidence to "**hold the defendant to answer,**" which means allowing the prosecution to go to trial on the charges. The prosecution's evidence must establish that it is more likely than not that the defendant committed the crime charged. This is called a *prima facie* (on its face) **case.** The judge relies on what each witness said and whether or not he/she believes the witness was telling the truth. If there was more than one charge filed, the judge must make a decision on each charge. Assuming sufficient evidence was presented, at the end of the hearing the judge announces that the defendant is bound over for trial.

If the judge holds the defendant to answer, the prosecutor will prepare the appropriate form, usually called an "**information.**" The information is similar in form and wording to the complaint. If the judge does not hold the defendant to answer on all of the original charges, the information will only contain the charges authorized by the judge. The prosecutor may also drop charges from the case at this time. The information will be filed in the clerk's office of the court where the trial will take place. A second arraignment (at a higher court in some states) will be held on the information.

2-5 Grand Jury

The purpose of the grand jury in criminal cases is to take testimony, review evidence, and decide if the suspect should be charged with a crime. Grand juries have other duties as well, primarily verifying efficient and honest county government. The grand jury is composed of citizens, not prosecutors.

Grand jurors are typically chosen by lot at a drawing held once each year. They come from lists of names submitted by judges, people who have volunteered for grand jury service, or the list from which trial jurors are selected. Each state is free to establish its own rules on how grand jurors are selected provided there is no racial or gender discrimination involved. States also set the size of the grand jury and how many grand juries can be empanelled at the same time.

For historical reasons, the grand jury operates separately from either the police or the prosecutor. The grand jury has the right to investigate criminal activity on its own, but in many states it rarely does this. The prosecutor can also present cases to a grand jury. This can be done either before or after the suspect is arrested.

No matter which route the case takes, the grand jury can call witnesses and ask questions regarding the crime. The proceedings are held in secret; the suspect does not have to be informed that he/she is being investigated. The suspect does not have the right to be at the grand jury proceedings unless called to testify, and while testifying he/she does not have the right to have an attorney present in the grand jury room; he/she does not have the right to call witnesses, be present when others testify or have an attorney cross-examine witnesses called by the prosecutor. Some states even refuse to give defendants a copy of the transcript of the grand jury proceedings after they have been indicted. State laws prohibiting witnesses from discussing their testimony after they appear before the grand jury violate the First Amendment. The U.S. Supreme Court held that prosecutors are not required to present evidence to the grand jury that tends to show that the suspect is not guilty of the crime; some states have either statutes or case law that mandates that grand jurors receive this information.

The minimum number of grand jurors who must vote for prosecution in a case is set by state law; unanimity is not required. Some states allow all charges to go to trial if the grand jury is convinced that any one of the alleged felonies was committed by the suspect. If the grand jury decides the suspect should be brought to trial, a document usually called a "True Bill of Indictment" will be filed with the court clerk. At this point the defendant will be considered indicted. If the suspect is not in custody, a warrant will be issued and bail will be set (if the offense is bailable) by the court. An arraignment will be held on the indictment, usually in the court where the trial will be held.

2-6 Suppression Hearing

The purpose of a **suppression hearing** is to allow a judge to decide if evidence can be used at trial. Most states require the defense to make suppression motions prior to trial if they know of any legal grounds to object to evidence due to illegal search and seizure or an illegally obtained confession. Some states also allow other evidentiary issues to be decided at the suppression hearing. By knowing what evidence can be used before the trial starts, both sides can more efficiently plan their trial strategy. If enough of the evidence in the case is suppressed, the defense can successfully ask for the case to be dismissed.

Unless local court rules state a time for the suppression hearing, the defense may schedule it anytime before trial. In practice, suppression hearings are normally held after the preliminary hearing in felony cases. There are two main reasons for this: if the case is dismissed at the preliminary hearing no suppression hearing will be necessary, and testimony given at the preliminary hearing may alert the defense to the need for a suppression hearing.

The normal rules of evidence apply at suppression hearings. This gives both sides the right to call witnesses and cross-examine. If the issue is the admissibility of the defendant's confession or the defendant is charged with possession of the item in question (for example, possession of marijuana), the defendant's testimony at the suppression hearing cannot be introduced at trial. If this rule was not used, a person could not claim the Fourth or Fifth Amendment without admitting guilt. Many states allow the defense to submit the suppression motion solely on the transcript of the preliminary hearing if the defense believes the sworn testimony at that proceeding established that the evidence was obtained illegally. The prosecution, of course, would have the right to call witnesses to refute the defense's claim.

The judge will either make a decision on the motion at the time of the hearing or take the matter "under submission" and issue a ruling at a later date. Some states permit either party to appeal the ruling before trial. Due to the fact that this is done before the trial begins, the defense cannot claim **double jeopardy** if the decision is reversed on appeal.

Examples of Issues Heard at Suppression Hearings

Motion to suppress drugs found in the defendant's pocket. Defense alleges that the police did not have probable cause to stop the defendant, therefore the drugs were found during an illegal search.

Motion to suppress guns found during the execution of a search warrant. Defense alleges that the warrant should not have been issued because the facts in the affidavits do not state probable cause for the search.

Motion to suppress stolen jewelry found during the execution of a search warrant. Defense alleges that the officers improperly executed a warrant authorizing them to look for assault rifles. Therefore the jewelry found in a drawer was not legally seized.

Motion to suppress the defendant's confession. Defense alleges that officers questioned the suspect after the arrest and *Miranda* warnings were not given until after the first incriminating statement was made.

2-7 Discovery

The idea behind **discovery** is that each side should have ample warning of what the other will present at trial. This should make the trial more efficient and promote the process of truth finding. It also cuts down on the number of times it is necessary to stop the trial so that either side can try to challenge surprise witnesses. The growing practice of pretrial discovery has eliminated most of the dramatic surprises at trial.

Discovery (the right to know what evidence the other side has) varies greatly from state to state. There are two areas where the U.S. Supreme Court has required discovery:

1. The name of an informant must be disclosed when the true identity of this person is necessary for the defendant's case.
2. The prosecution must disclose any evidence it has that tends to indicate the defendant is not guilty. This material is often referred to as "*Brady* material" because the case of *Brady v. Maryland* established the rule.

Until recently, discovery in criminal cases was largely one-sided. The prosecution had to disclose information to the defense, but the defense was allowed to withhold information from the prosecution. The reason for this was the interpretation of the Fifth Amendment protection against self-incrimination. Neither side is required to disclose privileged information, such as legal opinions on what strategies it plans to use at trial. Reciprocal discovery is a growing trend. Both sides must disclose names of witnesses, physical evidence, copies of laboratory tests performed on evidence, and statements potential witnesses made to investigators. Statements by the defendant to his/her attorney are still considered exempt from discovery.

Examples of Items Covered by Discovery Rules in Many States
- List of all witnesses each side intends to call.
- Recorded statements made by people on the witness list.
- Itemized list of the physical evidence in the case.
- Results of lab tests performed on the evidence that will be introduced in court.
- Reports made by expert witnesses that are scheduled to testify in the case.
- Statements made by all co-defendants.

Requiring a defendant to notify the prosecution that an alibi defense is planned does not violate the privilege against self-incrimination. Disclosure of where the defendant claims to have been at the time the crime was committed and the names of alibi witnesses have been upheld. Statutes that require both sides to make pretrial disclosure of intended witnesses have also been upheld.

Discovery can be conducted at either a formal or informal level. Informal discovery is conducted by the attorneys without making requests in court. Where the courts or the legislature have established clear-cut rules on what must be given to the other side, it is common for the attorneys to exchange information which they know the court would order them to provide to the other side.

Formal discovery motions are made in court for a variety of reasons, such as:

1. There is no established rule on releasing the information requested.
2. One side is claiming that the information should not be released.
3. The attorneys do not have a good working relationship.

A formal discovery motion must state exactly what is wanted (i.e., "all statements made by Mrs. Jones to the police").

When the defense requests information from the prosecutor, the prosecutor is responsible for disclosing what is in his/her file and what the police have in their files. Because of the prosecutor's duty to know what is in the police files, it is important that the police keep the prosecutor fully informed about the case.

Failure to comply with discovery rules can result in the items being declared inadmissible in court or the judge not allowing a witness to take the stand. The prosecutor's refusal to give information that the court ordered released can be grounds for dismissing the case. This applies even to cases where the prosecutor intentionally refuses to name an informant for fear the informant will be killed. A case can also be dismissed because the prosecutor erroneously said information did not exist, when the police had it in their files but did not tell the prosecutor about it.

2-8 Plea Bargaining

Plea bargaining is the process whereby the prosecution and defense work out an agreement for the defendant to plead guilty to one or more charges without a trial. In return, the prosecutor usually agrees to drop some of the original charges or sentencing demands. When the agreement is reached before the charges are filed, the process is called "**charge bargaining**"; after the charges are filed the process is called "**plea bargaining.**" It is now recognized as a legitimate part of the legal system in many jurisdictions. In some states, as many as 90 percent of defendants use plea bargaining to avoid trials.

Either the prosecutor or defense attorney may initiate the plea bargaining process. Many factors will be considered. One that is very important is the strength or weakness of the evidence in the case. Both sides will consider the police reports and testimony given at the preliminary hearing. Information from further investigations may be reviewed. The results of any laboratory tests will be scrutinized. Both sides will try to guess which witnesses the jury will believe. Non-evidentiary issues will also be considered; for example, what is the difference in the sentence if the defendant is convicted compared to the sentence if he/she agrees to the plea bargain? Are there mitigating circumstances that justify giving the defendant a less severe sentence? Is the court calendar so full that the case will be dismissed for lack of speedy trial? Has the defendant worked as an informant or in some way helped the police and thereby "earned" special treatment?

The final result is an agreement that the defendant plead guilty to one or more crimes and the prosecutor dismiss the rest of the original charges. For example, if there were five counts of burglary, the defendant may plead guilty to two counts of burglary and the remaining three will be dismissed. If the original charge was for driving under the influence, the defendant may plead guilty to a lesser charge of reckless driving.

The U.S. Supreme Court has set the following requirements for plea bargaining:

1. The defendant must have an attorney during plea bargaining if he/she would have the right to one at trial on the same charges.
2. There must be no threats or promises in the plea bargaining process.

Prior to accepting a plea bargain, the judge will ask questions to show that the defendant's rights have been protected. It is also generally recognized that the defendant has the right to withdraw a plea if the judge does not honor the agreement made by the prosecutor. Many states restrict plea bargaining, while others allow the prosecutor to enter into plea bargains on the charges, but not on the sentence the defendant will receive.

2-9 The Trial

The trial is the highest-profile action in the criminal case. In reality, trials are relatively rare because of plea bargaining and pretrial dismissals. Trials in most states follow the same format: selection of the jury, opening statements, prosecution witnesses, defense witnesses, rebuttal witnesses called by either side, closing statements, jury instructions on the law given by the judge, jury deliberations, and a verdict. Unique situations may arise that require departures from this format.

2-9a Jury Selection

The Sixth Amendment guarantees the right to a speedy trial by a jury of one's peers in criminal cases. While the U.S. Supreme Court has said this only applies to defendants facing more than six months in jail, many states provide jury trials in all criminal cases. Some states even allow jury trials for infractions. The defendant has the right to demand a jury. Although less commonly used, the prosecution also has this right. The case may be heard by a judge only if both the prosecution and defense agree to waive the right to a jury.

Historically, the criminal jury was composed of 12 persons. The U.S. Supreme Court has ruled that the Sixth Amendment sets a minimum size of six for juries in criminal cases. Each state legislature has the right to set the jury size as long as there are at least six jurors. Many states still require 12 jurors.

The idea of a jury of our "peers" has been interpreted to mean that the jury must be from a cross-section of the adult population. Discrimination on the basis of race or gender is not allowed in the jury selection process.

The initial phase of jury selection is conducted by the jury commissioner or someone at the courthouse who handles assembling jurors. A master list of everyone eligible for jury duty must be compiled. Traditionally, voter registration records were used for this purpose. More recently, the master jury lists have been enlarged in order to cover a greater portion of the population. Some states now combine voter registration and driver's license information.

Names of people to be called for jury duty are randomly selected from the master list. Each state has its own list of reasons a person may use to be legally excused from jury duty. Financial hardship, caused by loss of wages during jury duty, is commonly accepted in many jurisdictions. Those not exempt from jury duty will be told to report to the courthouse on a given date. The length of jury service varies. Some courts require jurors to attend daily for one or more months. Others require jurors to come in one day a week for one month, while some only ask for one day. Once selected to sit on a jury, they must serve until the trial is over, except when excused for cause by the judge.

Prospective jurors spend a great deal of time waiting to be called to a courtroom. There is usually a jury assembly room where they can read, watch television, etc. When a judge is ready to start jury selection, the Jury

Commissioner's office is asked for a group of prospective jurors. Thirty people are frequently sent to the courtroom; the judge may ask for more if this does not turn out to be enough. Names may be drawn randomly each time a jury panel is requested or some other method, such as assigning jurors to groups before they arrive at the courthouse, may be used.

Once in the courtroom, names are randomly drawn to fill the jury box. Prospective jurors take an oath to answer questions truthfully. *Voir dire* (the process of questioning to determine if a person is qualified) is conducted to determine if these people can consider the evidence in the case with open minds. While *voir dire* was traditionally done by the attorneys, many states now allow the judge to ask the questions in order to save time. When jury questionnaires are used, a set of written questions is completed by each prospective juror and the answers reviewed by the attorneys before *voir dire* begins.

Examples of Questions Jurors Are Asked during *Voir Dire*
1. Do you know the defendant in the case?
2. Have you heard anything in the news about this case?
3. Do you believe that the police always arrest the right person?
4. Do you understand that the defense does not have to prove that the defendant is innocent?
5. Have you been on a jury before today?

The attorneys will ask the judge to dismiss anyone whose answers during *voir dire* indicate that he/she will not decide the case solely on the facts introduced at trial and the law as stated in the jury instructions. This request is called a "**challenge for cause**" and may be used as often as believed necessary. Reasons for being excused at this stage include racial bias against the defendant, belief that police only arrest the guilty, and exposure to pretrial publicity to the extent that the prospective juror has already formed a conclusion regarding the defendant's guilt or innocence. In order to successfully "challenge for cause," the attorney must convince the judge that the prospective juror will not base his/her decision on what occurs inside the courtroom. Generalities, such as friendship with a police officer or even being a police officer, are not enough.

If a juror is excused, a new name will be drawn. The new juror will be asked similar questions, and the attorneys will have a chance to challenge him/her. This process is repeated until there are enough people in the jury box to form a jury.

Next come the "**peremptory challenges**." These are used to allow each side to replace jurors whom they subjectively feel cannot be fair. No reason need be stated for using a peremptory challenge, but a juror may not be excluded solely on the basis of race or gender. The prosecution and defense alternate in using their peremptory challenges. If a juror is excused, a new juror will be called, questioned, and possibly challenged. The jury selection is completed when either the maximum allowed peremptory challenges have been used or both sides agree to accept the people then seated in the jury box.

State law establishes how many peremptory challenges there are in any given case. A typical state might allow each side six for misdemeanors, 12 for felonies, and 20 in death penalty cases. When there is more than one defendant, the procedure becomes more complicated. Generally, however, the number of challenges is increased in proportion to the number of defendants.

Alternate jurors are normally selected last. They become members of the jury only if one or more jurors become unable to complete the trial due to illness or other reasons. Alternates also may be challenged for cause. A separate number of peremptory challenges to be used on alternates may be set by state law.

Once the jury and alternates are selected, they take an oath to decide the case on the evidence admitted at trial and under the rules of law given to them by the judge. "Jeopardy" attaches to the defendant(s) at this point. The trial officially starts when the jury is given the oath.

In most states, jurors are given paper and urged to take notes as the case is presented. They will be told that they are not to discuss the case with people who are not on the jury; discussions of the case among jurors should not start until deliberations at the end of the trial. Recent excesses by tabloid journalists in high-publicity cases have led some states to enact laws prohibiting jurors from accepting money for telling about the case even after the verdict is returned. The judge may order the jury "**sequestered**" if it is believed this is the best way to protect jurors from outside influences that might affect their vote.

When a jury is sequestered, the bailiff keeps the jury together and prevents all contact with non-jurors. In high-publicity cases, where jurors may be prejudiced by media coverage, sequestering the jury may include housing them in a local hotel at night and requiring them to eat all of their meals together under the watchful eye of the bailiff. Due to the expense to the government and inconvenience to the jurors, this type of sequestering of the jury is rarely done in the early stages of a trial. It is common during deliberations, however, to require the jury and bailiff to eat meals together without outsiders presents, but jurors are allowed to go home each night.

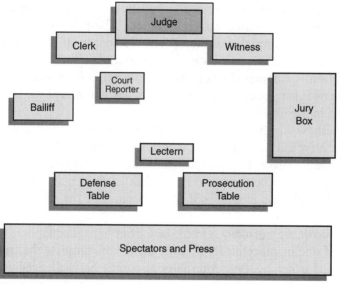

Figure 2-2
The Courtroom Setting

2-9b The Courtroom Setting

The center of attention in the courtroom is a dais on which the judge's desk and witness chair are located, usually enclosed by wood paneling. Facing the judge in the middle of the courtroom are two tables, one for the prosecution and the other for the defense. The prosecutor usually sits on the side of the room closest to the jury. There is usually a lectern for the attorneys to use when addressing the judge or questioning witnesses. The court clerk's desk is usually at the side of the judge's platform. If there is a court reporter, a small desk is usually located between the judge's platform and the tables for the attorneys. The bailiff's desk is frequently to one side of the room. The jury box is along one side of the room, perpendicular to the judge and attorneys. Facing the judge in the back of the room are seats for spectators and the press. Figure 2-2 illustrates the layout of a courtroom.

Technology is gradually coming to courtrooms, although the expense is still prohibitive for many jurisdictions. Whereas the only visual aids available in the past were chalkboards and easels with pads of newsprint, courtrooms may now be equipped with computer systems and large projection screens that make it possible to show the jury instantly each item the attorneys and witnesses are discussing. The attorneys may be required to have all photographs and diagrams transferred to CD or laser disc so that they can be shown in this manner. Videotapes may also be shown.

Another useful innovation is real-time stenographic reporting. In the past, the court reporter used the stenotype machine to keep a verbatim record of the proceedings, but only a person with special training could read the tape produced by the machine. Eventually the notes were transcribed and included in the court record. Computerized stenotype machines use software that automatically generates a transcript. Some courtrooms are equipped with monitors so the judge and attorneys can review the exact wording of questions if an objection is made or the witness asks to have the question repeated. The monitor can replace a sign language interpreter if a witness who has a hearing impairment is testifying. Some systems also allow the attorneys to mark the transcript with reference notes; such markings are confidential and not visible to other parties viewing the transcript on other monitors. Printouts of the transcripts are available at the end of the court session so the attorneys can prepare for the next day. This system also facilitates the process if the jury makes a request to have the testimony of a witness read to them during deliberations.

2-9c Opening Statements

An opening statement is a speech an attorney makes to the jury. It is *not* evidence in the case. Only evidence given at trial by witnesses under oath may be considered by the jury when they decide the case.

The purpose of the opening statement is to introduce the jury to the case. Two things are usually discussed in the opening statement—the facts of the case and the role of the jury in deciding guilt or innocence. Opening statements are particularly important in long cases because the jurors need help fitting the pieces of the puzzle together, especially if the facts will not be presented in chronological order.

Opening statements are optional. If the case is tried without a jury, it is common for both sides to skip the opening statement. When there is a jury, the prosecutor will normally give an opening statement. This will usually be the first thing that happens after the jury is sworn in and the charges are read.

Meanwhile, the defense has three options: (1) give an opening statement immediately after the prosecutor, (2) give an opening statement after the prosecution has called all of its witnesses, or (3) not give an opening statement at all. The defense attorney will make a tactical decision on what is the best way to proceed in each case.

The advantage of waiting to give an opening statement until after the prosecution has called its witnesses is that the presentation can be tailor-made for the evidence that has already been introduced against the defendant. It also allows the defendant to avoid revealing what the main defenses will be until after the prosecution has called all of its witnesses. The disadvantage of waiting is that the jurors will only hear the prosecution's side of the case prior to listening to the witnesses. This may result in the jurors placing too much weight on their testimony.

2-9d Prosecution's Case in Chief

The prosecution presents its case first. During the prosecution's case in chief the prosecutor must establish every element of each crime charged beyond a reasonable doubt. Each witness will be called to the witness stand, given the oath, and asked questions. Questioning by the attorney who called the witness is **direct examination.** During direct examination the attorney asks questions and the witness answers them. Questions are limited to things that are relevant to the case. A question that suggests the desired answer is called a **leading question** and is not usually allowed during direct examination; if asked, the opposing side may object. For example, on direct examination the prosecutor could ask "What color shirt was he wearing?" It would be considered a leading question to ask "Was he wearing a blue shirt?"

Questions are usually short and to the point so the witness can easily understand them. Argumentative questions, such as "Isn't it true that you drove the getaway car while he went inside the liquor store to commit the robbery?" are not allowed. Normally, the witness will be asked specific questions and will not be allowed to tell what happened in story form. A question that asks the witness "Tell me what happened," is called a narrative question and is rarely permitted.

Example of Direct Examination

Prosecutor: Where were you at 7:00 P.M. on October 27, 2003?
Witness: I was at John's house watching the World Series.
Prosecutor: Who was there with you?
Witness: John, my brother Bill, and some guy who is a friend of John but I don't know his name.
Prosecutor: Was there an argument?
Witness: Yes. John and Bill were yelling at each other about whether the umpire should have called a pitch a strike.
Prosecutor: Did you observe anything other than their shouting at each other?
Witness: Yes. John hit Bill.

While the prosecutor is conducting direct examination of a witness, the defense may make objections to the questions asked. The proper time to object is immediately after the question is asked and before the witness has a chance to answer. This is called the **Contemporaneous Objection Rule.**

The purpose of the rule is to allow the judge to decide if the question is proper before the jury hears the witness's answer. The attorney who made the objection will be required to state the legal rule which makes the question improper (for example, hearsay or a leading question). The attorney who asked the question will have a chance to explain why the question should be permitted before the judge makes a final decision. If the judge agrees that the objection is valid, the ruling will be "objection sustained" and the witness instructed not to answer the question. If the objection is considered improper, the ruling will be "objection overruled" and the witness told to answer it.

Example of Contemporaneous Objection Rule

Prosecutor:	Tell us what John said.
Defense:	Objection, your Honor. Hearsay.
Prosecutor:	Your Honor, John is the defendant in this case. His statements are admissible under the admissions exception to the Hearsay Rule.
Judge:	Objection overruled.

All evidence is introduced by calling witnesses to the stand. If any physical evidence, such as the murder weapon, is to be introduced into evidence, a witness must be called who can tell where the object was found and what happened to it since it was found. This is called **laying the foundation.** Once it has been shown that the object is relevant and it has been authenticated (shown that it has not been altered or tampered with), it will be given an identification number or letter. Frequently, objects introduced by one side are given numbers and the other side's evidence is given letters. For example, the prosecution may introduce the murder weapon and it will be marked "People's Exhibit 1," while the defense introduces fingerprints found at the scene and they are marked "Defense's Exhibit A."

Example of Laying the Foundation to Admit Physical Evidence

Prosecutor:	Did John hit Bill with his bare hand?
Witness:	No, he picked up a heavy ashtray and hit him with it.
Prosecutor:	Can you describe the ashtray?
Witness:	Yes, it was about four inches square and maybe two inches deep. I think it was made of glass. It had an Angel's logo on it.

Prosecutor:	Is this the ashtray?
Witness:	Yes.
Prosecutor:	How can you tell?
Witness:	I gave it to John for his birthday because he was an Angel's fan. I had it engraved "John, I hope your Angels win the series." If you look on the back of the ashtray, that is what it says.

The Sixth Amendment right to confront witnesses has been interpreted to mean that the defendant has the right to be present when prosecution witnesses testify. Reforms intended to ease the trauma child abuse victims suffer while testifying have had to comply with the Sixth Amendment. Screens or other physical barriers and closed circuit television can be used so that witnesses do not have to look at the defendant only if there is a clear showing that the physical confrontation would cause severe emotional trauma. The need for these protective measures must be determined on a case-by-case basis. The defendant and jurors watch the victim testify via television monitors. Though closed circuit television can be used when necessary to protect the abuse victim, the child who is testifying must be available for normal cross-examination.

After the prosecutor finishes questioning a witness, the defense attorney will have the opportunity to do so. This is called cross-examination. The purposes of cross-examination are to:

1. Follow up on statements made during direct examination.
2. Ask relevant questions that were not asked during direct examination.
3. Show that the witness should not be believed.

The Sixth Amendment confrontation clause gives the defendant the constitutional right to cross-examine all prosecution witnesses. Figure 2-3 shows how attorneys narrow the focus of a witness's testimony during questioning. Cross-examination is considered essential in the search for the truth. Most states follow the rule that cross-examination is limited to the scope of the direct examination (plus impeachment, see Chapter 5). This means that the cross-examination may only cover topics asked during direct examination. For example, if a prosecution witness testified about what happened during a robbery, the defense attorney could ask questions about details of the robbery that the prosecutor did not cover. But the defense could not ask about some other crime, such as a burglary committed by the defendant on a different day. The jury has the job of deciding who is telling the truth. Therefore, a witness may be cross-examined to show why he/she should not be believed. This is called

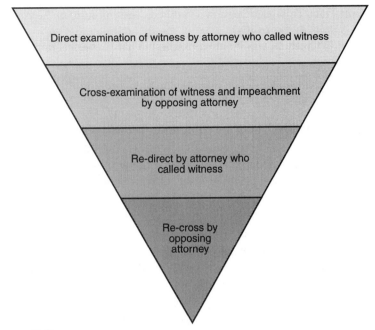

Direct examination of witness by attorney who called witness

Cross-examination of witness and impeachment
by opposing attorney

Re-direct by attorney who
called witness

Re-cross by
opposing
attorney

Figure 2-3
Narrowing Focus of Testimony

impeachment. Any witness who takes the stand can be impeached. Some of the ways to impeach are:

1. Showing that the witness is lying by submitting prior statements the witness made which are inconsistent with what he/she just said.
2. Calling witnesses to show that the person testifying has a reputation for dishonesty.
3. Proving that the witness is biased and might be distorting the facts.
4. Proving that the witness has a prior felony conviction.

If a witness is impeached, the attorney who called him/her may in turn attempt to show why the jury should believe the witness. This is called "rehabilitation." Impeachment and rehabilitation will be covered in more detail in Chapter 5.

Example of Impeachment and Rehabilitation

Defense: You testified that you heard John say, "If the Giants win I will kill you." Where were you when this statement was made?

Witness: On the other side of the room, maybe 10 feet away.

Defense: Do you have a hearing impairment?

Witness: Yes, I have a moderate loss in my left ear.

Prosecutor: (after cross-examination is finished): Are you sure you heard what John said correctly?

Witness: Oh, yeah, he was shouting. You would have to be deaf not to hear him.

After cross-examination the attorney who called the witness will have the opportunity to ask the witness more questions. This is referred to as re-direct examination. There are strict limits on what can be done during re-direct. It can be used to rehabilitate a witness who has been impeached or to ask questions aimed at clarifying what the witness said during cross-examination. Attorneys are not allowed to treat this as an opportunity to ask questions they forgot to ask earlier. After re-direct, the opposing attorney has a similar right to question the witness. This is referred to as re-cross-examination. The attorney conducting re-cross is allowed to ask questions to clarify information obtained during re-direct. Both re-direct and re-cross are optional and may be skipped if the attorney deems that further questioning is not necessary.

The trial will proceed with the prosecutor calling witnesses and conducting direct examination and the defense cross-examining them until the prosecutor is satisfied that each element *(corpus delicti)* of the crime(s) charged has been established beyond a reasonable doubt. The prosecutor is not required to call all possible witnesses, but the jury may decide that the case has not been proven if a person who apparently has important information is not called. When the prosecutor decides that no more witnesses will be called, he/she will inform the judge that the prosecution "rests its case."

Example of Prosecution Resting Its Case

Prosecutor: No more questions for this witness.

Judge: The witness may step down. Prosecutor, call your next witness.

Prosecutor: The prosecution rests.

2-9e Defense's Case in Chief

Since the burden of proof in a criminal case rests with the prosecution, the defense is not required to prove anything. At the end of the prosecution's case in chief, the defense may immediately make a motion to acquit the defendant. This motion would be based on the prosecution's failure to establish every element of the crime. The judge will normally grant such a request only if the prosecution has failed to introduce testimony regarding one or more elements of the crime.

The defense does not have to call any witnesses. The defense may use cross-examination of prosecution witnesses to show that the defendant should not be convicted. The defendant and his/her attorney will decide whether it is necessary to call defense witnesses. It must be kept in mind that any witnesses the defense calls can be cross-examined and possibly impeached by the prosecution. This includes the defendant if he/she decides to testify. The defense may rely on the fact that the prosecution did not prove its case beyond a reasonable doubt.

If the defense does call witnesses (which is usually the case), the defense attorney will conduct the direct examination of each witness followed by cross-examination by the prosecutor. One unique choice for the defense is calling character witnesses. The defense has the right to introduce evidence that the defendant has a good reputation for honesty, integrity, and other relevant traits. The defense hopes the jury will conclude that since the defendant is a "good person," he/she could not have committed the crime. If the defense does call character witnesses, the prosecution will be allowed to cross-examine them regarding both the defendant's character and the credibility of the character witness. The prosecution will also be allowed to call its own character witnesses during **rebuttal** to show that the defendant, in fact, has a poor reputation.

Example of Use of Character Witness

Defense Attorney:	Mr. Jones, are you familiar with the reputation of John, the defendant in this case?
Witness.	Yes.
Defense Attorney:	On what do you base your conclusions about his reputation?
Witness	I have lived next door to him for the last five years. Most of the neighbors are friendly and I have talked to them about John.
Defense Attorney:	Based on these contacts with the neighbors, what is John's reputation?
Witness:	Everyone thinks he is a good guy. He is very involved with his children. He is very gentle with them. He never gets angry. He is very helpful when someone is having trouble fixing something. If he gives you his word, he keeps it.

Once the defense has called all of its witnesses and they have been cross-examined, the defense rests.

2-9f Rebuttal and Rejoinder

Sometimes defense witnesses raise new issues, such as alibi or character. Rebuttal gives the prosecution a chance to call witnesses on these new issues. It is not used to fill gaps in the case accidentally left by the prosecution during the case in chief. The judge has the power to decide if the prosecution may call rebuttal witnesses. If rebuttal witnesses are called, the defense may cross-examine them.

Rejoinder is the calling of witnesses by the defense to attack the evidence introduced by the prosecution during rebuttal. If the judge allows rejoinder the prosecution will be allowed to cross-examine.

2-9g Closing Arguments and Summation

Closing arguments (also called summations) resemble opening statements in many ways. The main difference is that the attorneys may discuss only the evidence actually introduced during trial. The closing argument is each attorney's last chance to persuade the jurors to find for his/her side.

In most states the prosecution goes first. It will review the evidence and emphasize everything that points to the defendant's guilt. The defense follows, trying to show that the prosecution has not proven guilt beyond a reasonable doubt. The defense will stress its witnesses' versions of the facts and point out weaknesses in the prosecution's case. Many states allow the prosecution to reply after the defense has given its closing statement, providing the defense called witnesses during its case in chief. The reason for this is that the prosecution has such a heavy burden of proof.

2-9h Jury Instructions

Near the end of the case the judge will meet with the attorneys and select applicable jury instructions. Jury instructions are statements of law that will be read to the jury to tell them what rules to use when deciding the case. Important terms will be defined, such as "beyond a reasonable doubt," "malice," and "competency of a witness." Each crime will be defined. The jury will be told it has the right to decide which witnesses to believe and how important each witness's testimony was. The process of discussing the facts and voting on the verdicts will be explained.

Each attorney will prepare a list of jury instructions that he/she wants given. The individual instructions may be taken from a published book of jury instructions or written by the attorney. The instructions are usually based on the wording of prior court decisions or statutes. At their conference the judge will review prosecution and defense requests. Instructions requested by both sides will be included and given to the jury. If one side objects to the other's request, the judge will hear arguments from both sides and make a ruling. If no one has requested key instructions, the judge has the responsibility to add these instructions to the list.

Example of a Jury Instruction for Unarmed Bank Robbery

**Based on U.S. Court of Appeals for First Circuit
Model Criminal Jury Instructions for 18 U.S.C. § 2113(a)**

The defendant is accused of robbing the [bank, savings and loan association, or credit union]. It is against federal law to rob a federally insured [bank, savings and loan association, or credit union]. For you to find the defendant guilty of this crime, you must be convinced that the government has proven each of these things beyond a reasonable doubt:

First, that the defendant intentionally took money belonging to the [bank, savings and loan association, or credit union], from a [bank, savings and loan association, or credit union] employee or from the [bank, savings and loan association, or credit union] while a [bank, savings and loan association, or credit union] employee was present;

Second, that the defendant used intimidation or force and violence when he did so; and

Third, that at that time, the deposits of the [bank, savings and loan association, or credit union] were insured by the [_____]. [The parties have so stipulated].

Intimidation is actions or words used for the purpose of making someone else fear bodily harm if he or she resists. The actual courage or timidity of the victim is irrelevant. The actions or words must be such as to intimidate an ordinary, reasonable person.

After closing arguments, the judge will give the instructions to the jury. In some states this is done by reading the prepared statements. These states frequently give the jury a copy of the instructions to take to the jury room during deliberations. Other states allow the judge to instruct the jury about the case in a more informal manner.

2-9i Jury Deliberations

The judge will instruct the jurors regarding the selection of a foreman before they start deliberating the case. They will be told to discuss all the evidence before voting on any of the charges. Each charge must be voted on separately.

Jury deliberations normally take place in the jury room, which is usually located near the courtroom where the trial was held. The exhibits which were introduced into evidence are usually sent to the jury room. No one except the jurors is allowed in the jury room during deliberations. Alternate jurors are not present during deliberations unless they have taken the place of jurors who have been excused due to illness or other emergency. If a juror is excused after deliberations have begun, an alternate will be appointed, and the jury will be instructed to start deliberations over. Traditionally, total secrecy surrounded jury deliberations to the point that jurors could not even be called at a later time to testify about jury misconduct. Some states have changed this rule and now allow jurors to testify if the defendant moves to have a conviction reversed due to jury misconduct.

The jurors should discuss the case and consider each other's viewpoint. If there is disagreement about what a witness said, the jury can ask to have the verbatim record of key points of the testimony read to them. The judge will normally meet with the attorneys and discuss what should be said in response to these types of questions. Reading of testimony or giving additional instructions for the jury will be formally done in the courtroom with the prosecutor, defendant, and defense attorney present. Jurors will then return to the jury room.

The deliberation process allows the jurors to discuss the case and vote on each charge. If the vote is not decisive, they may continue the discussion and voting process. No time limits are set; deliberations may run from a few minutes to several days. Usually, the jury will finally agree on the outcome of the case; in other words—reach a verdict. Historically, criminal cases required an unanimous verdict. The U.S. Supreme Court has held that the Sixth Amendment only requires an unanimous verdict when the state uses six-member juries. When larger juries are used, unanimity is not necessary. The Supreme Court has approved verdicts of 9-3, 10-2, and 11-1. Each state's legislature must determine which standard will be used. Most states still require unanimous verdicts.

If the jurors cannot reach a verdict (i.e., are "deadlocked") the jury foreman will notify the judge of the problem. At this point neither side is told what the last vote was. The jurors return to the courtroom and the judge will ask questions to determine if there is any chance that the jurors can discuss the case further and reach a verdict. If any of the jurors indicates he/she might change his/her mind, the jury will be sent back for more deliberations. If the judge believes there is no chance of reaching a verdict, the jury will be dismissed and the trial will be over. This is referred to as having a "hung jury."

Example of a Jury Instruction Used When Jury Cannot Reach a Verdict

Based on U.S. Court of Appeals for Ninth Circuit Model Criminal Jury Instructions

Members of the jury, you have advised that you have been unable to agree upon a verdict in this case. I have decided to suggest a few thoughts to you.

As jurors, you have a duty to discuss the case with one another and to deliberate in an effort to reach a unanimous verdict if each of you can do so without violating your individual judgment and conscience. Each of you must decide the case for yourself, but only after you consider the evidence impartially with your fellow jurors. During your deliberations, you should not hesitate to reexamine your own views and change your opinion if you become persuaded that it is wrong. However, you should not change an honest belief as to the weight or effect of the evidence solely because of the opinions of your fellow jurors or for the mere purpose of returning a verdict.

All of you are equally honest and conscientious jurors who have heard the same evidence. All of you share an equal desire to arrive at a verdict. Each of you should ask yourself whether you should question the correctness of your present position.

I remind you that in your deliberations you are to consider the instructions I have given you as a whole. You should not single out any part of any instruction, including this one, and ignore others. They are all equally important.

You may now retire and continue your deliberations.

The defense usually requests that the charges be dismissed. If the case is dismissed the prosecutor cannot re-file the case. The judge rarely dismisses the charges unless the jury verdict was overwhelmingly in favor of the defendant (10-2, for example). If the charges are not dismissed, the prosecutor will have the right to re-file the case if he/she believes it is worth the additional time and effort.

2-9j Verdict

When the jury reaches a final decision, the foreman notifies the judge that a verdict has been reached. The defendant and all the attorneys will be told to return to the courtroom. Each charge and the corresponding verdict will be read. Figure 2-4 is an example of a verdict form that might be used in a trial. The attorneys have the right to ask each juror to state that he/she agrees with each verdict. This is called "**polling the jury.**" The purpose of polling the jury is to make sure that there has been no mistake. It also gives each juror one last chance to change his/her mind. After these procedures

> We the jury find the defendant, John Jones, Case No. CR-1234,
>
> ☐ Guilty
>
> ☐ Not Guilty
>
> Of the crime of murder in the first degree, Penal Code Section 187.
>
> Signed: _____   _____
>   Jury Foreman   Date

Figure 2-4
Example of a Verdict Form

have been completed, the court clerk will officially enter the verdict on each count (charge) into the court records.

2-10 Sentencing

If the verdict is guilty on any of the charges, the next step is sentencing. In many states, sentencing does not occur on the day the verdict is read. The main reason for this is the request by the court for a pre-sentence investigation report. Except when the statute gives the judge no choices regarding the sentence, this additional information will help the judge decide on the appropriate punishment. The exact content of these reports varies, but they usually include information on the defendant's past life and prior convictions (called a "social history"), as well as any aggravating or mitigating circumstances in the present case. Depending on the seriousness of the crime and local court rules, procedures range from having a probation officer prepare the report while the defendant is free on bail, to having a diagnostic study done while the defendant is confined in the reception center of the state prison. The defense is usually allowed to submit a similar report prepared by its own experts.

The purpose of the sentencing hearing is limited to determining what sentence should be imposed. The judge frequently has the option to sentence the defendant to probation, fine, and jail or prison. The length of the sentence, within limits set by the legislature, is also decided by the judge. Both sides usually have the right to call witnesses at the sentencing hearing. The person making the pre-sentence investigation report may be called and cross-examined. Victims may be given the right to make a statement to the judge. After reviewing all of the information, the judge will make a final decision at the sentencing hearing. Death penalty cases are somewhat unique because it is usually the jury, instead of the judge, that decides the sentence. Only a few states allow juries to sentence in non-capital cases.

Example of Judge Sentencing the Defendant

Judge: Mr. Jones, you have been convicted of the crime of robbery. I find that you committed this crime intentionally and there were no mitigating circumstances. I therefore sentence you to serve five years in the state prison. You are to pay a fine of $5,000 and make restitution to the victim in the amount of $3,251, the amount you took during the robbery. I hereby remand you to the custody of the State Department of Corrections.

At the close of the sentencing hearing, the defense attorney frequently informs the judge that an appeal will be filed. The judge will then decide if the defendant should be allowed out on bail while the appeal is in progress. The attorneys will be permitted to introduce evidence that the defendant is (or is not) likely to leave the state to avoid serving the sentence or that he/she may commit additional crimes if bail is granted. Figure 2-5 summarizes the stages of a trial.

2-11 Appeal

There are several ways to change a guilty verdict. After the jury returns a guilty verdict, the defense attorney may ask the trial judge to set aside the verdict and grant a new trial or enter an acquittal. The most common appeal is made to a higher court based on what happened at the trial. This is called a "**direct appeal.**" *Habeas corpus* can also be used to seek reversal, and is explained later in this section.

The most common reasons for setting aside a conviction are: (1) the jury convicted the defendant even though the judge believes no reasonable person could believe that he/she was guilty, or (2) the judge realizes there were legal errors committed during trial that are sure to result in a reversal on appeal. Double jeopardy prevents the prosecution from having the verdict set aside if the jury acquitted the defendant.

The direct appeal can be based only on what is included in the record of prior court hearings, including the preliminary hearing, any suppression hearings, and the trial. The record is frequently divided into two documents, the **reporter's transcript** and the **clerk's transcript.** The

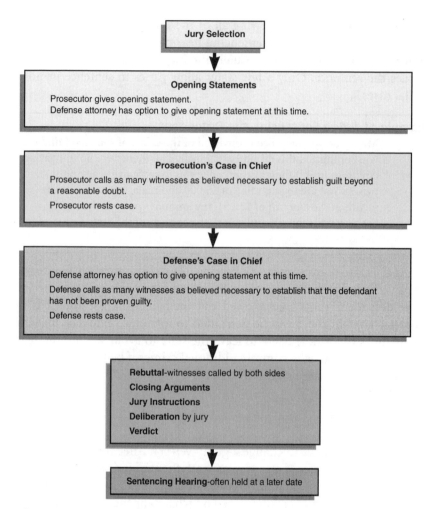

Figure 2-5
The Trial

reporter's transcript is a typed, verbatim record based on the notes the court reporter made at the proceeding (frequently with the help of a stenotype machine). It will include what the attorneys and judge said as well as what the witnesses said under oath. In courts where court reporters are not used, the attorneys are usually required to meet and agree on a statement of what happened during the trial. This is frequently called a "settle statement of facts."

The clerk's transcript includes copies of all documents filed with the court clerk during the case. This would include the complaint, information, indictment, any motions made to suppress evidence, requests for jury instructions and the entries of the clerk during court days. The daily entries list the names of the judge, defendant, and attorneys present, the purpose of the hearing, and the names of witnesses called (but not a summary of their testimony). During jury selection, the clerk's record lists the names of every person called to the jury box, as well as the names of the jurors selected. If a juror is excused and replaced by an alternate, this event is also indicated.

Direct appeals must be filed within a short time after conviction. The time for appeal is set out in the state statutes or court rules. Notice of appeal is usually required within 30 days or less after the sentencing hearing. The statutes or court rules also give the length of time the attorneys have to prepare briefs—30 days is common. The court can extend the length of time if the attorney makes a timely request and states a valid reason.

When the defense files a notice of appeal, the court will have the reporter's transcript and clerk's transcript prepared. Due to the expense of typing the reporter's transcript, it is usually not made prior to this time. If the defendant cannot afford the transcripts, the government is required to pay for them. The defense reviews all of the transcripts and then prepares a brief which will be filed with the appellate court. The brief usually begins with a summary of the facts of the case, listing the page numbers where this information can be found in the transcripts. Legal arguments for reversing the conviction follow. Each reason for reversal is usually discussed separately and includes statutes, court cases, and other legal references in support of the argument.

The American legal system places great reliance on the jury's ability to determine which witnesses are telling the truth. Therefore, cases are rarely reversed if the defense bases its appeal primarily on the credibility of witnesses. Occasionally a conviction is reversed because the court of appeals believes the case was so weak the jury should not have convicted. If a case is reversed on grounds of insufficient evidence, the legal consequences are the same as if the jury had acquitted the defendant. The prosecutor cannot re-file the case. Most appeals are based on legal problems with the case.

Examples of Issues That Can Be Raised on Appeal
- Confession obtained in violation of *Miranda* rules.
- Search violated the Fourth Amendment.
- Improper jury instruction given by judge.
- Judge improperly sustained objections and refused to allow a witness to testify on important questions.

Examples of Issues That Can Not Be Raised on Appeal
• Weight to be placed on testimony of individual witnesses.
• Credibility of each witness.
• Possible testimony of witnesses who were not called during trial.

Appellate courts often rule an error harmless even when the defense correctly points to errors that occurred at trial. The "**Harmless Error Rule**" allows the conviction to stand unless the court believes that the error had a substantial influence on the outcome of the case. If the conviction is reversed on one of these legal grounds, the prosecution has the right to re-file the case.

The defense can also appeal on the grounds that the judge improperly sentenced the defendant. If this is the only grounds for reversal, the case will be sent back to the trial court for a new sentencing hearing, but the conviction will still stand.

The defendant has the right to one appeal immediately after being convicted. The appellate court cannot refuse to review the case. If the defendant cannot afford to hire an attorney to handle the appeal, the court must appoint one for this purpose. After the first appeal, the court has the right to reject further appeals. Both the highest state court and the U.S. Supreme Court have formal procedures which allow the defendant to request review of the case, but only a small percentage of the cases are given full hearings. In many states, the highest court handles the first appeal if the defendant was given a death sentence.

Habeas corpus is a separate civil lawsuit used to challenge illegal confinement. Being in jail, prison, or on probation or parole due to an improper conviction is considered to be illegal confinement. The defense files a Petition for a Writ of *Habeas Corpus*. The petition briefly states why the person filing the petition believes the conviction should be reversed. The prosecution must file a reply giving reasons the conviction is valid. If the judge reviewing the petition believes there are valid legal grounds to consider the case, a hearing will be held. At this hearing, unlike on direct appeal, both sides can call witnesses who will be subject to both direct and cross-examination. Another dissimilarity between *habeas corpus* and the direct appeal is that *habeas corpus* can be filed at any time as long as the defendant is still in custody; direct appeals are restricted to the time period immediately following the trial.

Examples of Issues That Should Be Raised by *Habeas Corpus*
• Person was illegally arrested and is being held in county jail.
• Person was placed in a mental hospital against his/her will and claims to be legally sane.
• Person is in jail and has served the entire sentence but has not been released.

- Defendant was denied his/her right to an attorney at trial because the defense attorney was incompetent.

Examples of Issues That Should Not Be Raised by *Habeas Corpus*
- The judge did not give proper jury instructions during the trial.
- The evidence presented at trial was not sufficient to convict the defendant.
- The defendant was illegally arrested and therefore should receive monetary payment from the arresting officer and police department.

Habeas corpus is usually the best way to request reversal on the grounds that the defense attorney at trial was incompetent. The hearing is usually needed to determine how much research and preparation the attorney did prior to trial. *Habeas corpus* has also been successfully used when the U.S. Supreme Court made retroactive rules that affected cases that were beyond the time limits for direct appeals. One such case was *Gideon v. Wainwright,*[1] which declared that a criminal defendant who cannot afford to hire an attorney has a constitutional right to have the state provide a free lawyer for his/her trial.

Summary

The prosecutor may consider all facts and evidence available when deciding what charges to file. At the preliminary hearing witnesses must be called to testify regarding every element of each crime charged. A grand jury also needs to hear testimony regarding all elements of all crimes in the indictment.

Suppression hearings are based on testimony made under oath. This is either taken from transcripts of previous hearings, such as the preliminary hearing, or witnesses are called at the suppression hearing.

Attorneys exchange information during discovery. If a formal discovery motion is filed, it will contain legal references showing the right to receive what has been requested. Witnesses are not usually called at this hearing.

The trial process begins with jury selection. Jurors are under oath to truthfully answer questions regarding their ability to serve. Jurors who have already made up their minds about the defendant's guilt are excused. Attorneys also have the right to remove a limited number of jurors for other reasons.

The attorneys may preview the evidence in the case during opening statements, but opening statements are not evidence in the case. The attorneys have a duty to discuss only evidence that they believe will be presented during the trial.

The prosecution must convince the jury beyond a reasonable doubt that the defendant committed the crimes charged. This is done by calling witnesses and introducing physical evidence. When the prosecutor calls a witness, he/she conducts the direct examination of that witness. The defense attorney will cross-examine the witness in order to show that the direct examination left out information and to attack the truthfulness of the witness.

After the prosecution has finished calling its witnesses, the defense may call witnesses. When the defense calls witnesses the defense attorney conducts direct examination and the prosecutor will cross-examine. Since the prosecution has the burden of proof, the defense is not required to call any witnesses.

Closing statements are not evidence in the case. During closing statements the attorneys summarize the evidence, point out the weaknesses in the other side's evidence, and urge the jury to vote for their side.

The jury will be given instructions which the judge and attorneys have selected. The jury will go into deliberations and decide the outcome of the case based on the legal rules provided in the jury instructions. If the jury is unable to reach a verdict (hung jury), the prosecutor may retry the case unless the judge dismisses the charges.

Witnesses may be called at the sentencing hearing. Their testimony may cover any information the judge can use to decide what is an appropriate sentence. This frequently includes facts about prior crimes, physical trauma suffered by victims, and other information that would not be allowed at trial.

Neither the direct appeal nor the motion to set aside a verdict involve calling new witnesses. They are based on what happened at trial. Witnesses may be called at a *habeas corpus* hearing to show why the conviction is illegal.

Discussion Questions

1. What facts may the prosecutor consider when deciding what charges to file?
2. What is the standard of proof at the preliminary hearing?
3. What types of evidence may the prosecution and the defense introduce at the preliminary hearing?
4. Explain the role the grand jury serves in criminal cases.
5. What facts may the grand jurors consider when deciding what charges to include in the indictment?
6. What information must the prosecution and the defense exchange during discovery?
7. Discuss what evidence the defense may introduce at a suppression hearing.
8. Describe how juries are selected.
9. What is the purpose of the opening statement and the closing argument?
10. How does cross-examination differ from rebuttal evidence?
11. What is a jury instructed to do during deliberations?
12. Describe what happens if the jury cannot reach a verdict.
13. What evidence may be considered by the judge at the sentencing hearing?
14. What evidence may the judges consider when deciding a case on direct appeal?
15. What evidence may the judge consider when ruling on a Petition for Writ of *Habeas Corpus?*

Endnote

1. *Gideon v. Wainwright* 372 U.S. 335. 9 L.Ed. 2d 799, 83 S.Ct. 792 (1963).

Types of Evidence

Outline

Key Terms

- At issue
- Circumstantial evidence
- Conclusive presumption
- Corroborative evidence
- Cumulative evidence
- Direct evidence
- Documentary evidence
- Inference
- Judicial notice
- Limited admissibility
- Material evidence
- Presumption
- Probative value
- Real evidence
- Rebuttable presumption
- Relevant evidence
- Stipulation
- Testimonial evidence

After studying this chapter, you will be able to:

- Define relevant and material evidence and explain when each is admissible in court.
- Define circumstantial evidence and explain how it differs from direct evidence.
- Explain the difference between testimonial and real evidence.
- Define stipulation and judicial notice and explain how each applies in court.
- Describe presumptions and how they are used in court.

3-1 Relevant Evidence

In the study of the rules of evidence, there are several basic terms that must be understood before going to specific issues. This chapter will discuss the more important of these key terms.

One of the basic concepts of evidence is that only **relevant evidence** is admissible in court. There are situations, however, where even relevant evidence will not be admitted. One is where the evidence was obtained in violation of the defendant's constitutional rights. This rule will be discussed later in detail (see Chapter 10). Two other common reasons for excluding evidence are violations of the Hearsay Rule (see Chapter 8) or the information is privileged (see Chapter 9).

To put it as simply as possible, something is relevant if it tends to prove (or disprove) a disputed point or issue in the case. One of the keys to what is relevant is the question of what is "**at issue**" in the case. "At issue" refers to all disputed facts that are required to establish the elements of the crime(s) charged and the defendant's guilt beyond a reasonable doubt; facts necessary to establish the defense are also "at issue." When the defendant enters a plea of "Not Guilty," all the facts needed to establish the crimes charged are, in effect, disputed. Evidence can be admitted to establish these facts. If the prosecution feels it is necessary, more than one witness may be called to testify about the same fact or event. On the other hand, if the defendant admits something, such as the prior conviction, the facts regarding the crime which resulted in that conviction are no longer at issue. No evidence can be admitted to prove facts that are not at issue.

Relevant Evidence Defined

Relevant evidence is any evidence that tends to prove or disprove any disputed fact in the case. It merely needs to show that it is more probable that the fact exists than it appeared before the evidence was introduced. No single piece of evidence has to make a fact appear more probable than not.

Another key to admissibility is **probative value.** This means that the evidence must make it appear that a fact probably occurred. Sometimes there is one piece of evidence that conclusively proves the case. This is rare, however. More commonly there are a variety of pieces of evidence which, when considered together, convince the jury that the defendant is guilty beyond a reasonable doubt. It is hard to decide what weight any one piece of evidence will have in convincing the jury that the defendant is guilty or innocent. Any evidence that might have some impact on the jury has probative value. If an attorney makes an objection based on lack of relevance, the judge must decide if the evidence is likely to have any effect on the jury. If not, the evidence will not be admitted. This determination is made on a question-by-question basis during both direct and cross-examination.

Examples of Relevant Evidence
- Defendant's fingerprints were on the murder weapon.
- Defendant was the last person seen with the victim before her death.
- Defendant was the beneficiary of a large life insurance policy on the life of the victim.
- Defendant had previously threatened to kill the victim.
- Defendant disappeared the day after the victim died.

Relevant evidence must also be "**material.**" There currently appear to be two different definitions of material:

1. Evidence is material if it is logically connected with some fact that is at issue.
2. Material evidence is evidence that is important to the case—it cannot be too remotely connected to the facts at issue.

In practice, relevant evidence is material only if it meets both of these tests:

1. It must be relevant to some fact that is at issue in the case, AND
2. It must have more than just a remote connection to the fact.

There are several other limits to the admissibility of relevant evidence. These restrictions apply to evidence that does not have very great probative value. A balancing test is used to determine if the value of the evidence outweighs the problems it may cause at trial.

Relevant evidence is not admissible if it would be unduly prejudicial due to its emotional impact on the jury. The court is cautious about admitting evidence if it would be likely to arouse either hostility or sympathy toward either side. The defendant's prior convictions are in this category. In most cases the prior conviction has only slight relevance, but the chance that the jury will believe that the defendant was more likely to have committed the current crime merely because of the prior conviction is great. Therefore, evidence of prior conviction is usually not admissible by the prosecution during its case in chief. If the defendant takes the witness stand, his/her prior record may be used to impeach. Prior convictions are also admissible at the sentencing hearing.

On the other hand, pictures of the murder victim may arouse the hostility of the jury towards the defendant, but they are usually admissible because of their greater relevance to the case. Even in these types of cases, prosecutors face restrictions on the number of photographs or their size (e.g., limited to 8" × 10"); some judges permit black and white pictures but not color photographs.

Other reasons for rejecting relevant evidence are that it may distract the jury from the main issues of the case or that it would take too much court time to prove a fact that has only minimal relevance. An example of this is the court's reluctance to allow testimony regarding laboratory tests which do not have a record of very high accuracy. In one case a child had contracted a rare form of venereal disease when she was sexually molested. The court refused to admit the laboratory tests showing that the defendant had the same disease because the test could only show that there was a 20 percent probability that a person had transmitted the disease to the victim. Another example is the limitation placed on calling a witness to impeach someone who has already testified. If the testimony is being questioned because of inconsistencies on minor details, the judge will not allow the opposing side to call another witness because this is unduly time consuming and distracts the jury from the main issues of the case.

Cumulative evidence may also be excluded. Cumulative evidence merely restates what has already been admitted into evidence. For example, if there were ten eyewitnesses to the crime and they all gave basically the same account of what happened, their testimony would be cumulative. How many eyewitnesses will be allowed to testify is up to the judge. Probably, after two or three have said the same thing, the judge would sustain an objection that the testimony is merely cumulative and should not be allowed. On the other hand, if their testimony corroborates what has already been introduced, it is usually admissible.

Examples of Cumulative Evidence
- John testified that he was at 3rd and Main at 10:00 P.M. on November 3 and saw a man flee the scene in a Ford.
- Henry testified that he was at 3rd and Main at 10:00 P.M. on November 3 and saw a man flee the scene in a red Ford sedan.
- Jack testified that he was at 3rd and Main at 10:00 P.M. on November 3 and saw a man run from the store, get in a red car and leave in a hurry.

The distinction is that cumulative evidence basically repeats the same thing that has already been introduced, whereas **corroborative evidence** supports the prior testimony by providing additional evidence to confirm what the previous witness has said, without merely duplicating it. Real evidence may be used to corroborate testimonial evidence. For example, a ballistics test that shows a gun has been fired corroborates the testimony of a witness who said she saw the defendant fire the gun.

Examples of Corroborative Evidence
- Adam testified that he was at 1st and Cedar at midnight on November 3 and he saw a red car speed past. As it went by someone threw an apparently empty bank bag out the window.
- Sam testified that he walked through the intersection of 1st and Cedar at 11:55 P.M. on November 2 on his way to liquor store to buy cigarettes and there was nothing unusual on the ground. On his way home ten minutes later he found an empty bank bag in the street.

When there is a question about the admissibility of relevant evidence, the judge will be called upon to exercise discretion. Both sides will be allowed to argue why their requests should be granted. The judge will then make a ruling which may be appealed at the end of the trial. Such rulings are upheld as long as they are logical and do not violate common sense.

Evidence may be relevant if introduced for one purpose but irrelevant for some other purpose. This is called "**limited admissibility.**" For example, a prior statement of the defendant may be admitted to show inconsistencies between what he/she testified to in court and what was said to the police. The purpose of introducing this earlier statement is to show that the defendant is lying, and it is relevant for this purpose. The same statement, however, may be irrelevant if used to show that the earlier statement is true and the in-court statement is false.

Examples of Relevant Evidence

- Witness to bank robbery wrote down the license number of the "getaway" car. Records show that defendant owned the car with that license.

  This evidence is relevant because it makes it more probable that the defendant committed the robbery. It is, however, far from conclusive. The defense can introduce evidence to show that the witness did not copy the license number correctly or that the defendant's car was stolen the day before the robbery.

- Five minutes after a theft, the defendant was stopped near the scene. Defendant had a unique ring in his pocket that had been taken in the theft.

  This evidence is relevant because it makes it appear more probable that the defendant committed the theft. It is not conclusive. The defense can show that there is some other explanation for the defendant having the ring.

- In a trial for rape, the defendant has admitted that he had sexual intercourse with the victim. His defense is based on his claim that the victim consented to the sexual act. The prosecutor wants to admit evidence that the defendant matches the physical description given to the police by the victim immediately after the crime.

  Ordinarily this evidence would be relevant, but under the facts of this case it is not. Due to the defense of consent, the defendant has admitted that he is the person who had intercourse with the victim. His identity is not in issue. Therefore, evidence which shows that he is the person the victim described is not relevant.

3-2 Direct and Circumstantial Evidence

One method of classifying evidence divides all evidence into two types: direct and circumstantial. A conviction can be based on either direct or **circumstantial evidence** or a combination of both. The defense attorney's favorite argument, "It is only circumstantial evidence," may be reassuring to the defendant, but it is legally possible to convict a person solely on the basis of circumstantial evidence.

Direct evidence of a fact in issue is always relevant. In a criminal case, direct evidence usually involves eyewitness testimony regarding the commission of the crime. For example, it would be considered direct evidence if a witness testified that he saw the defendant shoot the murder victim. If the jury believes the witness is telling the truth, it has no choice but to conclude that the defendant shot the victim. On the other hand, it is only circumstantial evidence if the witness testified that he heard a gunshot and ran to the scene of the crime just in time to see the defendant run from the location with a smoking gun in her hand. This is not direct evidence because it is necessary to draw a conclusion from the facts given, namely that the person with the smoking gun is the same person who shot the victim. Even though the jury believes the witness, it can still conclude that someone else shot the victim and the defendant merely picked up the gun after the shooting and ran with it.

Direct Evidence Defined

Direct evidence is based on personal knowledge or observation of the person testifying. No inference or presumption is needed. If the testimony is believed by the jury, the fact it relates to is conclusively established.

Circumstantial Evidence Defined

Circumstantial evidence indirectly proves a fact. It requires the trier of fact to use an inference or presumption in order to conclude that the fact exists.

Circumstantial evidence may be so strong that it is nearly conclusive or so weak that it is immaterial. Admissibility of weak circumstantial evidence is at the discretion of the judge.

An **inference** is a logical conclusion that a person can make based on a fact or group of facts. The jury decides when to draw inferences. A **presumption** is a conclusion that the law requires the jury to make. In the example of the woman with the smoking gun, it is a logical conclusion that she shot the victim if there was no one else at the shooting scene between the time gunshot was heard and she was observed running away. The jury will make the final determination on whether to draw this conclusion. The defense may be able to offer a logical explanation for her conduct that convinces the jury that someone else actually shot the victim. If a presumption had been involved, the jury would have been told what conclusion the law required them to draw. (Presumptions will be covered in more detail later in this chapter.)

There are many common situations in which circumstantial evidence is frequently used in criminal cases. Some states have actually enacted these into law; others merely allow the jurors to use their common sense and draw the logical conclusions.

Examples of Direct and Circumstantial Evidence

- **Fact:** The defendant was seen running from the scene immediately after the crime occurred.
  Inference: The defendant committed the crime.
- **Fact:** The defendant was the only person who knew the combination to the safe.
  Inference: The defendant opened the safe.
- **Fact:** The victim had a reputation for being an obnoxious bully.

Inference: The victim started the fight and the defendant was acting in self-defense.
- **Fact:** Eyewitness saw defendant put poison in the food and watched while the victim ate it.
Inference: None. This is direct evidence that defendant poisoned the victim.

Direct and circumstantial evidence will be discussed in more detail in Chapter 4.

3-3 Testimonial and Real Evidence

Another method of classifying evidence is by the way it is presented in court. There are a variety of terms that are used for this purpose. This book divides evidence into two types: (1) testimonial and (2) real. You should note that this is a separate classification system. An item, such as the defendant's gun which was found near the murder scene, can be correctly classified as both circumstantial evidence and real evidence.

The key concept in **testimonial evidence** is that a person is testifying under oath or affirmation. *Note:* An affirmation is a solemn formal declaration used in place of an oath for those persons whose religious beliefs forbid oath-taking.

Testimonial Evidence Defined

Testimonial evidence is evidence given by a competent witness while testifying under oath or affirmation in a court proceeding. Affidavits and depositions are frequently included in testimonial evidence.

All evidence must be introduced through the testimony of a person on the witness stand. The verbal content of what the witness says is testimonial evidence. This includes both direct and cross-examination. If the witness tells about seeing the defendant shoot the victim, this is testimonial evidence. But if the gun is admitted into evidence, the gun is real evidence.

A witness must be under oath or affirmation. This is the normal procedure at trial. A written statement made out of court under oath or affirmation is called an affidavit. A deposition is a pretrial procedure mainly used in civil cases. An attorney for each side and a stenographic reporter are usually present when a deposition is taken. The witness is placed under oath and asked questions. Cross-examination may be permitted; attorneys are allowed to make objections. In many states, the transcript of this session may be read into evidence if the witness later becomes unavailable to testify. Testimonial evidence will be covered in more detail in Chapter 5.

There is some confusion regarding the correct term for objects that are admitted into evidence. **Real evidence,** physical evidence, demonstrative evidence, tangible evidence, and **documentary evidence** are all commonly used terms. Various authors define one term so that it includes the others. Students should be aware that the above terms are frequently used interchangeably.

Real Evidence Defined

Real evidence is anything (except testimonial evidence) that can be perceived with the five senses that tends to prove a fact that is at issue.

Many states only consider objects that are admitted into evidence as exhibits to be real evidence. Some authors use a broader approach and apply the term real evidence to items such as drawings on blackboards or butcher paper which were made while a witness was testifying but not formally introduced into evidence. Real evidence will be covered in more detail in Chapters 6 and 7.

Examples of Real Evidence
- Physical items: guns, knives, clothing
- Documents: checks, contracts, letters, ransom notes, newspapers, maps, deeds, wills, fingerprint cards, computer files
- Exhibits made for trial: models, scale drawings, charts, demonstrations
- Pictures: still photographs, enlargements, moving pictures, videos, digital images, photocopies, X-ray films

---

3-4 Substitutes for Evidence

There are some situations in which the jury is specifically told what facts to believe rather than having the opposing sides introduce evidence on the issue. These can be divided into three categories: (1) stipulations, (2) judicial notice, and (3) presumptions.

3-4a Stipulations

An agreement between the opposing attorneys to admit that one or more facts exist is called a stipulation. If the agreement is made before trial, the **stipulation** will usually be introduced in court in the form of a written document. When stipulations are reached during trial, they are usually stated orally for the record. The judge will tell the jurors that they must conclude that the stipulated fact exists and give it the same weight as if it had been proven during the trial. This statement may be made both at the time the stipulation is entered and again in the jury instructions.

Attorneys may agree to make a stipulation for a variety of reasons. Probably the most common is that one side knows the other side can easily prove the facts involved. For example, all the prosecution has to do to prove that the defendant has a prior conviction is to give the judge a certified copy of the conviction. For this reason, the defense frequently agrees to stipulate to the prior.

Another reason for stipulating may be that the facts would prejudice the jury against the defendant. For example, the prosecutor is charging that the defendant has a prior felony conviction. Since the prior is for a gruesome crime almost identical to the present one, the defendant does not want the jury to hear the details. By agreeing to stipulate to the prior, the defendant can keep the prosecution from telling the jury the details of the prior crime.

Stipulations are also made on minor points of the case. Both sides agree that proving these small details is too time consuming, therefore, they stipulate to them.

Since stipulations involve a voluntary agreement between the attorneys, there are also cases where there obviously should have been a stipulation, but there was none. This can be caused by antagonism between the attorneys, failure to communicate, or lack of preparation. Occasionally it is a trial tactic.

Examples of Stipulations

- The charges include the fact that the defendant has a prior conviction. The defense may be willing to stipulate that the prior conviction exists and prevent the prosecution from introducing details of that crime.
- The event happened at 10:00 P.M. Both sides may be willing to stipulate that the crime occurred at night. *Note:* This fact could also come in under judicial notice.
- In a drunk driving case, it may be stipulated that the emergency room staff used proper techniques in taking the blood sample from the defendant.

3-4b Judicial Notice

Judicial notice is a procedure where the judge, on his/her own authority, tells the jury to conclude that a fact exists. The jury is required to follow this instruction. An attorney may request that the judge take judicial notice of some point or the judge may decide to do it without a request.

The idea behind judicial notice is that it is a waste of time to require proof of commonly known facts. Some states break this down and make it mandatory that judicial notice be taken, if requested, of the state's own laws, the federal Constitution, and well-known scientific facts. They let individual judges decide whether to take judicial notice of lesser known facts and out-of-state law.

As used in judicial notice, "commonly known facts" refers to facts that are well known in the community, including the scientific community. The judge's personal knowledge of the fact is not important. If the judge has a doubt about how well-known the fact is, it is the duty of the attorney who requested judicial notice to convince the judge that the fact qualifies.

Judicial notice is not requested if the parties enter into a stipulation. If the attorneys know that the judge will automatically grant judicial notice, they may not bother to draft a stipulation. On the other hand, one side may request judicial notice because the other side refused to stipulate. In these cases the opposing counsel may argue that judicial notice is not properly taken. It seems to be a contradiction that there could be dispute on what are "commonly known facts." The issues would most likely arise when the attorney requesting judicial notice is attempting to abuse the procedure or the attorney objecting to it is unfamiliar with local law on judicial notice. In the case of scientific facts, it is also common to see debates on the propriety of judicial notice when the scientific fact involved has been recently established or is still controversial.

Examples of Items Subject to Judicial Notice

- Law: U.S. Constitution, state constitution, United States Code, state codes. Out-of-state laws and foreign laws usually have to be shown to the judge before judicial notice is taken
- Court records and court rules
- Scientific facts: temperature at which water freezes, time of sunset and sunrise, probabilities of occurrences of various blood types, accuracy of properly maintained radar equipment used to determine the speed of a car, high and low tides
- Local facts: which cities are in the court district, which streets run north-south, location of landmarks, fact that a given area is uninhabited.

3-4c Presumptions

When a presumption is involved, the judge instructs the jury to draw specific conclusions from the facts. Unlike stipulations and judicial notice, in order to use a presumption the attorney must convince the jury that at least some of the facts exist.

Presumption Defined

A presumption is a conclusion which the law requires the jury to draw from facts that have been established at trial. The judge instructs the jurors when they are to use a presumption.

There are two constitutional limitations on presumptions in criminal cases: they must be based on a logical assumption rather than mere policy, and, when used by the prosecution, the basic fact must be established beyond a reasonable doubt. A presumption that a person intends the ordinary consequences of his/her voluntary acts is unconstitutional because the jury could believe it shifts the burden of persuasion to the defendant.

The following presumptions have also been found to be unconstitutional: intent to commit theft by fraud is presumed when there is a failure to return rental cars within 20 days of the owner's demand, and a person is presumed to have embezzled a rental car if it was not returned within five days of the expiration of the rental agreement.

Some states list specific presumptions in their codes and specifically state the effect of each presumption. Others rely on the common law or the local state's case law.

Presumptions are generally divided into two types: conclusive and rebuttable. **Rebuttable presumptions** can be further divided into strong and weak. Which category a presumption falls into is governed by the social policy behind it. Not all states will find the same policy reason for a presumption, so it may not be considered to be in the same category in all states.

To understand how presumptions work you should think of two terms: the basic fact and the presumed fact. The basic fact is the fact that one side must prove to the jury in order for the jury to use the presumption. The presumed fact is the fact that the jury is told to conclude exists. In its simplest form, a presumption requires the jury to conclude that the presumed fact is true if the jury believes the basic fact has been established. In all presumptions the opposing side can try to convince the jury that the basic fact did not occur.

The role of the presumed fact changes according to the social policy involved. In cases where social policy is strongest (i.e., **conclusive presumptions**) no one is allowed to refute the existence of the presumed fact but attacks on the basic fact may be used to avoid the conclusion that the presumption directs the jury to draw. There are very few conclusive presumptions. When a rebuttable presumption is involved, the opposing side can attempt to disprove either the basic fact or the presumed fact. With a strong rebuttable presumption, many states give the opposing side the task of either disproving the basic fact or the presumed fact. Merely casting a doubt on the existence of the presumed fact is not enough. The lowest level of social policy is involved in weak rebuttable presumptions. These are usually created to expedite the trial rather than to enforce the interests of society. In these cases, the presumption completely disappears if the opposing side has introduced evidence to disprove the presumed fact; the jury will not even be told that the presumption exists.

It is helpful to work through several presumptions in order to understand how they operate. First, consider the conclusive presumption that a child born to a married couple who are living together was fathered by the husband unless the husband is impotent or sterile. There is a strong social policy favoring the legitimacy of children involved in this presumption. Some states refuse to consider DNA evidence that could scientifically disprove paternity. A growing number of states are abandoning this presumption and relying on scientific tests to accurately determine paternity.

The party wishing to use this presumption must convince the jury that all three of these conditions (the basic fact) are met. The opposing party may disprove the basic fact. If the jury concludes that all the conditions of the basic fact exist, it must conclude that the child is the legitimate child of the husband. The opposing side is not allowed to try to convince the jury that this is not true by introducing evidence to show that someone else is the father. The jurors are instructed that if they believe the married couple were living together and that if they believe he was not impotent or sterile, they must conclude that the child is legitimate.

Now let's look at a strong rebuttable presumption. A presumption that many states place in this category is that a person who has disappeared and has not been heard from in five years is presumed to be dead. The basic fact is that a person has disappeared and has not been heard from in five years. The presumed fact is that the person is dead.

The party that wishes to use this presumption must establish that the person has disappeared and has not been heard from in five years. If this is done, and the other side introduces no evidence on the issue, the jury must conclude that the person in question is dead.

The opposing side can attack the presumption in two ways: show that the person has been heard from during the last five years (disprove the basic fact) or show that the person is not dead (disprove the presumed fact). Testimony from people who claim to have seen the person recently can be used to attack the basic fact. Evidence that there was a motive for the disappearance, such as escaping prosecution for a serious felony, can be used to attack the presumed fact.

The jurors are usually instructed that if they believe the person has disappeared and has not been heard from, they must conclude that he/she is dead unless they believe the other side's explanation for the disappearance.

The next illustration involves a weak rebuttable presumption: a letter that is properly mailed (correctly addressed, stamped, and put in the U.S. mail) is presumed to reach its destination. This is a presumption established solely to facilitate the trial.

Everyone knows that the mail service is not perfect, but it is easier to start with the general assumption that a letter will get to its destination. If the opposing side tries to show that the letter was not correctly mailed (attacks the basic fact) the jury will be instructed that if they believe the letter was correctly mailed they must conclude that it got to its destination. On the other hand, if the opposing side introduces testimony that the letter never reached the addressee, the presumption ceases to exist, and the jury will not even be told about the presumption. Figure 3-1 illustrates each of the presumptions.

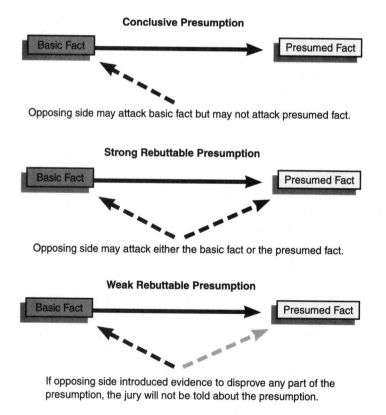

Figure 3-1
Conclusive, Strong Rebuttable, and Weak Rebuttable Presumptions

Summary

Only relevant evidence can be admitted in court. This means that the evidence must tend to prove something that is required in the case. Not only must it be relevant, but the value of the evidence must be sufficient to make the evidence material.

Evidence can be divided into direct or circumstantial. Direct evidence proves the point without the need to draw any conclusions. Circumstantial evidence requires the jury to draw a conclusion that some relevant fact occurred.

Another system of classification divides evidence into two categories: testimonial and real. Testimonial evidence covers what witnesses say under oath or affirmation. Real evidence includes all types of tangible objects.

There are three main substitutes for evidence. The opposing attorneys may agree that a fact exists without proving it to the jury. This is called a stipulation. A judge may take official notice of commonly known facts. Judicial notice is the name for this procedure. Presumptions require the jury to draw specific conclusions if certain basic facts have been established. In all of these situations the jury is told to assume that a fact has been proven when in fact it has not been. This is done to expedite the trial and, in some cases, to protect strong social policies.

Discussion Questions

1. Define *relevant* and *material evidence* and explain how they differ.
2. List two situations where relevant evidence would not be admissible in court.
3. Define *direct* and *circumstantial evidence* and give two examples of each.
4. Define *testimonial* and *real evidence* and give two examples of each.
5. Compare and contrast stipulation and judicial notice, and give two examples of facts that could be judicially noticed.
6. Define *inference*, and give an example of its application.
7. Differentiate between a rebuttable presumption and a conclusive presumption.
8. Give an example of a conclusive presumption and a rebuttable presumption.

CHAPTER **4**

Direct and Circumstantial Evidence

Outline

Key Terms

- Character
- Circumstantial evidence
- Credibility of the witness

- Direct evidence
- Matter of law
- *Modus operandi*

- Reputation
- Weight of each piece
  of evidence

After studying this chapter, you will be able to:

- Define both *direct* and *circumstantial evidence.*
- Explain how the jury determines the weight to be given to the testimony of each witness.
- Describe circumstantial evidence which can be used to show *modus operandi* and to establish motive.
- Identify situations in which the defendant's knowledge or skills can be used as circumstantial evidence of guilt.
- Describe the types of situations in which the defendant's acts prior to the crime may be used in evidence.
- Identify situations in which the defendant's acts after the crime was committed can be used as circumstantial evidence of guilt.
- Explain when character evidence is admissible at trial and describe how character is established at trial.

4-1 Basic Definitions

In Chapter 3, we briefly talked about direct and circumstantial evidence. The following were the key definitions:

Direct Evidence Defined
Direct evidence is based on personal knowledge or observation of the person testifying. No inference or presumption is needed. If the testimony is believed by the jury, the fact it relates to is conclusively established.

Circumstantial Evidence Defined
Circumstantial evidence indirectly proves a fact. It requires the trier of the facts to use an inference or presumption in order to conclude that the fact exists.

Direct evidence will be admissible if it was legally obtained and is not privileged. **Circumstantial evidence** is admitted at the discretion of the judge. The judge considers whether the evidence is relevant and balances other factors such as the amount of time it will take to introduce the evidence, confusion that may result from the evidence and the possibility that the evidence may be unduly prejudicial. Either direct and/or circumstantial evidence can be used to establish guilt. The law does not favor direct evidence over circumstantial. The jury decides whether the fact has been established.

4-2 Weight of Evidence

In American courts, questions of law are decided by the judge. Questions of fact are decided by the jury, unless the trial is being heard by a judge without a jury. Stipulations and items judicially noticed are determined as a "**matter of law**" by the judge; the jury decides all disputed facts.

The jury, as trier of the facts, is given the duty to decide the effect and **weight of each piece of evidence.** This requires them to decide which evidence to believe if there is a conflict in the facts. If there is more than one possible interpretation of the facts, the jury has to decide which one is correct. They also decide what inferences to draw from circumstantial evidence and which witnesses should be believed.

When direct evidence is introduced, the jury's main function is to decide the **credibility of the witness.** This usually revolves around two factors: the demeanor of the witness and the likelihood that what the witness said could have happened. Demeanor includes all types of body language. The jury also considers whether the witness was evasive or antagonistic. Common sense may be applied to the facts in order to decide if it was possible for the events in question to occur in the manner the witness described. Facts disclosed during impeachment, such as personal bias or prior felony convictions of the witness, may also be considered. Jury instructions usually explain all of this. Impeachment will be covered in detail in Chapter 5.

Examples of Ways to Test Credibility of a Witness
- The witness refused to look at the prosecutor or the jury.
- The witness gave evasive answers and refused to be pinned down on details.
- The witness cooperated with one side but was very hostile toward the attorney for the opposing side.
- The witness previously told the police a totally different story than he gave while testifying.
- The witness has previously been convicted for perjury.

Circumstantial evidence is more difficult to evaluate. The jury must decide the credibility of the witness, what inference should be drawn from the evidence, and the weight to be given to each piece of evidence. There is frequently more than one inference that can be drawn from the facts, and sometimes the possible conclusions are quite contradictory. Also, individual jurors will have different ideas on the correct weight for various pieces of evidence. All of these conclusions are obviously affected by the credibility of the witnesses. These issues must be resolved during jury deliberations. The jurors are told to listen to each other's opinions and try to reach a consensus. Lengthy discussions and many ballots may be required. If an impasse appears, the judge may intervene with additional instructions on the need to consider all points of view in order to reach a verdict, but the jurors are the only ones who can decide what conclusions to reach.

4-3 Circumstantial Evidence of Ability to Commit the Crime

Some crimes are committed in a manner that indicates that the suspect had special skills or abilities that the average person would not have had. The more unique the skill, the stronger the inference that the defendant is the one who committed the crime if he/she has that skill. Obviously, the case must be based on more than this one inference. The prosecutor hopes that the jury will conclude that the defendant is guilty if the defendant has the rare skill or ability that was required to commit the crime. The defense can also use the reverse of this approach. If the crime was committed by a person with a special skill or ability, the fact that the defendant does *not* have the requisite skill or ability can be used to infer that the defendant did not commit the crime.

4-3a Skills and Technical Knowledge

Most street crimes require few special skills or technical knowledge, but there are circumstances where even these crimes are committed in such a way that the suspect must have had some specialized training or experience. On the other hand, most white-collar crimes require uncommon skills or technical knowledge.

For example, "safe cracking" is a skill which the average person does not have. In a case where an unauthorized person opened a locked safe, the fact that the defendant has been known to "crack" safes in the past is relevant. This circumstantial evidence is not conclusive, of course, but combined with other admissible evidence it may convince the jury that the defendant committed the crime. The opposite approach can also be used by the defense. If the defense attorney can convince the jury that the defendant has no idea how to open a safe, the jury would likely conclude that the defendant did not commit the crime (at least not alone).

Computer crimes are another example. Many elaborate embezzlement schemes are accomplished by altering a company's computer software. High-tech extortion plots may involve the unauthorized use of computer access codes or the placing of "logic bombs" and "viruses" in a software program. The Internet may be used to obtain credit card numbers. These crimes require advanced programming techniques that the average person does not possess. In these types of cases, the fact that the defendant had the ability to do sophisticated programming is very relevant circumstantial evidence. Other examples of skills that can be used as circumstantial evidence include etching and printing (counterfeiting cases), locksmithing (burglary without signs of forced entry), bookkeeping (embezzlement), and advanced training in electronics (entry by avoiding highly sophisticated alarm system).

Examples of Skills and Technical Knowledge Needed to Commit the Crime
- The burglar bypassed an elaborate alarm system in order to enter the building.
- The door was opened with a "lock pick."
- Someone programmed the company computer to pay invoices submitted by a fictitious business.
- The artists made and sold paintings that looked exactly like famous masterpieces.

4-3b Means to Accomplish the Crime

The fact that the defendant had the means to accomplish the crime can also be used as circumstantial evidence if the average person would not have access to the necessary equipment or location. A simple example of this is if the defendant owned a gun which was the same caliber as the bullet taken from the body of the murder victim. If the bullet is damaged so that no further testing can be done, and there are many similar guns, the inference would be weak. On the other hand, if a ballistics test matches the bullet to the defendant's gun, the inference would be strong.

Examples of Means to Accomplish a Crime
- A person who worked at a company making explosives would have access to the chemicals necessary to manufacture bombs.
- A person caught with a lock pick in his/her possession may have committed a burglary without leaving signs of forcible entry.
- A person who had a large quantity of small, clear plastic envelopes might be selling illegal drugs.
- A person owns a rare gun that is the same make and model as the one used to commit the crime.
- A person was recently fired by the business that was burglarized and still has a key to the back door.

In a similar manner, the fact that the defendant had a stolen pass key for the area where the theft occurred can be used as circumstantial evidence that the suspect was in the area; unauthorized possession of the password for a computer which has been tampered with is circumstantial evidence that the defendant illegally used the computer; and possession of someone else's credit card numbers or telephone calling card numbers is circumstantial evidence that the defendant made the unauthorized charges.

4-3c Physical Capacity

Physical capacity can also be used to infer guilt in some cases. An obvious example is the defendant's height, if the physical facts show that only a very tall person could have committed the crime. The ability to run very fast, or the fact that the defendant is disabled and could not possibly have run that fast, can also be used if the situation makes speed relevant. The ability to lift heavy weights would be relevant if the suspect carried away heavy objects, or impotence may be relevant in sex crime cases.

Examples of Physical Capacity to Commit the Crime
- The burglar carried 50-pound bags out of the building.
- The burglar was a very thin person who entered the building through a window that would only open a few inches.
- The suspect was able to outrun the victim.
- The victim was severely injured by karate kicks to his head.
- The kidnapper picked up the victim and carried her a long distance.

4-3d Mental Capacity

Mental capacity may also be relevant. This is probably obvious if the defendant is pleading "not guilty by reason of insanity" or "diminished capacity." Juvenile cases may turn on the maturity and mental capacity of the child. Specific intent crimes and crimes requiring premeditation also make mental capacity more important.

On the other hand, since adults are presumed to know things that are common knowledge, the defense may need to establish that the defendant has minimal mental capacity and, therefore, did not know something that was obvious to everyone else.

The facts of a crime may also make mental capacity relevant. It can be inferred that sophisticated crimes could only have been committed by very intelligent people. Childish pranks may be circumstantial evidence that the suspect was an adult with below average mental capacity or that juveniles were the culprits.

Examples of Mental Capacity to Commit the Crime
- The defendant developed a very sophisticated plot to kill the victim.
- The ransom demand note was written in perfect Shakespearean English.
- The adult suspect acted like a 7-year-old.

4-4 Circumstantial Evidence of Intent

Circumstantial evidence is frequently needed to establish intent. This is doubly true in specific intent crimes. The two most common approaches to establishing intent are *modus operandi* and motive.

4-4a *Modus Operandi*

Modus operandi literally means the method of operation. Many criminals become creatures of habit and rather methodically commit the same crimes repeatedly in the same way. When this happens the prosecutor can introduce evidence of the defendant's prior crimes that were substantially similar to the current one, and let the jury conclude that the defendant also committed the crime he/she is now charged with. The fact that the defendant has been previously charged with violation of the same penal code section is not enough. There must be a great similarity in the method of committing the crime. If there are many common features, the jury will be more likely to infer that the defendant also committed the crime for which he/she is now on trial. The prosecutor may also be allowed to introduce evidence of very similar crimes committed by the defendant, even if the defendant was never charged with those offenses.

The judge has the discretion to admit or reject this type of circumstantial evidence. The normal rule is that prior crimes are not admissible. The jury should not infer that the defendant is guilty merely because he/she has been guilty of other crimes. The prosecutor must convince the judge that the method of committing the crime was sufficiently unusual to amount to the defendant putting his/her "signature" on it.

An example would be the person who enters liquor stores late at night, asks for a specific brand of cigarettes, and while the clerk is getting the cigarettes, pulls a gun and demands all the money in the cash register. The combination of time of day, type of store, and diversionary technique make this person's crimes distinctive. The prosecutor will be allowed to introduce evidence so the jury can see that the defendant has committed very similar crimes in the past. Based on this, the jurors will be allowed to conclude, if they see fit, that the defendant also committed the current liquor store robbery.

In a case involving a woman who was charged with bank robbery, the judge ruled that her prior conviction for bank robbery was admissible because there were very few women who rob banks. Normally the prosecutor will have to show several common features of the past and present crimes in order to convince the judge that the prior offenses can be introduced.

Examples of *Modus Operandi*—Same Method Used on Several Occasions

- Rape suspect frequented "singles bars" and offered to take the victim to dinner. On their "dinner date" he suddenly told the victim he would cook dinner for them. Once they had entered his apartment, he became very aggressive and raped the victim if she did not cooperate.
- Suspect knocked on the front door. If anyone answered he asked for Fred. When told that no one by that name lived there, he asked to use the phone. Once inside he stole expensive items.
- Man walked in parks where children frequently played. He would approach a child, show them a picture of a puppy, and tell the child he had lost his puppy. The child was asked to help find the puppy. If the child went to an isolated spot with the man, he would molest the child.
- Suspect avoided burglar alarms by entering through the roof. He used a grappling hook to scale the wall and then chopped a hole in the roof.

4-4b Motive

Motive does not have to be proven by the prosecution unless it is included in the definition of the crime. Even though it is not an element of the crime, it may be a key to convincing the jury that the defendant is guilty. This is particularly true when there is no direct evidence in the case. Depending on the facts of the case, possible motives could include hate, prejudice, revenge, retaliation, greed, lust, profit, economic need, love, mercy, and many more.

Greed is a motive in many crimes. In a murder case it usually means the criminal will profit financially from the death of the victim. This could include being hired to commit murder, inheriting money or something else of value from the victim, being the beneficiary of the victim's life insurance policy, eliminating business competitors, and preventing the victim or witness from reporting a crime. Any of these could be used as circumstantial evidence of intent to kill.

Hatred and prejudice also motivate many criminals. Hatred may be obvious if there has been a long running feud between the victim and the suspect. Racial prejudice may appear as the motive in other cases. Less obvious examples include gang violence and terrorism. Love and mercy may even be motives. "Lovers' triangles" (and other geometric patterns) can erupt into violence and even murder. Euthanasia, or mercy killing, may be based on the belief that a loved one should not be allowed to suffer.

Motive may also be important if the defendant is claiming that a murder was committed in self-defense or in the heat of passion. Evidence that there was a motive for the killing, such as revenge, jealousy, or hate, may help convince the jury that an opportunistic defendant's claim to mitigating circumstances is not valid.

Examples of Motive to Commit the Crime

- Husband was involved in an affair and wanted a divorce. The couple could not agree on a property settlement so the divorce was not completed. Wife was found dead.
- Business owner was deeply in debt. He falsified inventory records to show that many expensive items were stored in the warehouse. He took out a fire insurance policy. Two weeks later the warehouse burned to the ground.
- A woman had a double indemnity life insurance policy which did not cover suicide. Her husband, who was the beneficiary of the insurance policy, hid evidence that indicated the woman took her own life.
- Husband and wife were in the midst of a fierce custody battle. Mother coached one of the children to tell a police officer that the father had sexually abused him.
- Defendant had been charged with capital murder. Only one witness could positively identify the defendant as the killer. Someone killed the witness.

4-4c Threats

The fact that the defendant has threatened to commit the crime is circumstantial evidence that he/she committed the crime. While a person may make threats without planning to carry them out, the fact that the threat was made has some probative value. Specific threats will carry more weight than vague ones. How recently the threat was made, the credibility of the person reporting it, and other circumstances surrounding it will also be relevant. On the other hand, if it can be shown that someone else threatened to commit the crime, the defense can try to convince the jury that the other person committed the crime and the defendant is innocent.

Threats may also be relevant in self-defense cases. The standard used to determine if self-defense justified the use of force is whether a reasonable person would have used the same amount of force under the same circumstances. Jurors may consider the fact that the victim had previously threatened to harm the defendant. The question becomes what force would a reasonable person who had received the same threat believe was necessary to protect him/herself when confronted by the person who made the threats.

Examples of Relevant Threats to Commit the Crime

- Two days before the victim's death, the victim and suspect got into a fight. The suspect shouted, "I'll kill you for that!"
- Battered woman told her batterer that she was going to leave him. He made a menacing gesture and said, "If you ever leave me you will never see your kids again!" The next day the children disappeared.
- A bully continually threatened another high school student. He taunted, "I'm going to kill you!" One day the bully approached the student with his hand in his jacket pocket. Believing the bully was coming at him with a gun, the student grabbed a rock and hit the bully in the head.
- Someone repeatedly phoned and in a loud whisper said, "You won't live to see the morning sun." About 2:00 A.M. someone tried to open the back door. The person who received the calls became very frightened and shot through the door.
- Employee was caught stealing. He told the security staff that if he got fired they would pay for it. A week later someone slashed the tires on all the cars in the area where the security staff parked.

4-5 Circumstantial Evidence of Guilt

What the suspect does following the crime may also be circumstantial evidence of guilt. Flight to avoid prosecution, attempts to hide evidence, possession of stolen property, sudden wealth, and attempts to silence witnesses are commonly put in this category.

Although the average juror probably considers the fact that the defendant has invoked the Fifth Amendment to be evidence of guilt, the U.S. Supreme Court has made it clear that the jury must not draw this conclusion. Invoking *Miranda* rights also comes under the same protection. The Court's reasoning was that constitutional rights would be meaningless if the jury could conclude that a person is guilty if he/she used them.

4-5a Flight to Avoid Punishment

This category includes almost anything a suspect does to avoid conviction and serving a sentence. Probably the first to come to mind is fleeing from the scene of the crime. Later attempts to flee to avoid arrest are also included. Hiding raises a similar inference. After arrest the more common ways to avoid punishment include jumping bail and attempts to escape from jail.

Examples of Flight to Avoid Punishment
- The suspect ran from the scene immediately after the crime.
- The suspect fled the country after being released on bail.
- The police tried to arrest the suspect on an outstanding warrant. The suspect attacked the officer and escaped.

4-5b Concealing Evidence

Hiding or concealing evidence raises an inference of guilt, as does destroying evidence. Falsifying evidence or tampering with it can also be used to infer guilt.

Many fact patterns raise this type of inference. Some, such as arson to conceal theft or staging an auto accident to hide the fact the victim had been murdered, involve detailed planning and can only be disproved by testimony from expert witnesses. Others, such as throwing a ski mask in a trash can while running from the scene of a robbery, can be more easily established.

The defendant may try to hide evidence from the jury by asking witnesses to lie at trial. This information can be used as circumstantial evidence of guilt. The fact that the defendant tried to get a witness to alter testimony is admissible whether or not the witness agreed. It does not matter if the witness was willing to cooperate with the defendant, or if bribery, extortion, or some other means was used to get the witness to comply. The fact that the prosecutor does not plan to file charges for the perjury (lying under oath) or subornation of perjury (recruiting someone to lie under oath) is irrelevant.

Tampering with real (physical) evidence also raises an inference of guilt. This includes altering the evidence in the case or manufacturing evidence for use at trial.

Examples of Concealing Evidence
- The suspect killed the victim and set the house on fire to hide the murder.
- The suspect carved a hole in the wall, hid the evidence, and then paneled the wall to hide the hole.
- The suspect gave evidence to a friend and told him to hide it.

4-5c Possession of Stolen Property

In a theft case, the fact that the defendant was in possession of something taken during the theft is circumstantial evidence that the defendant was the thief. The inference is much stronger if the defendant had the property immediately after the theft. Receiving stolen property (called theft by possession in some states), rather than theft, may be a more appropriate charge when there is a substantial time lag between the theft and the discovery that the defendant had the property.

Examples of Possession of Stolen Property
- The suspect was stopped about a mile from the scene of the robbery. When he searched the suspect, the officer found cash in his pocket that was exactly equal to the amount stolen.
- The suspect had shiny new rims on his car that matched the description of ones stolen about a week before. He stated that he had received the rims as a birthday gift from his girlfriend.
- The suspect was wearing an antique ring that matched the description of one stolen in a recent home-invasion robbery.

4-5d Sudden Wealth

The fact that the suspect suddenly had a lot of money shortly after a property crime occurred can be used as circumstantial evidence. This is also true if the defendant profited from a violent crime such as murder. The prosecutor will ask the jury to infer that the money came from committing the crime. The jury may be told how much the defendant earns (or that he/she was unemployed), the defendant's normal spending habits, or that he/she recently tried to obtain charity or loans because he/she had no money. The defense will attempt to convince the jury that there was a legal source for this sudden wealth. Evidence that the defendant inherited a large sum of money from a recently deceased relative, won the lottery, or even won it by gambling may be used.

Examples of Sudden Wealth

- The suspect, who was unemployed, went to his favorite bar and paid cash for several rounds of drinks for everyone present.
- The suspect, who worked at a low-paying job, deposited $10,000 in cash into his checking account.
- The suspect, who previously took the bus to work, suddenly started driving an expensive automobile.

4-5e Threatening Witnesses

If the defendant threatens or abuses the victim or witnesses in order to prevent prosecution and conviction, it can be inferred that the defendant is guilty. Killing the victim, either during the original crime or later, in order to prevent the victim from testifying, is the most extreme case. The same inference also applies if threats were used in an attempt to prevent the victim or witness from reporting the crime, to pressure the victim to drop the charges, or to prevent the victim or witness from testifying in court. It does not matter if the defendant makes the threats or if he/she has someone else do it. The jury will decide how much weight the threats should be given based on what the defendant did.

These types of activities frequently amount to separate crimes. Their use as circumstantial evidence is separate from any prosecution for intimidating witnesses.

Examples of Threatening Witnesses

- Prior to leaving the scene of the crime, the robber told the victim, "You call the police and I'll come back and kill you!"
- Someone believed to be the defendant telephoned a person who had been subpoenaed to testify at trial and said in a menacing voice, "You'd better not show up in court if you love your kids."
- John, the defendant, had friends talk to the potential witness on several occasions. These friends appeared to be armed and they said, "We want what is best for John."

4-6 Character

"Character witnesses" are used to try to convince the jury that a person did something consistent with his/her character. Most states use reputation as evidence of character. For example, if a person has the reputation for telling the truth, the jury may infer that the person is currently telling the truth. This is circumstantial evidence, and the jury will have to decide how much weight to give the character evidence.

In most states, character witnesses are only allowed to testify about a person's reputation. **Reputation** is what other people believe about a person's character. **Character** describes what a person's moral traits really are. In some cases there may be a big difference between what the person is and what others believe he/she is.

The most common rule is that the character witness may only testify about what he/she knows of a person's reputation in the "community." Community usually means neighborhood, but it can also refer to the group of people who work together. To testify about reputation in the community, the character witness must tell what he/she has heard other people say. The personal opinion of this witness is not admissible under the traditional rule.

Some states have expanded the traditional rule and allow character witnesses to give their personal opinion of a person's character. This gives the jury more information to use when drawing a conclusion.

The use of character witnesses is restricted to three basic situations:

1. The defendant may try to use his/her good character to convince the jury that he/she did not commit a crime.
2. Specific character traits of the defendant may be used to infer that the defendant did (or did not) commit the crime.
3. Specific character traits of the victim may be used when relevant to the crime.

4-6a The Defendant's Character in General

The prosecution is not allowed to attack the defendant's character unless the defendant has placed character at issue. If the defense called character witnesses, the prosecution may also call character witnesses during rebuttal. The prosecution's character witnesses will testify that the defendant's reputation is not what the defense witnesses said it was. For example, the defendant may call his priest to testify that the defendant has a reputation for being an honest, law-abiding citizen. The prosecutor may call the defendant's former business partner who testifies that the defendant has a reputation for being a lying thief.

Cross-examination can be used effectively on character witnesses. Since the witness is supposed to be telling the jury what the defendant's reputation is in the community, showing that the character witness does not know what very many people think of the defendant reduces the impact of the testimony. The testimony of a character witness is also weakened if it is shown that the witness knows the defendant has done things that are inconsistent with his/her reputation. It is also easy to impeach many defense character witnesses for bias. Since the defendant's friends and family frequently testify about his/her good reputation, they probably view things in the light most favorable to the defendant. The character witnesses may also be shown to be liars. The defense, of course, will use the same tactics to impeach the prosecution's character witnesses.

Example of Evidence on Defendant's Character in General

- Defendant calls her pastor to testify that she is an outstanding member of the congregation and does many acts of charity.
- Prosecutor calls character witness after the pastor testifies. The prosecution witness states that the defendant is known to be a hypocrite who goes to church regularly but otherwise leads the life of a hardened criminal.
- Defendant calls a character witness who testifies that the prosecution's character witness has the reputation of being a liar.

4-6b Specific Character Traits of the Defendant

In some trials, one of the defendant's specific character traits may be relevant. Since this evidence is relevant to a specific issue, it can be raised by either side. The prosecution does not have to wait for the defense to call character witnesses first.

The use of specific character traits is most common in trials for violent crimes. If the trial is based on the defendant's killing his wife after finding out that she was having an affair, the defense may try to use his reputation for going into jealous rages in an attempt to reduce the murder charge to voluntary manslaughter. The defendant's reputation as a bully may be useful for the prosecution if the defendant is claiming that he/she acted in self-defense. On the other hand, the defense may try to establish a reputation for being timid, to show that the defendant would never have started the fight.

The defendant's reputation for being cautious or reckless may also be relevant in some cases. If the defendant is charged with manslaughter based on gross negligence, his/her reputation for being reckless may be very damaging to a defense based on the contention that the defendant was acting with due care when the death occurred. The defense could use the reverse of this if it could show that the defendant had a reputation for being careful.

Examples of Evidence of Specific Character Traits of the Defendant
- Defendant is charged with murder and claims self-defense. Defense calls character witnesses who testify that the defendant is known to be a gentle person who never becomes angry.
- Prosecution then calls a character witness who testifies that defendant has the reputation for threatening anyone who disagrees with him.
- Defense calls character witnesses who testify that on several occasions they heard that someone violently attacked the defendant but the defendant did not return the assault.

4-6c Character Traits of the Victim

Sometimes the character of the crime victim may be relevant. This is most common in cases where the defense is based on self-defense. If it can be shown that the victim was a violent person, it is much easier to convince the jury that the defendant acted in self-defense. The inference would be even stronger if the victim's reputation included being a bully. The prosecution can use the reverse of this approach; for example, showing the jury that the victim had a reputation for being a nonviolent person may defeat the self-defense claim.

At one time, the reputation of a rape victim was considered to be at issue. The oldest cases allowed the jury to conclude that the woman who was single and not a virgin would consent to sex with almost anyone. More recently, the reputation of the rape victim for being promiscuous has been used to infer that she consented. This type of questioning is now usually reserved for rape cases where the defendant admits having sex with the victim but claims that she consented. Some states now refuse to allow questions about the sex life of the victim unless there was a prior relationship between the defendant and the victim.

Examples of Relevant Character Traits of the Victim
- Defendant is charged with murder and claims self defense. Defense introduced a character witness who testified that the victim had the reputation of being very violent and getting angry very quickly.
- Defendant is charged with rape. Defense calls character witnesses who state that the victim has a reputation for making false accusations against men she dates.
- Defendant is a battered woman charged with killing her batterer. Defense introduced character evidence that the victim was violent and had beaten several of his former girlfriends.

4-7 Other Acts Evidence

"Other acts evidence" includes a variety of situations where prior actions of the defendant are relevant to the current case. In these situations, the prior acts can be used to infer that he/she committed the crime alleged in the current trial. Normally the defendant's history is not admissible. The use of this type of evidence is permitted in response to specific issues raised by the defense. Since introduction of this type of evidence is contrary to the normal rules, the judge must first decide whether the evidence is relevant and then whether the value of the evidence is outweighed by the potential prejudice against the defendant.

4-7a Identity

Prior similar crimes can be used to infer that the witness correctly identified the defendant. The defendant does not have to have been arrested or charged with the prior crime as long as the prosecutor can call a credible witness who can convince the jury that the defendant committed the crimes.

Circumstantial evidence is most commonly used in this way when an eyewitness claims that he/she saw the defendant commit the crime, but the defendant claims that it is a case of mistaken identity. This method of establishing identity is very similar to the use of prior crimes to show *modus operandi*. Unless there is a great deal of similarity between the current offense and the prior acts, the judge will not allow the prosecutor to admit the prior crimes because they would be unduly prejudicial to the defendant.

Example of Other Acts Evidence Used to Prove Identity

- A 72-year-old man is on trial for bank robbery. He claims the witness wrongly identified him as the robber. The prosecution is allowed to show that robberies by senior citizens are very rare and the defendant has been arrested for two bank robberies in the last three years.
- Defendant is charged in an elaborate fraud scene. Prosecution was only able to tie him to the crime by the use of fingerprints found on the documents involved. Defendant claims there is an innocent explanation for how the fingerprints were placed on the documents. Prosecution introduces evidence that the suspect has been involved in the same type of fraud scheme in three states.

4-7b Habit or Custom

The fact that the defendant had a habit or custom of doing something can be used to infer that he/she did it when the crime was committed. The victim's habits and customs can also be used to show he/she was not voluntarily involved in criminal conduct. Habits and customs are easily confused with character traits. Habits and customs are more specific than character traits. A person's character may include being a liar; lying about one's age can be a habit.

In most states, evidence is admissible if the person's habit or custom is so strong that it becomes a semiautomatic response to a particular type of situation. This creates stronger circumstantial evidence than a character trait would. Since the potential for prejudicial impact is less, the judge is usually more likely to admit it if it is relevant to the case. The habit or custom does not have to relate to doing criminal acts. It merely needs to be relevant to the way in which the crime was committed. This type of evidence can also be used to infer that the defendant did not commit the crime because it was his/her habit or custom to act in a different way than the way the person committing the crime did.

Habitual neatness could be relevant, for example, if the suspect went to great lengths to clean up after the crime was committed. A person's obsession for punctuality could be used to infer that he/she would be at a scheduled appointment unless forced to go somewhere else. In a homicide case where the body has not been recovered, habit or custom could be used to show that a missing person did not voluntarily leave town without telling anyone.

Examples of Other Acts Evidence to Prove Habit or Custom
- The victim was a very tidy housekeeper. When the police were called to the scene the house was a mess and the victim was gone. Prosecution asked the jurors to infer that the victim was forced to leave the scene against her will.
- The victim was an elderly man who was very frugal with his money. The prosecution asked the jury to infer that the large check written on the victim's account for an extravagant gift was not written by the victim.
- The victim was an old lady who was inseparable from her dog. When her house burned down they found her dead dog inside with bullet hole in his head. Police were never able to locate the old lady or her remains. The prosecution asked the jury to infer that the lady was kidnapped.

4-7c Lack of Accident

In some cases, the defendant admits doing the criminal act but claims it was done accidentally. In these situations the defendant's prior acts can be used to show that the current crime was not an accident.

A good example would be a theft case where the defendant knew that the victim carried something very valuable in his/her briefcase and attempted to switch briefcases with the victim. The defense might try to prove that picking up the victim's briefcase was an honest mistake. This defense could be very convincing until the prosecutor calls a witness who testifies that the defendant pulled a similar switch a few months back.

Another example would be the burglar who was caught in a secluded area of Al's Market shortly after closing time. His/her claim of not knowing that the store had closed could be countered by testimony of an employee of Bob's Grocery who caught the defendant shortly after the defendant had committed a similar burglary by hiding in Bob's Grocery at closing time.

Examples of Other Acts Evidence Used to Show Lack of Accident
- Defendant was charged with carrying a concealed weapon and claimed he did not know the law covered the type of weapon he had. Prosecution showed that defendant had previously been convicted for carrying the same model of a handgun.
- Defendant was at a party and left with an expensive coat that was not hers. She claimed it was an innocent mistake. Prosecution introduced evidence to show that similar incidents had occurred at two other parties the defendant attended that year.

4-7d Prior False Claims

If a person has previously filed false claims, it can be inferred that the current claim is also false. In fraud cases it may be very helpful to show that the defendant has previously filed false claims in order to recover on insurance policies. Some states also allow the prosecutor to show that the defendant has repeatedly filed claims and ask the jury to conclude that this is evidence that the current claims are false. This, of course, is weaker evidence than the situation where it can be shown that at least one of the prior claims was actually fraudulent.

A different use of this type of evidence is to discredit the complaining witness. If the witness can be shown to have previously made a false report of a crime, or falsely accused a person of committing a crime, it can be inferred that the present allegations are also untrue. This type of evidence usually comes out during cross-examination if the attorney has done his/her homework. Asking this type of question would only support the credibility of the witness if it turned out that no prior reports had been made.

Examples of Other Actions Evidence—Prior False Claims

- Defendant was charged with staging a traffic accident in order to defraud an insurance company. He claimed it truly was an accident. Prosecution introduced evidence that defendant had been involved in three similar accidents and filed excessive claims in each one.
- Defendant was on trial for rape. Defendant introduced evidence that the alleged victim had previously filed police reports for rape and then withdrew them when confronted with conflicting evidence.

4-8 Offers to Plead Guilty

If the jury knew that the defendant had tried to plea bargain, it would be likely to conclude that the defendant was guilty. Although this is a very logical conclusion, there are strong policy reasons for denying the jury access to this information. Making offers to plead guilty admissible would interfere with nearly all attempts to plea bargain. The need to expedite court proceedings through the use of plea bargaining is considered much more important than allowing the jury to know this evidence. For this reason most states do not allow the introduction of any testimony about attempts to plea bargain or the fact that the defendant entered a guilty plea but for some reason was allowed to withdraw it. A similar public policy usually covers attempts to settle civil cases. The Supreme Court held that statements made during plea negotiations are admissible, however, if there is an agreement between the defendant and prosecutor that stipulates that the statements can be used in court if the defendant fails to follow through with the actions he/she promised to take. This type of procedure is used when the prosecution offers a plea bargain in exchange for the defendant giving information about other suspects involved in the crime or acting as an undercover operative.

4-9 Circumstantial Evidence Involving the Victim

The victim's injuries can provide circumstantial evidence that a crime occurred. This usually requires testimony of an expert witness to explain that the injuries are inconsistent with the defense's theory of the case. For example, in a rape case where consent of the victim is claimed, a medical expert may testify that the genital bruises sustained by the victim rarely occur during consensual intercourse.

Parents frequently claim that an abused child was injured accidentally. An expert can testify that the X-rays show broken bones that were at different stages of healing. This is consistent with the battered child syndrome and indicates that there were multiple violent attacks on the child.[1] From this it can be inferred that the latest injuries were the result of battering and were not accidental. This type of evidence is admissible even though the defendant has not been previously charged with child abuse. The Supreme Court held that it is not necessary to establish beyond a reasonable doubt that the defendant has previously beaten the child.[2]

In addition to the physical evidence of the battered child syndrome, psychological evidence may also be introduced. This focuses on the child's behavior toward the abuser and others. Experts in psychology may testify to help the jurors understand the types of behavior that frequently result. For example, the abused child frequently is very loving and protective toward the abusive parent. Jurors might conclude that this is a sign that the parent is a loving parent while the behavior may be an attempt to prevent future abuse.

Behavior of the victim can be used to infer that the crime occurred. Not all victims conform to popular stereotypes of how a victim should behave, however. Many courts allow expert witnesses to testify about the Rape Trauma Syndrome and the Battered Woman Syndrome. The expert witness cannot positively state that the crime occurred but he/she can explain common symptoms so that the jury can make inferences from the victim's conduct.

The Rape Trauma Syndrome is used by the prosecution to overcome juror's stereotypes of how victims react after being raped. Symptoms include withdrawal from the external world, sleep disorders, exaggerated startle responses, guilt, memory impairment, difficulty concentrating, and avoidance of stimuli that make the victim recall the rape.[3]

The Battered Woman Syndrome has become an issue in the defense of women who kill (or attempt to kill) their abusive partners. This final act of aggression may come while the man is sleeping and clearly does not qualify as self-defense. In courts allowing this defense, expert testimony focuses on studies that show that battered women may accept abuse for years, downplay episodes of violence, defend the abuser by claiming he was justified in beating her, rarely report abuse to family or the police, and pass up chances to flee until some event causes her to strike back and kill.

The mental state of the typical abused woman is used to explain why the defendant feared for her life when she used deadly force.[4]

Examples of Circumstantial Evidence Involving the Victim

- In a trial for child abuse, X-rays are introduced that show numerous fractures. The expert witness concludes that the child was beaten on numerous occasions based on the state of healing shown for each broken bone.
- In a trial for sexually molesting a 3-year-old girl, witnesses may testify that the girl's behavior was very sexually orientated. An expert witness may testify that the behavior was not normal for a child that age and that such behavior usually indicates the child has been involved in sexual activities.
- In a trial of a wife charged with the murder of a husband, the defense claims that the wife acted in self-defense. The defense may introduce evidence that the husband had physically abused the wife on many occasions. An expert witness may testify that a battered woman frequently becomes hypervigilant and interprets small signs of aggression as indicators that a serious beating is about to happen.

Summary

Circumstantial evidence may be used to establish any element of a crime. It is usually weaker than direct evidence because the jury must infer that a fact exists in addition to assessing the credibility of the witness. The jury must also decide the weight to be given to each fact introduced into evidence.

Circumstantial evidence can be used to show that the defendant had the ability to commit the crime. This is done when the crime is committed in such a manner that the suspect must have had some ability that the average person would not possess. These situations may include special skills, technical knowledge, tools to accomplish the crime, access to the location where the crime occurred, or unusual physical or mental capacity.

Prior crimes, which are very similar to the current one, can be used to infer that the defendant also committed the present crime. The *modus operandi* needs to be quite distinctive to be used in this manner.

Motive can also be used as circumstantial evidence of guilt. A wide variety of motives can be involved in crimes. Greed, hatred, and jealousy are among the most common.

Prior threats can be used to show that the defendant probably committed the crime. Only fairly recent threats would carry much weight.

Attempts to avoid apprehension after the crime may be used to show guilt. These include flight from the crime scene, attempts to avoid arrest or trial, and intimidating witnesses.

Possession of the fruits of the crime infers guilt. Sudden wealth can also be used to indicate that a person profited from the crime.

Character witnesses may be called by the defense to establish that the defendant has a good reputation. The inference is that a person with a good character would not commit the crime. Once the defense has placed character in issue, the prosecution may also call character witnesses. In some crimes, specific character traits may be in issue; if so, either side may introduce character evidence on the relevant trait. The character of the victim is frequently relevant if self-defense is raised. Attacking the character of rape victims is now more restricted than in the past.

Some defenses may make additional circumstantial evidence relevant. Alleging mistaken identity will make evidence that the defendant committed very similar crimes in the past admissible. Habits and customs may be admissible if they are so firmly established that they are nearly automatic responses. Prior acts may be relevant to show that the current crime was not done by accident or mistake. The fact that a person has previously filed false claims, either to collect on an insurance policy or as crime reports, can be used to infer that the current claim is also false.

There is a strong policy reason, based on judicial efficiency, to exclude evidence that the defendant attempted to plea bargain the charges or that the defendant withdrew a plea bargain. It is not admissible because allowing this evidence into court would result in many more cases going to trial.

Discussion Questions

1. Define and compare *direct evidence* and *circumstantial evidence*.
2. Explain how the jury decides what weight to give each fact in evidence.
3. List three technical skills and three means of accomplishing the crime which can be used as circumstantial evidence. Describe a crime in which each would be relevant.
4. When can physical and mental capacity be used as circumstantial evidence? Give three examples of each.
5. Define *modus operandi*. Explain how it may be used as circumstantial evidence.
6. When is motive relevant? Give three examples of how motive can be used to infer guilt.
7. Explain how (1) threats, (2) flight from the scene, and (3) attempts to destroy evidence can be used as circumstantial evidence. Give two types of situations where each may be relevant.
8. Can possession of the fruits of the crime or recently acquired wealth be used as circumstantial evidence to infer guilt? Explain.
9. Explain what evidence a "character witness" may present to the jury and when the defendant's general character is admissible evidence.

10. When is the prosecution allowed to call "character witnesses," and when are the defendant's specific character traits admissible?
11. Under what circumstances is the victim's character admissible? Explain.
12. What circumstantial evidence is admissible if the defendant is claiming mistaken identity? Explain.
13. Distinguish "habit" and "character." Explain when "habit" is admissible.
14. What evidence can be used to discredit the defendant's claim that the crime was accidentally committed without criminal intent? Explain.
15. When, if ever, is the fact that (1) the defendant previously attempted to make false claims under an insurance policy, or (2) offered to plead guilty to the crime admissible? Explain.

Endnotes

1. Sylvia I. Mignon, Calvin J. Larson, and William M. Holmes, *Family Abuse: Consequences, Theories, and Responses* (Boston: Allyn & Bacon, 2002); Harvey Wallace, *Family Violence: Legal, Medical and Social Perspectives,* 3rd ed. (Boston: Allyn & Bacon, 2002), Chapter 2.
2. *Estelle v. McGuire,* 502 U.S. 62, 116 L.Ed. 2d 385, 112 S.Ct. 475 (1991).
3. Tammi D. Kolski, Michael Avriette, Arthur E. Jongsma, Jr., *The Crisis Counseling and Traumatic Events Treatment Planner* (New York: J. Wiley, 2001); Sylvia I. Mignon, Calvin J. Larson, and William M. Holmes, *Family Abuse: Consequences, Theories, and Responses* (Boston: Allyn & Bacon, 2002), Chapter 3. Harvey Wallace, *Family Violence: Legal, Medical and Social Perspectives,* 3rd ed. (Boston: Allyn & Bacon, 2002), Chapter 13.
4. Lenore E. Walker, *The Battered Woman Syndrome,* 2nd ed. (New York: Springer, 2000); Mark Costanzo, Stuart Oskamp, eds., *Violence and the Law,* (Thousand Oaks, Calif.: Sage Publications, 1994); Harvey Wallace, *Family Violence: Legal, Medical and Social Perspectives,* 3rd ed. (Boston: Allyn & Bacon, 2002), Chapter 8.

CHAPTER **5**

Witnesses

Outline

Key Terms

- Competent witness
- Corroboration
- Expert witness
- Hypothetical questions
- Impeachment

- Lay witness
- Opinion Rule
- Past Recollection Recorded Exception

- Present Memory Refreshed Rule
- Rehabilitation
- *Voir dire*

After studying this chapter, you will be able to:

- Define *competency of a witness* and give examples of incompetent witnesses.
- Explain the process of impeaching and rehabilitating a witness. List five ways a witness can be impeached.
- Explain the legal methods of refreshing the memory of a witness. Describe the process of introducing reports if the witness has no memory of the events described in the reports.
- State the Opinion Rule, and explain its application.
- Explain the prerequisites for allowing an expert witness to testify.
- List three types of evidence that require the testimony of an expert witness.
- Explain what a lay witness is allowed to testify about.

5-1 Competency of Witness

All evidence is introduced at trial by the testimony of a witness. Therefore, the role of the witness in the criminal justice system is very important. This chapter will address the following five key issues related to the trial witness:

1. Who is competent to testify
2. How the credibility of a witness is attacked
3. What can be done if the witness's memory is faulty
4. What a lay person is allowed to testify about
5. How and when expert witnesses are used

Every witness who testifies in court must be competent. In addition to being competent, the witness must possess relevant information. The standard for competency to testify refers to the person's ability to communicate with the jury. It is not equivalent to the test used to determine if the defendant is mentally competent to stand trial.

Competent Witness Defined

A **competent witness** is a person who:

1. Understands the duty to tell the truth
2. Can narrate the events in question

Competence is the first issue addressed. If a person is not competent, he/she will not be allowed to testify. If the witness is competent the adversary system unfolds. The attorney who called the witness asks questions. Opposing counsel should object if the question calls for an answer the witnesses is not qualified to answer. The judge rules on the objections. The jurors who watch this interplay must decide if they believe the witness and how much weight to give the testimony.

5-1a Duty to Tell the Truth

The most common oath administered to witnesses today includes the traditional promise to "tell the truth, the whole truth, so help me God." While each witness must understand the duty to tell the truth, neither the Bible nor swearing is currently mandatory. For the person who is an agnostic or atheist, swearing on the Bible may be a meaningless gesture. Also, some people have religious beliefs against taking an oath on the Bible. As discussed in Chapter 3, an "affirmation" is administered instead of an oath in such instances.

The purpose of the oath or affirmation is to make it clear to a witness that he/she is testifying under penalty of perjury. The witness swears to tell the truth but the jurors decide whether to believe the witness. No immediate action is taken if the witness is suspected of lying while on the stand. If the witness knowingly lies about a material matter, perjury charges may be filed at a later time. The threat of being punished in this manner is commonly assumed to be sufficient to keep witnesses from lying. The truth is, some witnesses lie but prosecutors rarely file perjury charges. In most situations, administering an oath or affirmation is all that is done to qualify a witness. There is a common exception in cases involving children as witnesses. Young children do not understand the meaning of the term "under penalty of perjury." So the attorney who calls a child as a witness usually has the task of showing the court that the witness knows that he/she is required to tell the truth. Simple questions are asked in language that a child can understand. A typical line of questioning focuses on the fact that the child has been taught that it is wrong to tell a lie. Once it is established that the child knows that lying is wrong and he/she will be punished for lying, the testimony is usually allowed.

A related problem is posed by the person who cannot distinguish fact from fantasy. Again, children pose the most frequent problem. Young children frequently have very active imaginations. They may have invisible friends who are quite real to them. Unfortunately, when a child is a crime victim, this same creativity that is a healthy part of childhood may result in a serious injustice. It is the task of the prosecutor to convince the judge, and later the jury, that the child is able to differentiate between fact and fantasy and to testify about events that actually took place.

Senility and certain types of mental illness can result in the inability to tell fact from fiction. The questions asked in court to determine if a witness knows what the truth is are not based on medical or psychiatric diagnosis. Factual questions are used in order to show that the potential witness is out of touch with reality. This is done before the person testifies in the presence of the jury.

Some courts have ruled that a person who has been hypnotized cannot testify about things discussed while under hypnosis. Proponents of hypnosis claim that a person can recall things under hypnosis that he/she cannot remember in the conscious state. Opponents claim that during hypnosis information can be embedded in a person's memory. When this occurs in hypnosis, the person believes that he/she is recalling what was previously observed but cannot distinguish between what actually happened and what was added to memory during hypnosis. Courts that exclude testimony enhanced by hypnosis usually exclude only testimony about topics that were covered in a hypnotic session. Statements made to the police before hypnosis are usually admissible. Controversy about the use of hypnosis will probably continue until there is conclusive scientific evidence on the effects of hypnosis on memory.

5-1b Ability to Narrate

To be a witness, a person must be able to communicate with the judge and jury and must be able to tell about the events in question. This is referred to as the ability to narrate.

Several problems may be raised. Probably the most obvious is the ability to coherently answer questions. To do this, the witness must have the ability to understand the questions. Severely mentally retarded persons, very young children, and people with certain other types of physical and mental illness may not be able to do this.

Other more practical problems may be raised. For example, the witness may not be able to speak English. This is usually solved by using an interpreter or translator. The witness will need an interpreter or translator to understand the questions, and the judge, jury, and defendant may need a translation of the answers. A similar problem arises if a witness speaks through sign language. Again, interpreters are the solution.

5-1c Procedure to Establish Competency

If there is a question of the witness's competency, a hearing will be held before the person takes the stand. The jury leaves the courtroom during this session. Questions will be asked of the witness to determine if he/she is competent to testify. This is called *voir dire.* The side wishing to call the witness will bear the burden of convincing the judge that the person is competent. Opposing counsel will be allowed to cross-examine.

This screening process is limited to the two key questions of competency—knowing that there is a duty to tell the truth and being able to narrate. The fact that one side suspects that the witness will commit perjury is not grounds to prevent that person from taking the stand. Neither is the fact that a prospective witness has a severe personality disorder as long as it does not affect the ability to narrate. Some states do not allow a witness to testify if he/she has previously been convicted of perjury.

Testimony taken during *voir dire* is not used to prove any of the issues in the case. If the person is found competent, he/she will then be put on the witness stand in the presence of the jury. Direct and cross-examination will proceed as with any other witness.

5-2 Impeachment

One of the key functions of cross-examination is convincing the jury that they should not believe the other side's witnesses; this is called **impeachment.** In some situations, witnesses may be called solely for the purpose of impeaching someone who has already testified.

A witness is impeached by asking questions. If the answers indicate that the witness lacks credibility, those answers will be emphasized by the opposing attorney during closing arguments. The witness is not asked to leave the witness stand nor is he/she prevented from testifying at future trials.

The opposing attorney must make a tactical decision on impeachment. While each witness may be attacked with any or all of the six impeachment methods, questioning usually zeros in on one or two that are believed to be the most effective. Both the vulnerability of the witness and the impact on the jury must be considered. Trying to intimidate a witness who has the jury's sympathy may backfire. Every witness, including the defendant (if he/she takes the stand), is subject to impeachment. This frequently discourages defendants in criminal cases from taking the stand if they have prior records. The prosecution is rarely allowed to show the defendant's past if he/she does not take the stand, but if the defendant does take the stand, both prior convictions and crimes that never went to trial may be admissible.

Impeachment Defined

Impeachment is the process of attacking the credibility of a witness. Six main methods of impeachment are allowed:
1. Bias or prejudice
2. Prior felony convictions
3. Immoral acts and uncharged crimes
4. Prior inconsistent statements
5. Inability to observe
6. Reputation

5-2a Bias or Prejudice

If a person is biased or prejudiced, either for or against one side of the case, it can be inferred that he/she cannot testify objectively. This includes bias or prejudice toward a defendant, a witness, one of the attorneys, or the police. Bias and prejudice, as used in impeachment, have very broad definitions.

A person can be biased due to friendship. Even though the witness has sworn to tell the truth, if he/she is called to testify against a close friend there may be a conscious or unconscious distortion of the facts. This friendship is a proper subject for cross-examination. The jury will have to decide if the witness was truthful or allowed the friendship to affect his/her testimony.

Example of Impeachment Based on Bias or Prejudice—Friendship

Prosecutor:	Mr. Green, you just testified that John, the defendant, was at your house on the evening of November 15.
Mr. Green:	Yes.
Prosecutor:	How well do you know John?
Mr. Green:	We have been friends for about five years.
Prosecutor:	Is John your best friend?
Mr. Green:	Yes.
Prosecutor:	Would you try to help John if he were in trouble?
Mr. Green:	Well, yes, I would do whatever I could.

Hatred and lesser degrees of animosity toward a party to the case may also cause a witness to distort the facts. During cross-examination, questions may be asked to explore bad feelings between the witness and others concerned with the case. Once again, the jury has the task of deciding how these personal feelings may have affected the testimony.

Example of Impeachment Based on Bias or Prejudice—Hatred

Defense:	Mr. Brown, you testified that John hit you on November 15. Did you know John prior to November 15?
Mr. Brown:	Yes.
Defense:	Describe your prior encounters with John.
Mr. Brown:	John dated my sister Mary for about a year.
Defense:	During that year did you and John become friends?
Mr. Brown:	No.
Defense:	Why didn't you become friends?
Mr. Brown:	He done my sister wrong. He cheated on her and he hit her several times.
Defense:	Describe your feelings toward John.
Mr. Brown:	I hate him. I hope he gets what's coming to him.

Family ties are generally assumed to form strong bonds which would cause a witness to testify more favorably toward a relative. Obviously, some family feuds result in just the opposite bias. Cross-examination is once again the key to discovering the extent of the distortion.

Example of Impeachment Based on Bias or Prejudice—Family Ties

Prosecution:	Mrs. White, you just testified that you observed a fight on November 15. Did you know any of the people involved?
Mrs. White:	I know John but not the other guys.
Prosecution:	How well do you know John?
Mrs. White:	He is my son.
Prosecution:	Do you have a good relationship with your son John?
Mrs. White:	Yes. He is a very good boy.
Prosecution:	Do you believe it is a mother's duty to provide love and support for her children?
Mrs. White:	Yes, I do. There isn't anything I wouldn't do to help my children.

Racial prejudice can also cause a witness to distort the truth. Questions regarding racial bias would only be allowed if the facts of the case indicate they are relevant (e.g., the victim and/or defendant are from different racial groups than the witness or there is evidence that the witness is prejudiced about his/her own racial group). Prejudice toward the police officer or one of the attorneys might also be involved. However, the fact that the witness is a bigot is not admissible if there are no facts in the case that are likely to cause him/her to distort the facts.

Example of Impeachment Based on Bias or Prejudice—Racial Prejudice

Defense: Mr. Allen, you just testified that John, the defendant who is sitting over there, was the man that started the fight.

Mr. Allen: Yes. That is exactly what he did.

Defense: And you are sure it was John?

Mr. Allen: Absolutely.

Defense: Mr. Allen, are you prejudiced against African-Americans?

Mr. Allen: No.

Defense: Have you ever said, "They all look alike to me"?

Mr. Allen: Yeah, I've said that.

Other forms of bias or prejudice may arise in individual cases. Sexual biases may be relevant. For example, the witness may testify in a very critical manner at a rape trial because of a belief that women should not go to bars alone. Sexual preference may also become grounds for impeachment. A witness with very strong feelings on this topic (either anti- or pro-homosexuality) can be cross-examined on these attitudes if they are relevant.

Any relationship with the defendant, or anyone else in the case, that could result in a financial impact on the witness can also be used to impeach. This is based on the idea that a person would possibly alter testimony if he/she would be harmed (or helped) financially. For example, an employee may not be able to be totally objective on the witness stand if he/she fears being fired because of what was said. Whether consciously or unconsciously, a witness might also alter the facts if he/she could be promoted, earn a commission from a sale, or make a profit in the stock market if the side calling him/her wins the case.

Example of Impeachment Based on Bias or Prejudice—Financial Gain

Defense: Mr. Smith, are you the owner of the building involved in this case?

Mr. Smith: Yes.

Defense: Did you operate a business at that location?

Mr. Smith: Yes. A video game store.

Defense: Was your business profitable?

Mr. Smith: Don't I wish. We have been losing money for over a year.

Defense: Did you have fire insurance on the building and its contents?

Mr. Smith:	Yes. I always pay my insurance premiums.
Defense:	Has your insurance paid you for fire damages caused by the crime we are discussing today?
Mr. Smith:	Yes.
Defense:	How much were you paid?
Mr. Smith:	$51,000.

The list of possible biases is quite long (age, occupation, regional, religious, educational, etc.). Only the facts of the case determine what could be relevant in any one case. If there is a question of relevance, the attorneys will debate the issue with the judge outside the hearing of the witness and jury.

Motive to distort the truth or fabricate evidence can also be inferred from the fact that the witness is being paid to testify. The jury is more likely to conclude the payment influenced the testimony when a large amount of money is at stake. Expert witnesses can be impeached by showing the fees they receive for testifying. This also applies to the person who provides evidence in hopes of receiving a reward the city posted for information leading to a conviction. The witness who has accepted money from a journalist for information about the case fits in this category. Paid police informants are also suspect. Entering into a plea bargain in exchange for testifying against a co-conspirator also infers a motive.

Example of Impeachment Based on Bias or Prejudice—Motive

Defense:	Mr. Johnson, you just testified that you observed the fight involving John, the defendant in this case. What were you doing when the fight started?
Mr. Johnson:	I was talking to John.
Defense:	So you knew John prior to the events in question?
Mr. Johnson:	Yes, we were friends.
Defense:	Have you ever been arrested?
Mr. Johnson:	Yes.
Defense:	When and for what charges?
Mr. Johnson:	I was arrested at the same time John was. They said they were going to charge me with battery.
Defense:	Did they take you to court on the battery?
Mr. Johnson:	No. They told me that they wouldn't file the charges if I testified against John at his trial.

5-2b Prior Felony Convictions

We have a long history of distrusting convicts. At one time, anyone convicted of a felony was considered untrustworthy and not allowed to testify in court. While most states now allow everyone to testify, impeachment is permitted on prior felony convictions even if the prior crime is totally unrelated to the current case.

Prior convictions may be introduced at trial for two very different purposes. They may come in as "other acts" evidence, mentioned in Chapter 4 (Section 4-7). When used in this manner they infer that the defendant is guilty because the defendant has done very similar acts in the past. A separate use of felony convictions is to impeach a witness. Anyone who takes the stand is subject to impeachment. On cross-examination, opposing counsel can ask about prior felony convictions and thus undermine the credibility of the witness. The threat of impeachment is one of the main reasons that defendants with criminal records frequently do not testify at their own trials.

Most states allow impeachment on prior felony convictions. If the conviction was for a crime committed in another state, it must be similar to a felony as defined by the law of the state where the trial is held. Some states allow impeachment on crimes of moral turpitude. Moral turpitude usually includes all felonies, plus misdemeanors involving dishonesty. A few states include all criminal convictions as grounds for impeachment. Probably the newest, and least used, rule is that impeachment based on prior convictions is limited to crimes relevant to honesty on the witness stand. Truthfulness of the witness is always relevant, but violence would not be considered relevant to honesty.

Example of Impeachment Based on Prior Felony Conviction

Prosecutor: Mr. Adams, you just testified that John was provoked into hitting the victim.

Mr. Adams: Yes. That's what I said.

Prosecutor: Mr. Adams, have you ever been convicted?

Mr. Adams: Uhh, yes, I was. But only once.

Prosecutor: And was this conviction for a felony?

Mr. Adams: Yes.

Even when all prior felony convictions are admissible to impeach, judicial discretion can be used to exclude this evidence. Most commonly, this is done if the conviction is very old and the witness has had no other convictions. Some states have enacted laws that limit this type of impeachment to crimes that occurred in the last ten years (some use five years or some other number). Even when there is no specific law, judicial discretion can be used to prevent attacks on a witness with a long record of exemplary conduct.

If a witness denies a prior conviction, another witness may be called to show the jury that the conviction exists. This witness would usually testify about the court records on the conviction. A certified copy of those records might even be admitted into evidence.

5-2c Uncharged Crimes and Immoral Acts

Even crimes that did not result in convictions can be used to impeach. Immoral acts that do not violate any penal laws can also be used. The judge has more discretion since this evidence is very time consuming and may confuse the jury. Also, the witness has not had the right to a trial on the prior acts.

Generally, the same types of restrictions apply here as with prior convictions. The acts must be relevant to the truthfulness of the witness. Minor crimes are usually inadmissible. If a person has lived a law-abiding life for many years, old crimes are normally inadmissible.

Crimes that were charged but resulted in neither a conviction nor an acquittal may be used. In some situations, cases dropped due to procedural errors may be admissible. Good faith errors on searches and seizures would be in this category. Some states even allow impeachment based on convictions where the witness received a pardon.

Example of Impeachment Based on Uncharged Crimes and Immoral Acts

Prosecutor:	Ms. Young, you testified that you are an in-home aide for elderly patients. How many people have you cared for?
Ms. Young:	About 20, I guess.
Prosecutor:	And in caring for those 20 people, have you ever taken any of their possessions home?
Ms. Young:	Well, yes, I do that once in a while.
Prosecutor:	Did the patients give you permission to do that?
Ms. Young:	Not specifically.
Prosecutor:	So, you stole from your clients?
Ms. Young:	Hey, that's not the same as stealing. I never got arrested or anything.

5-2d Prior Inconsistent Statements

A witness can be impeached if he/she has previously made any statement that is inconsistent with the testimony at trial. The statement does not have to totally contradict the testimony; it merely needs to show that there is a reason to suspect the accuracy of the testimony.

The appropriate procedure is to ask the witness if he/she made a specific statement. The date, place, and name of the person to whom the statement was made are also given so that the witness has a fair chance to remember the event. If the witness denies making the statement, the judge may allow another witness to be called to testify about the statement in question. It is misconduct for an attorney to ask a witness about a prior statement unless the statement is believed to have been made.

Example of Impeachment Based on Prior Inconsistent Statements

Prosecutor: Mrs. White, you just testified that John was at your house on the evening of November 15.

Mrs. White: Yes, he sure was.

Prosecutor: Please think back to November 16. On that morning didn't you tell your friend Mabel that you visited your sister the night before?

Mrs. White: I sure don't remember saying that.

The U.S. Supreme Court has ruled that statements obtained in violation of *Miranda* may be used to impeach. The only restriction is that no coercion was used to obtain the statement. Most states follow this rule.

5-2e Inability to Observe

The credibility of a witness is weak if he/she was not able to clearly observe the events in question. Impeachment is used to raise this question. Inability to observe usually has one of the following causes: (1) physical handicaps of the witness; (2) obstruction at the scene; or (3) witness was too far away to see or hear the event in question. Sometimes more than one of these problems arise at the same time; for example, the witness might have a physical handicap (bad eyesight) and also be too far away to see clearly.

Since a witness can testify about anything observed with the five senses, a defect in any of these senses that is relevant to the case may be grounds for impeachment. For example, the eyesight of a person who identified the defendant at the scene could be challenged, though a hearing problem cannot be used to attack testimony about what the witness saw. The jury usually is not very impressed with minor impairments.

Suppose the witness claims to have observed a drug sale while standing across the street. A witness with 20/20 vision is more likely to have seen the transaction clearly than a person whose vision is 20/400. Poor vision may be irrelevant if the person wore proper corrective lenses.

Example of Impeachment Based on Inability to Observe— Physical Problem of Witness

Defense:	Mr. Allen, you testified that you saw John start the fight. Where were you sitting at the time you made this observation?
Mr. Allen:	I was on my front porch.
Defense:	How far is it from your front porch to the spot where the fight started?
Mr. Allen:	Maybe 50 feet.
Defense:	Mr. Allen, have you had your eyes checked lately?
Mr. Allen:	About six months ago.
Defense:	What did your doctor tell you about your eyesight?
Mr. Allen:	He said I needed new glasses really, really bad.
Defense:	And did you get new glasses?
Mr. Allen:	No. They cost too much.

The second problem is not with the witness but the layout of the crime scene. Something may be blocking the view, muffling sounds, etc. Weather and lighting conditions are important. Simple examples would be that there was a tree in the way, a bus drove by at the crucial moment, or it was a dark and stormy night. It might turn out that there was no window on the side of the building where the observation allegedly was made. Both of these avenues of impeachment require the police and attorneys to do their homework.

Example of Impeachment Based on Inability to Observe— Obstruction of View

Prosecutor:	Ms. Morris, you testified that you saw John being attacked before he hit anyone. Where were you at the time you made that observation?
Ms. Morris:	I was sitting in a chair in my front yard.
Prosecutor:	Why were you in your front yard?
Ms. Morris:	We were having a party and there were too many people to fit in the house. Anyway, it was hot in the house.
Prosecutor:	And you were sitting down.
Ms. Morris:	Yes. I was lucky. Most of the people had to stand up.
Prosecutor:	Were there any people between you and where John was?
Ms. Morris:	Yeah. A whole bunch of people.
Prosecutor:	And they were standing up while you were sitting down?
Ms. Morris:	Yeah.
Prosecutor:	With all those people in the way, how could you tell what was happening to John?
Ms. Morris:	I got little glimpses when someone moved.

5-2f Reputation

Impeachment based on reputation is usually restricted to the trait of honesty (also called truth and veracity). The credibility of a witness is easily diminished if it is shown that other people believe the witness is a liar.

As we discussed in the last chapter, reputation is usually shown by the testimony of people who claim to know what the community thinks about someone. For impeachment, the question rests on the general reputation of the witness for honesty.

Example of Impeachment Based on Reputation

Prosecutor:	Mr. Evans, do you know Mr. Brown who is a witness in this case?
Mr. Evans:	I don't know him personally.
Prosecutor:	Are you familiar with his reputation?
Mr. Evans:	Yes. I've heard a lot of people talk about him.
Prosecutor:	Have you heard people talk about Mr. Brown's honesty?
Mr. Evans:	Yes. I've heard a whole lot of people say that he is a liar. No one trusts him.

5-3 Rehabilitation

Rehabilitation is the restoration of the credibility of a witness. Once a witness has been impeached, the side that originally called the witness will try to convince the jury that their witness testified truthfully and should be believed. Redirect examination is usually used to attempt to rehabilitate witnesses. Sometimes the judge will allow new witnesses to be called to support the credibility of an impeached witness. Figure 5-1 shows the relationship of testimony to the impeachment and rehabilitation of witnesses.

Whereas impeachment focused on prior criminal conduct, rehabilitation frequently tries to publicize good deeds. If possible, the years of exemplary conduct since the last serious offense will be emphasized. Sometimes an attorney decides that the best defense is a strong offense. The witness's unsavory past may be acknowledged during direct examination so the impeachment will lack dramatic effect. Another tactic is to try to show that the witness can be objective despite a criminal record. The nature and extent of the criminal acts will probably be the most significant facts used to determine what rehabilitation will be attempted.

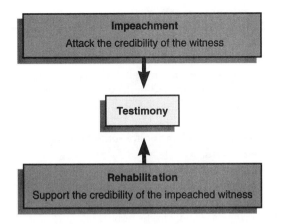

Figure 5-1
Impeachment and Rehabilitation of Witnesses

Example of Rehabilitation Based on Good Behavior

Defense: Mr. Williams, you just testified that you have a prior felony conviction. When did that conviction occur?

Mr. Williams: In 1978.

Defense: Was that your only conviction?

Mr. Williams: Yes.

Defense: And in the 20-plus years since that conviction, have you ever been arrested?

Mr. Williams: No.

Defense: In that 20-plus year period, have you committed any crimes for which you were not arrested?

Mr. Williams: No.

Three common approaches are used to rehabilitate a witness who was impeached by prior inconsistent statements. One is to try to convince the jury that there was a reason for lying earlier, but the witness is telling the truth now. These reasons might include fear of the police, intimidation by a co-defendant, or misunderstanding the questions. A second method of rehabilitation is to show that the statement used to impeach was taken out of context. The attorney may attempt to show there really was no inconsistency with testimony that tells about the whole conversation. The third method is to introduce statements that were made before the inconsistent statement. If these statements are consistent with the trial testimony the witness may be rehabilitated.

Example of Rehabilitation Based on Witnesses Currently Telling the Truth

Prosecution:	Ms. Benson, you just admitted to the defense attorney that you told the police, on the night we are discussing in this case, that John was not involved in the fight. Was your statement to the police true?
Ms. Benson:	No.
Prosecution:	Why did you tell the police something that was not true?
Ms. Benson:	I was afraid.
Prosecution:	Why were you afraid?
Ms. Benson:	John's friend was standing there. About 10 feet from me. And he kept staring at me and making a fist.
Prosecution:	So why did you lie to the police?
Ms. Benson:	I was afraid that I would get beat up if I told the police that John was involved.

A wide array of approaches can be used when the impeachment was based on inability to observe. Sometimes the witness explodes when attacked on cross-examination. For example, the elderly neighbor who is asked about wearing a hearing aid replies, "Even a deaf person could have heard them, the way they were shouting." Asking further questions in this type of situation is not necessary. More commonly, rehabilitation will take the form of asking the witness questions in order to show that the physical handicap(s) emphasized on cross-examination are not such severe impediments to the ability to observe as they might seem.

Example of Rehabilitation Based on Lack of Impairment by Handicap

Prosecution:	Mr. Allen, you just testified that you did not get new glasses when your doctor recommended them. Are you nearsighted or farsighted?
Mr. Allen:	I am farsighted.
Prosecution:	Does that mean you can see things that are far away?
Mr. Allen:	Yes. I can drive and see things just fine but I can't read a book without glasses. It's just stuff that is near to me, like within 5 feet, that I can't read.

Sometimes expert witnesses are called if the ability of one witness to observe is crucial to the case. These experts might discuss how lighting or distance would affect the ability to observe. Models may be constructed to demonstrate that a person at a given location could, or could not, have observed events in question.

Example of Rehabilitation by Use of Expert Witness

Prosecution:	Dr. Davis, is Mr. Allen one of your patients?
Dr. Davis:	Yes.
Prosecution:	When did you last give Mr. Allen an eye examination?
Dr. Davis:	About six months ago.
Prosecution:	Was Mr. Allen nearsighted or farsighted?
Dr. Davis:	He is farsighted.
Prosecution:	Please explain what farsighted means.
Dr. Davis:	In layman's terms, it means that a person is unable to focus properly on items that are close to the person. There is no impairment of vision for things that are far away.
Prosecution:	Based on your examination of Mr. Allen, could he clearly see an event that occurred 20 feet from where he was standing?
Dr. Davis:	Yes.

If reputation was used to impeach, there are usually two possible methods of rehabilitation. The credibility of the impeaching witness can be attacked. This is done during cross-examination. The other approach is to call reputation witnesses and try to convince the jury that these witnesses, who testify about a very good reputation, are the most credible. Table 5-1 summarizes the methods used to impeach and rehabilitate witnesses.

Example of Rehabilitation Based on Reputation

Defense:	Mr. Franks, do you know Ms. Benson who testified in this case?
Mr. Franks:	Yes.
Defense:	And do you know what other people say about Ms. Benson?
Mr. Franks:	Yes. We work at the same store so I know a lot of people who know Ms. Benson.
Defense:	Based on what the people you work with say, what is Ms. Benson's reputation?
Mr. Franks:	They think she is honest. Everybody trusts her.

5-4 Corroboration

The credibility of a witness is stronger if there is additional evidence to support the witness's testimony. This supporting evidence is called **corroboration.** Either the testimony of another witness or physical evidence may be used.

There are a few situations where corroboration is mandatory. One involves the testimony of an accomplice. When one party to the crime

T A B L E   **5-1 Summary of Impeachment and Rehabilitation of Witnesses**

	Impeach	**Rehabilitate**
Bias, Prejudice, Motive	Show witness may be less than objective	Show that despite apparent reason to distort the truth the witness is being objective
Prior Felony Convictions	Introduce evidence that witness has prior conviction	Show defendant led moral life after conviction
Immoral Acts and Uncharged Crimes	Ask questions about immoral acts and uncharged crimes that indicate the witness may not be testifying to truth	Testimony to show that despite past immoral acts and uncharged crimes the witness is currently telling the truth

testifies against the other, there is always the suspicion that this was done to reduce his/her own culpability. Due to this motive to falsify, a person cannot be convicted based solely on the testimony of an accomplice; there must be corroboration.

Many states also follow the common law rule that there must be some corroboration in cases of false pretenses. A few still follow the old rule that required corroboration in rape cases, although this has been highly criticized; nearly all other crimes can be established solely on the testimony of the victim.

Where corroboration is mandatory, the law usually does not require that all of the testimony be supported by other evidence. Most states merely require that there be some additional evidence to show that the testimony is true.

Even when corroboration is not required, both sides frequently try to introduce as much evidence as possible to corroborate the testimony of their witnesses. While the judge normally instructs the jury that neither party is required to introduce all possible evidence in the case, strong corroboration is likely to convince the jury that the witness should be believed. The jurors still retain the power, however, to reject the evidence because they do not believe either the original witness or the witness called for corroboration.

Example of Corroboration

Bob testified that he was at the corner of Third and Main at 7:30 P.M. on November 15 and saw John hit Sam. Bob said John was wearing black leather gloves at the time.

The following items were introduced to corroborate Bob's testimony:
1. A parking ticket that was dated November 15 at 7:29 P.M. It indicated that a car owned by Bob was parked at an expired meter in front of the store located at 301 N. Main Street. A city map shows that 301 N. Main Street is the first building north of the intersection of Third and Main.
2. A sales receipt which shows that John bought a pair of black leather gloves.
3. Laboratory tests that show that DNA tests done on tissue samples removed from a pair of black leather gloves matches a DNA sample taken from Sam.
4. Testimony by Tom that he was also at Third and Main at 7:30 P.M. on November 15 and he saw Bob there.

Corroboration must be distinguished from cumulative evidence. Evidence is corroborative if it confirms previous testimony by the use of another source. For example, Mr. Jones testified that he saw the defendant choke the murder victim. This would be corroborated by the autopsy report that indicated that there were bruises around the victim's neck. Physical evidence, such as the rope that the witness saw the defendant place around the victim's neck, could also be used to corroborate the testimony. Cumulative evidence merely repeats what was said. If another witness was called who testified that he/she also saw the defendant choke the victim, this evidence would be cumulative. The judge usually allows several eyewitnesses to testify even though it is cumulative but will eventually refuse to let additional witnesses take the stand on this issue.

5-5 Memory Failures

It is not uncommon, especially when there is a long period between the crime and the trial, for a person to forget details of the case. This includes both victims, witnesses to the crime, and the police officers. When this happens, it will be necessary to attempt to refresh the person's memory. This can be done either before taking the witness stand or by asking appropriate questions during direct or cross-examination.

The basic rule is that anything can be used to refresh memory. Witnesses must, however, be able to testify from memory and not merely repeat what was used to refresh their memory. Cross-examination is used to attempt to point out that the testimony is not accurate. It can also be used to show that the witness was coached to the point that the current testimony was memorized or that the attorney told the witness what to say and what not to say.

While unusual things may be used to refresh the witness's memory, the most common thing used is the report written about the event. Notes that were taken in a field notebook can also be used. For this reason, it is important that police officers take accurate notes and that they are not destroyed until all possibility of a trial (or retrial) have passed.

So far we have described what is called the **Present Memory Refreshed Rule.** The witness now remembers the events in question and can testify. Sometimes the attempt to refresh memory fails. When this happens, it may still be possible to introduce reports written near the time of the event in question. This is done through the **Past Recollection Recorded Exception** to the Hearsay Rule. The basic requirements for the admission of these reports are:

1. The statement would be admissible if the declarant testified at the current trial.
2. The witness currently has insufficient present recollection to testify fully and accurately.
3. The report was made at a time when the facts were fresh in the memory of the witness.
4. The report was made by the witness, someone under his/her direction, or by another person for the purpose of recording the witness's statement.
5. The witness can testify that the report was a true statement of the facts.
6. The report is authenticated as accurate.

The key to using this approach is that it can be established that an accurate report was made at a time when the events were fresh in the witness's memory. This approach is discussed in more detail in Chapter 8. Table 5-2 shows how a witness's present memory is refreshed and how a past recollection is recorded.

5-6 Unavailable Witnesses

Sometimes a witness is not available to testify at trial. This can be for a variety of reasons (e.g., death, relocation, witness has gone into hiding, etc.). Under the Hearsay Rule exception for former testimony, statements made under oath at a prior court hearing in the same case may be introduced at trial if the witness is not available to testify.

Many states have established other procedures to preserve testimony if it is believed that a material witness will be unavailable at trial. Some

TABLE **5-2 A Witness's Present Memory Refreshed and Past Recollection Recorded**

Present Memory Refreshed	Past Recollection Recorded
Event	Event
Memory dims	Memory dims
Read report, etc., to refresh memory	Read report, etc., to refresh memory
Memory revived	Memory still inadequate
Testify in court from memory	Introduce document written near time of original event

allow sworn testimony to be recorded on videotape for later use at trial. Others take sworn statements in a manner similar to depositions that are taken during discovery in civil cases. State laws vary on whether the opposing side is allowed to be present and cross-examine the witness when the statements are obtained.

A material witness can be arrested and detained in the county jail until trial. This is an extreme measure and usually requires a court hearing. A judge usually can require the material witness to post bond in lieu of being jailed if it appears this will be sufficient to guarantee appearance at trial. Some states permit the prosecution to have material witnesses jailed if it appears flight is a serious risk but do not provide similar measures to prevent defense witnesses from leaving the jurisdiction.

5-7 Types of Witnesses

The general meaning of "witness" is someone who observed something. When we talk about a witness at a trial, we mean the person who has been sworn and takes the witness stand. There are two main types of witnesses: **lay witnesses** and **expert witnesses.**

Most people testify as lay witnesses. They are the ones who saw the crime occur, talked to the suspect before or after the crime, or otherwise observed what happened and/or gave information to the police. The fact that a person routinely testifies in court as an expert does not affect his/her ability to testify as a lay witness if he/she saw the crime occur. For example, if a forensic pathologist observed a robbery while driving to work, he/she would be allowed to testify about the robbery as a lay witness. If he/she did the autopsy on the robbery-murder victim, he/she may also be called as an expert.

Lay Witness Defined

A lay witness is a person who observed an event that is relevant to the case on trial. Lay witnesses are allowed to testify about any relevant event that was observed with one or more of the five senses (sight, hearing, smell, touch, or taste). Lay witnesses are not allowed to give opinions.

Expert witnesses are called to help the jury understand the evidence. They are in court to explain things to the jury. Experts are not allowed if the facts can be understood by the jurors without their help. There are a wide variety of specialties where experts can be useful at trial. Some require extensive education while others are based on specialized training and experience.

Expert Witness Defined

An expert witness is a person who is called to testify about a relevant event based on his/her special knowledge or training. Expert witnesses are only allowed if some evidence in the case is beyond the understanding of the average juror.

5-8 Opinion Rule

The jury, or the judge if the jury has been waived, is the trier of the facts. For this reason, the general rule is that only facts may be introduced into evidence. Opinions of the witnesses are not admissible because it is the function of the trier of the facts to analyze the evidence. This is called the **Opinion Rule.** The trial process revolves around asking specific questions in order to obtain concrete answers. The Opinion Rule fits into this by seeking to eliminate testimony not directly relating to the facts. Conclusions are left to the jury. In practice, however, the rule really is that lay witnesses are generally not permitted to draw conclusions, but expert witnesses may give their professional opinions.

5-8a Lay Witnesses

Even the Opinion Rule has exceptions. While the older view was that lay witnesses were only allowed to express opinions when they were absolutely necessary, the more common practice today is to allow opinions for the sake of convenience. Some courts go so far as to follow Wigmore's view that lay opinions should only be rejected if they have no value to the jury.[1] Much is left to the discretion of the trial judge.

Opinion Testimony of Lay Witness Defined

If the witness is not testifying as an expert, his/her testimony in the form of opinions is limited to opinions or inferences which are:

1. Rationally based on the perception of the witness.
2. Helpful to a clear understanding of the witness's testimony or the determination of the facts in issue.

Some statements of opinion are so common that we do not realize they are opinions. For example, an eyewitness attends a lineup and identifies the defendant. This is really a statement of the witness that it is his/her opinion that the defendant is the person that he/she saw committing the crime. Another example would be the statement, "He was drunk." This is an opinion. The facts may have been that the person smelled of alcohol, had watery eyes, slurred speech, unsteady gait, poor muscular coordination, and did not talk rationally. Nearly all courts would allow both of these opinions into evidence.

A wide variety of lay opinions may actually be admissible. They include:

- Identification of someone's handwriting.
- Statements about the emotional state of someone (he/she was sad, angry, happy, etc.).
- Statements about physical condition of someone (e.g., he/she was weak, strong, sick, drunk).
- Voice identification.
- General statements about mental condition (e.g., he/she was coherent, smart, seemed to have low intelligence, etc.).
- Identity of a person based on in-person lineup or looking at a photograph.
- General statements about speed of vehicles (e.g., he/she was going too fast).

If one or more of these opinions is given, additional questions are usually asked so the jury will know the basis for forming the opinion. Cross-examination can also be used to show that there was an inadequate basis for the opinion or that a different conclusion could have been drawn. Table 5-3 presents examples of opinion testimony allowed and not allowed by a lay witness.

5-8b Expert Witnesses

Expert witnesses are allowed to give opinions based on their professional judgment. Even though experts have broader rights than lay witnesses,

TABLE **5-3** Opinion Testimony by Lay Witness

Allowed	Not Allowed
The man had bloodshot eyes and staggered when he tried to walk.	The man was drunk.
The man was disoriented and incoherent.	The man was crazy.
The man carefully aimed before shooting the gun.	The man maliciously killed the victim.
The car was driving faster than the other cars and left skid marks when it tried to stop.	The car was going 85 miles per hour.

TABLE **5-4** Comparison of Testimony by a Lay Witness and an Expert Witness

Lay Witness	Expert Witness
The man smelled of alcohol and failed the field sobriety test.	The man's blood alcohol was .12%
The man hid from everyone and said he was protecting himself from invisible rays.	The man suffered from paranoid schizophrenia.
The car was going faster than the other cars and was unable to stop before hitting the tree.	Based on the skid marks, the car was going 74 miles per hour.
There was a man at the scene of the crime who looks just like the defendant.	DNA tests on blood found at the scene and a sample taken from the defendant indicate that the blood came from the same person.

there are still some areas where they are not allowed to testify. Table 5-4 compares examples of testimony by a lay witness with testimony by an expert witness.

Experts' testimony cannot invade issues that the judge or jury is required to decide. This means that they usually may not state conclusions on legal issues. For example, a psychiatrist may state a diagnosis (paranoid schizophrenia), but in most states he/she cannot testify that a person is criminally insane.

5-8c Foundation for Expert Witness

In order to use an expert, a foundation must be laid that establishes three main things:

1. The jury needs the help of an expert.
2. There is a recognized area of expertise that applies.
3. The person called to testify has the appropriate background to qualify as an expert.

Experts are only allowed to testify if they are needed. If the facts can be understood by lay jurors, no expert witness will be allowed. Things that are common knowledge do not require an expert to interpret them. Before a judge will allow an expert to testify, he/she must be convinced that there is a sufficiently established body of knowledge on the subject. Even then, the courts may be reluctant to allow testimony. Psychiatrists have developed many diagnoses, including the 47XYY (abnormal gene) Syndrome, that the courts have been very reluctant to accept.

For years most state and federal courts followed *Frye v. United States* (1923), which held that a scientific technique was admissible in court *only if* it was "generally accepted" as reliable in the relevant scientific community.[2] The Supreme Court in *Daubert v. Merrell Dow Pharmaceuticals, Inc.* (1993) adopted a new standard for use with the Federal Rules of Evidence: the judge must make a preliminary assessment that the reasoning or methodology underlying the testimony is scientifically valid and that the reasoning or methodology properly can be applied to the facts in issue.[3] This permits use of newer tests that have not yet become established in the scientific community. The trial judge makes the key ruling on whether the test provides relevant information. The *Daubert* decision is binding on the federal courts. State courts are free to decide whether to adopt the *Daubert* rule or retain the *Frye* standard.

Sometimes the courts refuse to accept a new technique as sufficiently accurate. The polygraph is a good example. While many people believe a well-trained polygraph operator can accurately test for deception, the courts have been very reluctant to accept polygraph results in criminal cases. Opponents argue strongly that there are too many errors to justify giving the jury information that may sound like it is conclusive evidence that a person lied. Many states refuse to admit the results of polygraph examinations.

Still other types of expert testimony are excluded because the courts refuse to believe there is any "scientific" basis for the opinion. Psychics and astrologers would be in this class.

Before an expert witness can testify, the court must be convinced that this person has the appropriate background. The exact qualifications vary with the type of expertise. There is no rule that requires advanced college degrees and in some areas, such as accident reconstruction and ballistic examinations, a combination of training and experience is required. In other areas, such as the probabilities involved in a pyramid scheme or the chance of two people having the same blood type, purely theoretical study may be sufficient.

Even if a person is an expert, he/she cannot give opinions on many things. The testimony must be restricted to factual descriptions of observations, much as a lay witness does, and opinions within the area of his/ her expertise. Opinions that are outside the area of expertise are not allowed.

Experts do not have a special right to use privileged communications, such as statements made to a doctor or lawyer. They can base their opinions on these statements only if the privilege has been waived or there is an exception to the privilege that applies in the case. See Chapter 9 for a detailed discussion of privileged communications.

5-8d *Voir Dire* of Experts

The expert will be subjected to *voir dire* to establish his/her qualifications before testifying unless the opposing side is willing to accept the witness without a challenge. *Voir dire* is done without the jury present. The side calling the expert will ask relevant questions to show that the witness has the necessary education and experience. Opposing counsel can cross-examine and attempt to show that the expert does not qualify.

5-8e Examination of Expert Witnesses

Immediately after the expert witness takes the stand, questions will usually be asked regarding his/her professional background, education and training. Since this has already been covered in *voir dire,* the only function of these questions is to impress the jury. It is common to have experts called by both sides in a case. Therefore, the jury needs to know about the expert's qualifications to help them decide how much weight should be given to the testimony.

On direct examination, the expert may be asked about his/her inspection and testing of the evidence in the case. Opinions based on this evidence may be given. Additionally, experts may be asked **hypothetical questions.** Hypothetical questions ask the witness to draw conclusions based on the facts given in the question.

Examples of Hypothetical Questions

"Based on your microscopic examination of the slides containing lung tissue specimens that were prepared during the autopsy, is it your professional opinion that the victim was dead prior to being placed in water?"

"Based on the fact that the room in question was illuminated with a 60-watt bulb and there were no windows, would you conclude that a person with normal eyesight could accurately determine if the currency was counterfeit?"

"Based on the testimony regarding the defendant's prior mental illness, the defendant's repeated claims that he was from Mars, and the fact that the defendant repeatedly said, 'You are the devil!' prior to shooting the victim, would you conclude that the defendant understood the nature and quality of his acts?"

It is not necessary that the witness has personally examined any of the evidence in a hypothetical question. For example, a civil engineer might be asked, "Would it be safe to drive a car with good tires on a dry surface at 55 miles-per-hour if there was a 10 percent downhill grade with a 90-degree turn that was banked 5 degrees?" The engineer would be allowed to give a professional opinion even though he/she had never seen the curve that was actually involved in the case.

In addition to the normal methods of cross-examination, experts may be questioned regarding the sources of information used to form their conclusions. The expert may be asked who he/she considers the leading authors and texts in the field. This also includes asking if he/she has read specific books or articles. If he/she admits reading a given work, questioning may continue on why the expert agrees or disagrees with the opinions stated in it.

Some experts always testify for the defense while others always testify for the prosecution. This can be used to impeach for bias. The amount of the expert's fee is also subject to cross-examination. If the fee appears too large, the jury may discredit the testimony.

5-8f Examples of Expert Testimony

Insanity. A lay witness can describe symptoms that he/she observed, but an expert witness is required in order to introduce diagnosis of mental disorders. The expert can explain the effect of the condition on the personality and how it probably affected the defendant's actions. Opinions can also be given on the defendant's ability to form criminal intent, premeditation, or to comprehend what was going on. While the expert psychiatrist or psychologist usually examines the defendant, hypothetical questions are also utilized. In most states, the expert may not testify that a person is criminally insane because this is a legal, not medical, opinion.

Example of Expert Witness Testimony on Issue of Defendant's Sanity

"Based on my diagnostic interview of the defendant which lasted six hours, I diagnosed the defendant as having a bi-polar disorder. Due to this condition I believe the defendant knew what he was doing but could not premeditate the murder."

"After reviewing the reports submitting by the two court-appointed psychiatrists, it is my professional opinion that the defendant suffers from severe depression with suicidal tendencies. It is my opinion that the defendant planned to commit suicide and was unaware that any other person was in the area."

Ballistics. Firearms tests can often reveal if a recovered slug could have been fired from a specific gun, depending on the condition of the slug. The pattern of lands and grooves in the barrel of the gun imprints a pattern on the bullet as it leaves the gun. Since manufacturers use the same configuration in all their guns, the pattern can be used to state what type of gun was used. Microscopic comparison of the recovered slug and one that was test-fired is required to make a positive match. Firing pin marks on the shell casing can also often be matched with a suspect gun.

Example of Expert Witness Testimony about a Ballistics Test

"After comparing Exhibit A, the bullet recovered from the victim, with Exhibit B, the bullet that was test fired from the gun found in the possession of the defendant, it is my opinion that the two bullets were fired from the same gun."

"I have studied the two bullets, Exhibits C and D, under a comparison microscope and it is my professional opinion that the two bullets were not fired from the same weapon."

Blood and Tissue Matching. Blood testing is important because the blood contains substances that can be used to match blood samples to saliva, tears, perspiration, semen, vaginal fluids, mucus, gastric contents, etc. In the past, blood testing was limited to typing by the ABO system. If the suspect did not have the appropriate blood type he/she could be eliminated, but if there was a match it still was not possible to indicate that the suspect committed the crime. If the suspect had Type A blood, test results were not very useful because Type A is present in 40 percent of the American public.

Today we have much more sophisticated tests. For example, scientific analysis of the DNA (deoxyribonucleic acid) molecule, found in all cells, reveals the body's genetic code and can identify blood, hair, semen, or skin left at the crime scene as accurately as fingerprints. Each state will decide on the admissibility of each new technique as it becomes recognized in its respective scientific community.

Example of Expert Witness Testimony on DNA Testing

"As I have explained, DNA testing was done on semen recovered from the victim when the rape kit was done at the emergency room. Similar tests were performed on a blood sample taken from the defendant at the time of booking.

Based on these tests, there is a 1 in 20,000,000 chance that the two samples came from two different individuals."

"DNA tests were performed on blood samples taken from the rape victim, the defendant, and the child born to the rape victim. Based on these tests I can conclusively state that the defendant is not the father of this child."

Summary

All trial witnesses must be competent. This means that they must understand the duty to tell the truth and be able to answer questions about the events in issue. If there is doubt about the competency of a witness, a *voir dire* examination will be conducted.

The truthfulness of each witness is in issue. The opposing side may ask questions for the purpose of convincing the jurors that they should not believe the witness. This is referred to as impeachment. A witness can be impeached because he/she is biased or prejudiced toward a person involved in the case. The prior crimes committed by the witness, whether or not there has been a conviction, can be used to infer that current testimony is not true. Prior statements which are inconsistent with what the witness said during direct examination may be used to show that the current testimony is not true. A witness can be impeached because he/she could not have accurately observed the events in question. The reputation of the witness for untruthfulness can also be used to impeach.

If a witness is impeached, the side that called the witness will have a chance to attempt to convince the jury that the testimony should be believed anyway. This is called rehabilitation and is usually done on redirect examination.

When a witness cannot remember the events in question, attempts may be made to refresh his/her memory. If this is successful, the witness will testify just like any other witness. Memory problems, of course, will probably be emphasized on cross-examination. If the memory cannot be refreshed, an accurate report made by the witness near the time of the event may be used instead of testimony.

Testimony can be corroborated by another witness or physical objects related to the case. Very few cases require corroboration, but attorneys frequently introduce this additional evidence to help support their case.

A lay witness is allowed to testify about anything observed with the five senses. Opinions are allowed only if they are expressions in such common usage that the jury will understand. Even then, a good attorney will ask the witness to explain what facts led to the conclusion.

Expert witnesses are allowed to express professional opinions. Before an expert can testify it must be established that the jury needs assistance with the facts. It also must be shown that there is a recognized body of knowledge that applies.

Each expert must show that he/she has the necessary education and experience to qualify as an expert. On the witness stand, the expert can testify about the facts and give opinions. Hypothetical questions may be used so the expert can give an opinion even if he/she has not personally examined the evidence.

Discussion Questions

1. Define *competency of a witness*, and explain the procedure for establishing the competency of a witness.
2. Give two examples of incompetent witnesses. Explain why each one is incompetent.
3. Define *impeachment.* Explain how impeachment is done, and give six ways a witness can be impeached.
4. Define *rehabilitation of a witness*, and give two examples of how a witness can be rehabilitated.
5. Explain how the memory of a witness can legally be refreshed, and list the requirements for introducing a document under the Past Recollection Recorded Rule.
6. State the Opinion Rule, and explain how it affects testimony.
7. Explain what a lay witness may testify about, and give three examples of opinions a lay witness can give.
8. When is an expert witness used in a criminal case? What arguments must be made to the judge before a specific type of expert witness may be called to the stand?
9. What is the purpose of *voir dire* of an expert witness? Why are the qualifications of an expert witness given to the jury?
10. Explain what hypothetical questions are, and tell how they are used.
11. Give three examples of how an expert witness can be impeached.
12. Give three examples of the use of expert witnesses in criminal trials.

Endnotes

1. Wigmore is one of the famous legal scholars on the subject of evidence.
2. *Frye v. United States*, 293 F. 1013 (D.C. Cir. 1923).
3. *Daubert v. Merrell Dow Pharmaceuticals, Inc.*, 509 U.S. 579, 125 L.Ed. 2d 469, 113 S.Ct. 2786 (1993).

CHAPTER 6

Crime Scene Evidence, Experiments, and Models

Outline

Key Terms

- Ballistics expert
- Blood alcohol
- Blood typing
- Chain of custody

- DNA testing
- Experiment
- Laying the foundation
- Latent prints

- Models
- Real evidence

After studying this chapter, you will be able to:

- Properly mark and package real evidence found during the investigation of a criminal case.
- Maintain the chain of custody for real evidence found at a crime scene.
- Explain the importance of scientific evidence in a criminal case.
- Describe how the prosecutor lays the foundation for the admission of crime scene evidence, experiments, and models.
- List commonly accepted laboratory tests used in criminal cases, and explain their respective evidentiary value.
- Explain what conditions must be met before experiments can be introduced into evidence.
- Describe common types of experiments used in criminal trials.
- Explain the most common conditions which must be met before a model or diagram can be introduced into evidence.

6-1 Introduction

In Chapter 3 we defined **real evidence** to include anything that can be perceived with the five senses except trial testimony. This includes physical items, documents, exhibits, and pictures. Since this is such a broad category, it will be divided into two chapters. Evidence recovered at the crime scene and by criminal investigations, scientific evidence, experiments, models, and diagrams will be covered in this chapter. Chapter 7 will discuss documents and pictures.

All types of real evidence have two things in common: they must be marked and formally introduced into evidence, and the attorney who wishes to introduce them must lay a foundation to establish the admissibility of the items in question.

The formal process of marking evidence has four steps. First, the item must be shown to opposing counsel before testimony about it is introduced. This gives the attorney a chance to see what is to be discussed and form appropriate questions. Second, the side that intends to introduce the item has the court clerk assign it a number (or letter) for identification purposes. Third, the foundation is laid to establish that the item is admissible. Lastly, a formal request is made to admit it into evidence. If the judge rules that the item is admissible, it is given an exhibit number (or letter) and becomes evidence in the case. The following example illustrates the process involved for the prosecution to introduce the murder weapon (e.g., a gun) into evidence.

Example of Procedures for Introduction of Evidence

Prosecutor shows gun to defense attorney and allows him/her to examine it if desired.

Prosecutor: "Your Honor, the prosecution requests that the clerk mark this .38 caliber revolver for identification as People's No. 1." (Gun is given to clerk who attaches tag to gun with "People's No. 1" written on it.)

Prosecutor calls witness(es) and lays foundation to show that gun is the one found at crime scene and that ballistics tests show slug test-fired from this gun matches slug removed from victim's body.

Defense cross-examines and raises objections to admission of the gun into evidence.

Prosecutor: "Your Honor, the prosecution requests that the gun that was marked for identification as People's No. 1 be admitted into evidence as Exhibit No. 1."

Judge: "Let the gun be received into evidence as Exhibit No. 1." (Clerk attaches tag that reads "Exhibit No. 1.")

Exhibits that have been admitted into evidence may be examined by the jury and can usually be taken to the jury room during deliberations.

The two requests to mark the gun, first for identification and later as an exhibit, appear to be a waste of time. The reason for marking it twice is that not all items displayed during trial will be admitted into evidence. To keep the trial record straight, all of those items are marked for identification purposes. The prosecutor or defense attorney may use something to illustrate a point or help a witness describe an event but not ask to have it introduced as evidence in the case. Opposing counsel may successfully argue that the item is inadmissible. Sometimes the testimony of several witnesses is needed to lay the foundation. Assigning the identification number makes it easier to determine which piece of evidence is being discussed. By the time all of these witnesses have testified, other items may have been introduced into evidence. In order to have the items which are introduced into evidence numbered consecutively, exhibit numbers (or letters) are only assigned after the judge rules they are admissible. To avoid confusion, one side usually uses letters and the other numbers. For example, the prosecution might begin with "1" while the defense starts with "A." If a large number of exhibits is anticipated, each side will be assigned a block of numbers, such as 100 to 299 for the prosecution and 300 to 599 for the defense.

6-2 Crime Scene Evidence

All items that are admitted as exhibits must be authenticated. Authentication means to show that an item is genuine. To authenticate evidence found at the crime scene, or during other parts of the investigation of the case, it is necessary to show that the item is the same one described by the witness. The item needs to be in the same condition it was at the time it was found by the police unless it was necessary to conduct laboratory tests on it. If tests have altered its appearance, this must be explained to the jury. Careful handling of evidence and accurate report writing are crucial. Most police department procedure manuals give detailed instructions on how to handle many different types of crime scene evidence.

At the crime scene it is very important to protect evidence so that it is not destroyed or damaged. Restricting public access to the area is important to prevent people from stepping on evidence, handling it, or removing it from the scene. Officers must also be careful not to accidentally damage potential evidence. No one should be allowed to try to clean up the area before the investigation is completed because evidence could be destroyed.

The police usually try to save everything that might have evidentiary value. The prosecutor will make the final decision on what is needed at trial. Things that are not properly preserved will not be admissible. *It is much better to have many items in the evidence locker that are not used than to discover that something which is needed was not kept.*

The series of questions that the attorney asks witnesses in order to establish that a piece of real evidence is admissible is called "**laying the foundation.**" The first step in laying the foundation for the admission of crime scene evidence is to have someone identify the object and testify about where the item was found. For example, "Yes, this is the gun that I took from the defendant's pocket at the time of the arrest." If the item has a serial number or some other unique form of identification this process is easier. Merely describing it, even in rather specific terms (Smith & Wesson .38 caliber revolver), is usually not good enough if there were more than one of these items made. After the piece of evidence has been identified, one or more witness(es) will be needed to testify about what has been done with it since it was taken into the custody of the police.

The most common solution to this problem of identifying an object is to make a mark, usually the officer's initials, on the item at the time it was originally collected. It is very important, though, that identifying marks are only made in locations where they do not interfere with the use of the item as evidence. Marks should not be placed where they will be in the way when laboratory tests are done. Extreme caution must also be used to preserve fingerprints, traces of blood, etc., that may be on an object.

The officer needs to be familiar with what laboratory tests may be done in order to be able to handle crime scene evidence properly. For example, blood-stained clothing needs to be air dried before packaging because mold and mildew which grow in airtight containers where damp clothing is stored can interfere with tests for blood types. On the other hand, charred remains from a suspected arson fire need to be stored in airtight containers immediately to avoid evaporation of gasoline or other volatile fluids used to start the fire. Knowing the types of tests that can be performed will also help the officer decide what evidence should be collected.

Before collecting and packaging evidence for storage, the officer should make a detailed record of the crime scene with clear indications of where each item was found. This can be done by sketching the location, taking photographs of the area, or making detailed notes. Ideally, all three will be done. Figure 6-1 is an example of a police sketch of a crime scene.

Sketches should be to scale, with all relevant facts, such as locations of doors, windows, and furniture, included. Distances between key objects should be noted in the drawing. The points of the compass are usually included to help orient the viewer. Photographs also need to show these facts. Additionally, photographs need to have something in them that clearly indicates the size of the items shown. A ruler is frequently placed near the object that is the focus of the picture for this purpose.

The process of packaging evidence for storage is very important. The evidence needs to be preserved for trial so that it will not be damaged, evaporate, or be contaminated by other things. Each piece of evidence must be packaged individually. It is useful to have a variety of clean envelopes and containers on hand for this purpose. Appropriate packing materials, such as sterile cotton, should also be kept on hand. Extra precautions may need to be taken to avoid damaging the evidence if it will be mailed to the crime laboratory.

The evidence should be marked or tagged and the container should have the necessary identification information on it because the evidence may be removed from the envelope for examination and laboratory tests. Each container should be labeled so that it is not necessary to open it to find out what is inside. This reduces the chance of losing or damaging the evidence. There should also be space (either on the envelope or on a form attached to the package containing the evidence) so that each person who handles it can indicate the time, date, and reason for having it. This detailed procedure is used to establish the "**chain of custody**" (also called continuity of possession). It will be necessary to account for everyone who has had possession of the evidence in order to show the judge and jury that the evidence has not been tampered with. Figure 6-2 illustrates the appropriate steps for collecting evidence at a crime scene.

6-3 Scientific Evidence

The modern forensics laboratory can perform a wide variety of scientific tests. Forensic evidence can be used to establish the elements of the crime, conclusively associate the defendant with the crime, and/or help reconstruct the crime.

6-3a Types of Cases Commonly Using Scientific Evidence

Research by Peterson[1] showed police are far more likely to clear a case if scientific evidence is gathered and analyzed. Prosecutors are less likely to plea bargain in these cases and judges tend to give more severe sentences. Results of a survey suggested that jurors gave scientific evidence serious consideration but that it usually was not the key element in deciding the case.

Peterson also reported on a nationwide survey of crime labs. About two-thirds of their caseloads involved drugs, narcotics, and drunk driving cases. Only about one quarter of their work was related to crimes against persons or property.

He also reported on a study of the use of forensic evidence in court in 1975, 1978, and 1981. The study focused on a sample of six metropolitan areas. From 60 to 80 percent of the forensic evidence introduced involved drugs or fingerprints. The next most common categories were firearms, blood and bloodstains, and semen. The use of these types of evidence declined from 1975 to 1981. Specialized tests, like those used to match hair, fibers, glass, paint, and soil, were rarely used in routine criminal cases.

Forensic evidence was used in nearly all murder and drug possession cases. Use in rape prosecutions varied considerably between the jurisdictions (from 30 to 70 percent). Burglary, robbery, and attempted murder or aggravated battery cases were less likely to have tests from a crime laboratory introduced.

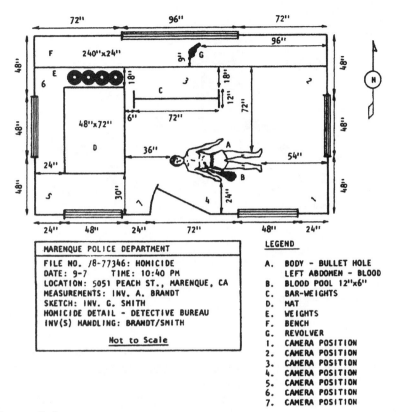

Figure 6-1
Typical Police Sketch of Homicide Crime Scene

6-3b Laying the Foundation

The foundation for the introduction of scientific evidence involves successfully answering three questions: (1) is this a valid scientific test? (2) was accurate equipment used for the test? (3) was the test performed in an appropriate manner by a qualified person?

The first question, which requires the side offering the test results to establish the scientific validity of the test, is in many ways similar to the requirement that expert witnesses may only be called if there is a valid field of scientific knowledge. This is no problem when a test has become widely accepted. In fact, in those situations it is rare for either side to even ask questions about the scientific basis for the test. Fingerprint comparisons are a good example of the well-established test. Newer tests must be carefully explained to the judge. This is done on *voir dire*. Expert witnesses will be called to provide the necessary background on the test and explain

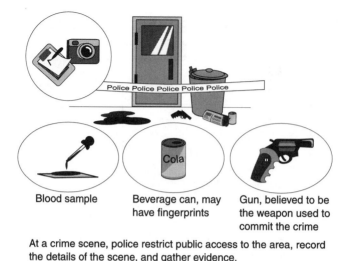

Blood sample

Beverage can, may
have fingerprints

Gun, believed to be
the weapon used to
commit the crime

At a crime scene, police restrict public access to the area, record
the details of the scene, and gather evidence.

Figure 6-2
Collecting Evidence at a Crime Scene

the scientific principles behind it. The federal courts and many state courts allow the judge to determine if the test is sufficiently reliable to be admitted. Factors the judge considers are these: whether a theory or technique presents scientific knowledge that will assist the jury; whether it has been subjected to peer review and published in professional journals; the known or potential rate of errors; and how widespread the acceptance of the test is.

The opposing side can cross-examine and call its own experts. After the witnesses have given their testimony, the judge will decide if the test is sufficiently accepted in the appropriate scientific community. Due to the highly technical nature of these scientific explanations, they are seldom repeated for the jury.

Any test can be attacked on the basis of faulty equipment. States frequently require certain types of equipment, such as the machines designed to measure breath alcohol, to be checked regularly and to be certified as accurate. Failure to have the machines tested can cast doubt on the test results. If the results appear to be wrong, the opposing side will attempt to show defects in the test equipment even if routine testing and maintenance have been done. This tactic may be used merely because the test results are damaging to its case. Doing this is the equivalent of impeaching the laboratory equipment. Although the trend in discovery is to share evidence and require each side to reveal the results of laboratory tests before trial, there is no duty to preserve evidence in order to allow the other side to perform tests on it.

Human error can also cause inaccurate test results. The side introducing the test will call the technician who performed it. Questions will be asked to show that the technician has had the appropriate training and that the test was done correctly. The questions will try to point out the skill of the operator and how carefully the required procedures were followed. Cross-examination will be used to try to show that deviations from the required testing procedures could cause the results to be inaccurate. Redirect can be used to try to establish that minor mistakes made during the test were not likely to affect the results. Sometimes expert witnesses will be called to testify about the effect of procedural errors on the test results.

6-4 Commonly Accepted Scientific Tests

Many scientific tests are so well established that they are admitted at trial without a challenge to their validity. This does not mean that the opposing side will not challenge the equipment used or the way the test was performed. This section will discuss the basis for accepting a few of the most common scientific tests.

6-4a Fingerprints[2]

Use of fingerprints for identification purposes in the United States dates back to 1901 when the New York City Civil Service Commission first used fingerprints for certifying all civil service applicants. Law enforcement began using fingerprints shortly thereafter. Centralized fingerprint files, which evolved into the National Crime Information Center (NCIC) files maintained by the FBI today, were started in 1924.

Fingerprint identification is based on three key principles: (1) a fingerprint is an individual characteristic; (2) fingerprints remain unchanged during an individual's lifetime; (3) fingerprints have general ridge patterns that permit them to be systematically classified.

Identification of a fingerprint is based on a study of the ridge pattern characteristics. Both the number and relative location of the characteristics are considered. In the 90 years that fingerprints have been collected, no two have been found that were identical.

The typical fingerprint may have as many as 150 ridge characteristics. There has been considerable debate about how many ridge comparisons must match before it can be concluded that the fingerprints are from the same person. Some experts have said anywhere from eight to 16. In 1973, the International Association for Identification concluded that there is no number that can answer this question in all cases. The final determination is based on the experience, skill, and knowledge of the fingerprint expert.

The ridge characteristics of the finger are formed where the epidermis and dermis meet. Perspiration, salts, and skin oil on the fingertips combine to leave a pattern on surfaces which the skin touches. An injury must produce a scar that goes one to two millimeters beneath the skin's surface to affect the fingerprint. Even then, there are usually enough matching points left to allow an expert to make a comparison. Also, a scar itself can be used for identification purposes.

There are three classes of fingerprints: loops (60 to 65 percent of population); whorls (30 to 35 percent of population); and arches (5 percent of population). Each of these classes can be subdivided into distinct groups. Figure 6-3 shows the six common fingerprint patterns. Classification systems, used to help locate fingerprints on file, were based on the presence of one type of pattern on each of the ten fingers. Such classification systems are now largely replaced by automated filing and searching.

In the past, individual prints had to be compared to prints on file by skilled fingerprint examiners. Now, advanced computer technology is making it easier to match single prints. Flying spot scanners can be used to input fingerprints. All ridge characteristics are given numeric identifiers which can be compared with those already in the database.

A separate question that must be answered when fingerprints are used in court relates to how the prints were preserved. The easier part of the answer relates to how the comparison set of prints was obtained. This focuses on the act of making the fingerprint card that was used. Many attorneys do not question this, but some demand testimony about the procedure used to roll the comparison prints.

Fingerprints that are recovered at the crime scene or from other evidence are commonly called "**latent**" (not developed) **prints.** A detailed explanation of how the latent prints were recovered is usually required. For many years, prints on hard, nonabsorbent surfaces (e.g., mirrors, glass, painted surfaces) were obtained by applying fingerprint powder to the surface with a camel-hair brush. The powder stuck to the skin oil in the fingerprint, thus making it visible. The fingerprint, as seen by the pattern in the powder, was photographed. It was also preserved by "lifting" it from the surface with a special adhesive tape (which may be clear or opaque) made for this purpose. If the object with the print on it is small enough, the actual object bearing the print may be kept for evidence.

Prints on porous surfaces (paper and cardboard, etc.) were obtained by the use of iodine fuming, ninhydrin, and silver nitrate. Laser light has been discovered to produce fluorescent fingerprints which can be pho-

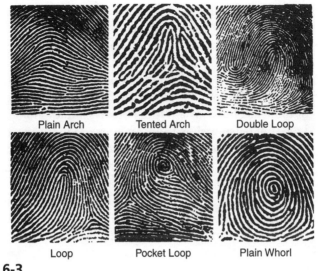

Figure 6-3
Six Common Fingerprint Patterns

tographed. Ninhydrin development, laser techniques, and cyanoacrylic ester fuming are now routinely used to obtain fingerprints on both porous and non-porous surfaces.

Caution must be taken, of course, when collecting and processing latent prints to avoid contaminating them with the fingerprints of investigators or others on the crime scene. The victim's attempts to clean the crime scene may also destroy valuable prints. Additionally, investigators must be aware of other types of laboratory tests that may be needed in the case because fingerprint powder or other substances used to develop latent prints may interfere with another test that must be performed.

6-4b Blood Alcohol[3]

The most common use of **blood alcohol** testing is in drunk driving cases. It is also used in cases where intoxication is an element of the crime and in other cases where the defendant's sobriety has a bearing on criminal intent.

Alcohol is absorbed into the body from the stomach and small intestine. Although it does not require digestion, absorption will be delayed if there is any food in the stomach. Alcohol is rapidly absorbed into the body's blood and circulatory system and distributed to all parts of the body. The molecular structure and weight of alcohol is such that it is able to cross cell membranes by a simple diffusion process. It can quickly achieve equilibrium in the body. The result is that alcohol rapidly becomes associated with all parts of the body in concentrations proportionate to body water content. It is therefore possible to estimate the total alcohol content of the body using a small sample of the blood.

The most common test for alcohol is done on breath samples; blood alcohol tests are also common. Capillary and arterial blood give the best prediction of brain alcohol concentration. Blood samples should be taken by qualified medical personnel (e.g., doctor, nurse, laboratory technician) and witnessed by a law enforcement officer. Special procedures are required, such as cleansing the skin with alcohol-free disinfectant, before taking the blood sample.

Kits are available with all the necessary supplies including chemicals to preserve the specimen until it reaches the laboratory. The chain of custody for the blood sample must be recorded. Having an officer witness the taking of the blood sample will eliminate the need to have the person who drew the sample testify in court.

Blood alcohol test results state the percentage of alcohol in the blood. Many states use the .08% level as conclusive evidence of driving under the influence; a lower standard may apply to juveniles. The number of drinks that it takes to achieve any specific level of alcohol in the blood varies with the weight of the person. Approximately one drink per hour can be removed from the body by the normal metabolic process.

6-4c Blood Typing[4]

There are many questions that a forensic serologist can help to answer: Is it blood? If so, is it human blood? If it is human blood, what group does it belong to? Can additional information be obtained by testing that will help identify the source of the blood?

Tests performed on a stain to determine if it is blood generally are based on the presence of blood cells or compounds characteristic of blood. These include the following: erythrocytes and leukocytes; blood serum proteins; and hemoglobin and its derivatives.

Once it has been determined that the sample is blood, the next step is to determine if it is human blood. If it is not, laboratory tests can also determine what species of animal the blood is from. Most of these tests are based on the response of the immune system to foreign substances in the blood.

Blood typing is done on human blood. The ABO system is the most common. Four major blood groups are used: A (41 percent of U.S. population), B (10 percent), AB (4 percent), and O (45 percent). The smallest subgroup in this system is present in 0.5 percent of the population.

Another blood group system is based on the Rh factor of the blood. This is totally separate from the ABO system. There are eight Rh determinants in common use. Their frequency in the U.S. population ranges from 33.2 percent for one of the Rh+ subgroups, to very rare occurrences in three of the Rh– subgroups. Forensic laboratories in the U.S. do not rely heavily on the Rh system.

A third blood group system is also in use. The MN system has nine categories. The frequency of these blood types in the U.S. Caucasian population range from 24 percent (MNS group) to 1 percent (NS group). This system is separate from both the ABO and Rh systems.

Each of these three blood typing systems has the same problem in court. If the defendant has a different blood type from the one found at the crime scene, it can be shown that it was not his/her blood. The tests cannot conclusively show that the blood came from one specific individual. Unless the suspect has a very rare blood type, the test only points to a large segment of the population. Scientists are constantly seeking better blood grouping systems so that blood can be identified on a more individualized basis.

6-4d DNA Testing[5]

Identical deoxyribonucleic acid (DNA) molecules are found in each cell of a person's body. With the exception of identical twins, each individual's DNA is unique. **DNA testing** can be performed on a blood stain the size of a quarter, or a semen stain the size of a dime, to determine if the evidence found at the crime scene matches a sample extracted from a criminal suspect. Tests can also be done on hair. Newer procedures reduce the size of the sample that is required to perform the DNA tests. Due to the uniformity of DNA throughout the body, a semen sample found at the crime scene can be matched to a blood sample taken at a clinical laboratory.

The laboratory test to match DNA samples is very complex. The dried material from the crime scene is treated with various chemicals and enzymes to wash away other materials and release the DNA. The DNA is then cleaned using enzymes and organic solvents. The DNA is then mixed with "restriction enzymes" which cut the DNA at sites where reoccurring gene patterns are found. The resulting pieces, called restriction fragments, are placed in a gel and electrical current is passed through this gel. This results in orderly patterns of DNA fragments in parallel lines. The gel is then transferred to a nylon membrane and radioactive DNA probes are applied. Each probe locks onto DNA segments that occur only once on the DNA chain. Exposure of these probes on X-ray film produces a DNA print which is used to match the samples being studied. The matching is done both by visual inspection and computer matching. Results of the test are given in two forms: a statement that there is (or is not) a match; and a probability calculation for such a match. For example, there is a 1 in 7,000,000 chance that the match would have occurred at random.

The most common type of DNA test currently in use is a technique known as restriction fragment length polymorphism (RFLP) analysis. It is done by comparing the length of certain fragments that tend to vary in length from person to person. A second method, called polymerase chain reaction (PCR), identifies an area of DNA in which there tends to be variation from one person to another and then "amplifies" the area by causing the DNA strands to replicate themselves. While PCR test are less accurate, they have the advantage that they can be performed on a smaller sample.

DNA testing, first used in criminal prosecutions in 1985, is now admissible in all states. While the scientific principle involved is unchallenged, there are a variety of errors that can occur. First, the sample recovered from the crime scene may be contaminated by bacteria, virus, or other non-human DNA. It may also be contaminated by detergents, salt and cleaning fluids. Second, the laboratory equipment, gel, enzymes, and DNA probe used in the test may be contaminated. These errors may result in DNA prints that are fuzzy or blurred. Although the major part of the matching technique is computerized, a technician makes the final determination that the total pattern matches; this means the technician's subjective impression is part of the matching process. Some authors estimate that the error rate caused by all of these factors is between 1 percent and 4 percent. Finally, and subject to the most controversy, the probability calculation has been attacked because the current database is too small and based on a nonrandom sample. Each testing laboratory maintains its own database; most are developed from samples obtained from blood banks and hospitals. DNA patterns vary for different racial groups and subgroups. The result is that the databases currently being used may not adequately reflect the variety of racial groups in the U.S. population.

6-4e Identification of Controlled Substances[6]

In cases involving possession, distribution, or manufacture of controlled substances, laboratory analysis plays a major role in the case. Testing for controlled substances is essentially qualitative and quantitative organic chemical analysis. As the number of drug cases has increased the demand on the criminalistics laboratory, new techniques have been developed to do the job faster and more accurately.

A variety of tests may be employed to determine what a substance is. These usually start with screening tests, but may also include separation tests, confirmatory tests, and quantitative analysis.

Samples are frequently tested rather than the whole quantity of suspected drugs. This is almost always the case when there was a large seizure. Laboratories follow different approaches to this problem. Some test a given percentage of the evidence. Others do screening tests on a large number of samples, but if the screening tests indicate that only one substance is present, further testing is only done on a small sample.

Representative sampling techniques are important. This is always true when only a sample is tested, but it is even more important when illegally manufactured drugs are in question, because of the lack of knowledge about their source. The evidence seized may not be homogeneous. Therefore, it is important to make sure that the sample comes from different locations within the seized containers. A visual inspection of both the sample and the entire quantity seized is useful to insure that the mathematical formula used produces a truly representative sample. These techniques need to be applied to solid substances, such as bricks of marijuana, as well as large barrels of pills.

When marked tablets are sent for analysis, the marks, along with the color and shapes of the tablets, may provide presumptive evidence of their content. Laboratories vary with regard to the amount of testing that is done on these samples. One screening test may be sufficient if there is a known tablet available for comparison which has the same appearance. The appearance of numerous counterfeit or "look alike" drugs increases the need to carefully test all samples. Due to the fact that capsules are easily tampered with, the presumption arising from their physical appearance is not as strong as the one for tablets.

If the quantity of drugs submitted for examination is very small (residue in a pipe, for example), it may be necessary to perform tests in a different order than usual. Those tests that can be done on small quantities of the questioned material and have a high degree of accuracy are done first. Screening tests that destroy the test substance, or tests that have a low probability of conclusively identifying the sample, may not be used at all.

Three main types of screening tests are used: spot tests, microscopic tests, and ultraviolet spectrophotometry. Based on the results of these tests, the chemist will select one or more appropriate tests to identify what the substance is. Additional tests may be done to confirm the identity of the substance tested.

Infrared spectrophotometry is the most popular because it is least expensive and easiest to use. Scientists also give gas chromatography-mass spectrometry high ratings because it only requires micrograms of material to do the test. Test instruments are frequently connected to computers which store extensive libraries of data on known compounds for comparison.

Due to the wide variety of tests which are now in use, individual crime labs may not be using the same tests. The fact that one specific test which has a high degree of accuracy was not used may be emphasized by the defense. It does not necessarily indicate that the lab work was shoddy.

6-4f Identification of Firearms[7]

Firearms can be identified from their fired bullets and cartridges. The firearms examiner is commonly called a **ballistics expert,** even though technically ballistics refers to the motion of projectiles rather than matching the expelled object to the weapon.

Pistols (revolvers, "semi-automatics" and "automatics"), rifles, assault rifles (i.e., automatic rifles such as the M-16), and machine guns and sub-machines guns are rifled firearms. Their barrels have spiraling lands and grooves which leave patterns of parallel scratches, called striations or striae, on the projectile. Shotguns, on the other hand, have smooth-bore barrels and do not leave striations.

The history of modern firearms examination in the United States began with Dr. Albert Llewellyn Hall in 1900. His technique of pushing, rather than firing, bullets through the weapon's barrel was in use until after World War I. A 1902 appellate case affirmed the use of firearms identification evidence in court, but the practice did not become commonly accepted until the 1930s. The admission of testimony regarding marks on fired cartridges began in 1906 and gained acceptance much faster than other methods of firearms identification.

Microscopic examinations of recovered bullets can be useful even if no weapon has been recovered. They can show the caliber of the gun and many facts about the barrel of the weapon involved. It may also be possible to determine that more than one gun was used.

Prior to testing a weapon for identification purposes, it should be checked for latent prints and trace evidence, such as blood and bits of skin or fat which may have been deposited on it if the gun was fired at close range. Recovered bullets should also be checked for these substances. Fibers from the pocket in which it was carried may also be present.

Preliminary examination of the weapon should cover make or manufacturer, type of weapon, caliber, serial number, model, number of shots, and barrel length. Prior to test firing, the functioning of the weapon's action and the operation of any safeties should be checked. One purpose of this is to determine if it is safe to test-fire the weapon; another is to refute any defense claim that the gun went off accidentally. Determination of the trigger's pull is also important for this purpose.

If the examiner determines that the bullet recovered from the crime scene has the same characteristics as the suspect's weapon, the gun will be test-fired into a bullet trap. Cotton waste or cotton waste soaked in oil is frequently used in a bullet trap; water traps are also used. The ammunition used to test-fire the gun should match that used in the crime as closely as possible. A comparison microscope and special bullet holders allow the examiner to simultaneously view a bullet recovered at the crime scene and one test-fired into the bullet trap.

The examination typically begins with careful checking for land impressions near the base of the bullets. It should then systematically proceed to check the land impressions on one bullet with those on the comparison sample until the entire surface of both bullets has been covered. The bullets are rotated synchronously to see if matching striation patterns are observed. Other distinctive markings, such as skid and shaving marks caused inside the barrel, may also be noted.

Rust in the barrel causes problems because rust particles can cause striations. Each firing may disturb the rust and result in different striations. Alterations in the barrel, including shortening, flattening, or bending, also cause variations in the striation pattern. Studies have shown that some guns, particularly .22 caliber rifles, may not produce identical striations, even when there has been no damage to the gun. Particularly in automatics and very inexpensive handguns (e.g., "Saturday Night Specials"), the firing of large numbers of bullets may cause wear that makes comparisons difficult.

Due to the fact that striations are caused by imperfections in the metal used to manufacture a gun, the marks left on a bullet are unique. Unfortunately, there is no exact standard for the number of striations that must match before it can be concluded that the bullets were fired from the same gun. If there is a match between the recovered bullet and the test-fired one, it can conclusively be stated that they came from the same gun.

The factors mentioned in the preceding paragraph indicate that the fact that two bullets do not match exactly is not conclusive evidence that the bullets were fired from different guns. One study showed that only about 20 percent of the striations on bullets fired from the same weapon matched. This means that many comparisons will result in inconclusive evidence.

Cartridge examinations should also begin with a check for latent prints and trace evidence. The initial examination with a low-powered microscope should note the size, shape, and type of cartridge. Size and position of the firing pin impression and location of extractor and ejector marks are also important. These can be used to determine the make and model of weapons that could have fired the cartridge. This is complicated by adapters that can be used to fire certain types of cartridges from guns designed for different ammunition. Alterations that may have been made to the weapon also interfere with accurate comparisons.

If these preliminary examinations indicate the cartridge could have been fired from the weapon in question, microscopic comparisons will be made of the recovered cartridge and one that was test-fired. The test-fired cartridge should be as similar as possible to the one in question. Special holders are used so that the cartridges can be mounted on a comparison microscope. Firing pin impressions, firing pin drag marks, and breech-block marks are usually compared first.

A match of these markings indicates that the same weapon was involved. Extractor and ejector marks, chambering marks, and magazine marks are compared next. These can indicate that the cartridges were run through the action of the same gun. A variety of problems may arise: (1) reloaded cartridges may bear markings from more than one gun; (2) low-powered cartridges may not produce enough force to be marked; and (3) the extractor may not grip the cartridge with enough force to mark it.

6-5 Tests That Are Not Commonly Accepted

Scientific tests must be accepted in their field before the courts are willing to allow their use at trial. The amount of evidence needed to show that a test is valid is left to the judge in most state and the federal courts. For this reason, newly developed tests are usually not admissible. Since the determination is made on a state-by-state basis, there is usually no nationwide agreement on the use of a test during its developmental stages. There have also been some instances where courts initially accepted a test but, based on research published at a later time, decided the test was no longer admissible. Spectrographic voice recognition ("voiceprints") and hypnotically refreshed memory fall into this category.

Some tests have been in use for many years but are still rejected by many courts. This section will look at two of them: polygraph examinations and hypnosis.

6-5a Polygraph[8]

The principal features of the polygraph are its ability to record changes in respiration, blood pressure, and pulse. Attachments can be added to record galvanic skin reflex (perspiration in hands), muscular movements, and pressures. Use of only one of these features is considered to be inadequate.

The skill of the polygraph examiner is of utmost importance. An internship is required in which the trainee can make frequent observations of an expert conducting polygraph examinations, as well as performing the procedure personally. Ideally, the polygraph examiner should have a minimum of six months of training.

The test itself should be conducted in a quiet, private location. Outside noise should be eliminated where possible. Police investigators should not be allowed to be present during the exam.

A pretest interview is done to explain the procedure to the subject. It also is used to gather information for test questions. Questions asked during the polygraph examination fall into three categories: control questions, relevant questions, and irrelevant questions. Control questions are designed to illicit a dishonest response to something that is not relevant to the case. This shows what the body's response is to lying. Relevant questions relate to the matter under investigation. Irrelevant questions have no bearing on the case, but give the examiner the chance to see the subject's response to questioning. During the pretest interview the subject is usually told what the irrelevant questions will be.

An assessment of truthfulness is made by comparing the responses to control questions with those to relevant questions. Deception is indicated if there is a greater response to the relevant questions than to the control questions. A good examiner should be able to discount the effects of nervousness. This is done in two ways: (1) the pretest interview is designed to relax the subject; and (2) nervousness should be indicated by uniformly irregular polygraph tracings—nerves have a similar effect on control, relevant, and irrelevant questions.

It is estimated that truthfulness/dishonesty are *clearly* indicated in about 25 percent of the cases. In 5–10 percent of the cases even a highly trained examiner will not be able to make a conclusive analysis. The remaining 65–70 percent of the cases yield subtle indications of truthfulness/dishonesty that trained examiners cannot fully explain to non-experts.

There are sizable numbers of experts on each side of the argument about polygraph examinations. In 2002, the National Research Council of the National Academy of Sciences published a report finding that polygraph testing is based on a weak scientific basis and that insufficient attempts have been made to verify the results. The Council concluded that polygraph tests should not be used for national security purposes.

The high frequency of inconclusive results makes the courts distrust the polygraph. Judges also fear that jurors will attach too much weight to the results of a polygraph examination. While states vary in their approaches to the admissibility of polygraph tests, most refuse to admit them. Some allow them in criminal cases if there was a pretest stipulation by both sides that the results may be used in court. When this type of stipulation is made, the polygraph examiner usually must be agreed upon in advance by both sides. If the suspect is in custody at the time of the examination, *Miranda* waivers must be obtained in addition to any other stipulations that are made.

6-5b Hypnosis[9]

Hypnosis is commonly described as a trancelike state in which the subject is unconsciously responsive to the suggestions and commands of the hypnotist It is this state of suggestibility that concerns the courts.

The Council on Scientific Affairs of the American Medical Association reviewed the evidence on hypnosis, and in 1984 concluded that there was no support for the assertion that hypnosis could aid accurate memory except in cases of amnesia. One member of the council concluded that when amnesia victims are hypnotized, the following safeguards should be used: (1) the hypnotist must be a psychiatrist or psychologist who is not affiliated with either side of the case; (2) the hypnotist should be provided with sufficient factual data on the case, but not have knowledge of details of the investigation; (3) the hypnotic session should be conducted with only the subject and hypnotist present; and (4) the entire session be videotaped.

On the other hand, numerous articles were written in the 1970s and 1980s about the effectiveness of hypnosis in criminal investigations. Some authors claim that new information can be obtained under hypnosis in 60–90 percent of the cases. At least 5,000 police officers have been trained to conduct hypnosis. Use of hypnosis has appeared in criminal cases as far back as 1898, but most courts are still hesitant to admit the testimony.

Several state court decisions in the late 1970s allowed testimony from hypnotically refreshed memory, but the more recent trend has been to make this type of testimony inadmissible. For example, a pair of cases decided by the New York Court of Appeal (*People v. Hults* [1990] and *People v. Schreiner* [1991])[10] reaffirm the state's rule that post-hypnotic statements (including testimony in court) cannot be used by the prosecution to establish the defendant's guilt or by the defense for impeachment. The decisions were based on three reasons: (1) the person who was hypnotized may be susceptible to suggestions given intentionally or unintentionally by the hypnotist or others present during the session; (2) the subject may confabulate or intentionally fabricate events in order to fill memory gaps; and (3) a witness who has been hypnotized may experience an enhanced confidence in his or her memory of an incident, thereby unfairly impairing cross-examination of the witness about the event. Today, testimony of witnesses who have been hypnotized is rarely, if ever, admitted in a criminal trial.

Psychiatrists sometimes make a different use of hypnosis when trying to evaluate competency to stand trial and "not guilty by reason of insanity" cases. Due to the fact that this technique is recognized in the field of psychiatry, it is admissible on the mental issues if the proper foundation has been laid. The foundation must include the following: (1) a showing that hypnosis is reliable for this purpose; and (2) that the witness is qualified as an expert on the psychiatric use of hypnosis. This testimony is not used to establish guilt or innocence, but has limited admissibility on the issue of the mental state of the defendant.

6-6 Experiments

The ideal **experiment** screens out all extraneous variables so that the experimenter can measure the impact of one factor. While there are numerous situations that lend themselves to experiments in criminal trials, few experiments are introduced in court. This is largely due to attorneys' lack of knowledge in this area. Some experiments are quite simple, like going to the crime scene under lighting conditions that are similar to those that existed at the time of the crime to determine if the stop sign is visible, or having someone walk from one location to another to determine if is possible to cover the distance in the time stated by the defendant. Others are very complex and require expensive equipment such as electron microscopes and X-ray analyzers.

Some basic concepts apply to experiments. One is that the conditions must be similar to those that existed when the event in question occurred. While this similarity is meant to control outside variables, courts are frequently very flexible when it comes to admitting experiments that were not conducted under totally similar conditions. Secondly, the experiments must be based on sound scientific principles. This is the same basic criteria that applies to all uses of expert witnesses and scientific evidence. Both the testing procedure and the equipment used must conform to standards generally accepted in the scientific community. Thirdly, the judge may refuse to admit experimental evidence if it will be confusing to the jury or take up an undue amount of time at trial. The weight to be given to an experiment is left to the jury.

The Federal Rules of Evidence and some states do not distinguish between experiments and other types of evidence. The normal rules of relevance are used to judge admissibility.

The normal procedure for introducing experiments is the following: (1) to have either the person conducting the experiment or someone who witnessed it take the stand; (2) lay the foundation, and (3) ask questions so that the witness can present the results of the experiment. The foundation should include that (1) the witness is familiar with the facts of the case; (2) the witness knows how to use the equipment used in the experiment; (3) the witness compares the actual event with the results of the experiment; and (4) the witness believes the experiment fairly simulates the events in question.

Experiments may be conducted to determine if it is possible to have committed a crime in a particular manner. For example, the prosecution may believe that the defendant packed the body of the murder victim in ice to prevent *rigor mortis* from setting in until after the defendant was able to establish an alibi. A pathologist would be consulted to determine all the necessary conditions that would need to be set up for the experiment. An object similar in size, weight, and retention of body heat to the victim's body would be used with the body temperature of a living person. It would then be packed in ice and placed in a room where the temperature was kept the same as the conditions where the body was believed to have been placed by the defendant.

At trial, the effect of temperature changes on *rigor mortis* would be established by an expert witness. A comparison would be made between what would be expected under the temperature present at the time of the crime and what happened when the body was packed in ice under those same weather conditions.

Test crashing of automobiles also is included within the category of experiments. Cars are set to collide under the same road conditions as were alleged in the case (e.g., weather, road surface, incline, angle, banking of the curve, and speed of the vehicle). Based on the results of the test crash, it may be demonstrated that one version of the facts is impossible.

Due to the expense of this type of experiment, it is rarely done. Models may be used instead. Computer simulations are becoming more popular.

6-7 Models, Maps, and Diagrams[11]

Most courts allow the witness to use models, maps and diagrams to illustrate his/her testimony. Some states permit these objects to be formally introduced into evidence, while others do not. Each judge usually retains a great deal of discretion on this matter. Whenever models, maps, or diagrams are used, it is important for the attorney to state for the record what the witness was pointing to (e.g., "Let the record show that the witness pointed to the northeast corner of the intersection"). If this is not done, the record on appeal will be very confusing (i.e., the witness said "I was here, he was there"). This also applies when the witness places marks on the drawings to indicate where someone was standing or the location of an important object.

Witnesses are frequently allowed to use a chalkboard or chart paper to draw the crime scene. After this is done, the attorneys will ask questions related to the drawing. The drawing, if the witness has any skill at all, usually helps the jury visualize the location. When this type of drawing is done, it is rarely to scale. For this reason, it frequently is not introduced into evidence. The better practice is to have the drawing on paper or some other medium that can be saved for later reference if there are any additional questions. This also preserves it for appeal.

If scale drawings are desired, they are usually made before trial. They are made large enough so the jury can see them while the witness is testifying. If the police reports included the exact dimensions of the scene and where all relevant objects were located, the drawing could be based on these measurements. Otherwise, someone will have to go to the crime scene and take appropriate measurements. Since everything is to scale, judges are usually willing to admit the drawing into evidence after it has been authenticated.

Sometimes scale **models** are used. Examples could be the models architects use to show proposed buildings and their surroundings or a three-dimensional model showing the inside of a room with all the furnishings done to scale. Anatomical models are also used to show the trajectory of bullets or the effects of other murder weapons. A key reason to admitting these types of models is to help the jury. The fact that they are to scale is important, but the judge can still decide that they are inadmissible if he/she feels the model would confuse the jurors more than help them.

Maps may be used to show the location of various places that are relevant to the case. Either official survey maps, road maps, or maps drawn specifically for the trial can be used. Computer software is available that can generate street maps for most cities in the United States. Sometimes aerial photographs which show the relevant streets and buildings are introduced into evidence. Maps that are to scale are usually admissible.

Computer-generated diagrams and three-dimensional animated videos are now commonly used at trial. These types of demonstrative evidence, like their non-computerized counterparts, must meet two requirements: they are made to scale from evidence that is admitted in the case, and they are relevant. For example, a defense attorney might produce a three-dimensional drawing depicting the positions of the attacker and the victim at the time the victim used a gun in self-defense. A program called Mannequin Designer, which creates three-dimensional human forms that can be positioned at virtually any manner and viewed from any angle, could be used for this purpose. For such a diagram to be admissible the defense must show that the actual dimensions of the people depicted were entered accurately into the computer, the positions accurately reflect the facts of the case, and that the software and hardware are reliable and accurate.

Summary

All real evidence must be marked before it can be introduced into evidence. The attorney must also lay a foundation to show that it is admissible. Evidence recovered at a crime scene must be carefully handled so that it is not damaged. Detailed records must be kept to show where it was found and what has been done with it since it was taken into police custody.

The foundation for scientific evidence includes a showing that the test used is valid, the person doing it is well-trained, and that the equipment used is accurate. The exact procedures used during the test are also subject to challenge.

There are many scientific tests that are currently recognized by the courts. Among the most common are fingerprint comparisons, blood-alcohol and DNA tests, and tests to identify drugs.

Latent print identification is based on the fact that each person has unique fingerprints. The prints recovered at the crime scene are compared with a set of fingerprints on file. If a match is found, it conclusively establishes that the person left the prints at the scene. There may, of course, be innocent explanations of how the prints got there.

When alcohol enters the human body it is rapidly distributed throughout the entire system in the same proportion. Blood tests can be used to establish the level of intoxication because the sample taken reflects the alcohol content of all parts of the body.

Laboratory tests can be done to determine if a stain was made by human blood. If it was, the blood type may also be determined. Although traditional tests have been able to identify a person's blood type, this has not been very useful in many cases because such a large proportion of the population has the same blood type. The fact that the blood types did not match can establish that the blood was from a different person. DNA testing provides a method that can conclusively identify one person as the source of blood, semen, or other body fluids.

Many tests have been developed to identify drugs. Caution should be taken to test an adequate sample of the seized drugs. This is especially true when illegally manufactured drugs are involved because clandestine drug labs do not have the same quality controls that the legitimate drug industry uses.

In many cases bullets and cartridges can be tested to determine if they were fired from a particular gun. Microscopic examinations are done to compare unique patterns that are left when the bullet exits the barrel or the cartridge is processed through the firing chamber. An exact match indicates that the gun that was test-fired is the same one used in the crime. Unfortunately, the fact that an exact match was not observed cannot exclude a gun.

The polygraph has not been accepted by most courts. The conflicting views of experts on the reliability of the polygraph have caused the courts to doubt its reliability. Hypnosis is in a similar situation. Although once claimed to enhance memory, it is now largely discredited.

Experiments must be conducted under similar conditions to those that existed when the event in question occurred. Maps, models, and diagrams may be admitted into evidence if they are relevant and to scale. Witnesses may be allowed to draw on a chalkboard or chart paper to help illustrate their testimony even if it is not done to scale but these drawings are not usually admitted into evidence.

Discussion Questions

1. Explain what should be done to protect evidence at a crime scene and list three things that should be done to document the scene before evidence is removed.
2. Describe how various items of crime scene evidence should be identified and packaged for storage.
3. Define *chain of custody* and explain how it is maintained for trial.
4. What scientific tests are most commonly introduced in criminal trials?
5. What foundation must be laid for the admission of a piece of evidence found at the crime scene and for the admission of the results of a scientific test?

6. Explain the scientific basis for fingerprint identification.

7. Explain the reason blood tests can accurately show alcohol levels in the body.

8. Describe how blood typing can be used in a criminal case.

9. Explain what can be determined by conducting scientific tests on bullets and cartridges.

10. Explain how DNA testing can be used to identify the defendant as the person who committed the crime.

11. Explain why the courts rarely admit polygraph test results and seldom permit witnesses to testify after having been hypnotized.

12. Define *experiment* and give two examples of experiments that could be used in criminal trials.

13. Give two examples of scale diagrams or models that would be admissible and describe a situation where a drawing that is not to scale may be used in a criminal trial.

Endnotes

1. Joseph L. Peterson, "Use of Forensic Evidence by the Police and Courts," *Research in Brief* (Washington, D.C.: National Institute of Justice) (Oct. 1987).

2. Andrea A. Mansions, "Novel Scientific Evidence in Criminal Cases: Some Words of Caution," *Journal of Criminal Law & Criminology* 84 (1): 1–21 (1993); Richard Saferstein, chap. 14 in *Criminalistics: An Introduction to Forensic Science,* 7th ed., (Englewood Cliffs, NJ: Prentice-Hall, 2000); National Institute of Justice, *NIJ Update: New Reagents for Development of Latent Fingerprints* (Washington, D.C.: U.S. Department of Justice, 1995).

3. Richard Saferstein, chap. 12 in *Forensic Science Handbook,* vol. I, 2nd ed. (Englewood Cliffs, NJ: Prentice-Hall, 2002).

4. Richard Saferstein, chap.12 in *Criminalistics: An Introduction to Forensic Science* 7th ed., (Englewood Cliffs, NJ: Prentice-Hall, 2000).

5. Richard Saferstein, chap. 3 in *Forensic Science Handbook,* vol. I, 2nd ed. (Englewood Cliffs, NJ: Prentice-Hall, 2002).

6. Richard Saferstein, *Forensic Science Handbook,* vol. II (Englewood Cliffs, NJ: Prentice-Hall, 1988), pp. 68–161.

7. National Institute of Justice, *The Future of Forensic DNA Testing* (Washington, D.C.: U.S. Department of Justice, 2000); G. W. Steadman, *Survey of DNA Crime Laboratories* (Washington, D.C.: U.S. Bureau of Justice Statistics, 1998).

8. National Research Council, Committee to Review the Scientific Evidence on the Polygraph, *The Polygraph and Lie Detection,* 2002; Andre A. Moenssens, Fred E. Inbau, and James E. Starrs, *Scientific Evidence in Criminal Cases,* 3rd ed. (Mineola, NY: The Foundation Press, Inc., 1986), pp. 698–723.

9. W. S. Hibbard and R. W. Worring, *Forensic Hypnosis,* Revised 1st ed. (Springfield, IL: Charles Thomas, 1996); A. W. Newman and J. W. Thompson Jr., "The Rise and Fall of Forensic Hypnosis in Criminal Investigation," *The Journal of the American Academy of Psychiatry and the Law* 29 (1): 74–85 (2001).

10. *People v. Hults* 76 N.Y. 2d 190, 556 N.E.2d 1077, 557 N.Y.S. 2d 270 (1990); *People v. Schreiner* 77 N.Y. 2d 733, 573 N.E. 2d 552, 570 N.Y.S. 2d 464 (1991).

11. E. X. Martin III, "Using Computer-Generated Demonstrative Evidence," *Trial* (September 1994): 84–88; Robert Simmons and J. Daniel Lounsbery, "Admissibility of Computer-Animated Reenactment in Federal Courts," *Trial* (September 1994): 79–83.

CHAPTER 7

Documentary Evidence

Outline

Key Terms

- Ancient documents
- Authentication
- Documentary evidence
- Parol evidence
- Posed picture (photograph)
- Primary evidence
- Secondary evidence
- Self-authenticating

After studying this chapter, you will be able to:

- Describe how documents are authenticated in court.
- Identify what a forensic document examiner can determine from a document.
- Define the Best Evidence Rule.
- Recognize the foundation necessary for admitting photographs into evidence.

7-1 Authentication

The term **documentary evidence** applies to all types of documents including deeds, contracts, checks, letters, pictures, movies, videotapes, audio recordings, compact disks, files on a computer's hard drive, computer-generated reports whether on paper or any other device, and even price tags and display items hanging from the ceiling in a store. The generic term "writing" is also used to refer to these items. Documentary evidence and writings, consequently, include more than what we normally think of as written material.

In addition to being relevant, all types of documents must be authenticated to be admissible as evidence. When we are discussing documentary evidence, the term **authentication** means showing that a writing is what it is claimed to be.

The reason for the authentication requirement is to prevent a person from fraudulently claiming a document is his/hers. Authentication also protects in situations where a person claims that a proposed contract is binding, when in fact, the negotiations on the contract broke down and no contract was ever finalized.

7-1a Self-Authenticating Documents

Self-authenticating documents are those which are automatically assumed to be made for their apparent purpose. Usually a seal or some other indication of authenticity is on, or attached to, the document. Even with self-authenticating documents, the opposing side can show that they are fraudulent.

Sealed government documents. As used here, government documents include all public documents that are made by the federal, state, or local government. These government documents are self-authenticating if they bear an official seal and are signed by someone who states the document is genuine. Government documents are also self-authenticating if they have a signed and sealed statement attached which states that the original signature is genuine. Government documents from foreign countries are self-authenticating if they are either sealed or accompanied by a certificate of genuineness which is signed by an appropriate person and sealed.

Certified copies of public records are also self-authenticating. A certified copy is usually signed by someone working in the clerk's office. A paragraph is usually added to the document which states that it is a true copy of an official document. It is then signed and, in many states, sealed. Births, deaths, marriages, and divorces are usually established by certified copies. Prior convictions are also introduced into evidence by producing a certified copy of the original court record of the conviction.

Examples of Sealed Government Documents
- A copy of the judge's order convicting the defendant of a crime. The court order must bear a seal of the court and a statement that the document is a true copy of the original.
- A copy of a death certificate with the state's seal.

Notarized documents. Notarized documents may be self-authenticating. The statement added by the notary public usually states what the notary is declaring to be authentic. In many cases, the notary asks to see identification, such as a driver's license, and then notarizes the signature as being genuine. Sometimes a notary will state that the document is intended to be a deed or some other document. If so, the document is self-authenticating for that purpose.

Examples of Notarized Documents
- A deed signed by the maker with a statement by a notary stating that the notary verified the identification of the person who signed the deed.
- A promissory note with a statement by a notary indicating he/she verified the identification of the person who signed the note.

Acknowledged documents. The exact form of an acknowledgment is governed by state law (or federal law if made in a federal enclave). Wills are usually acknowledged. The person making the will must show the will to the witness and state that this document is intended to be his/her will. The witness then signs or acknowledges the will. The witness does not have to read the will or know what is in it. All he/she must know is that the document was intended to be the maker's will.

Examples of Acknowledged Documents
A will with a statement at the bottom which the witness signed. The statement includes the fact that the witness watched the person sign the document and that the person who signed the document stated that the document was his/her will.

Official publications. Official government publications are self-authenticating. These documents include the officially published codes and case reporter. When it is necessary to establish a penal code section in court, the bound volume may be handed to the judge. Due to the fact that the judge can take judicial notice of all codes of the state where the court is located, it is rare to see this done except when a law from another state is questioned. While the judge may be shown the bound volume when a case is cited for precedent, it is more common for the attorneys to quote from the case and give the citation for the case in their briefs.

Examples of Official Publications
- A book, published by the official state publisher, entitled *Penal Code.*
- A book, published by the official state publisher, entitled *Illinois Appellate Reports.*

Other self-authenticating documents. A variety of other documents are usually considered to have such a minimal likelihood of forgery that they are considered self-authenticating. Newspapers and periodicals are in this group. Note that the newspaper is self-authenticating but that does not guarantee that the stories are accurately reported. So are brand-name labels fastened to merchandise to show the name of the manufacturer. Commercial documents, such as letters of credit, are self-authenticating if they comply with the requirements stated in the Uniform Commercial Code.

Examples of Other Self-Authenticating Documents
- The page of the *New York Times* for the date in question giving the closing figures for stocks traded on the New York Stock Exchange.
- The page of the *Chicago Tribune* giving the weather for the local area for the day in question.

7-1b Methods to Authenticate Documents

There are a variety of ways to authenticate documents. All of them are subject to challenge by the opposing side. The jury makes the final decision on authenticity.

Testimony of a witness. The most obvious way to authenticate a document is to call one or more witnesses who can testify about the making of the document in question. If the document has been in the possession of the police, witnesses will also need to establish the chain of custody.

Examples of Using Testimony of a Witness
to Authenticate a Document

- Friend of victim states that she was there and saw the extortion victim write a check to the person who was threatening him.
- Bank teller states that he observed the victim endorse the check before asking the teller to cash it.

Lay opinion on handwriting. If any part of the document is handwritten (including the signature), anyone who is familiar with the handwriting of the person in question or who saw it being written or signed may authenticate it.

Examples of Using Lay Opinion
to Authenticate a Document

- The witness states that the person who allegedly wrote the letter has been a friend for a long time and he recognizes the handwriting.
- A secretary testifies that she has worked for the same boss for several years and that the signature on the document is her boss's signature.

"Handwriting expert." A written document can also be authenticated by the testimony of a handwriting expert. To do this, it is usually necessary to provide the expert with a handwriting exemplar (sample) of the person who allegedly made the document. More details on this type of authentication will be given in Section 7-2 about forensic document examiners.

Examples of Using a "Handwriting Expert"
to Authenticate a Document

- Forensic document examiner testifies that she compared the allegedly forged check with a handwriting exemplar provided by the defendant and believes that the defendant made the signature on the check.
- Forensic document examiner testifies that he examined the document and, in his expert opinion, the written portions of the document were made by more than one person.

Distinctive characteristics. A document can be authenticated by showing that it contained distinctive characteristics, like words, phrases, or "doodles," used by the person who allegedly made the document. The fact that it contains information known only to the maker, or a very small group of people, can also be used.

Examples of Using Distinctive Characteristics to Authenticate a Document
- Wife testifies that the signature on the check was not made by her husband because her husband's signature, although hard to read, was very distinctive and not similar to the one on the forged check.
- Secretary testifies that she does not believe the will in question was the one prepared by the lawyer she works for because wills made in her office always started with the phrase "being of sound mind and having the intent to distribute my earthly possessions to my loved ones" rather than the phrase found on the will in question.

Public records. The fact that a report was made and filed in accordance with local law can be used to show that the event occurred. Police reports fall in this category. Since it is a crime to make a false police report, it is assumed that the event reported actually happened. Obviously, not all reports made to the police are true.

Examples of Using Public Records to Establish That an Event Occurred
- Birth certificate, signed by doctor who delivered the baby, and filed with the county's Recorder of Vital Statistics.
- Death certificate, signed by personal physician of the deceased, and filed with the state's Department of Vital Statistics.
- Report of suspected child abuse filed by a school teacher who is a mandated reporter of child abuse.

Ancient documents. **Ancient documents** are accepted without authentication if they appear to be genuine and the document has been treated as if it were what it claims to be. A document appears to be genuine if there is no sign of alteration or forgery. The fact that the people who made the document have kept the document in an appropriate place, such as a safe deposit box, also shows they believed it was genuine.

At common law, a document had to be at least 30 years old to qualify as an ancient document. Many states still use this rule. Others have established a shorter time period. The Federal Rules of Evidence require the document to be 20 years old.

Examples of the Use of Ancient Documents
- Entry in family Bible stating that John and Martha were married on July 15, 1956. John and Martha lived together as husband and wife until John died in 2002.
- Deed dated August 1, 1957, stating that John and Martha purchased a house at 123 N. Main Street. John and Martha lived in this house for 40 years and paid off the mortgage.

Process or system used. Some documents can only be authenticated by reliance on the process or system used to make them. The most common example of this is the X-ray. The court must rely on the technology involved in the X-ray machine. No independent proof of what the bones look like is usually available. Computer printouts are also subject to reliance on the operating system and software that produced them.

7-2 Forensic Document Examiners[1]

A forensic document examiner may testify if the authenticity of a document is challenged. When we mention questioned documents, we usually think of forged checks. The term can be used to apply to a broader range of things including anything on paper, fabric, cardboard, or even written on walls. While the most common cases involve written or typed materials, pictures, graffiti, and other forms of graphic presentations can also be examined. Fake passports, diplomas, and trademarks may be involved in a criminal case.

The forensic document examiner is involved in four main types of activities: (1) handwriting comparisons; (2) typewriter comparisons; (3) tests to determine if a document has been altered; and (4) paper and ink comparisons. Other situations arise in more specialized cases.

The questioned document should be delivered to the examiner in the same condition it was found. It should not be folded, cut, torn, marked, paperclipped or stapled. Documents should be kept in protective, stiff, transparent folders or envelopes. They should be stored at room temperature in a dark place and delivered to the crime lab as soon as possible. The chain of custody must also be maintained.

7-2a Handwriting Comparisons

As a child learns to write, his/her handwriting takes on habitual shapes and patterns. These form a unique subconscious pattern. Variations exist in angularity, slope, speed, pressure, letter and word spacing, relative dimensions of letters, connections, pen movements, writing skill, and finger dexterity. Additionally, a person may develop distinctive habits of arranging his/her writing on the page—margins, spacing, crowding, insertions, and alignments. Spelling, punctuation, phrasing, and grammar may also help identify the writer. One handwriting sample may have from 500 to 1,000 different individual characteristics.

In order to determine who wrote a questioned document, the examiner must have an adequate sample of the suspect's handwriting. If possible, a handwriting exemplar is obtained from the suspect; the suspect is usually told to copy, in his/her own handwriting, a paragraph provided by the examiner which contains all the letters in the alphabet. A suspect cannot invoke the Fifth Amendment privilege against self-incrimination as grounds for refusing to provide an exemplar. A law-enforcement agency cannot, however, take a suspect to the station in order to obtain the exemplar unless there is either probable cause to arrest the suspect or he/she consents to go to the station.

All characteristics found in the sample must be compared with those in the questioned document. While any one handwriting characteristic could be found in someone else's writing, the combination of many similar characteristics indicates that the same person wrote both documents. The examiner will be able to make a more valid comparison if there is a large sample of the suspect's handwriting. If possible, the exemplar should be made with the same type of writing instrument (ballpoint pen, pencil, crayon, etc.) as used in the questioned document. Exemplars made for the purpose of comparisons may not be useful if the suspect is intentionally trying to alter his/her normal writing style. Even then, if the exemplar is long enough, the suspect usually reverts to some of his/her normal handwriting characteristics.

As with fingerprint and ballistic comparisons, the number of matching characteristics is important in handwriting comparisons. Unfortunately, there is no specific number of matching characteristics that is used to show a positive comparison. The skill of the examiner and the facts of the individual case are used as the basis for the expert opinion. Obviously, if there are only a few matching characteristics, the opposing side will attempt to convince the jury that the expert's conclusion is wrong.

7-2b Typewriting Comparisons

The most common questions involving typewriter comparisons are the following: What make and model of typewriter was used to make the document? Was the document typed on a specific typewriter? While there are only two common type sizes used on typewriters (pica and elite), there are many minor variations between the typefaces used on different makes and models of typewriters.

Fifty years ago, typewriter companies made their own typebars. Most of these could be distinguished by comparing the document in question with a complete reference collection of typefaces used in typewriters. In a kidnapping, for example, this process could be used to determine if the model of typewriter the defendant owns could have been used to type the ransom note. Today, many typewriter companies buy their typebars from other sources. The result of this change is that different makes of typewriters may have the same typefaces. The use of interchangeable typing elements and daisy wheels has further complicated this process because one typewriter can use more than one typeface. This also makes it possible to destroy the element used to type a document without harming the typewriter. The advent of computer printers has resulted in fewer documents being prepared on typewriters, necessitating the development of different comparison techniques.

Matching the document with one specific typewriter is based on the fact that the use of a typewriter, like all mechanical devices, results in wear and damage to moving parts. This results in unique type patterns. There may be variations in vertical and horizontal alignment of the letters (i.e., too high, too low, or too far to one side), perpendicular misalignment (i.e., letter leans to one side), or one or more of the characters may have a defect. An exemplar is made on the typewriter in question and then compared to the questioned document. Ideally, the exemplar should be made with the same typewriter ribbon as the questioned document. If the typewriter has variable touch control, the exemplar should include portions made at each setting. If it is not possible to make an exemplar on the typewriter in question, an examiner may be able to work from other documents known to have been typed on the same machine.

7-2c Alterations, Erasures, and Obliterations

Documents may be altered to change their meaning, alter the original intent of the maker, alter important dates, or perpetrate forgery. Erasers, sandpaper, razor blades, and knives are used for this purpose. All of these methods cause disturbances in the upper fibers of the paper which are apparent when the document is examined under a microscope. While the microscope can show that an erasure has been made, it cannot show what the original document said if the erasure removed the original contents. If chemicals were used to obliterate portions of the original documents, tests can usually be performed to show what was removed. Infrared photography can also be used to reveal the contents of documents that have been charred in a fire.

7-2d Comparisons of Paper and Ink

Exact determination of the age of the ink used in a document is very difficult, but it is frequently possible to determine that two different inks were used in a document. If the two inks contain chemicals used in the manufacture of ink at different time periods, it is possible to state that part of the document was written at a later date. Many sophisticated tests have been developed for this purpose. A common problem in ink identification is that there is very little ink available for testing unless the handwritten portion of the document was lengthy.

The Bureau of Alcohol, Tobacco and Firearms (ATF) maintains an ink library. For many years, ink manufacturers have given samples of their ink to the library on a periodic basis. Every time a new ink is used, a sample is also sent to ATF. By comparing an ink sample to information in the library, it is possible to determine the approximate date when the ink was made. This is useful when trying to establish that a document was backdated or a forgery made long after the year it is claimed to have been made. Since 1968, ATF has also encouraged ink manufacturers to add unique, nontoxic, chemically recognizable substances to their ink each year. When this is done, it is possible to determine the exact year the ink was manufactured.

The ink in typewriter ribbons can be tested in much the same manner as ink from pens. When the ink was manufactured and who manufactured it can be determined. It may also be possible to show that two different ribbons were used to type one document.

While it may be possible to determine when the ink was manufactured, there is currently no reliable system to determine when a document was written. To determine how long ink has been on a document, it would be necessary to show temperature, humidity, and exposure to light and handling since the document was made. Testing is almost always impossible because all of these variables are seldom known.

Paper may be matched based on general composition, form dates, cutting marks, and thickness. The presence of synthetic brighteners, adhesive components, and synthetic fibers may also give some indication of when the paper was made. The exact formula used for paper varies enough that it is frequently possible to tell that two pieces of paper were not manufactured by the same company. Watermarks are imprinted on paper to identify the manufacturer. Since some manufacturers change watermarks yearly, these marks can be used to date a document. It is important to note that being able to determine the date the paper and ink were manufactured merely sets a starting point, it does not establish the date the document was written.

7-3 The Best Evidence Rule

The Best Evidence Rule was first established about 1700. Its purpose was to prevent fraud. The origins of the rule go back to a time when the only way to make a duplicate was to copy the document by hand. In the process of copying, mistakes could be made either intentionally or accidentally. It was also believed that the document was a more accurate source of what was written down than the memories of the people who made the document. Some states no longer use the title "Best Evidence Rule" but most utilize the same concepts for establishing the admissibility of a written document or its content.

Best Evidence Rule Defined

In proving the material terms of a writing, the original document must be produced unless it is unavailable for some reason other than the serious fault of the party that wants to introduce it into evidence (*McCormick,* 1984).

The rule applies to all types of documentary evidence. Whether a letter, book, photograph, videotape, audiotape, or X-ray is involved, the original must be produced in court or accounted for. If it is only necessary to show that the document was made, but proof of the content of the document is not required, the Best Evidence Rule does not apply.

7-3a Primary Evidence

Primary evidence is the original document or a duplicate, according to the Best Evidence Rule. The "original" is the document itself and any copies that the person making the document intended to have the same effect as the original. "Duplicate" (sometimes called duplicate original) refers to copies made with the same stroke of the pen (carbon copies), produced from the same negative or offset master, printed from the same set of fixed type, etc. The idea is that the contents are exactly the same. Photocopies made in the normal course of business are now generally accepted as duplicates. Microfilms and microfiches usually receive similar treatment.

It would be very impractical to remove the original of a public record from the file and take it to court. For this reason, certified copies of public records, such as birth certificates, are usually admitted as originals. Business records are often treated in a similar manner. If the custodian of the records prepares an affidavit stating that the photocopy is a true copy of the original, the original does not have to be sent to court. Some states require the custodian of the record to testify in court while others allow the introduction of the documents based on the affidavit alone. This procedure does not apply to cases where it is alleged that the business records have been altered.

**Examples of Using Primary Evidence
to Establish the Content of a Document**

• The ransom note received by the parents of the kidnapped child.
• A photocopy of the original contract signed by the parties if the copy was made in the normal course of business.
• A carbon copy of a sales receipt.

Most courts now admit duplicates in place of originals unless there is some indication that the original has been altered or for some other reason it would be unfair to admit the duplicate. Duplicates must be authenticated before they are accepted into evidence.

Computerized information storage obviously does not fit the original rule. Providing the jury with a floppy disk, computer chip, or magnetic tape would be useless. Either by statute or court decisions, computer printouts are now admissible to show the content of information and software stored in the computer. If there is any allegation that the printout is unreliable or does not accurately show the information in question, the opposing side is allowed to introduce its own evidence on the issue. Some states then require the side introducing the computerized information to carry the burden of proof on the validity of the printout.

7-3b Secondary Evidence

Secondary evidence includes all other evidence that can be produced to establish the content of the original. This may be documents, such as the rough draft of a contract, or testimony about what was stated in the document. Testimony introduced to show the contents of a document is called **parol** (pronounced the same as parole) **evidence.**

Parol evidence is not allowed to show the information in public records unless it is impossible to obtain certified copies. The majority of states follow the "American Rule," which prefers certain types of secondary evidence to others. Written copies are preferred to oral testimony. Immediate copies are usually preferred to more remote ones. The exact order of preference varies from state to state. The remaining states follow the "English Rule," which does not recognize degrees of secondary evidence. This allows any type of secondary evidence to be used when primary evidence is not available due to one of the reasons listed next. The Federal Rules of Evidence follow the English Rule.

**Examples of Using Secondary Evidence
to Establish the Content of a Document**
- The rough draft of a contract with penciled notes made by both parties.
- The tape from the dictating machine the secretary used to type the contract.
- Testimony from the head accountant for the company that was the victim of embezzlement about the content of checks that the company did not authorize to be drawn on its account.

There are four main reasons to admit secondary evidence of the contents of a document:

1. The original was destroyed (except when done in bad faith by the side seeking to introduce secondary evidence) or cannot be found after a thorough search of all appropriate places.
2. It is impossible to obtain the original by a subpoena *duces tecum* or other court order.
3. The opposing side has the original and refuses to produce it in court.
4. The document is only introduced to establish something that is not closely related to the main issues in the case.

When the contents of a large volume of records is relevant to the case, it is usually possible to present summaries, charts based on all of the records involved, or otherwise make it possible for the judge and jury to review them more quickly. If this is done, the opposing side must have the opportunity to review the original and verify that what is presented in court is accurate and not misleading.

7-4 Photographic Evidence

Photographs must meet three criteria to be admissible: (1) they must be relevant to some disputed fact in the case; (2) the Best Evidence Rule must be satisfied; and (3) the picture must not be unduly prejudicial. Pictures can either illustrate the testimony of a witness or be independent evidence in the case. While we normally think of still pictures when we use the term *photograph,* the same rules apply to motion pictures and videotapes. X-rays are also photographs, but their admissibility is governed by the rules applied to scientific evidence.

The proper foundation must be established before a photograph can be admitted into evidence. To do this, a witness must state that the photograph accurately depicts the scene as it existed when the photograph was taken. Any witness who was at the scene can do this if he/she has a good memory of the details shown in the picture. It is not necessary to call the photographer to the witness stand. The judge retains the right to refuse to admit pictures that might confuse the jury or be unduly prejudicial. The number of photographs of the same scene that can be admitted is also within the discretion of the judge. Photographs that are merely cumulative are not admissible.

Color photographs and enlargements are judged by the same standards. They must accurately portray the scene without causing undue prejudice. Gruesome pictures taken at murder scenes cause the most problems. Pictures that emphasize the gory nature of the crime may be excluded because of their prejudicial impact on the jury. For example, in a case where the victim's body was dismembered with a chain saw, the prosecutor sought to admit four color pictures which showed a torso covered by a blanket, two severed legs, and a bloody piece of blue jeans that covered one leg. The purpose set forth for introducing the pictures was that the treatment of the victim's body showed malice. The judge ruled that the color pictures of the dismembered body parts were inadmissible. Any juror with average intelligence could imagine what the body looked like. It was feared that the jurors who saw the gruesome photographs might convict the defendant without weighing other evidence.[2] Some judges allow black and white pictures of these types of crime scenes while excluding color photos.

Another problem with pictures is visual distortion. The angle of the camera, lighting, and other factors may result in deceptive representations of the scene. For example, an ordinary flight of stairs may appear very steep if the camera angle is altered; or the lighting at the time the picture was taken may indicate that visibility at the crime scene was much better (or worse) than it actually was at the time the crime occurred. The opposing side has the right to object to the admission of pictures that do not accurately show the facts.

Enlargements and close-ups pose similar problems. Field evidence technicians usually include a ruler or some other standard-sized item in a picture as a point of reference. Aerial photographs are covered by the same considerations. The jury must be able to relate the picture to the total crime scene. These types of photographs are generally admissible as long as the picture will not mislead the jury.

Sometimes one side claims the pictures have been altered and do not represent the facts. This can be done by retouching the negative or superimposing one picture on another. It is usually necessary to call an expert witness to show that these techniques have been used.

New computer software has made it possible to alter photographs. These programs, some of which cost as little at $100, make it possible to retouch photographs so that tampering cannot be detected. Photographs can be scanned into the computer; digital pictures are already in computer-usable form and can be altered pixel by pixel. Possible alterations may be as slight as changing the shading or may be overtly misleading such as adding or removing a person or cleaning up a scene or a bloody victim. This potential for alteration now makes it exceedingly important to maintain the chain of possession for both the photograph and negative in order to show that the photograph introduced in court is tamper-free. One sanctioned use of altered photographs is to ask a witness during cross-examination to identify the photograph and then point out that the witness is so unobservant that he/she identified a picture in which important details had been changed.

Posed pictures are sometimes made to illustrate the facts of the case. For example, investigators might take pictures of the swollen, black-and-blue face of a battered wife. Part of the foundation for these types of pictures will be testimony about when and where the photographs were taken. The pictures are usually admitted into evidence if they accurately reflect the testimony in the case. If they unfairly show controversial facts to the advantage of one side, they are frequently excluded.

More recently, motion picture or videotaped reenactments of the crime have been produced. Videotapes of a drunk driving suspect taking the field sobriety test are now quite common. While older court decisions required expert testimony about the process used to produce these films, they are now accepted without question. The accuracy of the facts depicted in the films must still be established by testimony at trial prior to admitting the films. If there is a question regarding the accuracy of the pictures or their prejudicial impact, the judge will usually preview the film out of the presence of the jury. In rare cases it will be necessary to call expert witnesses who have examined the film to testify on whether or not the film has been spliced or altered.

Some cases even use animation to show the same events from different perspectives.[3] Animation produced by computers is subject to the same foundation as any other computer-generated document. As advancing technology makes it possible to produce new audiovisual aids, the rules of evidence gradually develop methods to introduce them for the benefit of the jury.

Sound recordings are treated in the same manner as photographs. They must be relevant and meet the requirements of the Best Evidence Rule. The tape used at trial must be accurate, and editing must not substantially alter the content of the conversation. Audio tapes of nonverbal sounds can also be used at trial. For example, a tape recording may contain the sound of screeching tires, screaming, or moaning and groaning.

Summary

All documents must be authenticated, (i.e., shown that they are what they claim to be). Many documents that bear seals, have acknowledgments, or are notarized are self-authenticating. Official government publications are also self-authenticating. When it is necessary to authenticate a document, several methods may be used: (1) testimony of a witness who has knowledge of the circumstances surrounding the making of the document; (2) testimony (expert or lay witnesses) that the handwriting in the document matches that of a specific person; (3) distinctive characteristics of the document; (4) document is public record; (5) the Ancient Document Rule applies; or (6) the process or system used to make the document is established in court.

A forensic document examiner may testify about the authenticity of a document. This expert can determine if the handwriting in the document matches that in an exemplar. Typewriter comparisons can also be made. Both ink and paper can be compared to establish their source and possible date. Computer-generated printouts made with ink jet, dot matrix, or laser printers can be compared. Tests can also be done to determine if a document has been altered or erased.

The Best Evidence Rule requires the original document to be introduced into evidence. Duplicates, such as carbon copies, are only admissible if the original is unavailable. Modern statutes have relaxed the rules on duplicates, especially for photocopies. When the original and duplicates are not available, secondary evidence may be admissible. Witnesses may testify (parol evidence) about the content of the document, but courts usually give preference to written documents that indicate the content of the missing original.

Photographs are admissible if they are relevant, satisfy the Best Evidence Rule, and are not unduly prejudicial. A witness must establish that the photograph accurately shows the scene, but the photographer is not required to testify. Color pictures, close-ups, enlargements, posed pictures, motion pictures, and videotapes are all admissible as long as they accurately represent relevant facts in the case. The judge has the discretion to refuse to admit photographs if they distort the facts.

Discussion Questions

1. Define *authentication*. List three types of documents that are self-authenticating, and describe how a prosecutor authenticates the prior convictions of the defendant.
2. List five ways to authenticate a document.
3. Can a lay witness authenticate a handwritten document? Explain.
4. Explain how a forensic document examiner determines if a document and a handwriting exemplar were made by the same person.
5. Explain how a forensic document examiner can determine what make and model typewriter was used to make a document and how he/she can determine if a document was typed on the suspected typewriter.
6. How does a forensic document examiner determine if a document has been altered after it was originally made?
7. What evidence can a forensic document examiner find by examining the paper and ink used to make a document?
8. What is the Best Evidence Rule? When using this rule, what is primary evidence? What is secondary evidence?
9. Under the Best Evidence Rule, when may parol evidence be used to establish the contents of a document?
10. What foundation is necessary for the admission of a photograph?
11. Who determines how many and what type of photographs of the crime scene are admissible? What is the basis for this decision?
12. Are posed photographs admissible? Explain.

Endnotes

1. Richard Saferstein, ed., chap. 13 in *Forensic Science Handbook Vol. I,* 2nd ed. (Englewood Cliffs, NJ: Prentice Hall, 2001); Richard Saferstein, *Criminalistics: An Introduction to Forensic Sciences,* 7th ed.(Englewood Cliffs, NJ: Prentice Hall, 2000); Andre A. Moenssens, Fred E. Inbau, and James E. Starrs, *Scientific Evidence in Criminal Cases,* 4th ed. (Mineola, NY: The Foundation Press, 1995); Andre A. Moenssens, "Novel Scientific Evidence in Criminal Cases: Some Words of Caution," *Journal of Criminal Law & Criminology* 84 (1): 1–21 (1993); C. E. Chaski, "Who Wrote It? Steps toward a science of authorship identification," *NIJ Journal* (U.S. Department of Justice) (September 1997).
2. H. L. Blitzer and J. Jacobia, *Forensic Digital Imaging and Photography* (Academic Press, 2001); S. S. Phillips, C. Squiers, and M. Haworth-Booth, *Police Pictures: The Photograph as Evidence* (Chronicle Books, 1997); R. P. Siljander and D. D. Fredrickson, *Applied Police and Fire Photography,* 2nd ed.(Springfield, IL: Charles C. Thomas, 1997); Steven Staggs, *Crime Scene & Evidence Photographer's Guide* (Springfield, IL: Charles C. Thomas, 1997).
3. *Forensic Animation Evidence* (West Group, 1999); J. D. Foley et al., *Computer Graphics: Principles and Practices in C,* 2nd ed. (Addison-Wesley Publishing, 1995).

CHAPTER 8

Hearsay and Its Exceptions

Outline

Key Terms

- Admissions Exception
- Adoptive admission
- Ancient Documents Exception
- Authorized admission
- Business Records Exception
- Contemporaneous declaration
- Declarant
- Declaration against interest
- Double hearsay
- Dying declaration
- Excited utterance
- Former Testimony Exception
- Hearsay Rule
- Negative hearsay
- Past Recollection Recorded Exception
- Present sense impression
- Prior consistent statement
- Prior identification
- Prior inconsistent statement
- Public Records Exception
- Reputation Exception
- Spontaneous statement
- Statement
- Tacit admission

After studying this chapter, you will be able to:

- Define *hearsay.*
- List the requirements for the use of admissions and confessions.
- Identify three types of declarations against interest.
- Explain how to identify spontaneous statements and contemporaneous declarations.
- List the requirements for making a dying declaration admissible.
- Identify what falls under the Business Records Exception to the Hearsay Rule.
- Explain what is admissible hearsay to show character.
- Identify what is admissible as former testimony.
- Describe which prior statements are admissible to impeach and rehabilitate.
- Explain what is admissible as ancient documents.
- Explain when hearsay is admissible to show reputation.

8-1 Basic Hearsay Principles

Our legal system usually requires that a case be decided solely on the basis of sworn testimony given in the presence of the trial judge or jury. The general rule is that out-of-court statements may not be used as evidence unless they fall under one of the exceptions to the **Hearsay Rule.** This chapter defines hearsay and discusses 14 of the most common exceptions to the rule.

People frequently misuse the term *hearsay.* This makes it very important for you to understand the term in its legal context. Rule 801(a)(2) of the Federal Rules of Evidence, which follows, is the definition adopted by approximately half of the fifty states.

Hearsay Defined

Hearsay is a statement, other than one made by the declarant while testifying at the trial or hearing, offered in evidence to prove the truth of the matter asserted.

The Hearsay Rule focuses on three things:

1. What is a statement?
2. Who is a declarant?
3. What is meant by "offered in evidence to prove the truth of the matter asserted"?

A "**statement**" may include several types of communication: oral, written, recorded on audio or video tape, and nonverbal. In fact, anything a person says is a statement. So are his/her letters, business records, will, etc. But technically, the legal word *statement* is even broader. It also includes body movements done with the intent to communicate. Specifically, it includes actions such as shaking your head "yes" or "no," and pointing in answer to the question, "Which way did he go?"

Statements are hearsay if they were not made in court at the hearing or trial that is currently being conducted. The common idea that "What you say is hearsay, but what I say is not" is not correct; statements originally made by the person who is now testifying are hearsay. This means that even the sworn testimony of the witness which was given at the preliminary hearing is hearsay when offered at the subsequent trial; the witness's account of what he/she said while the crime was being committed is also hearsay.

The **declarant** is the person who made the statement. If the witness is telling what he/she heard someone else say, the person who originally made the statement is the declarant and the statement is hearsay. If the person on the witness stand is telling what he/she previously said, the witness is the declarant and the statement is also hearsay. It is important to determine who the declarant is. The facts surrounding the declarant's statement are considered when determining if an exception to the Hearsay Rule applies.

Something is "offered to prove the truth of the matter asserted" when the attorney wants the jury to believe the answer. Most testimony is admitted for this purpose. Sometimes, however, an attorney will ask a question for some other reason.

Examples of Hearsay and Non-Hearsay

- Prosecutor asks a police officer to tell the jury what the defendant said when he confessed. This is offered to show the truth of the matter asserted—that the defendant committed the crime as described in the confession—and is hearsay.
- If the defense wants to show that the defendant was insane, it might try to admit the defendant's statement, "I am Napoleon," to show that the defendant obviously did not know who he was. Since it is not used to show that it is true—we all know the defendant is not Napoleon—it is not hearsay.
- Prosecutor asks the witness to repeat the defendant's original alibi even though she later made a confession. The purpose of this is to show that the defendant is a liar, not to show that the alibi was true. When used this way, the original statement is not hearsay.
- Prosecutor wants to admit the note that was given to the teller during a bank robbery that says, "Hit the alarm button and I will kill you." This is a written document that contains hearsay. It is also a document and must be authenticated.

8-2 The Hearsay Rule

The basic Hearsay Rule is very simple—hearsay is not admissible in court. There are, however, many exceptions to this rule which will be discussed in Section 8-3. A statement is admissible in court when it falls under an exception to the Hearsay Rule. There are several reasons for the Hearsay Rule, the most important of which is a basic distrust for testimony that was not made under oath. Since the hearsay statement was made without any fear of prosecution for perjury, it is not considered as trustworthy as one made under oath. Another thing that makes courts suspicious of hearsay is the fact that the jury cannot see the person who originally made the statement. The attorneys cannot question and cross-examine the person who originally made the statement. They can only question the witness to make sure he/she is accurately repeating what was said. All of these factors make us distrust hearsay.

The Sixth Amendment to the U.S. Constitution gives the criminal defendant the right to confront and cross-examine those who accuse him/her of a crime. When hearsay is used these rights are denied. The only witness the defendant can cross-examine is the person who tells about something he/she heard said out of court. The Supreme Court, in *Crawford v. Washington* (2004), held that testimonial hearsay is admissible in a criminal trial only if the witness is unavailable and the defendant had a prior opportunity to cross-examine that witness. The Court specifically applied this rule to the introduction at trial of statements made at the preliminary hearing, before a grand jury, or at a former trial, and answers given during police interrogations.

Despite the fact that these are very good arguments for not admitting hearsay into evidence, there are some situations where out-of-court statements obviously should be used. These situations have been grouped together and form the exceptions to the Hearsay Rule. Most of the exceptions are based on facts surrounding the making of the statement that shows that the statement is trustworthy. Some are based on necessity, such as the dying declaration where the deceased cannot be called to the witness stand.

Other exceptions are based on the concept of fair play. For example, it would be unfair to the prosecution to exclude the defendant's confession solely because it was not made under oath. The current trend has been to allow new exceptions to the Hearsay Rule if there is sufficient reason to believe the statement is trustworthy.

Some states allow police officers to testify at the preliminary hearing and/or grand jury about conversations with victims and witnesses even though the officer could not give the same testimony at trial due to the Hearsay Rule. The purpose of this procedure is twofold: it makes the process more efficient; and it minimizes the inconvenience for victims and witnesses of taking time off work to testify in court.

8-3 Exceptions to the Hearsay Rule

Only statements which fall under one of the exceptions to the Hearsay Rule are admissible in court. When the police or the prosecutor review a case involving hearsay to decide if there is enough evidence to convict, what they are really looking for are statements which fit within the exceptions to the Hearsay Rule.

Several other points should be kept in mind. Hearsay varies greatly. Some is so convincing it constitutes key evidence in the case. Other statements will be nearly frivolous. Finding the appropriate hearsay exception, so as to get certain evidence admitted, merely insures that the jury will hear it. The jury, of course, will decide how much weight to give the evidence.

In some situations more than one exception will apply. Examination of the requirements for the various exceptions may reveal technical reasons why one will be more appropriate to use than another.

Sometimes we come upon "**double hearsay.**" Double hearsay is hearsay included in another hearsay statement. For example, if Jane told you what Mary said, whatever Jane told you is hearsay. But if Jane is repeating what Mary said that Alice told her, the portion about what Alice said is double hearsay. The only times these types of statements are admissible is when there is a hearsay exception that applies to what Mary told Jane and an exception which covers what Jane told you.

All 50 states do not follow exactly the same exceptions to the Hearsay Rule. Approximately half of the states follow the Hearsay Rules listed in the Federal Rules of Evidence. The others follow their own rules, which may not be the same as the Federal Rules. Each student must do a little research and discover what rules apply in his/her local state courts. The Federal Rules list at least 30 exceptions to the Hearsay Rule. The most commonly used exceptions are covered in this chapter.

8-4 Admissions and Confessions

Out-of-court statements made by the defendant appear to be within the definition of hearsay and are treated that way by some states. The Federal Rules of Evidence declare that statements by parties to the lawsuit are not hearsay (Rule 801[b][2]). States following this approach include: Louisiana, Montana, Nebraska, Nevada, New Mexico, Oregon, Texas, and Wisconsin. Another approach is to use the standard definition of hearsay but state that admissions of parties are not excluded by the Hearsay Rule, i.e., create an exception to the Hearsay Rule that allows admissions to be introduced in court. California, Florida, Kentucky, Pennsylvania, and Tennessee are among the states that follow this approach.

Statements of a party (the defendant in a criminal case) will be admissible if the attorney establishes the appropriate foundation. This foundation is remarkably similar regardless of whether the statement must qualify under the **Admissions Exception** to the Hearsay Rule or it is not considered hearsay. For that reason, it is important to understand the requirements for the Admissions Exception even when testifying in a state that does not recognize statements of parties as hearsay. Once the foundation is established, the statements are admissible even though there may not be any sign of their trustworthiness. The traditional rationale is that a person would not make untrue statements that could be used against him/her.

Admissions of a party may be used against the person making them; the reverse is not true. A party cannot introduce his/her own self-serving statements to bolster the case. The only questions are whether the person made the statement and whether the person was mentally competent when the statement was made.

The Admissions Exception to the Hearsay Rule Allows the Use of Statements If:

1. The statement was made by a person who is a party to the lawsuit AND
2. The statement is used against the person who made it.

In a criminal case the defendant is obviously a party to the lawsuit. The defendant's confessions and other statements may be admitted under the Admissions Exception. By pleading "Not Guilty," the defendant denies committing the crime; therefore, any confession the defendant made can be used against him/her.

Examples of Statements Admissible under the Admissions Exception to the Hearsay Rule

- The defendant told a friend on the morning after the crime was committed, "I need you to cover for me. If anyone asks, tell them I was with you last night."
- The defendant told a police officer after being given the *Miranda* warnings, "Hey, I was there but I didn't do anything."
- The defendant told his girlfriend, "Don't worry about me. They can't prove I was there."

- When questioned at his home the day after the crime, the defendant said, "I've never been there. Last night I went to visit my mother."

There are two special situations where the Admissions Exception applies. One is the authorized admission. An **authorized admission** is a statement made by a person who is authorized to speak for someone else. For example, the president of a company is authorized to speak for the company, but the janitor is not.

Examples of Statements Admissible as Authorized Admissions under the Admissions Exception to the Hearsay Rule

- The store manager told the lady who slipped and fell while shopping, "I'm very sorry you got hurt. I'll tell my janitors to use a different wax next time so the floors aren't so slippery." The lady later sued the store.
- The CEO of the corporation issued a news release that said, "This company wishes to apologize to its customers for misleading advertising. The person responsible has been fired. In the future, you can rely on our ads." Criminal charges were filed against the corporation for fraud.

The other special case is the **tacit admission.** Sometimes this is also called an **adoptive admission.** This type of admission occurs when someone is accused of wrongdoing but does not deny the accusation. It is usually applied only to face-to-face confrontations. It does not apply when the police accuse a suspect of a crime. The tacit admission is not applicable during custodial interrogation because of the Fifth Amendment right to remain silent.

Example of Statements Admissible as Tacit Admissions under the Admissions Exception to the Hearsay Rule

- The suspect stole a lawnmower from a neighbor. The next day the neighbor confronted him and said, "Why did you take it? Why?" The suspect said nothing and quickly walked away.
- The suspect's mother confronted him when she visited him in jail and said, "How could you do such a thing and embarrass the whole family?" The suspect hung his head and said nothing.

In addition to the Admissions Exception, confessions must meet constitutional standards, such as giving *Miranda* warnings prior to custodial interrogation. When two or more defendants are being tried at the same time, it may be necessary to exclude confessions if the defendant who confessed refuses to take the witness stand. Admitting a confession made by a defendant who decides not to testify would deny the other defendants their Sixth Amendment right to cross-examination. One solution to this problem is to "sanitize" the confession by removing all references to what the other defendants did. Another solution is to have separate trials for the defendants.

Many states also admit statements made by co-conspirators. This rule closely mirrors the criminal law concept which makes each conspirator responsible for acts of other conspirators. Statements made by one conspirator during the conspiracy can be used against another conspirator. The statement must be made within the scope of the conspiracy and in furtherance of the purpose of conspiracy.

8-5 Declarations against Interest

Unlike the admissions exception, which only admits statements by parties to the case, **declarations against interest** are admissible no matter who made them—but the declarant must be unavailable.

A Statement Is Admissible under Declaration against Interest Exception to the Hearsay Rule If:
1. The person making the statement is not available to testify in court AND
2. The statement is against the interest of the person who made it.

According to Rule 804(a) of the Federal Rules of Evidence, a person may be considered unavailable for at least five reasons. They are as follows:

1. The witness refuses to testify on the grounds that the statements are privileged.
2. The witness refuses to testify even though there is a court order requiring that he/she do so.
3. The witness lacks sufficient memory of the event in question.
4. The witness died or currently has a mental or physical disability which makes it impossible for him/her to appear in court.
5. The witness cannot be found after a diligent search.

Note: The same definition of unavailability will be used in some other exceptions to the Hearsay Rule. Due to the length of the list, it will not be repeated each time. Most states have similar rules although they may not recognize all five of the above reasons. It is also important to remember that testimonial hearsay from an unavailable witness will only be admitted at trial if the defendant had the opportunity to cross-examine the witness at a prior proceeding. See *Crawford v. Washington,* p. 174.[1]

Originally a statement was considered to be against the interest of the person making it only if the statement could result in a financial loss. In more recent years, the definition has expanded. Confessions to crimes are now generally included. A few states, such as Montana, Nevada and Wisconsin, include statements that would make the person the subject of hatred, ridicule, or disgrace.

Examples of Statements Admissible under the Declaration against Interest Exception to the Hearsay Rule

- The fraud victim, who has since moved out of town and cannot be located, told a friend, "I can't tell my husband about this. I took money from an account at work to pay for those things. I feel like a fool falling for such an obvious swindle."
- The defendant tried to cash a forged check. The bank manager, who refuses to testify, told the teller, "Go ahead and cash his check. I don't have the time to call the other bank to verify the signature."
- The person who bought several stolen rings from the suspect told a friend, "Sure, I knew the rings were hot but he was selling them so cheap." The suspect is now on trial for theft. The person who bought the rings has been charged with receiving stolen property and is being tried separately.
- The loan officer said, "Yes, Mary paid off the loan."
- The bookkeeper said, "Yes, I took the money. My kids needed school clothes."

Declarations against interest are considered trustworthy because it is unlikely a person would make a statement that could be damaging to oneself unless that statement were true. Even then, the declarant's testimony from the witness stand is preferred. The out-of-court statement is only allowed if the declarant is unavailable.

You should note that if the defendant made a statement against his/her personal interest, the statement is admissible under the Admissions Exception to the Hearsay Rule. It is not necessary to show that the defendant is unavailable to testify.

8-6 Spontaneous Statements and Contemporaneous Declarations

Some states consider **spontaneous statements** and **contemporaneous declarations** to be two separate exceptions to the Hearsay Rule. Other states include them in the *res gestae* (literally, "things done") exception to the Hearsay Rule which covers a variety of statements to explain the actions that were being done at the time the statement was made. We will consider the two separately and note that they are quite similar.

Both of these exceptions to the Hearsay Rule are considered to be trustworthy because there has been no time for the declarant to think about what he/she is saying and make up a lie. These exceptions are rarely used for statements made by the defendant because it is usually easier to have things admitted under the Admissions Exception.

A Statement Is Admissible under the Spontaneous Statement (Also Called an Excited Utterance) Exception to the Hearsay Rule If:

1. It tells about something the declarant observed with one of the five senses (saw, heard, smelled, tasted, or touched) AND
2. It was made spontaneously while the declarant was still under the stress and excitement of the event.

The declarant must have personally observed the event he/she is commenting on. The statement must be made very near to the time the event happened. Normally, the statement must be made without any questioning. Self-serving statements, such as statements the defendant made to make him/herself look good, are not admissible under this exception. The defendant may make spontaneous statements but this exception is normally used to admit statements by other people because everything the defendant said is admissible under the Admissions Exception to the Hearsay Rule.

Examples of Statements Admissible under the Spontaneous Statements Exception to the Hearsay Rule

- Immediately after a traffic accident a bystander said "Did you see that? He just ran the red light and broadsided that car!"
- During a robbery the victim said, "No! No! Please don't take my money."
- The victim grabbed his stomach and said, "Oh, that hurts. Why did he hit me?"

A Statement Is Admissible under the Contemporaneous Declaration (Also Called a Present Sense Impression) Exception to the Hearsay Rule If:

1. It was made by the declarant to explain what he/she was doing AND
2. It was made at the time the declarant was performing the act he/she was trying to explain.

To fit under this exception the comments and the acts must happen at the same time (i.e., be contemporaneous). There is no requirement, however, that they be spontaneous. This means that statements will be admissible even if a police officer asked questions such as "What are you doing?"

Examples of Statements Admissible under the Contemporaneous Declaration Exception to the Hearsay Rule

1. The doctor said, "I am going to have to operate to save your life."

2. A man entered the bank and said, "This is a stick-up. Give me all the money."
3. The victim said, "OK, I'll give you the money, but don't shoot me!"

8-7 Dying Declarations

The **dying declaration** is considered trustworthy on the premise that a person would not go to meet his/her Maker with a lie on the lips.

The traditional rule allowed dying declarations only in criminal prosecutions for the homicide of the declarant. Many states now allow the statements in both criminal and civil trials. The Federal Rules (Rule 804([b])([2])) and a few states allow the statement to be used even if the declarant does not die.

A Statement Is Admissible under the Dying Declaration Exception to the Hearsay Rule If:
1. The declarant had a sense that he/she would die very soon AND
2. The declarant had firsthand knowledge of what he/she was saying AND
3. The statement is about the cause and circumstances of the death AND
4. The declarant is now dead.

One of the keys to admissibility of dying declarations is the declarant's belief that he/she will die almost immediately. This is the basis for trustworthiness. If the declarant has any hope of recovery, the statement will not fall under this exception.

Dying declarations can only be about the events surrounding the death—usually it is a statement by the victim about who inflicted the fatal injury. Statements about past crimes or other things are not admissible. The declarant must speak from personal knowledge and be mentally competent. If the dying person is in severe pain or under heavy medication the question of mental competence may be a problem.

Dying declarations do not have to be spontaneous. In fact, it is frequently necessary to ask the homicide victim questions in order to find out if he/she believes death is imminent. Questions regarding the crime are also allowed.

Examples of Statements That Are Admissible under the Dying Declaration Exception to the Hearsay Rule
- The victim said, "I'm dying, man. That jerk, Peter, shot me."
- The victim said, "Get a priest. I need the Last Rites. John shot me after we had an argument over the money we got in the bank robbery."

Examples of Statements That Are Not Admissible under the Dying Declaration Exception to the Hearsay Rule

- Battered wife said, "He tried to beat me to death. I'm going to divorce that brute."
- The victim said, "I know I am dying. I want to confess to the bank robbery I committed last week and get it off my chest."

8-8 Mental and Physical State

This exception to the Hearsay Rule is used to introduce statements made about mental, emotional, or physical states. The statement must relate to the declarant's mental, emotional, or physical state at the time the statement was made.

A Statement Is Admissible under the Mental or Physical State Exception to the Hearsay Rule If:
1. The statement relates to the person's state of mind, emotion, or physical sensation at the time it was made AND
2. The statement is offered to prove the declarant's state of mind AND
3. The circumstances indicate the statement is trustworthy.

This exception is useful to show intent, plan, motive, design, mental feeling, pain, or health. The statement is admissible even if the declarant is available at the time of the trial. It must be noted that the statement is admitted to show that the declarant said it, but it is not admissible to show that what the declarant originally said was the truth.

Most states allow the admission of statements relating to physical or mental state that were made for the purpose of medical diagnosis or treatment. They must, of course, be relevant to the case. In some states these statements are included in the Mental and Physical State Exception to the Hearsay Rule; in others there is a separate exception for them. A few states have a separate exception to the Hearsay Rule for medical records. Where this does not exist, the issue of business records or public records must be addressed. Another issue involved is whether or not the medical records can be excluded because they are privileged. Chapter 9 addresses this issue.

Statements regarding irrational behavior are not usually admitted under this hearsay exception. While they are definitely relevant if the insanity defense is used, in most states they are not considered hearsay. This is because they are not offered to show that what was said was true. In fact, they are offered to show just the opposite—that the declarant was irrational and did not know what was happening.

Examples of Statements Admissible under the Mental or Physical State Exception to the Hearsay Rule
- The robber said, "Give me your money or I will kill you."
- The owner of the stolen car said, "No! You cannot use my car."
- The battered woman screamed, "I hate you!!"
- The torture victim repeatedly screamed, as if in extreme pain.

8-9 Business Records and Official Documents

Most businesses keep records on employees, inventory, customers, etc. A well-run business will have established procedures to collect this information, making it more trustworthy than information obtained by a less systematic method. Due to this apparent reliability, an exception to the Hearsay Rule has been established for business records.

Section 90.803(6) of the Florida Statutes (which is similar to the rule followed in many other states) sets out the requirement for admissibility under the **Business Records Exception** to the Hearsay Rule. It applies to memoranda, reports, records, or data compilation, in any form, of acts, events, conditions, opinions, or diagnoses.

The term *business* includes every kind of business, governmental activity, profession, or occupation and calling, whether conducted for profit or not.

There are really two keys to admissibility under this rule. First, someone with firsthand knowledge must have made the record near the time the event occurred. This includes filling out a report, cash register tapes, making entries in a log book or a computer database, or dictating the information to someone else. Failure to make the record promptly makes the record less trustworthy.

A Document Is Admissible under the Business Records Exception to the Hearsay Rule If:
1. The document is made at or near the time of the underlying event AND
2. The document is made in the regular course of business AND
3. The custodian or other qualified witness testifies as to its identity and mode of preparation AND
4. Sources of information and method and time of preparation were such as to indicate its trustworthiness.

Second, the records must be kept as a routine part of doing business. Whatever procedures the business has established must be followed. Even then, the court can rule information inadmissible if it has been shown that the business kept inadequate records or frequently made fraudulent entries in its records.

It is not necessary to have the person who made the record testify in court. Depending on how the business is organized and the type of record sought, the witness may be someone from personnel, accounting, or the records office.

Business records can be used to establish many things. Some criminal cases, such as embezzlement, cannot be prosecuted without them. If a company keeps strict payroll records, the timecard can be used to show that the employee was (or was not) at work on a given date and time. Hotel and airline records can be used to show that a person was at a given location on a given date. Although none of these is conclusive because someone could have used a false identity, the evidence can be admitted, and the other side will have to convince the jury that the defendant was (or was not) there.

If a company keeps good business records, the fact that it has no record of an event can be used as evidence that the event did not occur. For example, the fact that the defendant did not punch his time card can be used to show that he was not at work at that time. This is sometimes called "**negative hearsay.**"

Examples of Statements That Are Admissible under the Business Records Exception to the Hearsay Rule

- Gun store records can be used to show that the defendant purchased a gun similar to the murder weapon prior to the death of the victim.
- Hospital emergency room records can be used to show the extent of the victim's injuries on the day in question.
- Cash register receipts can be used to show that no one purchased an item similar to the one that the defendant stole. Cash registers with scanners that itemize the purchase and give date and time are particularly useful for this purpose.
- Telephone records can be used to show that calls were made to the extortion victim from the defendant's telephone.

Official Documents. Official records of public agencies, including police departments, are covered by a rule similar to business records. These records are of two types: (1) records kept on what the agency does and (2) records that others are required by law to file with the public agency. The latter group includes birth, death, and marriage certificates. The requirements are basically the same as for business records.

Information Is Admissible under the Public Records Exception to the Hearsay Rule If:

1. The record was made by, and within the scope of duty, of a public employee AND
2. The record was made at or near the time the event occurred AND
3. Sources of the information and method and time of preparation indicate the record is trustworthy.

Examples of Information Admissible under the Public Records Exception to the Hearsay Rule

- Police logs showing that Mary Jones reported domestic violence incidents on September 1, 2003; October 2, 2003; and November 3, 2003.
- Portion of police report stating that Officer Green arrived at Jones's residence on December 4, 2003, and observed John Jones with "smoking gun" in hand. He was crying hysterically and said, "I killed her." (This statement would be a spontaneous declaration and also an admission).

Records of Vital Statistics Are Admissible under the Public Records Exception to the Hearsay Rule If:

1. The maker is required by law to report the event to a public agency AND
2. The maker of report filed it as required by law.

These rules make it easy to admit birth, death, and marriage certificates. They also apply to many other operations of government.

Examples of Vital Statistics That Are Admissible under the Public Records Exception to the Hearsay Rule

- Certificate filed with the county by a priest stating he officiated at the marriage of John and Mary Jones on June 3, 2003.
- Death certificate filed with the county by Dr. Smith stating that Mary Jones died of a gunshot wound on December 4, 2004.

Police reports, however, are a problem. Anything that is observed by the officer will be admissible. Information given to the officer by others is less reliable. As a general rule, this secondhand information is only admissible if another exception to the Hearsay Rule makes it admissible.

8-10 Reputation

Reputation is what others say about someone's character. It is by its very nature hearsay. In fact, it is frequently nothing but gossip. Nonetheless, historically, there has been an hearsay exception for **reputation.**

Statements Are Admissible under the Reputation Exception to the Hearsay Rule If:
1. The statement relates to the reputation of a person among his/her associates OR
2. It relates to the reputation of a person in his/her community.

As a general rule, the character witness is not allowed to give his/her personal opinion about the person whose reputation is in question, but should report on what the person's associates or the community thinks. (Refer to Chapter 4 for a discussion of when reputation is admissible.)

Examples of Statements Admissible under the Reputation Exception to the Hearsay Rule
- Defense character witness said that defendant had a reputation in the community for being a peaceful, law-abiding person.
- Prosecution character witness said that defendant had a reputation among co-workers for being hot-tempered and violent.

Some states have expanded the rule and allow character witnesses to give their personal opinions, as well as stating the reputation in the community.

8-11 Former Testimony

The **Former Testimony Exception** to the Hearsay Rule covers testimony taken under oath at a prior court appearance or other legislative authorized proceeding such as a deposition or arbitration proceeding. This is one of the easiest exceptions to the Hearsay Rule to justify. Since it was under oath it is considered trustworthy. The fact that the witness is no longer available makes the exception necessary. The reason it is restricted is that the witness cannot be cross-examined at the current trial.

When this exception is used, the former testimony is introduced as evidence in the present case. If the former testimony is used to impeach, it comes in under the Prior Inconsistent Statement Exception.

In criminal cases, the former testimony exception is most commonly used at trial to introduce testimony taken at the preliminary hearing. Testimony of any witness the defendant called at the preliminary hearing can be admitted by the prosecution. If it is the testimony of a prosecution witness, the defendant must have had the opportunity and motive to cross-examine. If the defense decided not to cross-examine, the testimony will still be admissible.

Testimony Is Admissible under the Former Testimony Exception to the Hearsay Rule If:

1. The former testimony was recorded under oath at a prior hearing (each state code will specify which hearings apply) AND
2. The person whose testimony is introduced is not available to testify at the present court proceeding AND
3. The former testimony is offered:
   (a) against the person who offered it in evidence on his/her own behalf when the former testimony was given; OR
   (b) the party against whom the former testimony was originally offered was a party to the proceeding and had the right and opportunity to cross-examine the declarant with a motive similar to what he/she now has.

Testimony might also have come from a previous trial of the same case if there was a hung jury or the case was reversed on appeal. When there is more than one defendant, it is possible that the testimony came from the preliminary hearing of another defendant. In all of these situations, there must have been at least one defendant present with a motive to cross-examine that is similar to the motive the current defendant has.

Examples of Statements That Are Admissible under the Former Testimony Exception to the Hearsay Rule

1. Transcript of testimony at a preliminary hearing given by an elderly victim who died prior to trial.
2. Transcript of testimony of defense witness who made statements implicating the defendant in the crime while testifying at a prior trial.
3. If the prior trial ended in hung jury the prosecutor can introduced a transcript from the prior trial if a witness can no longer be found.

8-12 Prior Inconsistent Statements

Prior inconsistent statements can be used to impeach a witness. Opposing counsel may ask questions about them during cross-examination (see Chapter 5). Many authorities on evidence claim that they are not hearsay because they are not offered to show that they are true. Instead, they are offered to show that the witness may not be telling the truth. The Federal Rules of Evidence (Rule 801[b][1][A]) and a number of states follow this approach. Some states list prior inconsistent statements as a separate exception to the Hearsay Rule and for that reason they are discussed here. Under either approach the prior statements are admissible.

Prior Inconsistent Statements Are Admissible if the Following Occurred:

1. The statement is inconsistent with the testimony given on the witness stand AND
2. While on the witness stand in the current trial, the witness was asked about the inconsistent statement and given a chance to explain.

If the witness admits the inconsistent statement, no other witnesses are called to impeach. But if he/she denies making the statement, a witness may be called to restate what was said. The purpose of asking about the inconsistent statement first is to save court time. It also gives the witness a chance to explain if the statement has been taken out of context or is not accurate.

Examples of Statements That Are Admissible as Prior Inconsistent Statements

1. Defendant gave Officer Green an alibi when questioned prior to arrest. On the witness stand, he gave a totally different account of where he was and denied having given the first alibi. Officer Green can be called to testify regarding what the defendant said.
2. Defendant testified that she had never met the co-defendant prior to her arrest. On cross-examination she was asked if she remembered telling someone at her office on January 6, 2003, that the defendant was her new boyfriend. She admitted making the statement at the office. No other witness will be called regarding the statement.

8-13 Prior Consistent Statements

Prior consistent statements are used to rehabilitate a witness who has been impeached by prior inconsistent statements. They can also be used if there is a charge that the witness recently fabricated his/her testimony, is biased, or has other improper motive for testifying. The status of prior consistent statements as hearsay is subject to the same debate as prior inconsistent statements: they are offered to show that the person made the statement, not that the statement is true. The Rule 801(a)(1)(B) of the Federal Rules of Evidence and a number of states do not classify prior consistent statements as hearsay although some states do. The topic is discussed here because some states specifically list them as exceptions to the Hearsay Rule. Either way, the statement will be admissible.

Prior Consistent Statements Are Admissible if Any One of the Following Exist:

1. The witness has been impeached by prior inconsistent statements and the prior consistent statement was made before the prior inconsistent statement OR
2. During cross-examination it was alleged that the witness recently changed his/her testimony and the prior consistent statement was made before the date the testimony was allegedly changed OR
3. During cross-examination it was alleged that the witness altered his/her testimony due to bias or other bad motive and the prior consistent statement was made before the date the witness allegedly altered his/her testimony.

Rehabilitation is normally done during redirect examination of the witness. Because of the restrictions on this type of evidence, it is very important to establish when the statement was made. Additional witnesses are not usually called for this purpose.

Examples of Statements That Are Admissible as Prior Consistent Statements

1. The prosecution alleged that the witness altered his testimony due to a bribe given on July 1, 2004. The defense is allowed to introduce a copy of a statement made by the witness on May 3, 2004, in which the details are the same as the testimony given during direct examination.
2. The witness was impeached by showing that she could not identify the defendant at a police lineup. The prosecution was allowed to show that she had identified the defendant when the police allowed her to look at him the day before the lineup.

8-14 Ancient Documents

The **Ancient Documents Exception** is necessary because after many years there is frequently no one available who can testify about the exact events that surrounded the making of the documents. This most commonly involves deeds and wills.

Documents Are Admissible under the Ancient Documents Exception to the Hearsay Rule If:
1. The document appears to be genuine AND
2. People have acted as if the document is genuine AND
3. The document is at least as old as required by the legislature.

The length of time to qualify for the Ancient Documents Exception varies and is usually set by the state's legislature. For example, both the Federal Rules and the Arizona Rules of Evidence require 20 years; Pennsylvania and Tennessee require 30 years.

Examples of Documents That Are Admissible under the Ancient Documents Exception to the Hearsay Rule
1. Deed dated 1956 showing that John Smith purchased a residential lot located at 123 Elm St., Hometown, from John Doe. Deed does not appear to have been altered. John Smith moved into the house in 1956 and lived there for 32 years.
2. Will dated 1945 showing that Jane Doe gave land at 123 Elm St., Hometown, to her son John. Will was probated without challenge and a deed given to John.

8-15 Past Recollection Recorded

The **Past Recollection Recorded Exception** can be used to introduce information even though the person who wrote it down can no longer remember the facts. While it is unlikely that someone would forget the facts in a homicide investigation, it occurs at times with lesser crimes and traffic tickets.

Evidence Is Admissible under the Past Recollection Recorded Exception to the Hearsay Rule If:
1. The statement would be admissible if the declarant testified at the current trial AND
2. The witness currently has insufficient present recollection to testify fully and accurately AND
3. The report was made at a time when the facts were fresh in the memory of the witness AND
4. The report was made by the witness, someone under his/her direction, or by another person for the purpose of recording the witness's statement AND
5. The witness can testify that the report was a true statement of the facts AND
6. The report is authenticated as accurate.

The reason this information is considered trustworthy is that the original report was accurately made near to the time the event occurred when memory was at its best. It does not have to be in the handwriting of the person who observed the event.

As used here, a "report" is any writing. It includes both formal business records and scraps of paper with notes written on them. A statement a victim or witness made to the police would qualify if the information was put in a police report. To use this exception, the witness must have a poor memory of the incident, and at the same time testify that the report is accurate. This sounds like a contradiction. The way it is done is to show a habit of making accurate reports. Normally, a person rereads the report, makes any necessary corrections, but never signs the report until convinced that it is correct. By seeing the signature, he/she can testify that the report must have been accurate.

Only things that would otherwise be admissible can be admitted under this exception. In other words, any parts of the report that are inadmissible hearsay, privileged, or not relevant would not be admissible.

At one time most courts required that the witness have no memory at all about the incident. Now the more common view is that the witness has insufficient memory to be able to testify fully and accurately. The judge, of course, will determine when this occurs.

Once something has been ruled admissible as past recollection recorded, the report is read into the record. The document is not given to the jury unless the opposing side requests that the jury be allowed to see it. Allowing the jury to use it as an exhibit is believed to give the contents of the report more weight than it deserves.

Examples of Documents That Are Admissible under the Past Recollection Recorded Exception to the Hearsay Rule

- Police report for petty theft observed in progress by officer. Officer has no current memory of event. She testified that she always reviews her reports and corrects them before signing them. This report has been signed.
- Notes that the witness made on a scrap of paper while talking to an extortionist on telephone. She testified that she has blacked out the incident, but remembers going over the demands twice and writing them down very carefully.

8-16 Prior Identification

Some states have created a special hearsay exception for the **prior identification** of the suspect by the victim. The Federal Rules of Evidence, and many states that follow them, do not consider testimony about prior identifications to be hearsay. In general, jurisdictions that do not consider admissions of parties to be hearsay also do not classify testimony about prior identification(s) as hearsay.

Evidence of a Prior Identification Is Admissible under an Exception to the Hearsay Rule if All of the Following Are Met:

1. The witness has testified that he/she accurately identified the person who committed the crime AND
2. The witness identified the defendant or another person as the person who committed the crime AND
3. The identification was made when the crime was fresh in the witness's memory.

This exception is used to introduce testimony about both correct and incorrect identifications. The key is that the identification was made at or near the time of the crime, and that the person who made the identification testified that he/she correctly identified the person selected as the criminal. If a lineup was held but the person called to view it did not select anyone, testimony regarding that lineup would not be admissible under this exception to the Hearsay Rule.

Examples of Statements That Are Admissible under the Prior Identification Exception to the Hearsay Rule

1. Robbery victim testified that he viewed a police lineup two days after the crime and made a positive identification of the defendant. The robbery victim can testify in court about making this identification.
2. Burglary victim testified that he viewed suspect that a police officer pointed out a few minutes after the crime and made a positive identification of the burglar. The burglary victim can testify in court about making this identification.
3. The defense can call an eyewitness to the crime to testify about a lineup at which he selected a man as the person he saw murder the victim. The defense would introduce this testimony because the person the witness selected was not the defendant.

Summary

The Hearsay Rule reflects the tremendous faith we put in our juries. By watching the witness testify under oath, the jury is expected to determine who is telling the truth. Out-of-court statements are therefore disfavored. Strict enforcement of this rule would be impractical, so many exceptions have been allowed.

One of the most important exceptions in criminal cases is the Admissions Exception which allows the defendant's statements to be introduced. This includes statements of co-conspirators.

Statements people make against their own financial interest or that could cause them to be criminally prosecuted are admissible as a declaration against interest. These can only be used if the declarant is unavailable at trial.

Dying declarations cover statements made by a homicide victim after the fatal wound was inflicted. The declarant must believe that death is imminent. The statement must relate to the circumstances of the homicide; it typically identifies the person who inflicted the mortal injury.

Statements a person makes that accompany what he/she is doing or has just observed can be admitted under one of three exceptions: Spontaneous Statements, Contemporaneous Declarations, and Mental and Physical State. The lack of time to think up self-serving statements is considered to make these statements trustworthy.

The Business Records and Public Documents exceptions cover all types of records kept in the course of business and government as long as established procedures for recording events promptly have been complied with. Vital statistics, such as birth, marriage, and death records, that the law requires doctors, the clergy and others to report to the government, are also covered. The Past Recollection Recorded Exception also recognizes the value of good recordkeeping. This is helpful when the witness cannot remember an event. If accurate notes were made at the time of the event, the notes may be read to the jury.

The Former Testimony Exception permits the introduction of testimony previously taken under oath when the declarant is no longer available.

The Prior Inconsistent Statement and Prior Consistent Statement Exceptions permit the introduction of statements for impeachment and rehabilitation.

The Ancient Documents Exception makes it possible to introduce old documents without trying to find witnesses from 20 or 30 years ago.

The Prior Identification Exception covers pretrial identification procedures. If the witness testifies that he/she identified the defendant at a pretrial procedure, someone who was present when the identification was made may be called to confirm or deny that the witness picked the defendant.

Discussion Questions

1. Define *hearsay,* and explain the rationale behind the Hearsay Rule.
2. Who is the declarant? List three exceptions to the Hearsay Rule that require the declarant to be unavailable.
3. What is an adoptive admission, and how does it differ from an authorized admission?
4. What types of interests are covered by declaration against interest?
5. What is a spontaneous declaration? Do contemporaneous statements have to be spontaneous?
6. When are statements of a person's mental state admissible?
7. What types of businesses are covered by the Business Records Exception? What types of public records are admissible hearsay?
8. What is admissible to show reputation?
9. What facts must be established at trial before an attorney can introduce the transcript of a witness's testimony at the preliminary hearing?
10. What must be shown before a prior inconsistent statement can be introduced?
11. List two situations where prior consistent statements can be introduced at trial.
12. How old must a document be to qualify for the Ancient Documents Exception?
13. When is the Past Recollection Recorded Exception to the Hearsay Rule used?
14. What must the prosecutor show before a police report can be read to the jury under the Past Recollection Recorded Exception?
15. When can the Prior Identification Exception be used to introduce a correct lineup identification of the defendant?

Endnote

1. *Crawford v. Washington* 541 U.S.__, 124 S.Ct. 1354; 158 L.Ed. 2d 177 (2004).

Privileged Communications

Outline

Key Terms

- Attorney-client privilege
- Clergy-penitent privilege
- Confidential communication
- Husband-wife privileges
- News media privilege
- Physician-patient privilege
- Police informant privilege
- Police personnel files privilege

After studying this chapter, you will be able to:

- Explain why the law regarding privileges allows relevant information to be excluded from trial.
- Identify conversations between an attorney and client that are privileged.
- List the privileges which apply to confidential communications between husband and wife.
- Recognize the privilege not to testify against one's spouse.
- Explain the physician-patient and clergy-penitent privilege.
- Describe the purpose and function of the police-informer privilege.
- Identify the reasons for considering police personnel files privileged.
- Describe what information obtained by the media is privileged.

9-1 Basis for Privileges

Our legal system operates on the basic concept that what a person says can be used against him/her. One well-known exception is the privilege against self-incrimination (see Chapter 14). Another major exception is the exclusion of privileged communications from evidence.

Over several centuries society has determined that there are certain relationships where it is important to maintain and encourage confidentiality. For example, in order to promote honest communications within a marriage, a husband-wife privilege was developed under common law. No matter how relevant the defendant's statement to his/her spouse may be, it is not admissible without the defendant's permission. Total confidentiality, however, would be contrary to public policy in some situations; for example, if the husband attempted to kill the wife. Therefore, exceptions were developed to make such statements admissible.

Communications covered by the various privileges are also hearsay. If an exception to the privilege applies, the communication is not automatically admissible. There must be both an exception to the privilege and an exception to the hearsay rule before the information can be used in court.

When a privilege is established, there is a corresponding rule that the holder of the privilege cannot be punished for using the privilege. The U.S. Supreme Court made this point when it refused to let prosecutors comment on the fact that a defendant had invoked the right to remain silent. It would be unjust to lead a jury to conclude that the only reason for invoking the privilege is that the defendant had something to hide.

Basic Rules for Privileged Communications

1. Statements must be made under circumstances that indicate confidentiality is expected.
2. Relationship between the individuals must be recognized as entitled to privilege.
3. Parties must not reveal confidential statements to others.
4. Privileged communications are admissible only if there is an exception to the privilege that covers the communication.

Other Evidentiary Rules That Must Be Considered:

1. Statement must be relevant.
2. All privileged communications are hearsay.
3. Statements are admitted into evidence only if covered by an exception to the Hearsay Rule.
4. Privileged communications that are in writing:
   Must be authenticated,
   Must satisfy the Best Evidence Rule.

Two things must be shown in order to utilize privileges: (1) there must be a **confidential communication,** and (2) the appropriate relationship must have existed between the parties.

While we usually think of privileged conversations, the rules extend to both oral and written communications. The term *conversation* will frequently be used in this chapter to mean both oral statements and written communications. Confidentiality can be shown by the fact that two people excluded everyone else from the room while they talked or otherwise made an effort to keep anyone from overhearing what was said. On the other hand, if they were shouting at each other and someone heard the conversation, no privilege would apply. Written communications are confidential if delivered in sealed envelopes and stored in a manner so that others cannot see them; confidential material sent by FAX usually has a cover sheet stating that the information is privileged.

A person can voluntarily give up (waive) a privilege. Most commonly this is done by revealing the privileged information to a third party. For example, if someone tells a friend all the details of a conversation he had with his attorney, the attorney-client privilege is waived. When a witness is called and voluntarily testifies to privileged communications, the privilege is considered waived both for the current and future proceedings. There is one exception. If a witness claims a privilege and the judge incorrectly rules that the privilege does not apply, the witness must testify but the privilege is not waived.

Over the years, other privileges have developed that are not based on the idea that a close relationship requires confidential communication. Two of these involve law enforcement agencies: (1) the identity of police informants is frequently considered confidential; and (2) police personnel records are considered privileged. Only under special circumstances can these two types of information be used in court.

One of the newest privileges involves the news media. The U.S. Supreme Court has denied that there is a constitutional privilege for the press, but many states have statutory privileges that enable the media to protect their sources of information.

9-2 Commonly Used Privileges

At common law there were very few privileges. Gradually, however, state legislatures have added new ones. Congress has followed suit. This chapter will cover the most commonly used privileges. Students are encouraged to review their local laws and find out what privileges apply in their jurisdiction.

9-3 Attorney-Client Privilege

The **attorney-client privilege** goes back to the time of Elizabeth I in England, and is firmly established in common law. It is based on the concept that an attorney cannot properly handle a case without full disclosure of the facts by a client.

The initial consultation is covered even if the client decides not to hire the attorney. Privilege does not depend on the payment of a fee for the lawyer's services. If payment is received, it also does not matter who is paying the lawyer. For example, if a father hires an attorney to represent his son, the son has the privilege—not the father.

Because the client is the holder of the privilege, the client can prevent the attorney from disclosing privileged information. Most states require the attorney to invoke the privilege unless the client has specifically ordered it waived.

Attorney-Client Privilege Described
Attorney: A person the client reasonably believes is licensed to practice law. The fact that the attorney is not actually licensed does not invalidate the privilege.
Client: A person who consults with an attorney for the purpose of obtaining legal advice.

What is covered: Confidential communications between attorney and client regarding the legal services sought. Consultation in furtherance of future crimes is not privileged.
Who holds the privilege: Client.

The client must be seeking legal advice. If the lawyer is sought out as a business advisor, or as a friend, the privilege does not apply. The more common view is that both what the client said and what the lawyer said are privileged. The lawyer can be compelled to give the names of clients and the dates of consultations but not the reasons legal advice was sought. The privilege continues to exist even after the death of the client.

Confidential communications normally require that no one except the attorney and the client be allowed to participate in the communications. There is a minor exception to this rule which allows the privilege even though members of the attorney's office staff are present. This is necessary for the functioning of the law office—secretaries, law clerks, and paralegals must have access to the case file.

Also, if an expert witness is going to testify, it will be necessary for the attorney to discuss the case with that expert prior to trial.

On the other hand, the privilege will not apply if the client has a friend present during an interview with the attorney unless some other privilege applies. For example, if a husband brought his wife with him when he visited an attorney, the husband-wife privilege would apply.

The privilege only applies to communications regarding legal services. The client cannot stretch the privilege by asking the attorney to hide incriminating physical evidence. For example, if a defendant hires an attorney to defend him on a robbery charge, their conversation regarding the robbery is privileged. However, the client cannot make the gun used in the robbery privileged by giving it to the attorney. If the attorney becomes actively involved in concealing evidence or helping the client commit crimes, the attorney may face criminal liability as an accessory.

While our legal system respects the right of every criminal defendant to have legal counsel at trial, it does not extend the attorney-privilege to planning crimes. There is no privilege if the client is seeking help for the commission of a crime in the future. Arranging to have perjured testimony given at trial falls in this category and is not privileged.

A new exception to the attorney-client privilege has emerged in several states. It applies if the attorney has reason to believe that the client will inflict serious bodily harm or death on a person in the near future. These states impose a duty on attorneys to warn the person who is in danger and/or notify authorities. Once these warnings have been made the confidentiality is broken and the same information can be introduced in court.

Examples of Use of Attorney-Client Privilege
- Defendant confessed to his defense attorney that he committed the crime.
- Defendant visited an attorney, outlined his case, and then decided to hire a different attorney.
- Business owner visited her attorney, outlined future business plans, and asked if the plans were legal.
- Man went to attorney, told about many personal problems, and asked for advice about filing for a divorce.
- Owner of a failing business went to attorney in order to file bankruptcy. During conversation a number of questionable business practices were revealed that did not amount to fraud.

9-4   Husband-Wife Privilege

In very early common law, neither the parties to the case nor their spouses were allowed to testify. The current version of the privilege emerged about 1850. There are now two **husband-wife privileges.** One protects confidential communications between husband and wife which are made during the marriage. The other applies when one spouse is called to testify in court against the other.

The privilege for confidential communications between husband and wife restricts courtroom use of statements made in confidence during the marriage. It applies only if there is a valid marriage; most states apply the privilege to couples who are legally married even though they are not living together. Some states officially recognize common-law marriages; in these states the privilege also applies to parties to a valid common-law marriage. To date, the courts have refused to extend the privilege to couples who are merely living together.

Husband-Wife Privilege for Confidential Communications Described
Husband and wife: Valid marriage is required. In states recognizing common-law marriages, parties to valid common-law marriage are covered.
What is covered: Confidential communications made during the marriage
Who holds the privilege: Both husband and wife. Either one can invoke it.
Exceptions common in criminal cases: Crimes committed by one spouse against the other spouse. Crimes committed by one spouse against the children of either spouse. Failure to support a spouse or a child. Bigamy.

About half of the states hold that confidential conversations that occurred during the marriage remain privileged even after the marriage has ended. In these states, a widow can refuse to disclose privileged conversations she had with her husband prior to his death. The same is true for divorced couples—they do not have to disclose confidential conversations they had during their marriage and they can prevent the former spouse from doing so in court.

The privilege covers all forms of communications (letters, phone calls, conversations, etc.) between husband and wife. They must, however, be made in a confidential situation. The presence of other family members, except for very young children, will usually defeat the privilege. The privilege is waived if the conversation is overheard because the husband and wife were in a public place, or if personal letters were left where someone else read them.

Many states hold that the privilege applies to actions as well as words. For example, if the wife saw her husband hide items stolen during a burglary, this would be considered privileged in states holding that actions are privileged.

Both husband and wife hold the privilege to refuse to disclose communications with a spouse and to prevent the spouse from disclosing those communications in court. While the normal rule is that a privileged communication that has been disclosed to a third party is no longer privileged, the husband-wife privilege is not waived because one spouse betrayed the confidence by disclosing information. Only the spouse who disclosed the information has waived (lost) the privilege.

The policy reason for the privilege is that requiring one spouse to testify against the other would damage the marital relationship. The exceptions generally cover those situations where the marriage is probably beyond repair.

There are several obvious situations where the privilege cannot be applied. If one spouse commits a crime against the other, such as domestic violence, there is no public policy reason for preventing the victim from testifying. This is also true if either spouse victimizes any of the children in the family. If one spouse is charged with neglect or desertion of the family, the privilege is also waived. The same is true in bigamy cases. Many states also have exceptions to the privilege for planning crimes. This applies if one spouse told the other about his/her plans to commit a crime as well as situations where both husband and wife were planning to commit a crime together. If a husband and wife are charged with conspiracy, either spouse may testify against the other.

Examples of Use of Privilege for Confidential Communications between Husband and Wife

- While in the living room with no one there except his wife, the husband said "I don't trust John. We just finished that job and I think he is planning on stealing the money from me."
- Wife whispered to husband, "You are flirting with Mary. I'll get even with you for that."

The second husband-wife privilege is the privilege not to testify. This issue is raised when one spouse is on trial and the other is being called as a witness. To invoke the privilege, the parties must show that they are currently married. The privilege ends when the marriage ends.

Husband-Wife Privilege Not to Testify against Each Other Described

- **Husband and wife:** Valid marriage is required. In states recognizing common-law marriages, parties to valid common-law marriage are covered.
- **What is covered:** Testifying in court.
- **Who holds the privilege:** One spouse—legislature or case law designates which spouse holds this privilege; the most common rule is that the spouse who is being called to testify holds the privilege.
- **Exceptions common in criminal cases:** Crimes committed by one spouse against the other spouse. Crimes committed by one spouse against the children of either spouse. Failure to support a spouse or child. Bigamy.

There is considerable variation between the states on who holds the privilege not to testify. Some jurisdictions allow the spouse who has been subpoenaed to refuse to testify; others allow the defendant to prevent his/her spouse from taking the witness stand. Several states do not recognize the testimonial privilege as separate from the confidential marital communication privilege.

The exceptions to the testimonial privilege are basically the same as those applicable to the confidential marital communication privilege. The same policy reasons apply. Some states do not apply the privilege if the defendant got married for the purpose of preventing the new spouse from testifying.

Examples of Use of Privilege Not to Testify against a Spouse

In state where spouse holds the privilege not to take the witness stand: Husband is on trial for robbery and wife is subpoenaed to testify. Wife may assert the privilege and refuse to take the witness stand.

In state where defendant holds privilege to prevent spouse from taking witness stand: Husband is on trial for burglary. Prosecution subpoenaed wife to testify. Husband can assert the privilege and block wife from taking the witness stand.

A key distinction between the confidential communication privilege for husbands and wives and the privilege not to testify is that the latter privilege allows someone not to testify at all. To invoke this right there must be a valid marriage on the court date. It does not matter whether the testimony would have been about events that occurred during the marriage or prior to it. On the other hand, the confidential communication privilege prevents testimony about conversations that occurred during the marriage. Whether or not the couple is still married at the time of the court appearance is not important in most states. Many times both privileges apply; the result is that the spouse does not take the witness stand.

9-5 Physician-Patient Privilege

The **physician-patient privilege** did not exist at common law. It first appeared in a New York statute in 1828. Despite this fact, some of the federal courts allow evidence to be excluded under this privilege. Some recent cases also exclude physician-patient communications under the constitutional right of privacy.

In many ways this privilege is similar to the attorney-client privilege. The patient is protected as long as there is a reasonable belief that the physician is licensed to practice medicine. The reason for the privilege is the belief that the doctor cannot adequately care for the patient unless he/she has full information about the patient's condition. The privilege makes it more likely that the patient will be completely honest with the doctor. While the definition varies a little from state to state, it usually includes MD's as well as osteopaths and chiropractors.

Physician-Patient Privilege Described
Physician: Person reasonably believed by the patient to be licensed to practice medicine.
Patient: Person who consulted physician for purpose of diagnosis or treatment.
What is covered: Information obtained by the physician for the purpose of diagnosis or treatment of the patient.
Who holds the privilege: Patient.
Exceptions common in criminal cases: Advice sought on how to conceal a crime. Advice sought to help plan crime. Information physician is required by law to report to authorities. Many states do not allow this privilege to be used in criminal proceedings.

Like the attorney-client privilege, the physician-patient privilege only exists if the physician and patient made reasonable attempts to keep the information confidential. The presence of an office nurse during the examination does not violate the privilege. Neither does the fact that a secretary typed the medical reports. Some states consider conversations privileged even though the patient was accompanied by a close family member. But the presence of other people during the consultation will result in the information not being privileged unless there is some other privilege involved.

Many states make information obtained by the physician privileged, rather than just restricting the privilege to communications between the physician and patient. "Information" refers to what the doctor observed during the examination, such as bruises, as well as what the patient told the doctor. On the other hand, the doctor can be ordered to give names of patients and the dates that they consulted the doctor (but no information about their conversations) even if the communications are privileged.

The law recognizes that there are a variety of situations in which a person goes to a doctor. The only ones that are privileged are those where the patient is seeking diagnosis or treatment. This includes referrals for a "second opinion."

Examples of Situations Covered by Physician-Patient Privilege

1. Woman went to doctor because she was badly bruised. When doctor asked how she sustained the injuries, she stated that her boyfriend beat her up.
2. Woman went to doctor for a HIV test. When asked why she wanted to be tested, she stated that she had been raped.
3. Man told his doctor that he had not been sleeping well and that he was hearing voices telling him to attack people who went into an abortion clinic.

Notes:
1. Some states do not allow the physician-patient privilege to be used in criminal cases.
2. If state law mandates that the doctor report a particular incident, the privilege does not apply. Incidents that must be reported vary from state to state; common examples are child abuse, gunshot wounds, etc.

Consultation for purposes such as a physical exam required by the patient's employer are not covered because the original intent was to disclose the information to someone else. Other situations that are not covered are listed next.

Examples of Situations Not Covered by Physician-Patient Privilege
- Blood and urine tests requested by the police in cases involving driving under the influence of alcohol.
- Blood tests done to obtain marriage licenses.
- Physical examinations done in order to obtain insurance.
- Court-ordered medical exams.
- Examinations done at the request of an attorney so that an expert witness can testify at trial.

Autopsy results are not usually covered by the privilege. This is based on the idea that a patient must be a living person.

The physician-patient privilege belongs to the patient. If a doctor is on the witness stand and is asked about a privileged conversation, the doctor should assert the privilege on behalf of the patient. If the patient testifies in court that he/she waives the privilege, the doctor will answer the questions. The patient can claim the privilege even if the physician has died or the medical practice has been sold. The privilege also continues after the death of the patient.

Some states do not allow the physician-patient privilege to be used at all in criminal proceedings. In states where this broad approach is not used, doctors can usually be compelled to testify if they helped plan or conceal a crime. For example, plastic surgery used to help the suspect avoid arrest would not be privileged. Consultations regarding altering fingerprints would not be privileged.

Many states require doctors to report gunshot wounds, fetal deaths, venereal disease, abused children, and a variety of other things. The privilege cannot be used as a reason for not reporting when the law mandates the event be reported. Under these circumstances, the doctor can also be required to testify in court about the incident.

Two variations of the physician-patient privilege are common: psychotherapist-patient privilege and psychologist-patient privilege. Some states include psychiatrists in the physician-patient privilege because psychiatry is a specialty within the practice of medicine; others have created separate statutory privileges. The student should consult local law to determine how to proceed with cases involving therapists.

9-6 Clergy-Penitent Privilege

There was no **clergy-penitent privilege** at common law, but most states now allow it.

Clergy-Penitent Privilege Described

Clergy: Priest, minister, or religious practitioner.
Penitent: Person who consults clergy for spiritual advice.
What is covered: Confidential communications.
Who holds the privilege: Both clergy and penitent.
Exceptions common in criminal cases: Traditionally: None. Some states now require the clergy to report incidents of child abuse.

The concept originated from the confidentiality of the confessional and has been expanded to include confidential communications with members of the clergy of all denominations. The courts usually look to the doctrines of the individual denominations to determine who is authorized to hear such communications. Many states only recognize the privilege if the denomination imposes a duty on the clergy to keep these communications secret.

The communication must have been made in confidence for the purpose of obtaining spiritual guidance. It does not cover situations in which a member of the clergy plays a different role, such as a marriage counselor. It also does not apply to observations made in a non-confidential setting; for example, seeing bruises on a child while shaking hands after the religious service or at the church picnic.

The clergy-penitent privilege is unique in that both the clergy and the penitent have the right to refuse to reveal what was said. The reason for giving a separate privilege to the clergy is that they are bound by the rules of their denominations not to disclose penitential communications. Corresponding to this respect for religious duties of the clergy is that traditionally there have not been any exceptions to this privilege. The result is that neither the prosecutor nor the defense can compel a member of the clergy to testify regarding the defendant's penitential communication. Recently, a number of states have expanded their child-abuse reporting laws to mandate that members of the clergy report suspected child abuse. Therefore members of the clergy, like doctors and teachers, are now required to file reports if they have at least a reasonable suspicion that someone has abused a child.

Examples of Situations Covered by the Clergy-Penitent Privilege

• Man went to confession and told the priest that he had had an affair.
• Woman met with her pastor in his study. She told him she had taken money from the Sunday School offering plate and asked if God would forgive her if she gave it back.

Examples of Situations Not Covered by the Clergy-Penitent Privilege
- Priest who taught in a school operated by the church noticed bruises on the face of a student. When he asked what had happened, the student replied that his father hit him.
- A woman met her rabbi at a party and told him that she had a bad habit. She loved to shop and frequently shoplifted.

9-7 Privilege for Official Information

There was a common-law privilege for official government documents if their disclosure would be against the "public interest." It was generally recognized to cover military and diplomatic secrets. It was not well developed in civil cases due to the fact that a person could not sue the government without the government's permission.

Recent legislation, such as the federal Freedom of Information Act, has made it easier to obtain many government documents. This statute, and many of its state counterparts, requires disclosure of information in government files but restricts access to facts about ongoing investigations. In some states the identity of informants and locations where surveillance is being conducted are privileged. Legislation frequently makes personnel records of government employees privileged. Table 9-1 summarizes how privilege is applied to certain types of information.

T A B L E 9-1 Types of Information and How Privilege Is Applied

Type of Information	Application of Privilege
Freedom of Information Act (federal)	Allows access to information retained by federal government. Exceptions apply.
Identity of Informant	Police have privilege not to disclose identity of informants but judge can order disclosure if it is crucial to defense.
On-going Investigation	Police have right to refuse to disclose information about an ongoing investigation. Privilege ceases once investigation is finished.
Personnel Records	Personnel records of government employees are privileged. Judge can order disclosure of relevant information.

These privileges apply to all levels and branches of law enforcement. It includes both traditional police forces and the investigative branches of other agencies, such as consumer affairs and environmental protection.

The **police informant privilege** allows the police to withhold the names of their informants, i.e., people who supply the police with information, with the understanding that they will not be called as witnesses. The information supplied is frequently used to develop other evidence which constitutes probable cause for an arrest.

Privilege to Withhold Identity of Police Informant Described

Police: Applies to all law enforcement agencies.
Informant: Person who supplies information to police in confidence.
What is covered: Name and address of the informer.
Who holds the privilege: Law enforcement agency.
Exceptions: Identity of informant must be disclosed if it is important in the defendant's case.

The U.S. Supreme Court held that there is a constitutional right to obtain the identity of an informant if it is crucial to the defense. Circumstances that would trigger this exception would be that the informant was the only eyewitness to toxic waste dumping or that the informant actually participated in the sale of drugs. If the informant provided information to the police, but the police investigated the case and developed probable cause, there is no need to disclose the identity of the informant.

When this issue is raised by the defense, the judge will review the police files *in camera* (in chambers) with only the prosecutor and police present. The identity of the informant is given to the defense attorney only after the judge decides that there is a constitutional right to know this information. Even at this point, the police may refuse to disclose the identity of the informant but refusal may result in dismissal of the case. The police and the prosecutor make the final decision on disclosing the identity of the informant; the informant cannot force them to withhold the information. If the life of the informant is in danger, or if concealing the identity of the informant is vital to other cases, it may be necessary to let the case be dismissed.

The police cannot prevent an informant from disclosing his/her own identity. If an informant does this, the relationship is no longer confidential and the police cannot continue to conceal the information.

Examples of Privilege Not to Disclose Identity of Informant

- Mr. Jones called police and reported that the man who lived next door appeared to be dealing drugs. Police set up surveillance on the neighbor's house and an officer witnessed several drug deals. The police would not have to reveal the name of the informant because all crucial observations were made by the police.

- As the result of a plea bargain agreement, Mr. Smith agreed to assist police in a stolen property investigation. Smith went "undercover" and made several purchases from burglars. Only Smith and the burglars were present when the purchases were made. The police would have to reveal Smith's name because his identity, and the ability to attack his credibility at trial, are crucial to the defense's case.

Many states consider **police personnel files** privileged except when there is litigation between the employee and the law enforcement agency. Certain facts, such as the dates of employment, are not privileged. The contents of these files are usually irrelevant in a criminal case.

There are a few recurring situations in criminal cases where the contents of police personnel files are relevant. If the defense claims the officer is committing perjury, the fact that other people have complained to the police department that the officer is untruthful is relevant. In a case of assault and/or battery on a police officer, the defendant may claim that he/she only acted in self-defense. Prior allegations of police brutality against the officer will be relevant.

Privilege to Withhold Personnel Files Described

Personnel files: Permanent personnel records on an employee. Police personnel files include investigations of an officer conducted by internal affairs.
What is covered: Records concerning the performance of the officer and investigations of his/her conduct.
Who holds the privilege: Law enforcement agency.
Exceptions common in criminal cases: Must disclose information relevant to the defense.

The procedure in these cases is for the defense to file a discovery motion asking for the police files. If the police department refuses to give the files to the defense, a hearing will be conducted before the judge. The judge will review the files *in camera* and determine if there is anything in them that is relevant. If there is, the judge will order that the relevant portions of the file be given to the defense. The order may include: (1) dates and locations of alleged incidents; (2) names and addresses of victims; and (3) witnesses to these incidents. The opinions of internal affairs investigators are not given to the defense.

Many states have set limits on this type of disclosure. It is common to limit the period during which allegations of misconduct must be disclosed; a five-year limit is common. Discovery may also be denied if there is any non-confidential source for the same information.

Examples of Privilege for Police Personnel Files

- The defendant claims the officer has falsified the evidence so the defense attorney subpoenaed the officer's personnel file. The judge reviewed the personnel file at the *in camera* hearing and determined that the only complaint against the officer was by his ex-wife who stated he was not paying child support. The defense would *not* be allowed to see the personnel file.
- The defendant was charged with assault on a police officer but the defendant claims she was acting in self defense. The officer's personnel file was subpoenaed. The judge reviewed the personnel file at the *in camera* hearing and found two complaints of police brutality filed against the officer in the last 3 years. The defense *would* be entitled to a copy of these complaints but not other documents in the personnel file.

9-8 Media Reporter Privilege

The news media plays a very important role in our society. We rely on them to keep us informed of what is going on around us and to investigate the misdeeds of government. The importance of their role is reflected in the First Amendment's protection of freedom of the press. The news media have argued that the First Amendment gives them a privilege not to disclose their sources. This argument is based on the assumption that the press would be not be able to obtain sensitive information if the reporter could not guarantee that the identity of the informant would remain confidential.

Privilege for News Reporter Described

News reporter: Person employed by the media to investigate stories and report on them. Media includes print media as well as radio and television.
What is covered: Reporter's notes and identity of informants.
Who holds privilege: Reporter.
Exceptions common in criminal cases: Some states make an exception in the prosecution of serious crimes if it can be shown that there is no other source for the information requested.

There was no privilege for the press at common law. The U.S. Supreme Court held that the First Amendment does not mandate an absolute privilege. Since 1970, many states and the federal government have enacted statutes creating a **news media privilege.** While these laws are not identical, it is common to give reporters immunity from being cited for contempt of court if they refuse to tell the court or a grand jury the sources of information used in a story.

When there is a statute in this area, it usually gives a very broad definition of "reporter." Publishers, editors, and reporters for newspapers, magazines, and periodicals are usually covered, as are those working for wire services. Similar protections are given to those working for radio, television, and cable networks. It is not clear whether the privilege extends to freelancers who are not employed by the media at the time they investigate or write stories.

The privilege generally covers all information discovered by the reporter that has not been published. This includes the sources directly related to the published story. It also covers items used only for background by the reporter and information collected, but not included, in the published version of the story. Notes, photographs, tapes, and out-takes (material edited out) are usually covered.

The most common procedure is to allow the reporter to be subpoenaed and take the witness stand. The judge may hold an *in camera* hearing to determine if there is a right to invoke the privilege. A *subpoena duces tecum* (subpoena to produce documents in court) may also be used to attempt to obtain documents from a news agency.

Some states require a reporter to give the names of sources if there is no other way to obtain vital information for the prosecution of a serious crime. The prosecution would have the burden of convincing the judge that there is no other way to obtain the evidence and that the reporter has enough relevant information to warrant violation of the confidence placed in him/her. This would be done at an *in camera* hearing.

There is an apparent conflict between this statutory privilege and the fact that the Supreme Court has allowed the police to obtain search warrants for newsrooms and reporters' desks. See Chapter 10 for a detailed discussion of the warrant process.

Examples of Media Privilege
- Notes the reporter made while investigating the case. What was actually published is no longer privileged, but notes on portions of the story that were not published are privileged.
- Film clips taken by a TV news crew that were not shown on the air.
- Audio tapes a reporter made of an interview done while researching a story. The newspaper later decided not to run the story.

Summary

Privileges have been established to protect the need for confidential communications. Each legislature has decided which relationships should receive protection. Even when a privileged relationship exists, the communication will not be admissible unless the parties have attempted to keep the communications confidential. Voluntary disclosure defeats a privilege. The information will also be admissible if it falls under one of the exceptions to the privilege.

The attorney-client privilege protects confidential communications between an attorney and client. It covers discussions about crimes that have already occurred. This privilege, however, does not apply to conversations in which the client seeks advice on how to commit crimes or escape punishment.

Confidential communications between a husband and wife while they are married are privileged. Common exceptions cover situations where one spouse is charged with committing a crime against the other spouse or their children.

Many states also allow one spouse to refuse to testify against the other spouse. Some reverse this and allow one spouse to refuse to let the other spouse testify against him/her. The same exceptions usually apply to this privilege and the privilege for confidential communications between husbands and wives. Unmarried cohabitants are not covered.

The physician-patient relationship usually has a privilege similar to the attorney-client relationship. Confidential communications are privileged except when planning or concealing a crime. Some states do not allow this privilege to be used in criminal cases at all.

There is a privilege for people who seek spiritual guidance from their clergy. Both the penitent and the clergy hold the privilege and can refuse to disclose their conversations.

Some government records are privileged. Two were covered in this chapter: (1) identity of police informants and (2) police personnel files. The defendant has a constitutional right to know the identity of a police informant if the information this person provided is crucial to the defense. Police personnel files are privileged except when they contain information relevant to the case. The defense cannot obtain facts to be used in general character assassination of the police officer, but previous accusations that the officer committed perjury can be discovered; earlier allegations of police brutality are discoverable if relevant to the current case (e.g., the defendant is charged with assault on a police officer and claims he/she was acting in self defense).

Although there is no constitutional or common-law privilege for the news media, many states have enacted statutory privileges for the media. These laws usually take the form of giving the media immunity from citation for contempt when they refuse to identify the sources of information for a story. Some states make an exception if there is no other way to obtain information about a serious crime.

Discussion Questions

1. Define the attorney-client privilege, and list its exceptions.
2. Define the privilege for confidential communications between husband and wife, and list three exceptions.
3. Define the privilege of one spouse not to testify against the other, and give three exceptions.
4. Define the physician-patient privilege. Explain the common exceptions.
5. Define the clergy-penitent privilege, and explain the exceptions, if any.
6. When may the police keep the name of an informant secret?
7. Explain the procedure the defense would use to obtain the name of a police informant.
8. Identify two situations where police personnel files would be relevant to a criminal case. Explain how a defendant can obtain the files.
9. Do the media have a First Amendment privilege to protect their sources? Explain.
10. Define the statutory privilege for the media to withhold the identity of their sources. Explain the procedure used to invoke the privilege.

CHAPTER **10**

Developing Law of Search and Seizure

Outline

Key Terms

- Affidavit
- Anonymous informant
- Confidential informant
- Exclusionary Rule
- Execution of a warrant
- Fruit of the Poison Tree Doctrine
- Good Faith Exception
- Independent Source Exception
- Inevitable Discovery Exception
- Knock-and-announce procedure
- Probable cause
- Protective sweep
- Public Safety Exception
- Return (of search warrant)
- Substantial compliance
- Valid on its face

After studying this chapter, you will be able to:

- Describe the history of the Fourth Amendment.
- List what acts of law enforcement are considered to be "searches" and "seizures."
- Define *probable cause* and how it is used in arrest and search situations.
- Define the legal meaning of the term *standing*.
- Identify what information is needed to obtain a search warrant and explain how a search warrant is executed.
- Define the Exclusionary Rule and its effect on evidence.
- Identify the Fruit of the Poison Tree Doctrine, its exceptions, and application.
- Define the independent source rule.
- Identify those court proceedings where the Exclusionary Rule is not used.
- Explain the constitutional limits placed on the use of physical force to obtain evidence.

10-1 History and Development of the Fourth Amendment

The principle that "a man's home is his castle" existed in England long before the colonies were settled in America. The English Bill of Rights was enacted by Parliament in 1689 and gave even the poorest peasant the right to exclude the King from his home. Yet, in Colonial America the British freely used the "general warrant" which gave unlimited rights for soldiers to search homes for whatever evidence they might find.

Many of the original states expressed their disapproval of the "general warrant" by including a prohibition against unreasonable searches and seizures in their constitutions. When the U.S. Constitution was ratified it did not contain any mention of searches and seizures or any of the other protections now in our Bill of Rights. Many of the states that ratified the Constitution insisted that additional protections against the power of the federal government be included. The first 10 amendments to the Constitution, known collectively as the Bill of Rights, were added in 1791, only four years after the Constitution was ratified. Their wording has not been changed since.

Fourth Amendment

The right of the people to be secure in their persons, houses, papers and effects, against unreasonable searches and seizures, shall not be violated, and no Warrants shall issue, but upon probable cause, supported by Oath or affirmation, and particularly describing the place to be searched, and the persons or things to be seized.

There are three broad concepts in this amendment:

1. Protection is provided for the person, home, and belongings.
2. Unreasonable searches and seizures are prohibited.
3. Warrants must be based on probable cause and specifically describe what is to be seized.

These concepts will be explained in detail in the remainder of this chapter and in Chapters 11–13.

10-2 Definitions

Prior to considering what police conduct violates the Fourth Amendment, four basic definitions must be discussed: (1) search; (2) seizure; (3) probable cause; and (4) standing.

Search Defined
An examination of a person, his/her house, personal property, or other locations when conducted by a law enforcement officer for the purpose of finding evidence of a crime.

A search involves the act of looking for something that otherwise would not be seen. If something is left out where the police can see it, there is no search. Even if there is a search, it may not violate the Fourth Amendment. Only unreasonable searches are prohibited. The Supreme Court has spent a great deal of time deciding what is "reasonable" and what is not.

Examples of Searches
- Police officer has suspect empty his/her pockets and carefully examines each item.
- Police officer sees a suspicious car parked behind a store late at night. The officer opens the unlocked door and looks for stolen merchandise.
- Police officer goes to a farm and looks in a field for marijuana plants.

Police "seize" evidence when they take it into their possession. When a person is seized, it is called an arrest. Even when there is no search (for example, something was left out in the open where the police could see it), officers still must have the legal right to seize it. If police observe something inside a house by looking through a window, they still may not have the right to enter the house to seize it without a search warrant.

Seizure Defined
The act of taking possession of a person or property.

Examples of Seizures
- Police stop a man carrying an object that appears to be a gun. They immediately seize the object.
- When the suspect is booked into the city jail, officers remove all personal belongings in the suspect's possession.
- Officers go to a bank and obtain a copy of the suspect's checking account records.

In criminal cases, **probable cause** is required in three key situations:

1. Probable cause that a crime was committed.

2. Probable cause that the suspect is the person who committed the crime.

3. Probable cause that seizable evidence is at a specific location.

Probable Cause Defined
A reasonable belief that a person has committed or is committing a crime or that a place contains specific items connected with a crime. Under the Fourth Amendment, probable cause must be shown before an arrest warrant or search warrant may be issued.

The Fourth Amendment specifically refers to issuing warrants based on probable cause. Probable cause is also important in many police activities conducted without warrants.

Examples of Probable Cause
- Police arrive at scene and witness the suspect hitting another person with a baseball bat.
- Woman calls 911. When the police arrive at her house, they observe that the woman has red marks on her face indicating she has recently been hit. The woman tells the officers that her husband hit her six times with his open hand.

"Standing" refers to the right to ask the court to take legal action. Only a person with standing can activate the Exclusionary Rule by asking the judge to rule that evidence cannot be used at trial because it was illegally seized. After many years of struggling with the concept, the U.S. Supreme Court adopted "reasonable expectation of privacy" as a guide and no longer uses the term "standing." A person can only ask to have evidence excluded due to a violation of the Fourth Amendment if it can be shown that his/her privacy was violated by the police. The results of having standing and having a reasonable expectation of privacy that was violated are frequently the same.

Standing Defined
Standing is a party's right to make a legal claim or seek judicial enforcement of a duty or right.

Some examples illustrate this approach. If a person's house is searched unconstitutionally, the resident's reasonable expectation of privacy has been violated; he/she can have the evidence suppressed. An overnight guest who was present when the house was searched also has had his/her expectation of privacy violated if his/her personal belongings were searched. If a friend left something in the same house, but was not present when the illegal search was conducted, the friend's reasonable expectation of privacy was not violated. The friend could not successfully ask the court to suppress the evidence, even though the police had conducted the search illegally. The Supreme Court refused to extend the rule to people who stop briefly at a home or apartment for business purposes; the business visitor cannot have the illegally seized evidence suppressed.

Rights under the Fifth Amendment are also personal. Only the person who made the confession can successfully make a motion to suppress it. If the confession implicated someone else in the crime, the person who was implicated would not have the right to have the confession suppressed even though *Miranda* had been violated.

Examples of the Right to Have Evidence Suppressed
- Suspect was stopped by the police and his car was searched. The suspect has standing to ask the court to suppress the evidence if it was found illegally.
- At a party, the man gave a woman a small bag containing illegal drugs and asked her to put it in her purse. The police raided the party and found the drugs. The man does not have standing to ask the judge to suppress the drugs at his trial because they were not in his possession. The woman would have standing to ask the judge to suppress the drugs at her trial because they were in her possession. Once the motion was considered, the judge would rule on whether or not the Fourth Amendment had been violated by the police when they raided the party.

10-3 Warrant Requirements

The Fourth Amendment specifically states that: (1) no warrant shall be issued unless there is probable cause; (2) probable cause must be established under oath or affirmation; and (3) the warrant must particularly describe the place to be searched and the person or things to be seized. It does not say that all searches must be authorized by warrants.

The Supreme Court has decided many cases addressing the issue of whether or not warrants are required. It has stated a preference for warrants; but it has also recognized that there are situations when officers do not have to obtain them. Search warrants may be issued to search nearly any location including residences, newsrooms, and doctors' and lawyers' offices.

In non-criminal situations, such as inspections to determine if buildings conform to electrical codes, search warrants are also required if no one will consent to the inspection. For these "administrative warrants," probable cause is satisfied if there is a reasonable legislative purpose for the inspection.

The basic principle is that warrants are mandatory except when the facts fit within one of the exceptions to the warrant requirement. This chapter deals with the procedures used to obtain warrants. The numerous exceptions authorized by the Supreme Court are dealt with in Chapters 11 and 12.

10-3a Information Needed to Obtain a Warrant

The warrant process was created to allow a neutral magistrate to review the facts and decide if the police should be authorized to conduct a search or make an arrest. To do this, the magistrate must have the facts of the case. The Fourth Amendment requires that these facts be taken under oath or affirmation. The written document used for this purpose is called an **affidavit.**

Prior to the 1960s, some judges relied on the officer's decision that there was probable cause. For example, the affidavit might read, "This officer has received information from a reliable informant which causes him/her to conclude that there is probable cause to search the house located at 123 N. Main St., Hometown, for stolen property." In 1964, the Supreme Court ruled that this was not acceptable.[1] It held that a warrant is only valid if the judge determined that probable cause existed. To do this, the judge must personally review the facts.

Search Warrants. Facts given in an affidavit are usually very detailed and must convince the judge that there is evidence that the officers have a

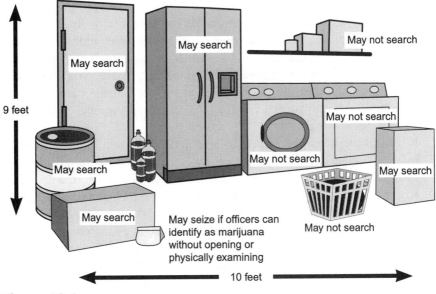

9 feet

May search

May search

May search

May search

May search

May search

May not search

May not search

May not search

May not search

May seize if officers can identify as marijuana without opening or physically examining

10 feet

Figure 10-1
Execution of a Search Warrant
The search warrant stated officers may search this garage for an assault rifle and a 55-gallon drum of methamphetamine pills.

legal right to seize. The warrant may be for the seizure of illegal drugs or other contraband, fruits of the crime, items used to commit the crime, or other items that can be used in the case. The facts need to provide detailed information about the crime involved, as well as an explanation of why the officers want to seize the items in question.

In addition to showing what is to be seized, the affidavit must give facts that show where the items to be seized are located. The description of the location to be searched must be as exact as possible. Since the reason for requiring search warrants is to protect people's privacy, the warrant should be worded so that the police are restricted to as small an area as possible. Figure 10-1 shows what can and cannot be searched with a warrant that authorizes the search of a garage for an assault rifle and a 55-gallon drum of methamphetamine pills. The officers may open refrigerator, for example, because it would be possible to conceal the assault rifle there; the washer and dryer may not be opened because they are too small to hide the rifle. Since the search warrant mentioned a 55-gallon drum, and not small quantities of pills, cupboards and boxes too small to conceal this large drum or the assault rifle cannot be searched.

Street addresses are usually given, but the location should be described even more precisely, if possible. For example, "the living room of the house at 456 S. Grand Ave.," or "the garage of the house at 789 W. First St." Case law generally upholds warrants that include a correct verbal description of the location even when the street address is wrong. Examples would include "the blue house on the corner of Market and Third," even though it turned out that 301 N. Market was the wrong address; or "the third floor apartment at the head of the stairs at 321 S. Broadway," when it turned out that the apartment number given in the warrant was wrong.

A problem unique to search warrants is the requirement that the information be fresh. If the facts are stale, they may not be a reliable indicator of where the items to be seized are currently located. In a drug case where the dealer is known to do a high volume of business and change locations frequently, information two or three days old may be stale. If the case involves the use of stolen building materials at a construction site, the information is not likely to become stale if the stolen property is being incorporated into a building. It is important for the police to have current information to avoid rejection of the affidavit due to staleness.

Example of Facts the U.S. Supreme Court Ruled Were Sufficient to Establish Probable Cause to Obtain a Search Warrant

The badly burned body of Sandra Boulware was discovered in a vacant lot in the Roxbury section of Boston at approximately 5 A.M., Saturday, May 5. An autopsy revealed that Boulware had died of multiple compound skull fractures caused by blows to the head. After a brief investigation, the police decided to question one of the victim's boyfriends, Osborne Sheppard. Sheppard told the police that he had last seen the victim on Tuesday night and that he had been at a local gaming house (where card games were played) from 9 P.M. Friday until 5 A.M. Saturday. He identified several people who would be willing to substantiate the latter claim.

By interviewing the people Sheppard had said were at the gaming house on Friday night, the police learned that although Sheppard was at the gaming house that night, he had borrowed an automobile at about 3 A.M. Saturday morning in order to give two men a ride home. Even though the trip normally took only 15 minutes, Sheppard did not return with the car until nearly 5 A.M.

On Sunday morning, police officers visited the owner of the car Sheppard had borrowed. He consented to an inspection of the vehicle. Bloodstains and pieces of hair were found on the rear bumper and within the trunk compartment. In addition, the officers noticed strands of wire in the trunk similar to wire strands found on and near the body of the victim. The owner of the car told the officers that when he last used the car on Friday night, shortly before Sheppard borrowed it, he had placed articles in the trunk and had not noticed any stains on the bumper or in the trunk.

Note: These facts were held sufficient to issue a search warrant for Sheppard's residence for the victim's clothing, rope and/or wire matching samples found on the body, a blunt instrument used to kill the victim, and blood-stained clothing.

Massachusetts v. Sheppard 468 U.S. 981 (1984).

Example of Facts the U.S. Supreme Court Ruled Were Not Sufficient to Establish Probable Cause to Obtain a Search Warrant

In August 1981, a confidential informant of unproved reliability informed an officer of the Burbank Police Department that two persons known to him as "Armando" and "Patsy" were selling large quantities of cocaine and methaqualone from their residence at 920 Price Drive in Burbank, California. The informant also indicated that he had witnessed a sale of methaqualone by "Patsy" at the residence approximately five months earlier and had observed at the time a shoebox containing a large amount of cash that belonged to "Patsy." He further declared that "Armando" and "Patsy" generally kept only small quantities of drugs at their residence and stored the remainder at another location in Burbank.

On the basis of this information, the Burbank police initiated an extensive investigation focusing first on the Price Drive residence and later on two other residences as well. Cars parked at the Price Drive residence were determined to belong to Armando Sanchez, who was had previously been arrested for possession of marijuana, and Patsy Stewart, who had no criminal record. During the course of the investigation, officers observed an automobile belonging to Ricardo Del Castillo, who had previously been arrested for possession of 50 pounds of marijuana, arrive at the Price Drive residence. The driver of the car entered the house, exited shortly thereafter carrying a small paper sack, and drove away. A check of Del Castillo's probation records led the officers to Alberto Leon, whose telephone number Del Castillo had listed as his employer's. Leon had been arrested in 1980 on drug charges, and a companion had informed the police at that time that Leon was heavily involved in the importation of drugs into this country. Before the current investigation began, the Burbank officers had learned that an informant had told a Glendale police officer that Leon stored a large quantity of methaqualone at his residence in Glendale. During the course of the investigation, Burbank officers learned that Leon was living at 716 South Sunset Canyon in Burbank.

Subsequently, the officers observed several persons, at least one of whom had prior drug involvement, arrive at the Price Drive residence and leave with small packages; observed a variety of other material activity at the two residences as well as at a condominium at 7901 Via Magdelena; and witnessed a variety of relevant activity involving respondents' automobiles. The officers also observed Sanchez and Stewart board separate flights for Miami. The pair later returned to

Los Angeles together, consented to a search of their luggage that revealed only a small amount of marijuana, and left the airport.

Note: This warrant application was found insufficient because the facts used to corroborate the reliability of the informant were either stale or only related to innocent activity.

United States v. Leon 468 U. S. 897 (1984)

Arrest Warrants. For an arrest warrant, facts must be given to establish every element of each crime listed in the warrant. Additional information must be included to show that the person named is the one who committed the crime(s). The physical description of the person to be arrested, along with his/her birth date (if available) or approximate age, is usually required so the officers making the arrest can verify that they have the correct person. It is possible to obtain an arrest warrant even if the name of the suspect is not known if a detailed description, usually including an alias or street name, is given.

Example of Facts That Establish Probable Cause for an Arrest Warrant

While on routine patrol on the evening of December 10, 2003, the undersigned officer observed a person in the alley behind 123 North Park Ave., Hometown. Said individual had an object in his hand that appeared to be a tire iron. The individual was using the object to pry open a garage door. The undersigned officer ordered the individual to halt. Rather than complying with the command, the individual ran and the officer was unable to apprehend him. A tire iron was recovered at the scene.

Latent fingerprints were recovered from the tire iron by Officer Fred Smith. Based on a comparison made by Officer Sam Green, fingerprints recovered from the tire iron match fingerprints in the files of this department that were taken from John Q. Doe when he was booked on May 2, 2002.

For the reasons stated above, an arrest warrant is requested for John Q. Doe for the offense of attempted burglary, Penal Code Section 459, at 123 North Park Ave, Hometown, on December 10, 2003.

Reliability of Facts in Affidavit. Due to the fact that the affidavit is usually reviewed by a judge without a chance to question the person providing the information, the affidavit must also convince the judge that the facts are reliable. If the officer making the affidavit observed the facts firsthand, the fact that the affidavit is made under oath is sufficient to establish reliability. Information provided by crime victims and eyewitnesses is usually assumed to be reliable unless there is a motive to falsify.

Informants who are themselves criminals create the biggest problem. Due to their past convictions, or a bad motive for incriminating someone else, they lack credibility. In *Spinelli v. United States* the Supreme Court established a rule that required applications for warrants to establish probable cause for the action sought (search or arrest) and separate probable cause that the informant is credible.[2] Some states still follow this rule while others have adopted the more lenient standard established in *Illinois v. Gates* (see below).

When a warrant is sought in a state that follows the *Spinelli* standard, facts stated in the affidavit must establish the reliability of the informant. The most common method used to do this is to give specific examples of useful information that the informant has given the officers in the past. If, in previous cases, officers checked out the facts supplied by the informant and found they were correct, the informant's reliability in the current case is enhanced. Another method is to verify the information provided in the present case. When reliability is established by verifying facts, the Supreme Court insisted in *Spinelli* that the facts that were checked showed criminal activity. Merely verifying innocent facts, such as addresses and telephone numbers, is not enough.

In 1983, in *Illinois v. Gates*, the Supreme Court ruled that anonymous tips could be used to obtain search warrants.[3] The Court relaxed the older rule which required that facts supporting the informant's reliability be given in the affidavit. In states that follow this rule, it is possible to support the reliability of the information by showing that the facts given are so detailed that they must be true. When an anonymous informant is used, it is especially important that as many facts as possible be given in the affidavit. Even so, the police must verify as much of the information as possible prior to seeking a warrant.

A distinction must be made between confidential informants and anonymous ones. **Confidential informants** give police information on the condition that their names will not be revealed. This information can be used in a warrant without giving the name of the person who provided it. At a later time the defendant may request the name of the informant, but the judge will only require the police to disclose it if the identity of the informant is crucial to the case (*McCray v. Illinois*).[4]

People whose identities are unknown, referred to as **anonymous informants,** frequently provide information for the police. They may call a hotline, such as "We Tip," and leave a message on an answering machine, or they may talk directly to an officer without identifying themselves. It would be impossible for the police to give the names of these people to the defense. It is also impossible, of course, to establish their prior reliability.

10-3b Procedure to Obtain a Warrant

The Fourth Amendment merely requires that a warrant be issued by a neutral magistrate. In most policing agencies, however, the case is reviewed by the officer's supervisor prior to seeking a warrant. Additionally, the prosecutor usually reviews the file to determine if a warrant should be sought. The prosecutor usually prepares the proper forms and may help police draft the required affidavits.

The completed warrant application is presented to a judge or magistrate who must be neutral and not part of any law enforcement agency. Many years ago, some states authorized high-ranking police officials and members of their attorney's general staff to issue warrants. This procedure was specifically disapproved in *Coolidge v. New Hampshire* because all personnel in law enforcement agencies are considered to have a vested interest in apprehending criminals.[5] The Supreme Court considered this interest to be a potential conflict of interests that could interfere with an objective review of the facts in the affidavit.

If there is more than one judge in the jurisdiction, each judge has equal power to issue a warrant. While there is no requirement that a warrant be issued by a judge who is assigned to criminal trials, judges who are not assigned to the criminal calendar usually defer to those who are.

Once a request for a warrant has been rejected by a judge, it may not be taken to another judge in hopes of obtaining a more favorable decision. However, new affidavits containing more facts can be drafted and the process started again. This may require more work for the police in order to develop additional information, or it might merely mean that a careful review of the file shows that the original affidavit left out some key facts.

Most states restrict the authority to issue warrants to the geographical area where the court has jurisdiction. Search warrants may be authorized for locations within the court's jurisdiction. Arrest warrants may only be issued for crimes that occurred within the jurisdiction.

Many states require that search warrants be executed in the daytime (typically defined as 6 A.M. to 10 P.M.) unless the judge specifically indicates they may be served at night. Arrest warrants for misdemeanors commonly cannot be served at night unless the suspect is in a public place. There are usually no similar restrictions on felony warrants.

Search warrants must be served within a few days after they are issued. State laws vary, but search warrants usually expire within 10 days. The reason for this short time period is the same as the policy which rejects affidavits containing stale information. The only reason to invade a person's privacy is to obtain evidence that can lawfully be seized by the police. If there is too much delay, there is no longer any reason to believe that the evidence is at the location.

Arrest warrants must be obtained before the statute of limitations expires on the crime in question. State laws establish how long an arrest warrant is valid. Misdemeanor warrants frequently do not expire for at least one year; most felony warrants are valid for three years or more, depending on the charge, while warrants for murder and a few other crimes may be valid indefinitely. The reason for enforcing old arrest warrants, but not search warrants, is that the passage of time usually does not change the probable cause that the suspect committed the crime.

10-3c Execution of Warrants

A warrant directs a peace officer to take specific action (i.e., search or make an arrest). The act of doing this is called the **execution of a warrant.** If necessary, a police officer may take civilians along when executing the warrant; for example, if the warrant authorizes a search for jewelry stolen during a residential burglary, the owner of the jewelry may go along to help identify the items in question. On the other hand, taking the news media along when officers enter a private home violates the privacy of the residents.

The officer executing the warrant is responsible for verifying that the warrant is **valid on its face.** This means that the warrant looks like it was legally issued, and it has not expired. The officer is not liable in a subsequent civil case if a judge issued a warrant without probable cause *unless* the officer knew there was a problem with the warrant. For example, in *Groh v. Ramieriz* (2004), an officer prepared an affidavit that supplied probable cause for a search warrant but the warrant did not indicate the location to be searched or the items to be seized; the court found that this warrant was not valid on its face and the officer was not entitled to immunity when sued for violating the suspect's Fourth Amendment rights.[6]

Even with a warrant, officers are expected to respect people's privacy. This results in three requirements: (1) searches must be restricted to the area described in the warrant; (2) absent an emergency or consent of the occupants, homes may only be entered with a warrant; and (3) prior to entering a home, officers must comply with knock-and-announce procedures.

The Fourth Amendment specifically requires that search warrants "particularly describe" the location to be searched and the items to be seized. When executing the warrant, officers must restrict their movement to locations where they are reasonably likely to find the things specified in the search warrant. If a large item, such as a 25-inch color television, is to be seized, officers may not look in drawers or other places that are obviously too small to conceal such an item.

If the warrant mentions the location of the evidence, such as the kitchen, officers may not search other rooms. While the courts have been quite strict in interpreting these requirements, they have also given officers the right to seize other evidence they find while legally conducting a search. For example, if drugs are found in plain view while officers are looking for the stolen television, the drugs can be seized and appropriate charges filed. This will be discussed in more detail in Chapter 12.

The ancient "home is one's castle" doctrine has been interpreted in *Payton v. New York* to mean that a person can prevent police from entering his/her home unless the officer(s) have a warrant or there is an emergency.[7] An arrest warrant is needed to enter the suspect's home in order to arrest him/her; if the suspect is hiding in someone else's home, a search warrant is needed to enter that dwelling. Emergencies that would permit entry without a warrant include hot pursuit of someone who just entered the house or someone inside the house calling for help.

Mincey v. Arizona held that there is no automatic right to enter a dwelling even if it is the scene of a murder or other serious crime.[8] The officers are justified in entering if there is a possibility that there are injured people inside who need assistance. Once it is determined that no further emergency aid is needed, the officers must either obtain consent from someone who lives in the dwelling or secure a search warrant.

Prior to entering a house, officers must comply with the knock-and-announce procedure unless special situations exist.[9] This rule applies to the service of warrants as well as actions done while investigating crimes and making warrantless arrests. The procedure is only required for residential buildings.

The proper **knock-and-announce procedure** requires three basic actions: (1) police must knock or otherwise announce that they are there; (2) they must identify their official capacity (e.g., "Police."); and (3) announce why they are there (e.g., "We have a warrant for your arrest."). Once these steps have been complied with, officers must wait long enough to allow a cooperative person to open the door. The length of the wait will vary, of course, with the circumstances. If no one responds, officers may resort to forced entry if necessary.

Two types of situations permit officers to enter without complying with the full knock-and-announce procedure. If there are explicit facts that indicate that the officer's life may be in danger, immediate entry may be allowed. Following an armed suspect to the house would be an example of this type of emergency. Similar exceptions are allowed if taking the time to comply is very likely to result in the destruction of evidence or the escape of a suspect. To qualify for total avoidance of "knock and announce," the facts must clearly indicate that there is an immediate danger. Mere suspicion or the fact that criminals usually destroy the evidence is not enough. In *Richards v. Wisconsin* (1997)[10] the Supreme Court refused to allow judges to automatically waive knock-and-announce procedures when issuing search warrants in drug cases.

Substantial compliance is permitted if the facts that develop while officers are giving the appropriate announcements indicate that there is danger. This follows the same basic situations mentioned in the previous paragraph: (1) danger to the police; (2) destruction of evidence; or (3) escape of a suspect. "Substantial compliance" is only authorized if the officers, in good faith, have attempted to comply with the law, and while they are doing this, the suspect does something to indicate that further delay would jeopardize the case. Common examples are hearing someone running away from the door while the officers are announcing their presence, or the sound of toilets flushing when the officers are attempting to serve a search warrant in a drug case. In this type of situation, the Supreme Court indicated that the crucial question is how long it would take the suspect to destroy the evidence, not how long it would take a cooperative person to come to the door.[11]

Officers may conduct a **protective sweep** in order to prevent attacks on them when they execute a search warrant (*Maryland v. Buie*).[12] When executing a search warrant in a house, they may quickly look in adjoining areas to make sure no one is hiding there. To go to more distant parts of the building, the officers must have reasonable suspicion that someone might ambush them. A protective sweep does not allow officers to look in drawers or other areas too small to conceal a person. The Plain View Doctrine does, however, apply to things found when checking appropriate places.

Lastly, officers must file a "**return**" on the search warrant. The return is a document, sometimes printed on the back of the search warrant, which tells the court what actions were taken. The time and date the warrant was served are listed. If anything was seized, an inventory of all items taken is included in the return. A copy of the warrant and the return are given to the person whose premises were searched. If no one was there at the time of the search, the copies are left at the scene in a conspicuous place. If no one executed the search warrant, this fact is indicated on the return. After the officers complete the "return" it is filed with the court and becomes a part of the official record of the case.

10-4 Exclusionary Rule

Although the U.S. Supreme Court has had the power to interpret the Constitution and the Bill of Rights since its inception, few cases were decided prior to 1914 that dealt with the Fourth Amendment. *Weeks v. United States,*[13] decided that year, declared that evidence obtained by federal agents in violation of the Fourth Amendment could not be used in federal court. The rule, however, did not apply to state and local police. In fact, the rule was so narrow that the so-called "Silver Platter Doctrine" emerged. This doctrine, which lasted until 1960, allowed evidence obtained unconstitutionally by local law enforcement officers to be used in federal court.

In 1949, the U.S. Supreme Court declared that the Fourth Amendment was binding on state and local law enforcement officers. At the same time, however, it refused to rule that evidence illegally obtained under the Fourth Amendment had to be excluded from trials in state courts.

10-4a Exclusionary Rule and the Fruit of the Poison Tree Doctrine

Mapp v. Ohio,[14] decided in 1961, finally made the **Exclusionary Rule** binding on state courts. While *Mapp* made unconstitutionally obtained evidence inadmissible, it did not provide guidelines to help the police determine when the Fourth Amendment had been violated. The Court issued many decisions in the years following *Mapp* in an effort to clarify the application of the Fourth Amendment.

Over the years the Supreme Court has followed two key rationales in applying the Exclusionary Rule: (1) deterrence of unconstitutional police conduct and (2) judicial integrity. The deterrence rationale excludes evidence based on the belief that police officers will be more careful if they know their errors may mean they cannot convict the criminal. The reverse of this has also been seen: if the Court believes that application of the rule would have little deterrent value in a specific situation, the Court allows the evidence to be used even though it was obtained in violation of the Fourth Amendment.

The judicial integrity approach excludes evidence because the courts should not be tainted by unconstitutional acts of the police. If this were the only basis for excluding evidence, the effect of the court action on future police conduct would not be considered. Very few cases have made judicial integrity the sole basis for their decision. In the 1970s, some Supreme Court cases did not even mention it. Recent cases usually mention judicial integrity, but the dominant rationale is deterrence.

The Supreme Court's language in *Mapp* indicated that illegally seized evidence is totally inadmissible in court. Two years later in *Wong Sun v. United States*,[15] the Court went even further and declared that evidence derived from illegally obtained evidence was also inadmissible. This is called the **Fruit of the Poison Tree Doctrine.**

Example 1: If a briefcase was seized during an unconstitutional search, the briefcase and its contents would be inadmissible under the Exclusionary Rule. While searching the contents of the briefcase, the police found a key for a storage locker. They located the storage locker which contained stolen televisions, but the stolen televisions would be inadmissible under the Fruit of the Poison Tree Doctrine.

Exclusionary Rule	Fruit of the Poison Tree
Illegally seized briefcase and its contents	Stolen televisions would be inadmissible

Example 2: If there was an illegal arrest, in which case all items found during the search immediately following the arrest would be inadmissible under the Exclusionary Rule. If the person arrested was immediately given *Miranda* warnings and a confession obtained, the confession is usually inadmissible as "fruit of the poison tree."

Exclusionary Rule	Fruit of the Poison Tree
Search incident to an illegal arrest	Statements made during interrogation conducted immediately after the illegal arrest are inadmissible even though *Miranda* was given correctly.

At some point the taint of the original unconstitutional act evaporates. Various factors have caused this result: passage of time; exercise of free will by a person giving the police information; the fact a person has been released from police custody; a lengthy chain of events, etc. No one event automatically stops the Fruit of the Poison Tree doctrine. The courts analyze all of the facts.

Example 3: In the *Wong Sun* case mentioned earlier provides a good example. Narcotics agents had a tip from Hom Way that Blackie Toy was selling heroin. They illegally entered Blackie Toy's living quarters and interrogated him. Mr. Toy indicated that Johnny Yee sold drugs and kept heroin in his bedroom. Mr. Yee was arrested and surrendered nearly an ounce of heroin to the agents. He told officers that his supplier was Wong

Sun. When Wong Sun was arrested the officers who searched his apartment did not find any narcotics. Toy, Yee, and Wong Sun were arraigned on narcotics charges and released. A few days later Wong Sun was advised of his rights, including the right to have an attorney present, at the agents' office. He made damaging admissions that were used at his trial.

Exclusionary Rule	Fruit of the Poison Tree
Illegal entry into Toy's living quarters Entry was held to be illegal because Hom Way was not a reliable informant	**Inadmissible** • Statements made by Toy • Arrest of Yee • Heroin Yee gave to agents at time of his arrest • Arrest of Wong Sun **Admissible** because taint of original illegal actions had dissipated: • Statements made by Toy, Yee, and Wong Sun when interrogated while released from custody on their own recognizance *after* arraignment.

Despite the broad language in *Mapp* and *Wong Sun,* there are many situations in which unconstitutionally seized evidence is admitted in court.

10-4b Good Faith Exception

In 1984, the Supreme Court recognized a **Good Faith Exception** to the Exclusionary Rule *(United States v. Leon; Massachusetts v. Sheppard).*[16] Officers must be acting under an objective belief that what they are doing is constitutional. They must stay up to date on the law of searches, seizures and confessions. The facts must be such that a reasonable officer could have made an honest mistake. If the officer has an ulterior motive, this exception does not apply.

But acting in good faith is not enough. The rule only applies in a few distinct situations. It has been applied to actions done under search warrants that appeared to be valid on their face. An arrest made under a statute that appeared valid but was later ruled unconstitutional by the courts was also upheld. An arrest based on a check of computerized files that indicated there was an outstanding warrant for the suspect was held to fall under the Good Faith Exception even though it was later determined that the warrant had been recalled before the arrest was made. Table 10-1 summarizes the good faith exceptions.

T A B L E   **10-1** **Good Faith Exceptions
to the Exclusionary Rule**

Exclusionary Rule	Good Faith Exception to the Exclusionary Rule
Search warrant was obtained based on an affidavit that did not contain enough facts to establish probable cause.	Evidence seized in plain view while executing the warrant will be admissible if the warrant appeared to be valid and the officers executing the warrant did not know there was a problem with the warrant.
Arrest made based on a statute that the arresting officer believed to be valid.	Evidence found during the search incident to the arrest will be admissible if the officer in good faith relied on the statute even though the statute was declared unconstitutional after the arrest was made.
Arrest made based on information the officers received from the dispatcher indicating that there was an outstanding arrest warrant for the suspect. This information was erroneous; the warrant had previously been recalled.	Evidence found during the search incident to the arrest will be admissible if the officers in good faith relied on the information in a database maintained by the courts which stated that there was an outstanding warrant for the suspect.

10-4c Inevitable Discovery

The **Inevitable Discovery Exception** to the Exclusionary Rule is based on the idea that the police would have found the evidence even if they had not used unconstitutional procedures. In *Nix v. Williams*,[17] the case which the Supreme Court used to establish the rule, the fact that hundreds of volunteers were searching for a murdered child was used to show that the discovery of the body was inevitable. The fact that improper interrogation procedures were used to induce the suspect to tell police where the body was located did not make the body inadmissible because the police would have discovered it anyway. Each case will, of course, turn on its unique facts. The prosecution must bear the burden of convincing the judge that the evidence would have been found by legal methods.

Example: Inevitable Discovery

Exclusionary Rule	Inevitable Discovery Exception to the Exclusionary Rule
Illegally obtained statement by Williams that told officers where the body of the victim was located.	The body of the victim, and any evidence discovered on it, was admissible because there were hundreds of people searching for the victim and it was inevitable that it would have been found legally.

10-4d Independent Source

To admit evidence under the **Independent Source Exception,** the prosecution must be able to convince the judge that the police discovered the evidence without relying on unconstitutional procedures. In *Segura v. United States*,[18] evidence had been illegally seized when the police entered the suspect's apartment immediately after arresting him. Later, the police obtained a search warrant based on legally obtained information, authorizing the search of the same apartment. Evidence not observed during the first search was seized. The Supreme Court found that the search warrant provided an independent source for the evidence seized during the second search. This would not have been so if the illegally seized evidence had been used to obtain the warrant.

Example: Independent Source

Exclusionary Rule	Independent Source Exception to the Exclusionary Rule
Evidence observed in apartment immediately after illegal arrest of occupant is inadmissible.	Officers legally obtained a search warrant based on facts that were independent of the search incident to the illegal arrest. When executing this search warrant in the apartment, they found the same evidence the other officers had observed but not seized.

The Independent Source Exception was also applied in *Murray v. United States*.[19] Federal agents illegally entered Murray's warehouse and observed numerous bales of marijuana. They did not seize anything at that time. Instead, they obtained a search warrant based on legally obtained information. When executing the search warrant, the marijuana they had previously seen was seized. The Court affirmed the admission of the marijuana at trial.

As the Court pointed out in *Murray,* the ultimate question is whether the facts in the affidavit and the execution of the search warrant are genuinely independent of the prior unconstitutional activity. The credibility of the police officer(s) involved is the crucial factor in this analysis.

10-4e Public Safety

The **Public Safety Exception** is based on the idea that the police are justified in acting to protect the public from immediate danger, even if it is necessary to violate someone's constitutional rights to do so (*New York v. Quarles*).[20] In this situation, there must be an immediate danger, such as a gun left where children can play with it. The fact that the area is closed to the public at the time the questioning is conducted does not change the rule because the danger will continue until the weapon is found.

In *Quarles,* the police arrested a man suspected of rape who was believed to be armed. They found an empty holster but no gun. An officer immediately asked the suspect where the gun was; the suspect indicated the location. Introducing the gun in court was upheld based on the Public Safety Exception to the Exclusionary Rule even though the *Miranda* warnings had not been given prior to questioning. Another example of the Public Safety Exception would be asking the suspect, immediately after an arrest for kidnapping, where the victim was being held. Only brief, urgently needed questions are permitted under this exception; attempts to get a full confession would not qualify.

Example: Public Safety

Exclusionary Rule	Public Safety Exception to the Exclusionary Rule
Police arrested rape suspect shortly after the crime. They noticed he was wearing a holster that was empty. They asked him where the gun was without giving him the *Miranda* warnings.	Statement about the location of the gun was admissible because it was important for public safety to recover the gun before anyone else could be harmed.

10-4f Procedural Exceptions

A variety of situations have been found to be outside the scope of the Exclusionary Rule.

Harmless Error. The case will not automatically be reversed because the judge admitted unconstitutionally obtained evidence. The Harmless Error Rule applies to most constitutional violations (*Chapman v. California*):[21] the case will be reversed *only if* the appellate judges are convinced, beyond a reasonable doubt, that the illegally obtained evidence influenced the jury's decision in the case.

Example: Harmless Error

Exclusionary Rule	Harmless Error Exception to the Exclusionary Rule
Illegally seized gun should not have been admitted at trial.	Trial judge erroneously allowed the illegally seized gun to be admitted at trial. Appellate court would reverse conviction only if it was convinced that the admission of the gun influenced the jury's decision in the case.

Grand Jury. The right of the grand jury to investigate criminal cases is deeply embedded in our legal history. In *United States v. Calandra,* the Supreme Court held that this tradition is stronger than the Exclusionary Rule.[22] Unconstitutionally obtained evidence may be considered by the grand jury when considering an indictment, even though the same evidence will be inadmissible at trial.

Example: Grand Jury

Exclusionary Rule	Grand Jury Exception to the Exclusionary Rule
Police illegally arrested a man. During search incident to arrest cocaine was found in his pocket. The illegally seized cocaine would *not* be admissible at trial.	The illegally seized cocaine *could* be introduced during the grand jury hearing.

Impeachment. While the Exclusionary Rule prevents the prosecution from using illegally obtained evidence to establish its case, the rule is not a license for the defendant to commit perjury. In *Harris v. New York* the Court held that if a defendant testifies during trial, statements he/she made to the police can be used for impeachment.[23] The statements must relate to the topics raised during direct examination. Confessions obtained by coercion may not be used for impeachment, however, because they are inherently untrustworthy and violate due process. The right to use unconstitutionally obtained statements for impeachment only applies to the defendant; the credibility of other witnesses may not be challenged in this manner (*James v. Illinois*).[24]

Example: Impeachment

Exclusionary Rule	Impeachment Exception to the Exclusionary Rule
Police interrogated Mary after her arrest and did not give *Miranda* warnings. Mary admitted her role in committing the crime. This statement would *not* be admissible during the prosecution's case-in-chief to establish that Mary committed the crime.	At trial during the defense's case-in-chief, Mary took the witness stand and denied any involvement in the crime. During cross-examination, the prosecution *could* use Mary's statement to the police in order to impeach her.

In a few cases, this rule also applies to the results of illegal searches (*United States v. Havens*).[25] Evidence previously excluded must be relevant to a specific issue in the current case. For example, a suspect had been arrested on drug possession charges, but the case was dismissed because illegal methods were used to find the drugs. In a later case, the same suspect took the stand and categorically denied ever being involved with drugs. The arresting officer was allowed to testify about the earlier seizure of a large quantity of drugs the suspect was carrying in order to impeach this testimony.

Civil Cases. The Exclusionary Rule does not apply in civil cases. This is true even if the evidence was seized by the police. In *United States v. Janis,*[26] police illegally seized evidence while investigating gambling. After the prosecutor refused to file charges, the evidence was turned over to the Internal Revenue Service. The IRS filed civil charges of tax evasion, relying on the illegally obtained evidence. The Supreme Court held that this did not violate the Fourth Amendment. It justified its decision on the grounds that police do not seize evidence for the purpose of civil suits; therefore, exclusion of the evidence would have no deterrent value.

Example: Civil Cases

Exclusionary Rule	Civil Case Exception to the Exclusionary Rule
Police illegally entered residence and seized evidence of illegal gambling. The prosecutor refused to file criminal charges because the evidence would be inadmissible in criminal court.	The gamblers were sued in civil court by IRS for tax evasion based on the evidence seized by the police. This evidence would be admissible, even though it was seized illegally, because the case is in civil court.

Deportation. The Supreme Court also ruled that unconstitutionally obtained evidence could be used in hearings held by the Immigration and Naturalization Service to deport aliens. The ruling in *Immigration and Naturalization Service v. Lopez-Mendoza* applies to both civil and criminal INS proceedings.[27]

Example: Deportation

Exclusionary Rule	Deportation Exception to the Exclusionary Rule
Police illegally detain suspect and search him. They discover a large quantity of illegal drugs. The drugs are *not* admissible in criminal court because they were illegally seized.	It is discovered that the suspect was a legal resident alien in the United States. The illegal drugs *could* be used in court when an attempt is made to deport him due to his involvement in the illegal drug trade.

Sentencing. While the Supreme Court has not specifically ruled on the question, many lower courts permit illegally obtained evidence to be used at sentencing hearings.[28] The reason given for these rulings is that only marginal deterrence would result from excluding the evidence. The courts believe that police conduct their investigations for the purpose of obtaining convictions. Excluding evidence from sentencing hearings would have a deterrent effect only if the police obtained it solely for use at the sentencing hearing.

Example: Sentencing

Exclusionary Rule	Sentencing Exception to the Exclusionary Rule
Police legally arrested John. When conducting the search incident to the arrest the officers found a stolen watch worth $50 in his pocket. They extended their search into the next room and found $10,000 worth of stolen jewelry. The $10,000 worth of jewelry would *not* be admissible at trial because the scope of the search incident to the arrest was beyond what is legally authorized.	The $10,000 worth of jewelry *could* be used at the sentencing hearing in an attempt to convince the judge to use his/her discretion and give John a longer sentence for the theft of the watch.

Parole Revocation Hearings. The Exclusionary Rule does not apply at parole revocation hearings.[29] The Supreme Court weighed the need to deter unlawful conduct by parolees against the likelihood that law enforcement officers would be motivated to conduct illegal searches so that parole would be revoked, and decided in favor of maintaining controls on parolees. Similar standards would logically apply to probation revocation hearings.

Example: Parole Revocation

Exclusionary Rule	Parole Revocation Exception to the Exclusionary Rule
Pat, who was on parole, was illegally detained while walking down the street. He was searched and marijuana was found in his pocket. The marijuana would *not* be admissible at trial if Pat was charged with possession of marijuana.	Pat's parole officer attempted to revoke his parole because he violated a condition of parole which required that Pat violate no laws. The marijuana *could* be used at the parole revocation hearing.

Search by Private Person. The Bill of Rights was designed to protect people from an overbearing central government. Since *Mapp,* the Fourth Amendment has also been used to protect against actions by state and local governments. Even with this expansion, the Fourth Amendment does not protect against actions by people who are not working for a government agency. Evidence seized by a private person does not become inadmissible under the Exclusionary Rule.[30] To qualify for this exception, the private person must be acting on his/her own. If the police encourage a person to do what the police cannot do, the items seized are treated as if the police have conducted the search.

Example: Search by Private Person

Exclusionary Rule	Search by Private Person Exception to the Exclusionary Rule
Alan is suspected of buying stolen merchandise. He leaves his garage door open. The police enter the garage, look through boxes, and discover stolen items. These stolen items would *not* be admissible because the police illegally searched the garage.	Bill, Alan's next door neighbor, suspected that Alan was selling drugs. When Bill saw that the garage door was open he went into the garage and looked through several boxes. He found the stolen items and took them to the police. The stolen items *could* be used at trial if it is established that the police had not directed Bill to search the garage.

10-5 Impermissible Methods of Obtaining Evidence and Apprehending Suspects

There are certain boundaries imposed by our society that cannot be crossed by the police in their search for criminals. The Supreme Court has said that the police may not use methods that "shock the conscience" or "offend the sense of justice." These concepts come from the due process clause rather than any one amendment.

Rochin v. California[31] is the landmark case in this area. Rochin attempted to swallow the evidence. The police responded by having his stomach pumped. The Court found that this procedure was very painful and could not be tolerated in a civilized society. The use of the "third degree" to obtain confessions is on a similar footing. Due process is violated when coercion is used during interrogation (*Hayes v. Washington*).[32]

More recently, the Court considered the question of performing surgery on the suspect to obtain evidence (*Winston v. Lee*).[33] These cases typically involve the recovery of a bullet that lodged in the suspect when he/she was shot by the crime victim or by police while fleeing the scene. A search warrant or other court order is a necessary prerequisite to performing the operation without the subject's permission.

Although the Court has not totally ruled out the use of surgery, it established a balancing test which heavily favors the privacy of the individual. Surgical procedures that pose any threat to the suspect's health cannot be done. The prosecution must show a compelling need for the evidence. If there are other witnesses who can supply the needed information, surgery is not a reasonable alternative. Surgery also would not be allowed if the facts indicate that it will probably be impossible to conduct conclusive tests on the evidence recovered.

High-speed police pursuits are dangerous and occasionally result in fatal accidents. The Supreme Court ruled that due process is implicated *only if* the officer intentionally tried to cause harm unrelated to the legitimate objective of arresting the suspect; reckless driving alone does not raise constitutional issues. (*County of Sacramento v. Lewis*).[34]

The Fourth Amendment controls the level of physical force used by the police.[35] Deadly force may only be used when the life of the officer or a bystander is in imminent danger. Deadly force is never permissible to apprehend non-violent people who are fleeing felons or suspected of committing property crimes. Officers are allowed to use reasonable force in all situations. Reasonable force means the amount of force that a reasonable person, faced with the circumstances as they appear to be, would believe is necessary to stop the violence. Once the violent confrontation is under control, any type of force would be unreasonable. Each case must be considered on its own facts. A detailed analysis is needed, frequently on a second-by-second basis, to compare the level of force that was necessary to the force that was actually used.

Summary

The Fourth Amendment was enacted to protect citizens from an oppressive central government. It mandates that warrants be issued by neutral magistrates based on facts given under oath or affirmation. To satisfy the Fourth Amendment, the judge must review the affidavits and determine whether the facts establish probable cause to issue the warrant. The judge also needs to know why the information in the affidavit is reliable. Search warrants cannot be based on stale facts. The area to be searched must be described in as much detail as possible so that officers will not unnecessarily invade someone's privacy.

When serving a warrant at a residence, officers must comply with "knock and announce" unless there is an immediate threat of harm to the officers, destruction of the evidence, or escape of the suspect. If no one responds to the knock, the officers may use force to enter.

While executing a search warrant, the officers must confine their search to places where the evidence listed in the warrant could be located. This includes staying out of areas where the warrant does not authorize entry, as well as restricting the search to places where items of the size indicated could be hidden.

The Exclusionary Rule prevents unconstitutionally seized evidence from being admitted at trial. The Fruit of the Poison Tree Doctrine excludes evidence derived from illegally obtained evidence. Even though the police violated constitutional rights, evidence may be admitted at trial if the violation was done in "good faith" reliance on an apparently valid warrant, a statute that was believed to be constitutional, or computerized information indicating that there is an outstanding arrest warrant for the suspect.

Evidence will be admitted under the Inevitable Discovery Exception if the court is convinced that it would have been found even if there was no unconstitutional activity. The Independent Source Exception also allows evidence to be admitted despite unconstitutional actions. To qualify under this rule, there must have been a genuinely independent and constitutional search that led to the evidence.

If immediate action is required to save someone's life, police may act under the Public Safety Exception. This exception authorizes only brief questioning aimed at preventing serious injury.

Cases are not dismissed for violations of the Exclusionary Rule if the Harmless Error Rule applies. This rule allows cases to be affirmed if the appellate judges are convinced that the introduction of inadmissible evidence at trial did not affect the verdict.

The Exclusionary Rule is not applied in a variety of situations. Grand juries may use unconstitutionally obtained evidence. The prosecutor can use it to impeach a witness or at the defendant's sentencing hearing. Unconstitutionally obtained evidence can be used in civil suits and in INS cases. None of the protections of the Fourth Amendment apply to actions of private persons acting on their own.

Evidence may not be obtained by means which offend our sense of justice. Surgery and other medical procedures that are particularly painful or dangerous are carefully scrutinized by the courts. Confessions may not be coerced. These situations violate due process. The Fourth Amendment allows officers to use reasonable force. Deadly force is permissible only if a life is in imminent peril. Non-deadly force must be reasonable and proportionate to the type of force encountered by the officers.

Discussion Questions

1. Define:
   (a) search
   (b) seizure
   (c) probable cause
   (d) standing
2. Explain what must be in an affidavit for a search warrant. How does a judge determine if an affidavit is reliable?
3. Explain what procedures must be followed prior to entering a house to serve a search warrant.
4. What areas may be searched when executing a search warrant?
5. Describe two situations in which police may enter a residence without a warrant.
6. Explain when officers are allowed to conduct a protective sweep when executing a search warrant.
7. Explain the Exclusionary Rule and the Fruit of the Poison Tree Doctrine.
8. Explain the Inevitable Discovery Exception to the Exclusionary Rule. How does it differ from the Independent Source Exception to the Exclusionary Rule?
9. Explain three exceptions to the Exclusionary Rule that are not listed in Question 8.
10. Explain two types of police tactics prohibited by due process.

Endnotes

1. *Aguilar v. Texas* 378 U.S. 108, 12 L.Ed. 2d 723, 84 S.Ct. 1509 (1964).
2. *Spinelli v. United States* 393 U.S. 110, 21 L.Ed. 2d 637, 89 S.Ct. 584 (1969).
3. *Illinois v. Gates* 462 U.S. 213, 76 L.Ed. 2d 527, 103 S.Ct. 2317 (1983).
4. *McCray v. Illinois* 386 U.S. 300, 18 L.Ed. 2d 62, 87 S.Ct. 1056 (1967).
5. *Coolidge v. New Hampshire* 403 U.S. 443, 29 L.Ed. 2d 564, 91 S.Ct. 2022 (1971).
6. *Groh v. Ramirez* __ U.S. ___, 157 L.Ed. 2d 1068, 124 S.Ct. 1284 (2004).
7. *Payton v. New York* 445 U.S. 573, 63 L.Ed. 2d 639, 100 S.Ct. 1371 (1980).
8. *Mincey v. Arizona* 437 U.S. 385, 57 L.Ed. 2d 290, 98 S.Ct. 2408 (1978).
9. *Wilson v. Arkansas* 514 U.S. 927, 131 L.Ed. 2d 976, 115 S.Ct. 1914 (1995).
10. *Richards v. Wisconsin* 520 U.S.385, 137 L.Ed. 2d 615, 117 S.Ct. 1416 (1997).
11. *United States v. Banks* __ U.S. ___, 157 L.Ed. 2d 343, 124 S.Ct. 521 (2003).
12. *Maryland v. Buie* 494 U.S. 325, 108 L.Ed. 2d 276, 110 S.Ct. 1093 (1990).
13. *Weeks v. United States* 232 U.S. 383, 58 L.Ed. 652, 34 S.Ct. 341 (1914).
14. *Mapp v. Ohio* 367 U.S. 643, 6 L.Ed. 2d 1081, 81 S.Ct. 1684 (1961).
15. *Wong Sun v. United States* 371 U.S. 471, 9 L.Ed. 2d 441, 83 S.Ct. 407 (1963).
16. *United States v. Leon* 468 U.S. 897, 82 L.Ed. 2d 677, 104 S.Ct. 3405 (1984); *Massachusetts v. Sheppard* 468 U.S. 981, 82 L.Ed. 2d 737, 104 S.Ct. 3424 (1984). See also *Illinois v. Krull* 480 U.S. 340, 94 L.Ed. 2d 364, 107 S.Ct. 1160 (1987); *Arizona v. Evans,* 514 U.S. 1, 131 L.Ed. 2d 34, 115 S.Ct. 1185 (1995).
17. *Nix v. Williams* 467 U.S. 431, 81 L.Ed. 2d 377, 104 S.Ct. 2501 (1984).
18. *Segura v. United States* 468 U.S. 796, 82 L.Ed. 2d 599, 104 S.Ct. 3380 (1984).
19. *Murray v. United States* 487 U.S.533, 101 L.Ed. 2d 472, 108 S.Ct. 2529 (1988).
20. *New York v. Quarles* 467 U.S. 649, 81 L.Ed. 2d 550, 104 S.Ct. 2626 (1984).
21. *Chapman v. California* 386 U.S. 18, 17 L.Ed. 2d 705, 87 S.Ct. 824 (1967).
22. *United States v. Calandra* 414 U.S. 338, 38 L.Ed. 2d 561, 94 S.Ct. 613 (1974).
23. *Harris v. New York* 401 U.S. 222, 28 L.Ed. 2d 1, 91 S.Ct. 643 (1971).
24. *James v. Illinois* 493 U.S. 307, 107 L.Ed. 2d 676, 110 S.Ct. 648 (1990).
25. *United States v. Havens* 446 U.S. 620, 64 L.Ed. 2d 559, 100 S.Ct. 1912 (1980).
26. *United States v. Janis* 428 U.S. 433, 49 L.Ed. 2d 1046, 96 S.Ct. 3021 (1976).
27. *Immigration and Naturalization Service v. Lopez-Mendoza* 468 U.S. 1032, 82 L.Ed. 2d 778, 104 S.Ct. 3479 (1984).
28. *United States v. Butler* 680 F. 2d 1055 (5th Cir. 1982); *United States v. Larios* 640 F. 2d 938 (9th Cir. 1981).
29. *Pennsylvania Board of Probation & Parole v. Scott* 524 U.S. 357, 141 L.Ed. 2d 344, 118 S.Ct. 2014 (1998).
30. *Burdeau v. McDowell* 256 U.S. 465, 65 L.Ed. 1048, 41 S.Ct. 574 (1921); *United States v. Jacobsen* 466 U.S. 109, 80 L.Ed. 2d 85, 104 S.Ct. 1652 (1984).
31. *Rochin v. California* 342 U.S. 165, 96 L.Ed. 183, 72 S.Ct. 205 (1952).
32. *Hayes v. Washington* 373 U.S. 503, 10 L.Ed. 2d 513, 83 S.Ct. 1336 (1963).
33. *Winston v. Lee* 470 U.S. 753, 84 L.Ed. 2d 662, 105 S.Ct. 1611 (1985).
34. *County of Sacramento v. Lewis* 523 U.S. 833, 140 L.Ed. 2d 1043, 118 S. Ct. 1708 (1998).
35. *Tennessee v. Garner* 471 U.S. 1, 85 L.Ed. 2d 1, 105 S.Ct. 1694 (1985); *Graham v. Connor* 490 U.S. 386, 104 L.Ed. 2d 443, 109 S.Ct. 1865 (1989).

CHAPTER 11

Field Interviews, Arrests, and Jail Searches

Outline

Key Terms

- Booking search
- Canine searches
- Citizen's arrest
- Field interview
- Frisk

- Jail searches
- Plain feel
- Probable cause
- Protective sweep
- Reasonable force

- Reasonable suspicion
- School searches
- Search incident to arrest
- Temporary detention

After studying this chapter, you will be able to:

- Recognize the standard that allows police to detain a person without making an arrest.
- Describe the extent of the search permitted when police stop a person who is not under arrest.
- Define the standard for making legal arrests.
- Describe the extent of the search police may conduct when an arrest is made.
- Explain when a warrant is needed to make an arrest.
- Identify the type of search permitted when someone is booked into jail.
- List the types of searches permitted in a jail without a search warrant.

This chapter focuses on the rights of the police to detain people against their will. Every time the police are allowed to detain, they are also given the right to conduct at least a limited search if the circumstances indicate it is needed for their protection. The rights of the police vary according to the strength of the reasons for detaining the person. Three types of situations cover most police encounters: field interviews, arrests, and booking. Searches of jail and prison inmates will also be discussed.

11-1 Field Interviews

Police frequently observe something that indicates that further investigation is called for. Many times the initial observation does not give the police officer enough information to arrest someone but indicates there is definitely something going on that needs to be checked out. Based on what they find during the **field interview,** the police may either make an arrest or release the person involved.

11-1a Right to Detain

The U.S. Supreme Court agreed with the police that officers should have the power to act even though the facts do not indicate that an arrest should be made. The leading case is *Terry v. Ohio.*

Standard for Temporary Detention

The police may temporarily detain someone for questioning if there are specific articulable facts that lead a reasonable police officer to believe that criminal activity is occurring.[1]

The standard for this type of stop is frequently called **reasonable suspicion.** It differs from the standard for making an arrest in several ways.

Reasonable suspicion does not require as many facts as are needed to make an arrest. The officer must be able to cite specific facts that caused him/her to believe criminal activity was present, but it is not necessary to identify a specific crime believed to be in progress. To make an arrest, the officer must believe that it is more probable than not that the suspect committed a crime. Reasonable suspicion only requires that a reasonable officer would believe that some criminal activity is occurring. An arrest is based on what a "reasonable person" would conclude; temporary detention can be based on what a "reasonable officer" would believe.

Anytime an officer has the right to detain someone, the officer has the right to use force to prevent that person from leaving. This applies to both temporary detentions and arrests. The **force** used must always be **reasonable** under the circumstances. Deadly force is only justified if a life (including the officer's life) is in danger.[2] The Supreme Court set this standard in *Tennessee v. Garner,* a case that dealt with the right to use deadly force to make an arrest. The justification for the use of force is even less when officers are only investigating to determine if a crime has occurred. Only a situation perceived as life threatening will ever justify using deadly force.

Even though the Court allows the police to detain someone against his/her will without making an arrest, the police still cannot stop people any time they feel like it. An officer may stop someone on reasonable suspicion but not randomly, on "mere suspicion," or based on a hunch. The officer must have specific facts that can be stated to justify detention—sometimes called "articulable suspicion."

The Court has never set a specific time limit on **temporary detentions.** The length of time must allow the officer to conduct a brief investigation. How long that investigation may take varies with the circumstances. One case involving a 90-minute detention was ruled unreasonably long. Cases involving 20-minute stops have been upheld. The detention should last no longer than necessary to determine if the person stopped was actually involved in a crime. The important thing is that the police diligently pursue reasonable investigative techniques in order to decide if the suspect should be arrested.

The courts have interpreted the temporary detention standard quite freely, permitting many police actions. For example, the Supreme Court recently held that the fact that a person ran from the scene when a police officer approached is sufficient grounds to detain the individual for questioning (*Illinois v. Wardlow*).[3] Merely associating with other known criminals or loitering in a high-crime area, however, is not sufficient to make a stop.

While most temporary detentions are based on the police officer's firsthand observations, often someone else provides the information. The Supreme Court, in *Adams v. Williams,* indicated that the police may use facts supplied by others if there is sufficient reason to believe the person supplying them is reliable. The totality-of-the-circumstances test is used to make this determination, even if the information came from an anonymous informant.[4] An anonymous tip, unconfirmed by the police, is not enough to detain someone even though the informant stated that the suspect was armed (*Florida v. J. L.*).[5]

The right to detain temporarily is not restricted to crimes in progress. Police may also stop someone on the basis of a wanted flyer (*United States v. Hensley*).[6] In these situations, the wanted flyer usually creates reasonable suspicion; additional details supplied by the law enforcement agency circulating the flyer establish probable cause for the arrest. If the flyer turns out to be based on insufficient evidence, the arrest is illegal (*Whiteley v. Warden*).[7]

Examples of Temporary Detentions

Legal Detentions
- Police observed two suspects who appeared to be armed outside a liquor store intently watching the clerk count money.
- Police saw car with lights out driving rapidly away from scene of "burglary now" call.
- Police saw person matching description of robbery suspect running away from scene shortly after crime occurred.

Illegal Detentions
- Police stopped person who had been standing on corner near location where drug dealers frequently make sales.
- Police stopped person who was jogging at night in industrial area.

11-1b Searches during Temporary Detention

The Supreme Court, recognizing that it is frequently necessary to search suspects in order to protect the officer, established standards governing these searches.

This limited search, frequently called a **frisk** or a "pat down," is designed solely for the protection of the officer. There is no automatic right to search every person stopped. Officers must have a reasonable suspicion that the search is needed for their protection. If a person is stopped, for example, because there is reasonable suspicion that a violent crime has been committed or is in progress, the right to search logically follows. If

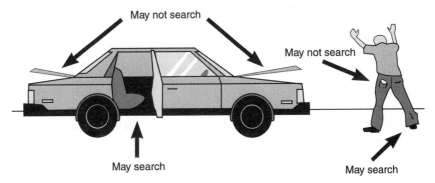

Figure 11-1
Search during Temporary Detention
There was recently a shooting in the area, and the police officer is reasonably suspicious that this person may be armed.

the situation involves a property crime, there may be little or no right to search.

Standard for Search during Temporary Detention

Reasonable suspicion to stop someone does not automatically give the officer the right to search the individual. During a temporary detention *if, and only if,* the officer has a reasonable suspicion that the suspect is armed or dangerous he/she may conduct a pat down of outer clothing for weapons. If the officer feels an object believed to be a weapon, he/she may reach into the clothing and remove it.

The scope of the search is limited to what is necessary to protect the officers. As previously indicated, in most cases, this involves patting down the suspect for weapons. If officers feel something they believe is a weapon, then they may retrieve it. Sometimes this search may be a bit broader. For example, in *Terry v. Ohio* the suspects were wearing heavy coats because it was a cold winter day. The Court approved a search that included checking inner pockets for items that could not be detected during a pat down because of the bulky nature of the coats. Figure 11-1 depicts the extent of a legal search when a person driving a car was detained based on *Terry v. Ohio* and there was reasonable suspicion that he was armed or that there were arms in the car.

When police, acting on reasonable suspicion, retrieve what they believe is a weapon, it is a legal search. This falls under the Plain View Doctrine. If, in fact, the object they seize is not a weapon, whatever they seize will still be admissible. The right to retrieve items in "plain view" was expanded slightly in *Minnesota v. Dickerson*, the officers were allowed to remove items that did not feel like weapons if, by their distinctive feel, it could be determined that the item was contraband.[8] This has been called **plain feel.**

Examples of Searches during Temporary Detentions

Legal Searches
- Officers observe bulge in suspect's pocket. During pat down officer feels hard object the shape of a knife. When object is retrieved it turns out to be a package of rock cocaine.
- Officers stop a man who fits the description given by a robbery victim. The victim described the robber as having a gun. The crime occurred ten minutes before the suspect was stopped and about half a mile from where detention occurred. An officer immediately frisked the suspect and retrieved a gun from the pocket in his pants.

Illegal Searches
- Officer has no reason to believe suspect is armed but conducts pat down.
- During a legal pat down an officer feels a lump of something that he/she cannot identify in the suspect's pocket. He orders the suspect to empty the pocket and discovers that the lump was a package containing methamphetamine.

11-1c Special Situations

A variety of situations have come before the Supreme Court. You should be familiar with the rights of the police to act in each of them.

> ***Car Stops.*** There is no special right to stop a car or other vehicle. Nor do police have the right to randomly stop a car merely to check its registration or to see if the driver has a valid license (*Delaware v. Prouse*).[9] In *Pennsylvania v. Mimms,* the Court recognized the right of the police officer to order the driver to get out of a vehicle during a traffic stop.[10] Other occupants may be ordered out of the car without particularized suspicion that they are involved in criminal activity (*Maryland v. Wilson*).[11] Someone may be searched if there is reasonable suspicion that that person is armed; for example, a bulge in the driver's pocket resembles a gun. A complete search of the suspect and the passenger compartment of the vehicle is authorized if an arrest is made.
>
> Cars are frequently stopped, however, because of vehicle code violations. These stops can be based on reasonable suspicion. At other times the facts may indicate that there is reasonable suspicion that the occupants of a car are involved in criminal activity. These cars can be stopped under the authority to detain suspects temporarily. When

this occurs, officers have the authority to conduct a search of the passenger compartment for weapons if there is an articulable and objectively reasonable belief that the suspect is potentially dangerous (*Michigan v. Long*).[12] This right to look for weapons exists even if the officers have decided to release the suspects. The rationale for this is that a suspect who has been released may return to the car and use the weapon against the officers.

Fingerprinting. The Supreme Court, in *Davis v. Mississippi* and *Hayes v. Florida,* heard cases involving taking suspects to the police station for fingerprinting.[13] Both times the Court ruled that this may not be done without probable cause to arrest. The most recent case indicated that it would, however, be legal to fingerprint a person at the scene.

Interrogation. *Miranda* warnings are not required when an officer questions a suspect during a temporary detention based on reasonable suspicion. The warnings will be required for questioning after an arrest is made. *Dunaway v. New York* held that transportation to the station for questioning can only be done if the suspect consents or has been arrested.[14]

School Searches. Searches by school officials are governed by standards similar to those that apply to temporary detentions.[15] There must be reasonable suspicion that the student has broken the law or violated a school regulation. These searches are not restricted to weapons. In *New Jersey v. T. L. O.,* the Supreme Court affirmed the search of a 14-year-old girl's purse for cigarettes.

Canine Searches. The Supreme Court has allowed customs agents to briefly detain luggage in order to have narcotics detection dogs check it for drugs.[16] *United States v. Place* held that there must be reasonable suspicion that the suitcases contain drugs. The luggage may not be opened prior to the canine inspection. Additionally, the detention must not be unreasonably long. The fact that a reliable, properly trained dog indicates drugs are present will establish probable cause.

11-2 Arrests

In Fourth Amendment terms, an arrest is the seizure of a person. More commonly, it is thought of as taking a person into custody for committing a crime. All arrests must be based on **probable cause.** Officers do not need

T A B L E **11-1 Comparison of Field Interview and Arrest**

	Field Interview Based on Reasonable Suspicion	Custodial Arrest
Grounds to initiate contact	Reasonable Suspicion—sufficient facts that would make a reasonable officer believe criminal activity is afoot.	Probable Cause—sufficient facts to convince a reasonable person that a crime has been committed and this is the person who did it.
Warrant requirement	None	Arrest warrant is mandated when officers will enter a home to make an arrest. Many states require a warrant to arrest for a misdemeanor not committed in the officer's presence.
Miranda warnings	*Miranda* warnings are not required.	*Miranda* warnings are mandated for all questioning after the person is taken into custody.
Right to use force	Officer may use reasonable non-deadly force to detain the person. They are restricted to the lowest level of force that will contain the situation. Deadly force may be used *only if* there is imminent danger to the life of the officer or a bystander.	Officer may use reasonable non-deadly force to arrest a person. Deadly force is never authorized to make a misdemeanor arrest. For felony arrests, deadly force is justified *only if* there is imminent danger to the life of the officer or a bystander.
Length of stop	Brief detention in order to ask the suspect questions. At the end of questioning the officers must decide whether to arrest the suspect or release him/her.	Once the arrest is made, the officers may take the time that is necessary to secure the scene and complete necessary paperwork. Suspect is then transported to station and booked.

to personally evaluate probable cause for the arrest if they are executing an arrest warrant or acting at the direction of another officer. Table 11-1 compares the field interview discussed in Section 11-1 with an arrest.

11-2a Probable Cause to Arrest

Probable cause consists of a group of facts that makes a reasonable person more certain than not that an event occurred. In an arrest situation, that reasonable person must be more certain than not that the person arrested committed a specific crime. This requires a higher level of certainty than the reasonable suspicion needed for a field interview. It is a considerably lower level of proof, however, than the "beyond a reasonable doubt" required for a conviction.

To decide if there is probable cause, the officer must determine that there is probable cause for each element of the crime. In many cases, an arrest is made for one crime, but different charges are filed by the prosecutor. This may be due to new evidence, such as drugs found when the suspect was searched incident to the arrest. It can also be due to information discovered by the police between the time of arrest and when the charges are filed. The arrest is still valid if, at the time of the arrest, the officer had probable cause to believe that the suspect committed the crime he/she was arrested for. This same rule applies even if the prosecutor refuses to file charges. The fact that the defendant was acquitted does not prove that the arrest was illegal; proof beyond a reasonable doubt that is required to convict is a much higher standard than probable cause for a legal arrest.

11-2b Powers of Arrest

At common law and in many states today, an officer may arrest if there is probable cause to believe a felony has been committed. For misdemeanors, officers are also required to have probable cause but can only arrest if the crime is committed in their presence. When the crime has occurred before the officer arrived at the scene, the arrest must be made by someone who witnessed it.

Having someone who witnessed the crime make the arrest (often the victim) is commonly called a **citizen's arrest.** For felonies, a citizen's arrest can be made by a person who knows of the existence of the crime even though he/she did not observe it occurring. Most states require the police to take custody of a person who has been arrested in this manner, although citations are now issued for many non-violent crimes.

Another approach to the problem of misdemeanors not committed in the officer's presence is to have the victim and/or witnesses state the facts in an affidavit. The victim or the police can then go to the prosecutor. This is commonly referred to as "swearing out a complaint." A judge will review the affidavit and, if probable cause has been established, issue an arrest warrant. This procedure can be used if it is not possible to make a citizen's arrest because the suspect left the scene. It is also used if the victim does not want to press charges at the time the crime occurred but later decides to pursue the case.

While the Supreme Court repeatedly has stated that obtaining a warrant is the preferred procedure, it has never required the police to obtain arrest warrants in cases where they have probable cause, even if there is no emergency requiring swift action. Neither is there a requirement that they arrest as soon as they believe they have enough evidence to establish probable cause.

Officers are required to obtain a warrant if the arrest is to be made in a home.[17] This rule, which the Supreme Court stated in *Payton v. New York,* applies whether officers are looking for the suspect in their own home or in someone else's house *(Stegald v. United States).*[18] Either an arrest or a search warrant can be used to enter the suspect's home to arrest him/her; a search warrant is needed if the officers must enter any other home to make the arrest. The foundation for this rule is the right of people to privacy in their homes. There is an emergency exception to the rule which applies if someone inside the house is calling for help, screaming, or apparently being attacked. If officers are in hot pursuit and the suspect runs into a house, the emergency exception also applies.

11-2c Search Incident to Arrest

Between 1914 and 1969, the Supreme Court repeatedly changed the rules on how far the police may search when they make an arrest. The current rule, which was established in *Chimel v. California* (1969), was originally based on three main criteria: (1) protection of the officer; (2) preventing destruction of evidence of the crime; and (3) seizure of contraband.[19] It allows officers to thoroughly search the person and area under the immediate control of the person being arrested.

The crime the suspect was arrested for has no bearing on the extent of the **search incident to arrest** *(United States v. Robinson; Gustafson v. Florida).*[20] The Supreme Court no longer follows the original rationale that one of the justifications for the search is to seize evidence of the crime. Even for offenses that have no physical evidence, such as driving without a license, if the person is arrested and taken into custody, the search may include the person and area under his/her immediate control.

The justification for the search is the arrest. Therefore, items found during the search cannot be used as a basis for the arrest. The search must be done contemporaneously with the arrest. Only searches done at the scene immediately after the arrest qualify. Those done later must be justified on some other grounds.

Standard for Search Incident to an Arrest

Immediately following an arrest, officers may conduct a thorough search of the person arrested and the area under the arrestee's immediate control.

Unlike the protective search done during field interviews, there are no restrictions on the thoroughness of the search conducted when the sus-

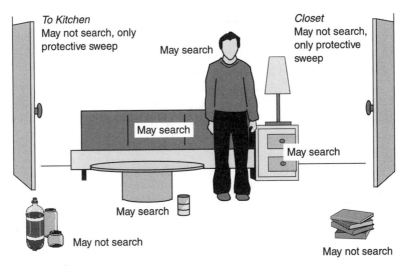

Figure 11-2
Search Incident to Arrest
This person was arrested in a living room, and the police officer will conduct a search of the area.

pect is arrested and taken into custody. Only the area searched is restricted. Anywhere the person arrested could reach to obtain weapons or destroy evidence can be searched. This "arms-reach" rule (also called the "wing-span" rule) is applied without considering the fact that the suspect was handcuffed prior to the search. Anywhere he/she could reach if not restrained is included. Some courts have permitted searches up to ten feet from the suspect. Officers are not restricted to places where evidence is believed to be. They may open drawers, look under sofa cushions, check in the clothes dryer, or anything else, provided it is within arms reach. Figure 11-2 depicts the extent of a legal search of a person who was arrested in the living room of a home.

Table 11-2 compares the officer's right to search during a field interview and when making a custodial arrest.

Whatever is found on the person or under his/her immediate control during the search incident to an arrest is admissible evidence. It does not have to be evidence of the crime he/she was arrested for. In many cases, the search incident to the arrest produces drugs or other contraband. Illegal weapons and evidence of totally unrelated crimes may be discovered. Additional charges may be sought based on what is found; it does not matter that the new charges are more serious than the ones that caused the arrest.

T A B L E **11-2 Right to Search during Field Interview
and Arrest**

	Field Interview Based on Reasonable Suspicion	Custodial Arrest
Right to search	Officer must have reasonable suspicion that the suspect is armed.	Search is allowed anytime a person is arrested and taken into custody. No suspicion that person is concealing evidence is required.
Reason for search	Sole justification of search is to retrieve weapons that could be used to harm the officer.	Originally the Supreme Court stated the purpose of the search was to retrieve evidence of the crime, weapons, and contraband. Later cases have allowed the search whenever there is a valid custodial arrest even if there were no grounds to believe the person was concealing anything.
Timing	Search must be done during the brief detention allowed by *Terry*.	Search must be contemporaneous with the arrest.
Search of the person	Pat down of person for weapons	Thorough search of the person
Search of surrounding area	None	Officers may search all items within the suspect's immediate control.
Search of vehicle	If person was in vehicle when detained, officers may search passenger compartment for weapons *if* there is reasonable suspicion that weapons are in the vehicle.	If person was in vehicle at time of arrest, officers may conduct thorough search of passenger compartment.

Whether or not a physical arrest is made is important. When the state law authorizes a custodial arrest, it shows that the offense is sufficiently serious to justify a major invasion of the individual's privacy. If the action is deemed less offensive to the state, officers may be authorized to cite and release the suspect on the spot. Obviously, a citation is a much smaller invasion of the suspect's privacy. Accordingly, intrusive searches are not permitted. Traffic stops present a typical example. If the suspect is released at the scene, the officers may not invade the suspect's privacy by doing a thorough search. The occupants of the vehicle can, however, be ordered out of the car. The right to search in these situations is similar to what can be done during a field interview (i.e., protective pat down for weapons) but even this is allowed only if there is reasonable suspicion that the person is armed. Due to the fact that the officers are only with the offender briefly, their need to protect themselves is not the same as when the offender is taken into custody.

Arrests frequently involve either the driver or passenger of a car. In the 1981 case of *New York v. Belton*,[21] the Supreme Court held that the entire passenger compartment, including the glove box and console, may be searched incident to the custodial arrest of an occupant of the car. *Thornton v. United States*[22] expanded this rule to include situations where the person being arrested is a "recent occupant" of the vehicle. The search must be done at the time of the arrest, but the suspect may be removed from the car before the search begins. The Court also authorized an extensive search of anything in the passenger compartment, including luggage and other parcels. The Closed Container Rule (see Chapter 12) does not apply. Other parts of the car, such as the trunk, require some other justification.

When an arrest is made in a home or other building, officers may make a **protective sweep.** A protective sweep is a quick, visual check for people who may be hiding nearby. At the time of an arrest and without additional facts indicating danger, officers may look in the area immediately adjoining the place where the arrest was made, such as a closet where someone could hide. To go beyond that, the Supreme Court requires that the officer conducting the search has a reasonable belief based on specific articulable facts that, taken together with the rational inferences from those facts, lead a reasonable officer to believe someone is present who might attack the officer (*Maryland v. Buie*).[23]

Examples of Searches Incident to Arrests

Legal Searches
- Immediately after the arrest, officers searched the suspect and found a small envelope containing heroin hidden in a cigarette pack found in the suspect's shirt pocket.
- Suspect was driving a car when arrested on an outstanding warrant. Officers placed the suspect in the police car and searched the entire passenger compartment of the suspect's car. Counterfeit money was found in the console.
- Suspect was standing near a desk when arrested. Officers searched the desk drawers and found records of a bookmaking operation.

Illegal Searches
- Suspect was stopped for speeding (non-custodial arrest). Officers searched the suspect and found a stolen ring hidden in a handkerchief.
- Suspect was arrested on the front lawn. Officers entered the house and found money taken in a robbery in the kitchen.
- Suspect was arrested at her home. After booking, officers returned to the house and conducted a detailed search of the area where the suspect had been standing when arrested.

11-3 Booking

Booking occurs when the person who has been arrested enters the jail or a holding facility. It also happens if a person reports directly to the jail to serve all or part of a sentence. Inmates who serve weekends or leave the facility daily on work furlough are included. Whether the person has been searched recently or not, the right to search at the time of booking is the same.

The reason for allowing **booking searches** is to prevent weapons and contraband from entering the jail. Searches done at the time of booking are usually divided into two types: (1) search of the person and (2) search of property.

Scope of Search at Booking
A booking search may include a thorough search of the person and any items in his/her possession at that time.

11-3a Search of the Person

The booking search is usually the most extensive search of the person that occurs. While both searches incident to arrest and booking searches allow thorough searches of the person, the booking situation provides the privacy necessary to do strip searches.

Due to the fact that weapons and drugs can easily be hidden, strip searches and searches of body cavities are permitted. Reasonable attempts to preserve privacy, such as shielding the strip-search area from public view and having searches conducted by officers of the same gender as the suspect, are still required. Combative inmates who defy control by booking personnel or those who attempt to flee the booking area waive protections of their privacy.

Several states have enacted legislation limiting the right to conduct strip searches and body cavity searches when inmates are booked into the jail. Many of these laws were triggered by public outcry over how an "average citizen," arrested for a very minor offense, was humiliated during a strip search. Most of the states that have enacted restrictions allow full searches for felonies, but limit them for misdemeanors. In misdemeanor cases, the police usually must have cause to believe that weapons or contraband will be discovered in order to do a strip search. Sometimes the statutes allow complete searches anytime the suspect is booked for drug or weapons charges, but require a factual showing to justify a strip search in all other cases. These restrictive statutes frequently require a court order prior to conducting a body cavity search. Several federal appellate courts have applied similar restrictions to booking searches of felony suspects but the U.S. Supreme Court has not considered this precise issue.

11-3b Property Searches

At booking, it is common to inventory and store all of the suspect's property, including clothing. Jail uniforms are frequently issued. These measures help keep weapons and contraband out of the jail facility and also reduce problems in the jail caused by thefts.

The Supreme Court has considered two cases dealing with inmate property at the time of booking. One dealt with sending clothing the inmate was wearing when booked to a forensics laboratory for examination. In *United States v. Edwards,* the Court held that anything in the inmate's possession that could have been searched at the time of arrest could be seized in the jail without a warrant.[24] No distinction was made between searches done at the time of booking and those done at a later time.

The second case, *Illinois v. Lafayette,* involved searching a shoulder bag the inmate carried at the time of booking. The Court held that any container or other article the inmate had in his/her possession at the time of booking could be searched.[25] The Closed Container Rule does not apply at booking. Everything taken from the inmate may be listed in an itemized inventory. Inventorying property at the time of booking is seen as necessary to prevent theft by jail employees; it also reduces the number of inmates making unfounded reports of theft. Information found during the inventory is also useful in positively identifying the person being booked.

Examples of Legal Booking Searches
- Inmate's clothing and everything she was carrying was thoroughly searched at the time of booking.
- Inmate booked for felony drug charges was strip searched by an officer of the same gender in a room in the booking area where no one else could observe.
- Purse inmate was carrying at time of arrest was searched during booking.
- Items removed from inmate's pockets at time of booking were searched at a later time.

11-4 Jail and Prison Searches

Once a person has been booked, his/her expectation of privacy is greatly reduced. In fact, it nearly disappears. The Supreme Court generally allows **jail searches** if a valid administrative reason can be given.

Inmates may be searched at any time. The randomness of these searches is seen as an important factor in maintaining security and reducing the flow of contraband in jails and prisons. *Bell v. Wolfish* held that even slight grounds to believe that an inmate may be concealing contraband can justify body cavity searches.[26]

Cell searches may also be done without cause. Inmates have no reason to expect privacy in their cells *(Hudson v. Palmer)*.[27] The need to maintain order and security within the facility justifies the intrusion into the inmate's cell. Some courts have allowed limited privacy interests in legal papers and diaries inmates keep in their cells.

This same need to maintain security in correctional facilities has justified limitations on what an inmate can possess. Many items that are legal outside the prison can be seized as contraband; for example, large paper clips may be prohibited because of the possibility they can be sharpened and bent to form weapons. Prison officials can also restrict what inmates receive from visitors and through the mail. Due process, however, requires that inmates be given reasonable notice of the rules.

Examples of Legal Searches in Jails and Prisons

- Correctional officer stopped inmate who was walking down a hall in jail and did a pat down. A makeshift knife was found in his pocket
- Two correctional officers ordered all of the inmates to leave their cell block. They then searched every cell. Illegal drugs were found hidden in two cells.

Summary

Police may briefly stop a person for questioning if there are specific, articulable facts that would lead a reasonable officer to believe that criminal activity is afoot. When this type of detention is made, a pat down of the outer clothing may be conducted for weapons *if* there is a reasonable suspicion that the detainee is armed. If a car is stopped, the officers have the right to search the passenger compartment for weapons *if* there is a reasonable suspicion that the car contains weapons. The right to detain a person for a field interview does not include the right to transport the suspect to the station for fingerprinting or interrogation.

All arrests must be based on probable cause. The officer must have facts that would cause a reasonable person to conclude that a specific crime has been committed and that this is the person who committed it. A totality-of-the-circumstances test will be used to determine if the officer had enough facts to justify the arrest.

Police usually have the right to arrest if there is probable cause to believe a felony has been committed, but in most states arrests for misdemeanors are restricted to situations where the officers observed the crime in progress. If the officers were not present when the crime occurred, the victim or someone else who observed the misdemeanor needs to make the arrest or swear out a complaint.

A warrant is normally needed to make an arrest inside a house. An emergency (sometimes called "exigent circumstances"), such as officers following a suspect into the house in hot pursuit or someone screaming for help, permits entry without a warrant.

When a custodial arrest is made, a search of the person and area under his/her immediate control is allowed. The search must be done at the time and place of arrest. Anything found is admissible. If the person was arrested while riding in a car, the entire passenger compartment may be searched.

A thorough search of the person (and anything in his/her possession) may be done at the time of booking. The Closed Container Rule does not apply. Strip searches and searches of body cavities must be done in a manner to protect the inmate's privacy.

Once the inmate enters the prison population, there are very few restrictions on searches. Probable cause is not required. The need to maintain security and control contraband justifies random searches of inmates and cells.

Discussion Questions

1. What is the standard for stopping a suspect for brief questioning when there are no grounds for an arrest? Explain.
2. How much force may be used to detain someone for a field interview? For an arrest? Explain.
3. Explain when a search is permitted during a temporary detention. How extensive may the search be? Explain.
4. When may a person be transported to the police station for fingerprinting or interrogation? Explain.
5. What is the standard for an arrest and when is a warrant required? Explain.
6. What area may be searched at the time of arrest? Explain.
7. What search is permitted if a person is arrested in a car? Explain.
8. Explain the extent of the search permitted at booking.
9. Can property seized at booking be searched at a later time without a search warrant? Explain.
10. Explain the right to search inmates in prisons and jails.

Endnotes

1. *Terry v. Ohio* 392 U.S. 1, 20 L.Ed. 2d 889, 88 S.Ct. 1868 (1968).
2. *Tennessee v. Garner* 471 U.S. 1, 85 L.Ed. 2d 1, 105 S.Ct. 1694 (1985); *Graham v. Connor* 490 U.S. 386, 104 L.Ed. 2d 443, 109 S.Ct. 1865 (1989).
3. *Illinois v. Wardlow* 528 U.S. 119, 145 L.Ed. 2d 570, 120 S.Ct. 673 (2000).
4. *Adams v. Williams* 407 U.S. 143, 32 L.Ed. 2d 612, 92 S.Ct. 1921 (1972); *Alabama v. White* 496 U.S. 325, 110 L.Ed. 2d 301, 110 S.Ct. 2412 (1990).
5. *Florida v. J. L.* 529 U.S. 266, 146 L.Ed. 2d 254, 120 S.Ct. 1375 (2000)
6. *United States v. Hensley* 469 U.S. 221, 83 L.Ed. 2d 604, 105 S.Ct. 675 (1985).
7. *Whiteley v. Warden* 401 U.S. 560, 28 L.Ed. 2d 306, 91 S.Ct. 1031 (1971).
8. *Minnesota v. Dickerson* 508 U.S. 366, 124 L.Ed. 2d 334, 113 S.Ct. 2130 (1993).
9. *Delaware v. Prouse* 440 U.S. 648, 59 L.Ed. 2d 660, 99 S.Ct. 1391 (1979).
10. *Pennsylvania v. Mimms* 434 U.S. 106, 54 L.Ed. 2d 331, 98 S.Ct. 330 (1977).
11. *Maryland v. Wilson* 519 U.S. 408, 137 L.Ed. 2d 41, 117 S.Ct. 882 (1997).
12. *Michigan v. Long* 463 U.S. 1032, 77 L.Ed. 2d 1201, 103 S.Ct. 3469 (1983).
13. *Davis v. Mississippi* 394 U. S. 721, 22 L.Ed. 2d 676, 89 S.Ct. 1394 (1969); *Hayes v. Florida* 470 U.S. 811, 84 L.Ed. 2d 705, 105 S.Ct. 1643 (1985).
14. *Dunaway v. New York* 442 U.S. 200, 60 L.Ed. 2d 824, 99 S.Ct. 2248 (1979).
15. *New Jersey v. T. L. O.* 469 U.S. 325, 83 L.Ed. 2d 720, 105 S.Ct. 733 (1985).
16. *United States v. Place* 462 U.S. 696, 77 L.Ed. 2d 110, 103 S.Ct. 2637 (1983).
17. *Payton v. New York* 445 U.S. 573, 63 L.Ed. 2d 639, 100 S.Ct. 1371 (1980).
18. *Stegald v. United States* 451 U.S. 204, 68 L.Ed. 2d 38, 101 S.Ct. 1642 (1981).
19. *Chimel v. California* 395 U.S. 752, 23 L.Ed. 2d 685, 89 S.Ct. 2034 (1969).
20. United States v. Robinson 414 U.S. 218, 38 L.Ed. 2d 427, 94 S.Ct. 467 (1973); *Gustafson v. Florida* 414 U.S. 260, 38 L.Ed. 2d 456, 94 S.Ct. 488 (1973).
21. *New York v. Belton* 453 U.S. 454, 69 L.Ed. 2d 768, 101 S.Ct. 2869 (1981).
22. *Thornton v. United States* __ U.S. __, 158 L.Ed. 2d 905, 124 S.Ct. __ (2004).
23. *Maryland v. Buie* 494 U.S. 325, 108 L.Ed. 2d 276, 110 S.Ct. 1093 (1990).
24. *United States v. Edwards* 415 U.S. 800, 39 L.Ed. 2d 711, 94 S.Ct. 1234 (1974).
25. *Illinois v. Lafayette* 462 U.S. 640, 77 L.Ed. 2d 65, 103 S.Ct. 2605 (1983).
26. *Bell v. Wolfish* 441 U.S. 520, 60 L.Ed. 2d 447, 99 S.Ct. 1861 (1979).
27. *Hudson v. Palmer* 468 U.S. 517, 82 L.Ed. 2d 393, 104 S.Ct. 3194 (1984).

Plain View, Consent, and Administrative Warrants

Outline

Key Terms

- Abandoned property
- Administrative warrant
- Aerial search
- Apparent authority
- Consent search
- Open Fields Doctrine
- Plain View Doctrine
- Right to inventory
- Roadblock

After studying this chapter, you will be able to:

- Define the Plain View Doctrine.
- Define the Open Fields Doctrine.
- Describe the right to search abandoned property and consent searches.
- Identify those situations in which police have a right to search cars.
- List the exceptions to the administrative warrant requirement.

12-1 Plain View and Open Fields Doctrines

The **Plain View Doctrine,** established in *Washington v. Chrisman, Coolidge v. New Hampshire,* and other cases, is one of the most useful exceptions to the warrant requirement.

Plain View Doctrine Defined

It is not an unreasonable search for officers who are legally on the premises to observe items left where they can be seen. Probable cause is needed to seize the objects observed in plain view.[1]

The Plain View Doctrine has three key elements:

1. Objects must be where officers can observe them.
2. The officers must be legally at the location where the observation was made.
3. There must be probable cause to seize what was observed.

12-1a The Observation

Finding objects in plain view is not considered a search because they are not hidden. However, under the Plain View Doctrine, officers are not allowed to move things or otherwise examine them for identifying marks (such as serial numbers). The item must be at a location where the officer can see it without disturbing anything. This does not prevent the officer from moving to a better vantage point to observe them, for example, walking around the room, stretching, or bending, as long as they stay in an area where they are legally entitled to be. Most courts also allow the use of flashlights and binoculars.

In *Horton v. California* the Supreme Court made it clear that items do not have to be discovered inadvertently to qualify for the Plain View Doctrine.[2] In that case officers had requested a search warrant to search for stolen property and weapons, but the judge had issued a warrant only authorizing a search for stolen property. While executing the search warrant, officers did not find any stolen property, but they did find weapons. The court held that these weapons were in plain view and legally seized, even though the officers suspected that they were there before going to the location.

Examples of Observations Covered by the Plain View Doctrine
- During a stop authorized by *Terry v. Ohio*, the officers believed the suspect was armed and did a pat down. A hard object in his jacket pocket was believed to be a gun but when the officer retrieved it, it turned out to be a roll of counterfeit money.
- While executing a search warrant for a large quantity of fake ATM cards, an officer opened a drawer and found numerous packets of heroin.
- A car was stopped for speeding. The officer looked through the window as he approached the vehicle and saw an illegal assault rifle in the back seat.

12-1b Legally on Premises

For the Plain View Doctrine to operate, the officers must be legally at the location where the observation was made. Probably the most common situations involve making arrests, field interviews, car stops, and executing search warrants. If the officer illegally entered the house, for example, nothing observed inside qualifies for the Plain View Doctrine.

Aerial searches are an extension of this concept. In *California v. Ciraolo,* the Supreme Court held that observations made from a police aircraft qualify for the Plain View Doctrine.[3] The fact that the defendant built a fence around his backyard indicated a subjective expectation of privacy, but the Court found that this did not matter when the police observed some marijuana plants with the naked eye from public airspace. Since this case arose from observations made from a chartered aircraft, it is clear that the observation does not have to be made during routine patrol or from a frequently used flight path.

Examples of Being Legally on the Premises
for the Plain View Doctrine
- Officers arrived at a house to serve an arrest warrant. They complied with "knock and announce" before entering. Three feet from the front door they observed a stack of uncut sheets of counterfeit $20 bills.
- Officers arrested the driver of the car for driving under the influence of alcohol. While they were taking inventory of the car prior to having it towed away, they opened the trunk and discovered ten bricks of marijuana.
- Officers discovered the suspect's car in a public parking lot. They walked around it and checked for damage consistent with it being involved in a recent hit-and-run accident.

- Officers chartered a helicopter and flew over the suspect's house. Parked in the backyard partially covered by a tarp, they observed a vehicle matching the description of the getaway car from a recent robbery.

12-1c Probable Cause to Seize

The fact that the item was in plain view and the officers were legally present indicates that there has been no unreasonable search. The final issue deals with the right to seize the item. To do this, there must be probable cause (*Arizona v. Hicks*).[4] Reasonable suspicion is not enough.

This probable cause requirement means the facts must indicate it is more likely than not that the item is evidence of a crime or is contraband. This decision must be made without searching the item for clues such as serial numbers. If probable cause exists, the item can be seized on the spot without a warrant.

Even when the facts do not establish probable cause, the observation may still be useful. It may provide leads in the investigation. The observation can also be included, along with other facts, in an affidavit used to obtain a warrant to conduct a full search of the location.

Examples of Probable Cause to Seize Item under the Plain View Doctrine

- When conducting a booking search of the suspect, an officer removed everything from a backpack the suspect had been carrying. The officer carefully inspected everything and discovered a watch that exactly fit the description of a unique watch taken in a recent robbery.
- While executing a search warrant for equipment used to make counterfeit money, an officer discovered seven TV sets. By walking around the TVs, the officer was able to copy down serial numbers. The officer had the dispatcher run the serial numbers and confirmed that they matched those on TVs taken during a recent burglary of an appliance store.
- An officer took inventory of a car found abandoned in the street prior to having the car towed to an impound lot. The officer found three hand-rolled marijuana cigarettes in the ashtray.

12-1d Open Fields Doctrine

The **Open Fields Doctrine,** established in *Oliver v. United States* and *United States v. Dunn,* relies heavily on history and the wording of the Fourth Amendment. Since farmland and other open spaces are not

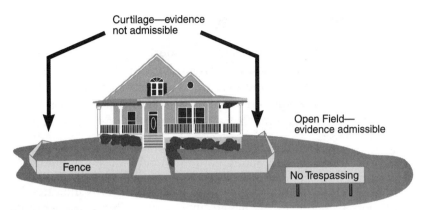

Figure 12-1
Open Fields Doctrine

included in the "persons, houses, papers and effects" specified in the Fourth Amendment, they are not protected. Historical protection of the "curtilage," or enclosed area immediately around the house, expands the Amendment to those areas but not beyond to open fields. Figure 12-1 illustrates where police officers can seize evidence under the Open Fields Doctrine.

Open Fields Doctrine Defined
Evidence found by officers in open areas that are not close to homes can be seized. This evidence is admissible even though the officers were trespassing at the time they seized it.[5]

The Open Fields Doctrine has little use in the urban setting, but can be used in rural areas. It is very useful in the search for clandestine marijuana cultivation. The Open Fields Doctrine applies even though fences have been built and "No Trespassing" signs posted. Areas where there are no established roads can also be searched under this doctrine.

Examples of Use of the Open Fields Doctrine
- Officers suspected that farmer was growing marijuana in the portion of his field farthest from the road. They walked down the rural road, climbed a fence that had a "No Trespassing" sign, and went to the back of the field. They found 100 healthy marijuana plants growing there.
- Police chartered a helicopter and flew over the suspect's farm. About 500 yards from the house they observed 10 cars in the process of being dismantled.

12-2 Abandoned Property

One of the key points in the Supreme Court's analysis of search and seizure issues is the expectation of privacy. Both an objective and subjective expectation of privacy must exist. The subjective part of the analysis focuses on the efforts a person took to protect his/her privacy. The objective aspect of privacy means that a privacy interest exists that society is willing to protect.

Seizing **abandoned property** is not an unreasonable search because there is neither an objective nor subjective expectation of privacy. In most cases, the fact that the property has been abandoned clearly indicates that the previous owner no longer has any interest in it. This is clear when the property has been left in a public place.

A more difficult question arises when trash has been sealed in opaque plastic bags and left at the curb for pickup by a garbage truck. While the opaque plastic may indicate a subjective expectation of privacy, the Supreme Court, in *California v. Greenwood,* ruled that there is no objective basis for this expectation.[6] This rests on the fact that strangers, animals, and snoops are free to look through trash. The person throwing out the trash also has no authority to prevent the garbage collectors from rummaging through it or giving it to the police. Leaving items for recycling results in the same conclusion because it should be anticipated that someone will sort through it.

The final part of this analysis is determining when something has been abandoned. Dumping it in a trash can in a public place or littering on the highway are obvious examples of abandonment. A person who merely puts an item in a wastebasket inside a private home still has the right to reclaim it. Hiding something in an open area that is accessible to the public, like under a rock in the forest, could be considered either way. Items that a person discards while being pursued by police, but prior to arrest, are considered abandoned.[7]

Examples of Use of Abandoned Property
- As a police officer chased the suspect, the suspect threw something away. After detaining the suspect, the officer went back to the location and found a small plastic bag containing illegal drugs.
- Police suspected that a man was involved in bookmaking. They put his house under surveillance and watched him put his trash bags at the curb and go back inside. They seized the trash bags and searched them for anything indicating bookmaking.

12-3 Consent Searches

Officers do not need a warrant if they have obtained consent to search. On the other hand, probable cause to search cannot be based solely on the fact that a person refused to give consent.

Consent Search Defined

A search conducted based on the voluntary consent of a person with apparent authority over the area to be searched does not require a search warrant.

Three key points must be considered to determine if a search can be based on consent:

1. The standard for obtaining consent.
2. Who can give consent.
3. What can be searched based on the consent given.

12-3a Standard for Consent

Schneckloth v. Bustamonte established that consent must be given voluntarily.[8] The Supreme Court has, however, specifically refused to require officers to warn suspects that there is a constitutional right to refuse to give consent for a search. Each case must be analyzed on the totality of the circumstances that were present when the officers asked for permission to search. Officers do not need reasonable suspicion to approach a person and ask for consent to search.

Some factors clearly indicate that the consent is coerced. Consent is not voluntary if the police inform someone that they have a search warrant. Allowing the police to enter under these circumstances is considered to be merely acquiescing to authority (*Bumper v. North Carolina*).[9] By stating that they have a warrant, the police, in effect, inform people that they do not have the right to refuse entry.

More commonly, the courts will look at all of the facts present when the request for consent was made. The fact that officers had their guns drawn weighs very heavily against the consent being voluntary. Other applicable factors include the education and intelligence of the suspect, attempts by the police to intimidate the suspect, and the fact the suspect already knew his/her rights. For example, in *Florida v. Bostick* uniformed officers approached a person on a bus and asked for permission to search his luggage.[10] The officers testified that they informed Bostick that he had the right to refuse to consent, and they never drew their guns or threatened Bostick in any manner with a gun. Bostick testified that he did not feel free to leave the bus. The Court held that consent was valid and saw no distinction between a stop in the close confines of a bus and one on the street.

Examples of Legally Obtained Consent

- During a routine traffic stop, the officer politely asked the driver, "Do you mind if I look in the trunk?" The driver consented.
- An officer handling a domestic violence call arrived after the batterer left. The officer asked the battered woman, "Do you mind if I look to see if there are any guns in the house? I can take the guns into custody so he won't be able to shoot you." The woman consented.

12-3b Who Can Consent

Consent must be given by someone with **apparent authority** over the area to be searched (*United States v. Matlock* and *Illinois v. Rodriguez*).[11] Officers may rely on reasonable appearances that a person lives in a house or owns a business.

Ownership, however, is not essential. In fact, the owner may not be able to consent. The key again is reasonable expectation of privacy. Landlords cannot consent to searches of a tenant's apartment, nor can hotel personnel grant permission to search a guest's room. Police cannot rely on consent from people whose personal privacy is not at stake.

If two people have equal rights to a location, either may consent to a search. This commonly applies to husband-wife and roommate situations. For example, either roommate can consent to a search of the kitchen, but if they have separate bedrooms one cannot consent to a search of the other's room.

The parent-child relationship is more complicated. If a young child is living at home, the parent can consent to a search of the child's room and possessions. Older children, however, may have their own privacy interests. Paying rent or the fact that the parents recognize the child's right to exclude them from the room may indicate that a parent cannot give consent. Even if the parent can consent to police entering the room, teenagers may still have an expectation of privacy regarding locked containers kept in their rooms.

Very young children do not have the authority to consent to police entering the house. Children generally do not have the right to consent to searches of their parents' room or other private parts of the house.

Probationers and parolees pose a different question. Some states permit searches of probationers and parolees on less than probable cause.

Others make consent to searches a condition of probation or parole. In *Griffin v. Wisconsin,* the Supreme Court approved of this practice because it is necessary to facilitate rehabilitation and deter criminal activity.[12] In the case before the Court, searches based on "reasonable grounds," but less than probable cause, were authorized under the supervision of the probation officer.

Examples of Who Can Consent to a Search
- Father called the police because he was afraid his 15-year-old son was using drugs. The police talked to the father but the son was not home. Father told the officer that his son stayed in the garage a lot. The officer asked if he could search the garage. Father said yes.
- Two roommates got into a fight. The police were called. Roommate A told the police that Roommate B was selling drugs. The officer asked where the drugs were kept. When told that they were in the freezer in the kitchen, an officer asked Roommate A for permission to look in the freezer. Roommate A said yes.
- A car carrying three adult males was stopped because it had been cruising the area all evening. The officer had all of them exit the car. He then asked the driver if he could search the car. The driver said yes.

12-3c Scope of the Search

The area to be searched and how long officers can search may be very broad or very limited. These factors are governed by the conditions that accompanied the consent. Once consent has been given, officers can search anything in that area (including closed containers) unless the person giving the consent has placed restrictions on what may be searched.[13] Consent can be withdrawn at any time and no justification needs to be given for terminating the consent to search.

What is found during the search may create probable cause for an additional search. If so, this probable cause can be considered by the officers when seeking a search warrant. It may also indicate that some other exception to the warrant requirement applies. Plain view accompanies a consent search. Anything seen during the search can be seized if there is probable cause to tie it to a crime.

Examples of the Scope of the Search When There Is a Consent Search
- During a routine traffic stop the officer asked to look in the trunk. Consent was given. When the officer was searching the trunk, the driver suddenly yelled, "Stop. Get out of my trunk. Now!" Consent was taken away and the officer had to stop the search.

- Officers entered a pawn shop and asked the sales clerk, "Do you mind if we look around?" The clerk nodded agreement. The officers slowly inspected everything behind the counter, writing down serial numbers to check later.

12-4 Vehicle Searches

Cars and other vehicles have become very important parts of our daily lives and are highly visible and heavily regulated. Their extensive exposure to public view, coupled with detailed licensing requirements and safety inspections, have resulted in a lesser expectation of privacy in vehicles than in homes. The mobility of vehicles is viewed as creating an urgency not present when evidence is found in buildings. For all of these reasons, the rules for searching vehicles are somewhat different than those for other locations.

Motor homes are usually treated like vehicles.[14] *California v. Carney* concluded that even though motor homes possess many of the characteristics of houses, they still have the ability to leave the scene. This creates an urgency not present with more traditional dwellings. If, on the other hand, the motor home is hooked up to utilities or otherwise immobilized, it is treated like a dwelling.

12-4a Vehicle Search Incident to Arrest

The search incident to a custodial arrest normally covers the person and area under his/her immediate control. If the occupant of a car is arrested, *New York v. Belton* permits the search to cover the person and the passenger compartment of the car. *Thornton v. United States*[15] expanded this rule to situations where the person arrested is a "recent occupant" of the vehicle. The entire passenger compartment is viewed as the area where the person may reach to obtain a weapon and/or destroy evidence or contraband. Unlike the non-vehicle arrest, the person arrested can be removed from the vehicle prior to the search. This does not change the requirement that the search be contemporaneous with the arrest.

Right to Search a Vehicle as Incident to Arrest Defined

When an occupant of a car is arrested, officers may conduct a thorough search of the person arrested and the entire passenger compartment.[16]

The passenger compartment is easily identified in a traditional sedan. It includes the area around the front and back seats, the glove compartment, and console. It does not extend to the trunk, the area under the hood, or to other parts of the vehicle. Vans, sports utility vehicles, and other models that do not have a physical barrier separating the driver and occupants from storage space require a factual determination of what is the equivalent of the passenger compartment.

Everything within the passenger compartment may be thoroughly searched. This includes items, such as briefcases, that would normally fall under the Closed Container Rule. The glove compartment and console may be opened. Since both weapons and other evidence may be seized, areas too small to hide a gun or knife may also be searched.

Examples of Vehicle Searches Done Incident to Arrest
- An officer arrested the passenger in a car based on an outstanding arrest warrant. Prior to taking the person to jail, the officer conducted a very careful search of the entire passenger compartment.
- An officer arrested the driver of a car for driving under the influence of alcohol, handcuffed him, and placed him in the back seat of the police car. An officer legally parked the car at the curb. While one officer watched the drunk driver, the other very thoroughly searched the passenger compartment of the vehicle.

12-4b Vehicle Searches Based on Probable Cause

Primarily due to the mobility of cars and other vehicles, the Supreme Court in *Chambers v. Maroney*[17] authorized searches without a warrant if the police have probable cause to believe that evidence is in the vehicle. Subsequent cases make it clear that these searches do not require any type of emergency to justify the failure to obtain a search warrant (*Michigan v. Thomas; Maryland v. Dyson*).[18] In fact, a probable cause search may be conducted after a car has been impounded for a reason totally unrelated to the case.

Right to Search Vehicle Based on Probable Cause Defined
Officers may conduct a search of a vehicle without a warrant if there is probable cause to believe that the vehicle contains something of evidentiary value that can legally be seized. The search is restricted to areas where there is probable cause to believe the items are located. It may be done at the scene or later at a more convenient location.[19]

The scope of a probable cause search of a vehicle is directly tied to the facts. For example, if an officer saw someone run from the scene of a robbery, throw something in the trunk of a car, and then flee the scene on foot, there would be probable cause to believe evidence of the robbery may be in the trunk of the car. The trunk may be searched immediately based on this probable cause. These facts, however, do not provide any justification to search other parts of the car. It is important to note that once a search is justified, the officer can search anything in the car that is large enough to conceal the item(s) sought. This would justify searching a purse that belongs to a passenger in the car who is not yet suspected of criminal activity (*Wyoming v. Houghton*).[20]

Sometimes probable cause searches and searches incident to arrests overlap. For example, if police pursue a getaway car leaving the scene of a burglary with occupants matching the description of the suspects, they will have probable cause to arrest the occupants and probable cause to search the car. On the other hand, if a person in a car is arrested on an old warrant there will be no probable cause to search the car.

There is no time limit on when a probable cause vehicle search must be done. It can be done at the scene or later. Officers can tow the car to a storage yard, the police station, or some other convenient location before searching it. One evidentiary issue must be considered, however. If the search is not done immediately, the prosecution will have the burden of showing that no one tampered with the vehicle or "planted" the evidence between the time the car was impounded and the search was conducted.

United States v. Ross held that the search of a vehicle based on probable cause can be as extensive as the one a judge could authorize if presented with an affidavit stating the facts known to the officers.[21] Closed containers can be searched on the spot. Officers are not required to seize them and obtain a warrant before opening them.

Examples of Vehicle Searches Based on Probable Cause

- Police saw a man run from a store with a clerk chasing him shouting "Thief! Thief!" The man threw something through the open window of a car and ran away. An officer reached through the open window and retrieved a brand new shirt with the sales tags still on it.
- Police stopped a car for speeding. As the officer walked up to the driver he smelled a strong odor of marijuana coming from the trunk. The officer demanded the keys to the trunk, opened it, and found 500 pounds of marijuana.
- Police observed what they thought was a drug deal. They chased the suspect's car and pulled it over for speeding. They observed approximately 25 baggies of marijuana on the passenger seat. They impounded the car. Two days later they searched the entire passenger compartment and found a number of other drugs packaged for sale.

12-4c Vehicle Search—Inventory of Impounded Vehicles

Whenever a car is legally impounded it may be inventoried. The reason for impounding the vehicle has no bearing on the **right to inventory.** The Supreme Court, in *South Dakota v. Opperman,* based the right to conduct the inventory on the protection of both the owner of the vehicle and the police. The police protect the owner by accounting for everything that is present and removing valuable items. The police are protected against unfounded claims of theft because a detailed report is available stating exactly what was in the vehicle at the time it was taken into custody.

Right to Inventory Vehicles Defined
Anytime a vehicle is impounded officers may inventory its contents.[22]

Any evidence found during the inventory is admissible. The primary question is whether the police were searching for evidence or conducting a legitimate inventory. Department policies that require all cars to be inventoried are usually admissible on this point. In general, the courts are satisfied that an inventory was being conducted if the police systematically go over the entire car. The inventory is more likely to be considered a pretext to search if the officers stopped as soon as evidence was found. Closed containers may be opened during an inventory if the department's policy indicates that this action is authorized.[23]

Another distinction between a search and an inventory is the extent of the search. An inventory usually involves merely itemizing observable items that could be removed from the car. This commonly includes opening the glove compartment and trunk. It does not involve inspecting the inside of the spare tire, removing rocker panels, or cutting the upholstery open to see if they contain drugs. Such acts would be considered searches.

**Examples of Vehicle Searches during Inventory
of Impounded Vehicle**
- Police had a car towed away because it was blocking a fire lane. When it arrived at the impound lot they inventoried it. In the trunk they found a jack, a tire iron, a spare tire, and a sack containing 100 counterfeit CDs.
- Police had a car towed away because it was inoperable after an accident. Prior to the arrival of the tow truck they inventoried it. In the glove compartment they found 10 forged checks and false IDs.
- Police arrested a suspected bank robber after a high-speed chase. The car was impounded as evidence. Prior to towing it, the car was inventoried. In the trunk they found a bank bag from the bank that was robbed and money wrappers from the same bank.

12-4d Vehicle Search during Stop Based on Reasonable Suspicion

Michigan v. Long stated two prerequisites for the search of a car for weapons during a field interview:

1. There must have been specific articulable facts that caused the officers to believe that at least one of the occupants of the vehicle was involved in criminal activity AND
2. There must have been at least a reasonable suspicion that the vehicle contained weapons the suspect might use against the officers.

Right to Search Vehicles during Stops Based on Reasonable Suspicion Defined

During a field interview, the passenger compartment of a vehicle may be searched for weapons if there is reasonable suspicion that the vehicle contains weapons.[24]

While this type of vehicle search permits police to search the entire passenger compartment, it is more limited than the search incident to a custodial arrest. Weapons are the only things officers are justified in looking for. This means that only areas large enough to conceal a weapon can be searched. Anything found while the officers are properly conducting this type of search is admissible under the Plain View Doctrine.

The search for weapons can be done while the suspects are out of the car if they will be permitted to return to it. This is allowed because as soon as the suspect is released he/she may retrieve weapons from the car and attack the officer.

Non-custodial arrests, such as traffic tickets, also fall under this rule. It is important to note that the second prerequisite, reasonable suspicion that the vehicle contains weapons, is not an automatic conclusion when a non-custodial arrest is made. Officers must be able to state specific facts that caused them to suspect that weapons were present.

Examples of Vehicle Search during Stop Based on Reasonable Suspicion

• A car is stopped based on reasonable suspicion that the occupants are about to spray graffiti on a nearby wall. Based on the behavior of the suspects, the officers believe they have weapons in the car. The passenger compartment is searched; two knives and six ounces of cocaine are recovered.
• A car is stopped because officers believe it is about to commit a drive-by shooting. The passenger compartment of the car is immediately searched for weapons. The officers find a sawed-off shotgun under the driver's seat.

12-4e Vehicle Search—Outside of Vehicle

The outside of a car parked in a public place falls under the Plain View Doctrine *(Cardwell v. Lewis; New York v. Class)*. What is seen may be used to establish probable cause for further action. For example, paint on the car may indicate that it has been in a collision. Samples may be taken, either at the original location or later at the impound lot, and sent to a forensics laboratory for testing. This rule also allows officers to look for vehicle identification numbers. It is important to note that this rule does not apply to cars parked on a private property.

Right to Search the Outside of a Vehicle Defined
Officers may inspect the outside of a vehicle that is parked in a public place.[25]

Examples of Vehicle Search—Outside of the Vehicle
• While the police questioned the suspect, another officer went outside and looked at the suspect's car which was parked on the street. A dent and paint the color of the vehicle pushed over a cliff were found on the front bumper.
• The police had the suspect under surveillance and noted that she always parked at the curb in front of her apartment. After the suspect went inside, an officer looked at the tags on the license plate and determined that they were not the ones issued for the car.

12-4f Vehicle Search during Non-Criminal Investigation

The Supreme Court authorized searches not related to the investigation of a crime as part of the "community caretaking function" of the police *(Cady v. Dombrowski)*. The case involved searching an impounded car in an unguarded lot for a gun the driver had the legal right to possess. The search was considered justified because it was done to prevent vandals from stealing the gun. During the search, much to the surprise of the officers, evidence of an unreported murder was discovered.

Right to Search Vehicle during Non-Criminal Investigation Defined
Under some circumstances, cars may be searched if there is a legitimate reason for the search not related to the investigation of a crime.[26]

This is an exception to the search warrant requirement that has not been fully developed by the Supreme Court. Officers should be very cautious in relying on it.

Examples of Vehicle Searches during Non-Criminal Investigations

- Police officers find a car parked beside a seldomly used road. It appears the vehicle has been there a long time. They open the door in order to find the registration. Once inside they detect the smell of marijuana.
- A Department of Motor Vehicles officer is checking paperwork at a local car dealer against the cars on the lot. This is done to verify that the dealer is paying appropriate fees on the cars. One car does not have any license plates. The agent opens the trunk to locate the license plate and finds several stolen license plates.

12-4g Vehicle Stops at Roadblocks

The seemingly contradictory rule that allows the police to stop all cars without cause but not to randomly stop a few cars was dicta in *Delaware v. Prouse,* a case which expressly prohibited random car stops for the purpose of checking drivers' licenses and vehicle registrations. It suggested that stopping all cars traveling on the street to check licenses and registrations would be legal.

Right to Stop Vehicles at Roadblocks Defined

Vehicles may not be stopped randomly but in some situations roadblocks may be established and all cars stopped briefly.[27]

Roadblocks have been used to conduct inspections of safety equipment, such as brakes and taillights. Roadblocks are not authorized, however, merely to check for outstanding arrest warrants. The Supreme Court approved the use of roadblocks for sobriety checkpoints after balancing the need to prevent drunk driving against the minimal intrusion such roadblocks make on the rights of individual motorists.[28] In a recent case, however, the Court refused to allow stopping cars at roadblocks that were set up to detect illegal drugs.[29] On the other hand, officers may set up a roadblock for the purpose of soliciting information from the public about a recent crime.[30]

Examples of Vehicle Stops at Roadblocks

- Officers set up a roadblock and stop every fourth car in order to give the driver a breath-alcohol test. Arrests were made for drivers whose blood alcohol was over the legal limit. Officers also arrested people when the officers observed drugs through the windows of the car.

- Officers set up a roadblock so they could check safety equipment on the car—brake lights, head lights, and turn signals. If the car did not have operative safety equipment the driver was given a "fixer" ticket. People were also cited if they were not wearing seat belts when they drove into the roadblock.

12-5 Administrative Searches

There are many reasons to search a building that are not related to normal police activity. For example, inspectors may need to check for compliance with the fire and building codes. The Supreme Court, in *Camara v. Municipal Court* and *See v. City of Seattle,* designed a modified warrant procedure for these situations.

The probable cause needed for an **administrative warrant** is very different from that mandated for search warrants. The purpose of the warrant is to protect people's privacy from invasion by public officials. It is also designed to prevent harassment by frequent, needless inspections.

Requirements for Administrative Warrant
Probable cause for an administrative warrant requires a reasonable legislative purpose for the search. This legislative purpose does not have to show that there is reason to suspect that there are violations in any specific building.[31]

The statement of legislative purpose merely restates the reason the law was created that authorized the search. For example, if the sanitation district is authorized to inspect each building once every four years, the fact that the quadrant of the city where the house in question is located is scheduled for inspection this year is sufficient probable cause. There is no need to state that there are facts indicating that the sanitation code is being violated at the address named in the warrant application.

Although the administrative warrant procedure applies to both residential and commercial buildings, the use of these warrants is rather rare. Most people are willing to permit inspectors to enter the building and perform their duty. When admission is denied, a warrant can be used to complete the inspection. The process can be used for building and wiring codes, inspection of restaurants for health code violations, sanitation inspections for rodents and other pests, and inspections to determine if the fire regulations are being complied with.

Supreme Court cases establish exemptions from the administrative warrant requirement for firearms dealers (*United States v. Biswell*),[32] establishments selling alcoholic beverages (*Colonnade Catering Corp. v.*

United States),[33] junkyards that dismantle cars (*New York v. Burger*),[34] and safety inspections under the Federal Mine Safety and Health Act of 1977 (*Donovan v. Dewey*).[35]

These are all businesses that are typically heavily regulated. The common theme for permitting warrantless inspections is:

1. The regulatory scheme is supported by a substantial government interest.
2. The warrantless inspections are necessary to further the regulatory scheme.
3. The statute must limit official discretion and advise the owners of businesses of the limits on their privacy.

Immigration and Naturalization Service agents are also exempted from the use of warrants when they enter businesses to check for illegal aliens employed there *(INS v. Delgado)*.[36] The Court found that, unlike the other exemptions, entering the business, including blocking the exits, did not constitute a seizure. If specific individuals were detained for questioning, normal Fourth Amendment standards would apply.

Several Supreme Court cases have refused to grant exemptions from the administrative warrant requirement. One is for OSHA (Occupational Safety and Health Administration) inspections. Inspectors may not enter a business to check for violations of health and safety rules without consent or an administrative warrant (*Marshall v. Barlow's, Inc.*).[37]

Fire inspectors pose several interesting problems. Fire fighters trying to put out a blaze, and those involved in the mop-up operation, obviously do not need any type of warrant. Inspections that are primarily regulatory in nature require administrative warrants. An administrative warrant is also required if there is suspicion of arson. Once arson investigators have probable cause to believe arson in fact occurred, they need a regular search warrant to enter the structure (*Michigan v. Tyler; Michigan v. Clifford*).[38] Burned-out structures may still have a protected privacy interest if the owners have tried to board them up or otherwise keep people out.

Examples of Administrative Searches

- The fire department is checking all businesses for compliance with fire regulations. When Business X refused to allow the inspection, the fire department obtained an administrative warrant for the inspection.
- The health department checks restaurants for compliance with sanitary requirements. When Big Burgers refused to allow the inspectors into the kitchen, the health department obtained an administrative warrant in order to inspect the kitchen.

- The Federal Bureau of Alcohol, Tobacco and Firearms (ATF) went to Gun Shop to check its records against the stock on hand. The owner of Gun Shop refused to allow the search. AFT agents forced their way into Gun Shop and searched it because firearms dealers are exempt from the administrative warrant requirement.

Summary

It is not a search to observe something that is in plain view. The Plain View Doctrine applies to whatever officers see without searching while they are legally on the premises. There must be probable cause in order to seize an item. A related rule, called the Open Fields Doctrine, admits evidence observed by officers even while trespassing. To qualify, the area must not be near a dwelling.

No matter where abandoned property is found, it is admissible. The Fourth Amendment does not apply to abandoned property due to the fact that no one's expectation of privacy is involved.

A search is legal if it is done with the consent of a person with apparent authority over the area. Officers must reasonably believe this person has a privacy interest in the area to be searched. The consent must be voluntary, but officers do not need to inform anyone of his/her constitutional right to refuse to consent. The person giving the consent may limit the area to be searched and/or restrict the length of time the police may spend searching.

The Supreme Court does not recognize as great a privacy interest in vehicles as in houses. If an occupant of a car is arrested, the entire passenger compartment may be searched. Specific parts of a car may be searched, immediately or after impounding the vehicle, if there is probable cause to believe evidence is concealed there. Any impounded vehicle may be inventoried. Evidence found during the inventory is admissible. If a car is stopped on reasonable suspicion that it is involved in criminal activity and there is also reasonable suspicion that weapons are in the vehicle, the passenger compartment may be searched for weapons. The exterior of a car parked in a public place may be inspected under the Plain View Doctrine.

A special search warrant must be obtained to enter a building to do an administrative inspection if no one will give consent. Probable cause for this warrant is established if there is a reasonable legislative purpose for the inspection. Gun dealers, junkyards, and establishments selling alcohol may be entered for inspection without a warrant.

Discussion Questions

1. Explain the requirements for the Plain View and Open Field Doctrines.
2. When may police search abandoned property? Explain.
3. What is the standard for determining if consent to search is valid? Who may consent? How detailed a search is permitted? Explain.
4. What areas may police search if they arrest the driver of a car? Explain.
5. When may officers search a car without a warrant? When may officers inventory a car? Explain.
6. What areas may be searched if a car is stopped because there is reasonable suspicion that a passenger is involved in criminal activity? Explain.
7. May officers randomly stop cars to check registration? Explain.
8. Can roadblocks be set up to check for drunk driving? Explain.
9. When is an administrative warrant required? How do officers obtain one? Explain.
10. Name three types of businesses that are exempt from the administrative warrant requirement.

Endnotes

1. *Washington v. Chrisman* 455 U.S. 1, 70 L.Ed. 2d 778, 102 S.Ct. 812 (1982). See also *Coolidge v. New Hampshire* 403 U.S. 443, 29 L.Ed. 2d 564, 91 S.Ct. 2022 (1971).
2. *Horton v. California* 496 U.S. 128, 110 L.Ed. 2d 112, 110 S.Ct. 2301 (1990).
3. *California v. Ciraolo* 476 U.S. 207, 90 L.Ed. 2d 210, 106 S.Ct. 1809 (1987).
4. *Arizona v. Hicks* 480 U.S. 321, 94 L.Ed. 2d 347, 107 S.Ct. 1149 (1987).
5. *Oliver v. United States* 466 U.S. 170, 80 L.Ed. 2d 214, 104 S.Ct. 173 (1984); *United States v. Dunn* 480 U.S. 480 294, 94 L.Ed. 2d 326, 107 S.Ct. 1134 (1987).
6. *California v. Greenwood* 486 U.S. 35, 100 L.Ed. 2d 30, 108 S.Ct. 1625 (1988).
7. *California v. Hodari D.* 499 U.S. 621, 113 L.Ed. 2d 690, 111 S.Ct. 1547 (1991).
8. *Schneckloth v. Bustamonte* 412 U.S. 218, 36 L.Ed. 2d 854, 93 S.Ct. 2041 (1973).
9. *Bumper v. North Carolina* 391 U.S. 543, 20 L.Ed. 2d 797, 88 S.Ct. 1788 (1968).
10. *Florida v. Bostick* 501 U.S. 429, 115 L.Ed. 2d 389, 111 S.Ct. 2382 (1991).
11. *United States v. Matlock* 415 U.S. 164, 39 L.Ed. 2d 242, 94 S.Ct. 988 (1974); *Illinois v. Rodriguez* 497 U.S. 177, 111 L.Ed. 2d 148, 110 S.Ct. 2793 (1990).
12. *Griffin v. Wisconsin* 483 U.S. 868, 97 L.Ed. 2d 709, 107 S.Ct. 3164 (1987).
13. *Florida v. Jimeno* 500 U.S. 248, 114 L.Ed. 2d 297, 111 S.Ct. 1801 (1991)
14. *California v. Carney* 471 U.S. 386, 85 L.Ed. 2d 406, 105 S.Ct. 2066 (1985).
15. *Thornton v. United States* __ U.S. __, 158 L.Ed. 2d 905, 124 S.Ct. 2127 (2004).
16. *New York v. Belton* 453 U.S. 454, 69 L.Ed. 2d 768, 101 S.Ct. 2869 (1981).
17. *Chambers v. Maroney* 399 U.S. 42, 26 L.Ed. 2d 419, 90 S.Ct. 1975 (1970).
18. *Michigan v. Thomas* 458 U.S. 259, 73 L.Ed. 2d 750, 102 S.Ct. 3079 (1982); *Maryland v. Dyson* 527 U.S. 465, 144 L.Ed. 2d 442, 119 S. Ct. 2013 (1999).
19. *Chambers v. Maroney* 399 U.S. 42, 26 L.Ed. 2d 419, 90 S.Ct. 1975 (1970).

20. *Wyoming v. Houghton* 526 U.S. 295, 143 L. Ed. 2d 408, 119 S. Ct. 1297 (1999).
21. *United States v. Ross* 456 U.S. 798, 72 L.Ed. 2d 572, 102 S.Ct. 2157 (1982).
22. *South Dakota v. Opperman* 428 U.S. 364, 49 L.Ed. 2d 1000, 96 S.Ct. 3092 (1976).
23. *Michigan v. Long* 463 U.S. 1032, 77 L.Ed. 2d 1201, 103 S.Ct. 3469 (1983).
24. *Michigan v. Long* 463 U.S. 1032, 77 L.Ed. 2d 1201, 103 S.Ct. 3469 (1983).
25. *Cardwell v. Lewis* 417 U.S. 583, 41 L.Ed. 2d 325, 94 S.Ct. 2464 (1974); *New York v. Class* 475 U.S. 106, 89 L.Ed. 2d 81, 106 S.Ct. 960 (1986).
26. *Cady v. Dombrowski* 413 U.S. 433, 37 L.Ed. 2d 706, 93 S.Ct. 2523 (1973).
27. *Delaware v. Prouse* 440 U.S. 648, 59 L.Ed. 2d 660, 99 S.Ct. 1391 (1979).
28. *Michigan Dept. of State Police v. Sitz* 496 U.S. 444, 110 L.Ed. 2d 412, 110 S.Ct. 2481 (1990).
29. *City of Indianapolis v. Edmond* 531 U.S. 32, 148 L.Ed. 2d 333, 121 S.Ct. 447 (2000).
30. *Illinois v. Lidster* __ U.S. __, 157 L.Ed. 2d 843, 124 S.Ct. 885 (2004).
31. *Camara v. Municipal Court* 387 U.S. 523, 18 L.Ed. 2d 930, 87 S.Ct. 1727 (1967); *See v. City of Seattle* 387 U.S. 541, 18 L.Ed. 2d 943, 87 S.Ct.1737 (1967).
32. *United States v. Biswell* 406 U.S. 311, 32 L.Ed. 2d 87, 92 S.Ct. 1593 (1972).
33. *Colonnade Catering Corp. v. United States* 397 U.S. 72, 25 L.Ed. 2d 60, 90 S.Ct. 774 (1970).
34. *New York v. Burger* 482 U.S. 691, 96 L.Ed. 2d 601, 107 S.Ct. 2636 (1987).
35. *Donovan v. Dewey* 452 U.S. 594, 69 L.Ed. 2d 262, 101 S.Ct. 2534 (1981).
36. *Immigration and Naturalization Service v. Delgado* 466 U.S. 210, 80 L.Ed. 2d 247, 104 S.Ct. 1758 (1984).
37. *Marshall v. Barlow's, Inc.* 436 U.S. 307, 56 L.Ed. 2d 305, 98 S.Ct. 1816 (1978).
38. *Michigan v. Tyler* 436 U.S. 499, 56 L.Ed. 2d 486, 98 S.Ct. 1942 (1978); *Michigan v. Clifford* 464 U.S. 287, 78 L.Ed. 2d 477, 104 S.Ct. 641 (1984).

CHAPTER **13**

Electronic Surveillance and Other Searches

Outline

Key Terms

- Border search
- Closed Container Rule
- Controlled delivery
- Electronic surveillance
- Fixed checkpoint
- Misplaced Reliance Doctrine
- Point of entry
- Roving checkpoint

After studying this chapter, you will be able to:

- Identify the requirements for obtaining an electronic surveillance warrant.
- Define the Misplaced Reliance Doctrine.
- Identify the situations when Border Patrol and Customs agents are allowed to detain people and conduct searches.
- Explain police authority to search closed containers.
- Describe the right to require employees to take drug tests.

13-1 Eavesdropping and Electronic Surveillance

Eavesdropping has probably been done since people began keeping secrets from each other. Electronic surveillance, however, only emerged after the technology developed. Both involve the seizure of private conversations. The key distinction in Supreme Court cases in this area is whether the person making the comments knows a listener is present, not whether electronic equipment is used.

13-1a Misplaced Reliance Doctrine

In situations where the suspect knew someone was listening, the Supreme Court has placed the burden on the suspect to make sure that he/she can trust everyone who can hear what is said. This is called the **Misplaced Reliance Doctrine.** It applies whether or not tape recorders or radio transmitters are used. The person who overhears the conversation may carry tape recorders or radio transmitters without the prior authorization of a judge.

Misplaced Reliance Doctrine Defined

No warrant is required to obtain conversations that can be overheard by the police or their agents based on the misplaced reliance of the suspect. Each person bears the burden of restricting his/her conversations to people who will not reveal them to the authorities.

The facts from two cases help explain this doctrine. *Hoffa v. United States* is one of the leading cases.[1] When Jimmy Hoffa was on trial in what is called the "Test Fleet" case, the Justice Department had another union official named Partin released from prison. Partin was instructed to join Hoffa's entourage and report on Hoffa's out-of-court activities. No electronic monitoring equipment was to be used. Partin frequented Hoffa's hotel room and overheard conversations about plans to tamper with the jury. The "Test Fleet" case ended with a hung jury. Evidence supplied by

Partin was used in a subsequent case where Hoffa was charged with attempting to bribe jurors. The Supreme Court found this was a case of misplaced reliance. Hoffa knew Partin was present and took the risk that Partin might report the jury tampering to the authorities. The fact that the Justice Department had planted Partin had no legal significance.

Federal narcotics agents used concealed radio transmitters in *United States v. White,* another leading case.[2] They recorded conversations between agents and the defendant in public places, restaurants, the defendant's home, and the informant's car. The informant also allowed an agent to hide in a kitchen closet and transmit conversations between the informant and the defendant. All of these recorded conversations were found admissible under the Misplaced Reliance Doctrine. Defendant White should have been more careful in deciding whom he could trust. This even applied to the agent in the closet. White should not have relied on his friend who allowed the agent to hide there.

Examples of Misplaced Reliance

- Mary told her friend Liz that she had stolen an expensive ring. Liz reported what Mary said to the police.
- Nancy got in an argument while talking to Phil on her cell phone. She became so upset that she started shouting. A passerby heard Nancy threaten to kill Phil and reported her.
- Rick was arrested for selling drugs. He tried to plea bargain. Officers told him that they would drop the charges if he wore a "body mike" while buying drugs from his supplier. Rick wore the "body mike" and the police obtained enough evidence to convict the supplier.

13-1b Electronic Surveillance

Electronic surveillance has particularly troubled the Supreme Court because it has such a great potential for abuse. In both wiretap and bugging cases the victim may be totally unaware the government is listening. The key decisions on this topic were made in the late 1960s and early 1970s. Since that time technology has rapidly advanced and the ability to eavesdrop is much greater than it was then.

Reasonable expectation of privacy, the current standard for Fourth Amendment protections, originally came from a wiretap case. Prior to that time, electronic surveillance cases had focused on trespassing. Anything the police could accomplish without physically trespassing on the suspect's property was permitted. Sometimes this went to the extreme of measuring how far a "spike mike" had gone into the common wall between two apartments in order to tell if there had been a trespass.

In *Katz v. United States,*[3] agents had probable cause to believe the suspect was using a telephone booth as part of an interstate gambling operation. A listening device was placed on the outside of a public telephone booth. There was no trespass. Even so, the Supreme Court held that the government had violated the Fourth Amendment. There was a reasonable expectation of privacy because Katz entered the telephone booth, closed the door and kept his voice down.

The issuing of warrants permitting electronic surveillance was reviewed by the Supreme Court in *Berger v. New York.*[4] Statutes authorizing these specialized search warrants must provide very precise requirements. This includes a description of the offense and the types of conversations the officers expect to seize. The warrant must be limited to a short period of time. While the Court did not specifically state what length of time was permissible, it found that two months was too long. Extensions of the original warrant must be based on a showing that probable cause exists for the continuance of the surveillance. The warrant must have a return.

Warrant Requirement for Electronic Surveillance Defined

A warrant is required to install electronic listening devices that invade a person's reasonable expectation of privacy. The warrant must contain a detailed statement of probable cause including a showing of why other investigative techniques will not work. The warrant must not permit electronic monitoring for extended periods of time.

Examples of Electronic Surveillance

- Based on a wiretap warrant, the police department had the telephone company connect a device that would record all conversations on the lines listed in the warrant.
- Based on an electronic surveillance warrant, the federal agents had a device secretly installed in the suspect's living room. The device contained a radio transmitter and the agents were able to monitor the conversations from a surveillance van parked a block away.
- Based on an electronic surveillance warrant, the police had a pager company install a device which recorded all messages left on the suspect's digital pager.

13-1c Federal Legislation on Electronic Surveillance

Immediately after *Katz* and *Berger* indicated the need for carefully drafted legislation authorizing electronic surveillance, Congress enacted the Omnibus Crime Control and Safe Streets Act of 1968. Title III of this act was devoted to electronic surveillance.

Omnibus Crime Control and Safe Streets Act of 1968.[5] Title III of
the Omnibus Crime Contorl and Safe Streets Act of 1968 made it a federal felony to willfully intercept any wire or oral communication by electronic or mechanical devices unless an electronic surveillance warrant has
been obtained. Oral communications, as defined in Title III, include any
communication uttered by a person with both objective and subjective
expectations of privacy. Wire communications include any communication made in whole or in part by aid of wire, cable, or other connection
operated by a common carrier. Employees of the telephone company or
other common carriers, such as telephone operators, who legally intercept
conversations are forbidden to disclose them.

Title III only covers the monitoring of audio and electronic messages
or messages sent by wire. Separate legislation, found in Title 18 of the
United States Code, Sections 2710 through 2711, enables federal judges
to issue search warrants for stored electronic communications such as
e-mail.

Pen registers are not covered by Title III *(Smith v. Maryland; United
States v. New York Telephone Co.)*,[6] but Congress enacted separate legislation requiring a warrant to install either a pen register or a "trap and
trace" device.[7] Neither of these devices seize (record) conversations. The
pen register merely records the numbers dialed. The Supreme Court
found no expectation of privacy in these numbers because the telephone
company has access to them.

Transponders (also called "bumper beepers") are not covered as long
as they do not enter residences *(United States v. Karo; United States v.
Knotts)*.[8] A transponder emits a signal that makes it possible to track a
vehicle or other item without constantly keeping it under visual surveillance. The Court found that the electronic device merely facilitates the
surveillance process. It drew the line, however, when the container with
the beeper in it entered the suspect's home.

Title III sets up detailed requirements to obtain electronic surveillance warrants. While this statute only applies to federal agents, it has
much broader implications because many states have either authorized
their officers to proceed under identical standards or have used it as a
basis for state statutes.

Electronic surveillance warrants may only be issued if crimes specified
in Title III are involved. These include espionage, sabotage, treason, terrorism, assassination of federal officials, offenses involving chemical weapons,
bribery and violent crimes directed at jurors, labor racketeering, gambling,
loan sharking and other offenses associated with organized crime, computer fraud, counterfeiting, bankruptcy fraud, narcotic trafficking, interstate transportation of stolen cars, and certain other violent crimes.

In addition to facts that would be in the affidavit when trying to obtain a search warrant, the application for an electronic surveillance warrant must include the following:

1. A particular description of the type of communication to be intercepted.
2. The length of time the surveillance will be conducted.
3. A full statement of other investigative procedures tried in the case.
4. Why it reasonably appears non-electronic techniques will not work.
5. A complete statement detailing all prior applications for electronic surveillance warrants in the case.

If the application is for an extension of an existing warrant, the application must also give details of what has been obtained so far or give a reasonable explanation why nothing has been obtained to date.

Another variation from normal procedure when seeking a search warrant is the prior screening by the attorney general or an assistant attorney general specially designated for this purpose. If a state empowers its officers to act under Title III, the screening is done by the principal prosecuting attorney of the county. The entire warrant application must be submitted for screening and may only be submitted to a judge after it has been approved.

The electronic surveillance warrant must correctly specify the identity of the person(s) whose communications are to be intercepted (if their names are known), where the interception is to be done, types of communications to be intercepted, agency authorized to intercept the communications, and the period of time during which interceptions can be made. It may direct a common carrier, such as the telephone company, to cooperate with the agents executing the warrant. The maximum length of interception under the warrant is 30 days. Shorter periods are preferred.

There is an emergency exception to the normal procedure. It applies if there is reason to suspect that a conspiracy threatening national security or organized crime activities requires surveillance before a warrant can be obtained. There must be sufficient grounds to obtain a warrant before an emergency interception can be started. An application must be made for a warrant within 48 hours of the start of an emergency interception. If the application is denied, or if no application is made, the interception must stop immediately and anything obtained during the interception is inadmissible in court.

The communications obtained under the electronic surveillance warrant must be tape recorded or otherwise retained. The recordings must be done in a manner that prevents later editing or alteration. These recordings must be made available to the judge when the surveillance has been completed. They must be kept for 10 years and may not be destroyed except by an order of a judge.

The persons whose conversations were intercepted must be served with a limited inventory within 90 days of the end of surveillance. They must be told:

1. An order was sought.
2. Date the order was issued.
3. The period interceptions were permitted.
4. Whether or not interceptions were made.

The judge has the discretion to permit the persons whose communications were seized to see the application for the warrant and to hear the taped interceptions. If evidence obtained during the surveillance is to be used in court, all parties must have access to the application and warrant at least 10 days before the testimony is introduced.

Title III contains its own exclusionary rule. It is stricter than the one created by the Supreme Court. Illegally obtained conversations may not be used in any hearing, trial, or other proceeding before any court, grand jury, government agency, regulatory body, or legislative committee of the United States or any of the states, counties, or cities. Anyone whose telephone or premises was monitored, and anyone whose conversations were seized, has standing.

The Supreme Court has decided several cases regarding Title III. Probably the most important to local law enforcement was *Dalia v. United States*.[9] The issue was whether agents using an electronic surveillance warrant could covertly enter a home to install listening devices. Congress had not addressed the issue. The Court found that the right to enter was a fundamental part of the right to use electronic devices. Re-entry to service the equipment and/or retrieve it at the end of the surveillance was included. No separate search warrant was required. Neither was it necessary to ask for authorization for covert entries when the original surveillance warrant was obtained.

The Court has also addressed the so-called "minimization" requirement. The idea of minimization is to protect privacy by limiting the monitoring of conversations. One aspect of this is the requirement that the suspects be named in the application for a surveillance warrant. Listing prime targets is not enough. *United States v. Donovan* applied this to all persons the government has probable cause to believe are involved in the crime and whose conversations are likely to be seized.[10] This does not make conversations inadmissible if police knew a person, such as the wife of the suspect in *United States v. Kahn*, was likely to be using the telephone but had no reason to suspect that she was involved in criminal activity.[11] Each case is to be decided based on an objective review of the facts. The officer's subjective intent is not binding (*Scott v. United States*).[12]

While Title III has an emergency provision that can be used in cases involving national security, the Supreme Court has narrowly interpreted it. It does not give the president, attorney general, or anyone else the right to authorize wiretaps on "domestic dissidents" *(United States v. United States District Court)*.[13]

Foreign Intelligence Surveillance Act of 1978 (FISA).[14] This act provides separate procedures for obtaining surveillance warrants for activities of foreign powers and agents of foreign powers. Groups working for foreign powers are included, as are international terrorist groups. The Act applies to "United States persons" (citizens and permanent resident aliens) and groups substantially composed of "United States persons," only if they are knowingly engaged in clandestine intelligence activities on behalf of a foreign government. It was amended by both the USA PATRIOT Act of 2001 and the Homeland Security Act of 2002.

In matters of national security, this act permits the president to authorize the attorney general to conduct electronic surveillance for up to one year without a warrant. This includes the right to conduct "wiretaps" and intercept e-mail as well as utilizing pen registers and "trap and trace" devices. Monitoring must be limited to channels used exclusively between or among foreign powers. Non-verbal technical communications can also be seized. A special certification process was set up for this. FISA also provides for search warrants to seize tangible objects.

For electronic surveillance of foreign agents not utilizing the exclusive channels mentioned above, the president must provide a written authorization for the attorney general to seek permission for the use of such techniques from a special federal court created for this purpose. The surveillance order is normally good for no more than 120 days; extensions can be for up to one year.

In the only case decided by the United States Foreign Intelligence Surveillance Court of Review since it was created in 1978, the court ruled that when FISA was used to issue wiretap orders, the information gathered could be shared with other government agencies for use in prosecuting crimes. Unlike some lower courts, the appellate court found no basis in the statute or debates when it was enacted by Congress to warrant creating a wall between the intelligence community and law enforcement.[15]

Examples of Use of Federal Legislation on Electronic Surveillance
- FBI agents are investigating organized crime's involvement in gambling. They have been able to trace banking records to a specific person but attempts to place this person under surveillance have failed. They obtain a Title III warrant for a wiretap on the person's home phone for 30 days.
- City police officers are investigating a kidnap-for-ransom case. They were assisted by the FBI because interstate transportation of the victim was suspected. The kidnapper is calling the parents and trying to arrange the delivery of the ransom money. FBI agents obtain a warrant to install a "trap and trace" device on the phone in order to determine where the kidnapper is.
- Federal agents believe that a person is involved with a terrorist cell sponsored by a foreign government that is plotting to blow up a federal building in the near future. The U.S. Attorney General authorizes a wiretap for 90 days.

13-2 Searches by Bureau of Citizenship and Immigration Services Agents and Customs and Border Protection Agents

Due to the compelling interest in protecting the integrity of our borders, the Supreme Court has identified criteria for many activities of border patrol and customs agents.

13-2a Searches at Border

People and physical items entering the United States may be routinely subjected to thorough searches without cause. This includes strip searches. To qualify for this unlimited right to search, the search must be done by border patrol or customs agents at the border or a point of entry. These **border searches** may be done randomly or on suspicion, however weak, that an undocumented alien is attempting to enter or something is being smuggled into the country. Table 13-1 summarizes when and what officers can search at a U.S. border or **point of entry**.

Right to Conduct Searches at U.S. Border Defined
Customs and immigration officers may conduct searches at the border or point of entry without suspicion. Reasonable suspicion is required before a person must submit to examination of body cavities.

T A B L E   **13-1 Right to Stop and Search at U.S. Border or Point of Entry**

Stop Vehicle at Border	No justification necessary
Detain People for Questioning	No justification necessary
Search People	No justification necessary except for searches involving X-rays and invasions of the alimentary canal
Search Items Being Brought into the United States	No justification necessary

In *United States v. Montoya de Hernandez,* the Supreme Court stopped short of allowing total discretion to search when it is suspected that a person is carrying narcotics or other contraband in his/her alimentary tract. These cases frequently involve couriers who swallow balloons containing narcotics. To detain for a rectal examination, X-ray, or to allow the foreign substances to be expelled from the body naturally requires reasonable suspicion.[16] Due to the nature of the examination, the time permitted for the detention will be longer than that normally permitted for a field interview. While the Court did not specifically address the issue, it would appear logical that this standard would apply to all types of body cavity searches.

Examples of Searches at the U.S. Borders
- Cars were stopped and searched as they entered Texas from Mexico. Agents were looking for undocumented people.
- Passengers on a flight from Bogotá, Columbia that landed at John F. Kennedy airport in New York were searched for drugs.
- Luggage of all passengers on a flight originated in Beijing, China, was searched at Los Angeles International Airport. Agents were looking for software that violated copyright laws.

13-2b Fixed Border Checkpoints

Fixed checkpoints are permanent Border Patrol stations on major highways near the United States border. They usually are well-lighted with signs telling motorists of the upcoming checkpoint. Based on federal legislation, they may be as far as 100 air miles from the international border. The Supreme Court has specifically mentioned the higher level of supervision that is present at fixed checkpoints as a reason to permit car stops on less cause than is required for other law enforcement activities. Table 13-2 summarizes when and what officers can search at fixed checkpoints.

T A B L E   **13-2 Right to Stop and Search
at Fixed Checkpoints**

Stop Vehicle in Street	No reason required
Brief Detention	Suspicion
Pat Down for Weapons	Reasonable suspicion that person is armed
Full Search	Probable cause

Various levels of searches may occur at a fixed checkpoint. Figure 13-1 illustrates these different levels of searches. The least intrusive action is for officers to stand in the roadway and stop cars. *United States v. Martinez-Fuente* held that no suspicion is needed to do this.[17] Cars may be sent to a secondary area (usually a parking lot adjacent to the checkpoint that was constructed for this purpose) for further questioning of the occupants. While this requires some suspicion, the Supreme Court, in *United States v. Ortiz*, allowed officers to consider a variety of factors including the fact that the occupants looked like foreign nationals. Officers may conduct a protective pat down for weapons under the *Terry v.*

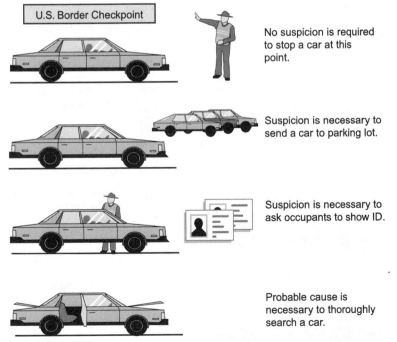

Figure 13-1
Search at Fixed Checkpoint

Ohio rule: There must be reasonable suspicion that the person is armed. To conduct a thorough search, officers need probable cause.[18]

Examples of Searches at Fixed Border Checkpoints

- Border Patrol agent stands in street and motions drivers to stop. The agent then looks in the car for suspicious people or objects.
- Border Patrol agent who is standing in the street notices that the trunk of one car is nearly scraping the pavement. The car is sent to a parking lot used as a secondary inspection area and searched.
- Border Patrol agent who is standing in the street sends a car to the secondary inspection area because the occupants of the car appear to be of Latino ancestry. An agent then asks the occupants of the car to produce proof that they are legally in the United States.
- When Border Patrol agents in the secondary inspection area notice a strong odor of marijuana coming from the trunk of a car, they search the trunk and find 1,000 pounds of marijuana.

13-2c Roving Border Checkpoints

Roving checkpoints are also set up near the border, but they are temporary in nature. Figure 13-2 illustrates what may occur when people are stopped at roving checkpoints. Typically two or more carloads of officers

Reasonable suspicion is required to stop a car at a roving checkpoint.

Reasonable suspicion is required to ask occupants to show ID.

Probable cause is necessary to thoroughly search a car.

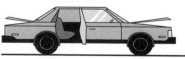

Figure 13-2
Search at Roving Checkpoint

T A B L E   **13-3 Right to Stop and Search
at Roving Checkpoints**

Stop Vehicle in Street	Reasonable suspicion
Brief Detention	Reasonable suspicion
Pat Down for Weapons	Reasonable suspicion that person is armed
Full Search	Probable cause

select a spot on a highway near the border and set up a checkpoint. There are no warning signs to alert motorists to the fact that they are approaching a checkpoint. The image of a few officers working alone on a dark highway has caused the Supreme Court to cautiously limit the power to stop and search. Table 13-3 summarizes the level of suspicion necessary for officers to stop and search people at roving checkpoints.

United States v. Brignoni-Ponce held that officers need reasonable suspicion in order to stop a car and question the occupants about their citizenship;[19] probable cause is needed to search the vehicle (*Almeda-Sanchez v. United States*).[20] Officers at roving checkpoints actually have no more power to make car stops or search people than any other police officer. The rules from *Terry v. Ohio* would allow a pat down for weapons if the officer has reasonable suspicion that the detained person is armed.

Examples of Searches at Roving Border Checkpoints
- Six Border Patrol agents establish a roving checkpoint on a rural highway about 25 miles from the U.S. border. An approaching car gets close enough to see the officers' uniforms and then makes a quick u-turn. Two officers pursue the car and stop it on reasonable suspicion.
- Once the car is stopped, officers look in the windows and see what appear to be three people lying on the floor of the back seat. They search the passenger compartment based on probable cause that the car is smuggling undocumented people into the United States.

13-2d Mail Searches

In *United States v. Ramsey*, the Supreme Court used the same reasons that are given for allowing searches of people entering the United States as justification for searching incoming mail. Customs officers may open and search all mail entering the country without probable cause. In *Ramsey*, the Court agreed with the prosecution's argument that reasonable suspicion justifies a search; the Court has never addressed the issue of whether a search could be done on a lower level of suspicion.[21]

Examples of Searches of the Mail
- Postal Inspectors find a bulky envelope postmarked in Thailand. The envelope is oddly shaped and when handled feels like it has sticks and dry leaves inside. The Postal Inspectors open it and find marijuana.
- Postal Inspectors find a large envelope that has a white powder leaking from it. The powder smells like baby powder. Knowing that baby powder is used to mask the smell of certain drugs, the envelope is opened. Instead of drugs, they find forged legal documents.

13-2e Boarding Vessels in Navigable Waters

Customs officers have the right to board vessels any place in the United States to check for customs violations and examine the manifest and other documents. Boarding may also be done in waters providing ready access to the open seas. Inbound vessels within four leagues (approximately 12 miles) off the coast may be boarded. The Supreme Court held that these stops may be done without any suspicion that the vessel is violating the law *(United States v. Villamonte-Marquez)*.[22] The inspection statutes were designed to protect important government interests. Only boarding vessels randomly can detect violations.

Examples of Searches by Boarding Vessels
- The Coast Guard randomly selects a boat in costal waters. The boat is boarded and inspected. A cargo of 50 pounds of cocaine is discovered.
- Customs officials stop a large cargo vessel in the San Francisco harbor. After searching containerized cargo for several hours, they discover 10 Chinese immigrants who have no legal papers permitting them to enter the United States.

13-2f Workplace Inspections

The Supreme Court has upheld the right of Immigration and Naturalization Service agents to enter factories and other workplaces to check for undocumented aliens (*INS v. Delgado*). Even though these workplace sweeps may involve blocking exits in order to temporarily detain everyone in the building, the Court found that they do not violate the Fourth Amendment.[23] The amendment would be violated if specific individuals were detained.

Example of Workplace Inspections
- INS agents go to a factory suspected of hiring undocumented workers. They leave an agent at each entrance while other agents stop and question employees. All undocumented workers are sent to an INS holding facility and the employer is fined.

13-3 Closed Containers

In 1977, the Supreme Court ruled that there was a greater expectation of privacy in closed containers than in many other items; hence the **Closed Container Rule.** Since that time, several exceptions have been made to this rule. Distinctions have also been made between closed containers that are opened by police and those that are opened by other people and then turned over to the police.

Right to Search Closed Containers Defined
Officers may seize closed containers based on probable cause but a search warrant is required to open them. This rule does not apply to booking searches or most vehicle searches.

Closed containers in the possession of the police that have been legally opened may be reopened. For this to apply to a package that has been returned to its owner, it must have been constantly under police surveillance after it was returned.

13-3a Police Seizure of Closed Containers

The first two cases regarding closed containers, *Arkansas v. Sanders* and *United States v. Chadwick,* involved luggage that the suspect was carrying immediately prior to being arrested.[24]

The Court took a two-step approach to the problem. Based on probable cause that the footlocker contained marijuana, police could seize it without a warrant. This was necessary to prevent it from being removed from the scene and the evidence destroyed. Probable cause, however, was not sufficient reason to search it. The officers were allowed to retain custody of it long enough to obtain a search warrant. Only after the warrant was obtained could the footlocker be searched.

Two clear exceptions to the Closed Container Rule have emerged. One involves cars.[25] Closed containers found in vehicles may be opened without a warrant if they are found incident to an arrest, during a probable cause search, or as part of an inventory. The second exception relates to booking searches.[26] *Illinois v. Lafayette* held that any closed container in the possession of the person being booked may be searched. A routine inventory of everything taken from the arrestee may include what is inside closed containers.

Examples of Police Seizure of Closed Containers

- Officers are chasing a suspected drug dealer who is carrying what appears to be a heavy box. As the officers are about to catch the man, he puts the box down and tries to escape. They arrest him about 50 feet from the box. The officers seize the box and store it while they obtain a search warrant.
- A man ships a suspicious footlocker believed to contain bricks of marijuana. Officers are on hand when the footlocker arrives at the shipping terminal. A man puts the footlocker on a cart and gets a taxi. The officers arrest the man after the footlocker is loaded into the cab but before the man gets in. They retrieve the footlocker and store it while they obtain a search warrant.

13-3b Legally Opening Containers

A totally different rule relates to containers that have already been opened legally. They may have originally been opened during a legal search by the police *(Illinois v. Andreas)*,[27] or after a container opened by someone else has been turned over to authorities *(United States v. Jacobsen)*.[28] Once legally opened, the expectation of privacy vanishes.

There are a variety of situations in which the police may legally open a package. For example, customs officials may open it at the border; police may open it during the search of a car based on probable cause; or it may be searched pursuant to a warrant. Common carriers, such as airlines and other freight companies, are frequently involved in cases where a container was legally opened and then turned over to the police. In *United States v. Johns*, the Supreme Court held that in all of these cases the police may reopen the container and search it. In the case of boxes found during a car search based on probable cause, this is true, even though the container was held in police custody for several days before the search.[29]

Sometimes the officers intentionally reseal the package. Surveillance is maintained while it is delivered to the addressee. This is called a **controlled delivery.** Constant surveillance is crucial for two reasons. First, if the package is allowed out of the sight of the officers, the contents may be changed. This greatly reduces the possibility that what is later found inside can be admitted into evidence. Secondly, and very important from a constitutional standpoint, the Court found that the recipient may develop a privacy interest in the contents if there is a substantial likelihood that he/she has altered the contents of the package.

Examples of Legally Opening Containers

- During the inventory of an impounded car, officers discover a shoe box that is taped shut. They open it and find $5,000 in $20 bills stolen during a bank robbery.
- A man is carrying a locked briefcase when arrested. Officers take the briefcase to the station where the man is booked. During the booking the briefcase is opened and its contents inventoried and placed in an evidence locker.
- A forklift operator for Federal Express accidentally gores a package. When agents try to repackage the box they discover it contains a white powdery substance they think is an illegal drug. They seal the box and then call the police. The police open the box, perform a field test, and determine that the box contains cocaine. They then obtain an arrest warrant for the person who shipped the package.
- A United Parcel employee opens a box because of a bad odor. Afraid that the contents are human remains, the police are called. The police instruct the employee to carefully repackage the box. A police officer dressed in a United Parcel uniform delivers the package so the police could identify the intended recipient.

13-4 Drug Testing

The Supreme Court has decided two cases involving drug testing of employees (*Skinner v. Railway Labor Executives Association; National Treasury Employees Union v. Raab*).[30] Both involved employees with jobs sensitive to public safety: railroad employees were subject to testing immediately after train accidents; U.S. Customs employees were subject to testing if they applied for a promotion or transfer to a position directly involving drug interdiction or requiring the carrying of a firearm. In both cases, the Court found that mandatory blood or urine tests do not violate the Fourth Amendment. No individualized suspicion is necessary. Neither a search warrant nor an administrative warrant is required. On the other hand, the Court held that Georgia's requirement that candidates for state office pass a drug test violated the Fourth Amendment.[31]

Drug testing in schools was addressed in *Vernonia School District 47J v. Acton* and *Board of Education of Independent School District No. 92 of Pottawatomie County v. Earls*.[32] The Court found that random drug testing of students participating in district-sponsored extracurricular programs did not violate the Fourth Amendment. The Court considered several factors: students had a lower expectation of privacy because they knew that they would be subject to testing if they signed up for the programs; the search was relatively unobtrusive; and the severity of the need to control the drug problem in the schools that were involved.

Examples of Drug Testing

- Police officers are required to submit to random drug testing. If an officer fails the test and cannot provide a medical reason for having drugs in his/her system, the officer is fired.
- The crews of trains are required to submit to drug and alcohol testing if their train is involved in an accident.
- Students participating in high school athletics are required to submit to random drug tests. If they test positive they must participate in a drug rehabilitation program. If they fail a second test, they can no longer be on the team.

Summary

Eavesdropping is covered by the Misplaced Reliance Doctrine. Anything overheard is admissible. The person speaking bears the burden of restricting his/her conversations to trustworthy people. This rationale applies even if someone is surreptitiously carrying electronic recording equipment.

Wiretapping and other electronic monitoring of conversations require a special warrant. Only specific serious crimes justify this type of invasion of privacy. Police must show that other types of investigative techniques are inadequate. The warrant is good for a maximum period of 30 days. Once the electronic surveillance warrant has been obtained, officers may covertly enter to install, maintain, and retrieve the equipment. Title III of the Omnibus Crime Control and Safe Streets Act of 1968 was designed to enable federal courts to issue electronic surveillance warrants. The Foreign Intelligence Surveillance Act of 1978 covers wiretaps and other devices used on agents working for foreign governments and terrorists.

Customs and immigration agents have almost unlimited power to search anybody and anything entering the United States at a point of entry. Reasonable suspicion is required to detain a person to determine if contraband is being smuggled in his/her alimentary tract. Border patrol officers may stop cars at fixed checkpoints for brief questioning if there is any suspicion that the occupants are in the United States illegally. Full searches require probable cause. The right to stop or search is more restrictive at a roving checkpoint. There must be reasonable suspicion to stop a car and probable cause to search it. A pat down for weapons may be done at either type of checkpoint if there is reasonable suspicion that the person is armed.

Mail may be searched by customs officers at a point of entry based on reasonable suspicion. Customs inspectors may board vessels anywhere in the navigable waters of the United States without suspicion. Immigration officers do not need probable cause to enter a business to check the citizenship status of people who work there.

Closed containers that are seized by police based on probable cause may not be searched without a warrant. Containers found in a car during a probable cause search, as part of a search incident to the arrest of a person in the car, or while taking inventory of an impounded vehicle are exempt from this rule. Containers that were resealed after being legally opened and were turned over to the custody of the police may be reopened without a warrant. If the package has been returned to the owner for any significant period of time, during which officers did not have it under surveillance, a warrant will be required to reopen it.

Discussion Questions

1. Is a warrant required if an informer is going to carry a tape recorder when talking to a suspect who has not been arrested? Explain.
2. When is an electronic surveillance warrant required? Explain.
3. Explain the requirements for obtaining a warrant under Title III of the Omnibus Crime Control and Safe Streets Act of 1968.
4. Explain the requirements for conducting electronic surveillance under the Foreign Intelligence Surveillance Act.
5. What are the rights of customs agents to search people at the United States border? At a fixed checkpoint? At a roving checkpoint? Explain.
6. Explain the Closed Container Rule and its exceptions.
7. Explain two situations where employees can be required to take drug tests.
8. When may school authorities require students to submit to drug testing? Explain.

Endnotes

1. *Hoffa v. United States* 385 U.S. 293, 17 L.Ed. 2d 374, 87 S.Ct. 408 (1966).
2. *United States v. White* 401 U.S. 745, 28 L.Ed. 2d 453, 91 S.Ct. 1122 (1971).
3. *Katz v. United States* 389 U.S. 347, 19 L.Ed. 2d 576, 88 S.Ct. 507 (1967).
4. *Berger v. New York* 388 U.S. 41, 18 L.Ed. 2d 1040, 87 S.Ct. 1873 (1967).
5. Title III of the Omnibus Crime Control and Safe Streets Act of 1968 can be found at 18 U.S.C. 2500 et. seq.
6. *Smith v. Maryland* 442 U.S. 735, 61 L.Ed. 2d 220, 99 S.Ct. 2577 (1979). See also, *United States v. New York Telephone Co.* 434 U.S. 159, 54 L.Ed. 2d 376, 98 S.Ct. 364 (1977).
7. See 18 U.S.C. 3121 et al.
8. *United States v. Karo* 468 U.S. 705, 82 L.Ed. 2d 530, 104 S.Ct. 3296 (1984); *United States v. Knotts* 460 U.S. 276, 75 L.Ed. 2d 55, 103 S.Ct. 1081 (1983).
9. *Dalia v. United States* 441 U.S. 238, 60 L.Ed. 2d 177, 99 S.Ct. 1682 (1979).
10. *United States v. Donovan* 429 U.S. 413, 50 L.Ed. 2d 652, 97 S.Ct. 658 (1977).
11. *United States v. Kahn* 415 U.S. 143, 39 L.Ed. 2d 225, 94 S.Ct. 977 (1974).
12. *Scott v. United States* 436 U.S. 128, 56 L.Ed. 2d 168, 98 S.Ct. 1717 (1978).
13. *United States v. United States District Court, Eastern Michigan* 407 U.S. 297, 32 L.Ed. 2d 752, 92 S.Ct. 2125 (1972).
14. The Foreign Intelligence Surveillance Act of 1978 can be found at 50 U.S.C. 1801 et. seq.
15. *In re: Sealed Case No. 02-001.* United States Foreign Intelligence Surveillance Court of Review 310 F.3d 717 (2002).
16. *United States v. Montoya de Hernandez* 473 U.S. 531, 87 L.Ed. 2d 381, 105 S.Ct. 3304 (1985).
17. *United States v. Martinez-Fuerte* 428 U.S. 543, 49 L.Ed. 2d 1116, 96 S.Ct. 3074 (1976).
18. *United States v. Ortiz* 422 U.S. 891, 45 L.Ed. 2d 623, 95 S.Ct. 2585 (1975).
19. *United States v. Brignoni-Ponce* 422 U.S. 873, 45 L.Ed. 2d 607, 95 S.Ct. 2574 (1975).
20. *Almeida-Sanchez v. United States* 413 U.S. 266, 37 L.Ed. 2d 596, 93 S.Ct. 2535 (1973).
21. *United States v. Ramsey* 431 U.S. 606, 52 L.Ed. 2d 617, 97 S.Ct. 1972 (1977).
22. *United States v. Villamonte-Marquez* 462 U.S. 579, 77 L.Ed. 2d 22, 103 S.Ct. 2573 (1983).
23. *Immigration and Naturalization Service v. Delgado* 466 U.S. 210, 80 L.Ed. 2d 247, 104 S.Ct. 1758 (1984).
24. *Arkansas v. Sanders* 442 U.S. 753, 61 L.Ed. 2d 235, 99 S.Ct. 2586 (1979); *United States v. Chadwick* 433 U.S. 1, 53 L.Ed. 2d 538, 97 S.Ct. 2476 (1977).
25. *United States v. Ross* 456 U.S. 798, 72 L.Ed. 2d 572, 102 S.Ct. 2157 (1982); *New York v. Belton* 453 U.S. 454, 69 L.Ed. 2d 768, 101 S.Ct. 2869 (1981); *Colorado v. Bertine* 479 U.S. 367, 93 L.Ed. 2d 739, 107 S.Ct. 738 (1987); *California v. Acevedo* 500 U.S. 565, 114 L.Ed. 2d 619, 111 S.Ct. 1982 (1991).
26. *Illinois v. Lafayette* 462 U.S. 640, 77 L.Ed. 2d 65, 103 S.Ct. 2605 (1983).
27. *Illinois v. Andreas* 463 U.S. 765, 77 L.Ed. 2d 1003, 103 S.Ct. 3319 (1983).
28. *United States v. Jacobsen* 466 U.S. 109, 80 L.Ed. 2d 85, 104 S.Ct. 1652 (1984).
29. *United States v. Johns* 469 U.S. 478, 83 L.Ed. 2d 890, 105 S.Ct. 881 (1985).
30. *Skinner v. Railway Labor Executives' Association* 489 U.S. 602, 103 L.Ed. 2d 639, 109 S.Ct. 1402 (1989); *National Treasury Employees Union v. Raab* 489 U.S. 656, 103 L.Ed. 2d 685, 109 S.Ct. 1384 (1989).
31. *Chandler v. Miller* 520 U.S. 305, 137 L.Ed. 2d 513, 117 S.Ct. 1295 (1997).
32. *Vernonia School District 47J v. Acton* 515 U.S. 646, 132 L.Ed. 2d 564, 115 S.Ct. 2386 (1995); *Board of Education of Independent School District No. 92 of Pottawatomie County v. Earls* 536 U.S. 882, 153 L.Ed. 2d 735, 122 S.Ct. 2559 (2002).

CHAPTER **14**

Self-Incrimination

Outline

Key Terms

- Custodial interrogation
- Double jeopardy
- Immunity
- Indigent suspect
- *Miranda* booking exceptions
- *Miranda* public safety exception

- *Miranda* waiver, intelligent
- *Miranda* waiver, knowing
- *Miranda* waiver, voluntary
- *Miranda* warnings
- Right to counsel
- Right to have attorney present

- Right to remain silent
- Self-incrimination
- Testimonial evidence
- Tolling statute of limitations

After studying this chapter, you will be able to:

- Define the scope of the Fifth Amendment protection against self-incrimination.
- Explain how the Fifth Amendment applies to nontestimonial evidence.
- Apply the Fifth Amendment to nontestimonial compulsion.
- State the *Miranda* warnings and explain when they should be given.
- Describe the standard for a waiver of *Miranda* rights.
- Explain how *Miranda* rights apply to sequential interrogations.
- List the procedures that are required prior to interrogating a person who has been indicted or arraigned.

14-1 Scope of the Privilege against Self-Incrimination

The Fifth Amendment protects a suspected criminal from being compelled to give testimony that might incriminate him/herself. It does not apply in civil cases.

Privilege against Self-Incrimination Defined

No person can be required to make statements which can be used against him/her in a criminal proceeding.

14-1a Situations Not Covered by the Fifth Amendment

Self-incrimination applies only if criminal charges could be based on the confession or admission. It does not apply in three situations that arise in criminal cases where it is impossible to file charges:

1. The statute of limitations has run.
2. The witness has been granted immunity.
3. The witness cannot be prosecuted due to double jeopardy.

It must be noted that even in these cases due process prevents police from using coercion to obtain confessions.

Statute of Limitations.   If the statute of limitations has run, no charges can be filed. Due to the fact that the **statute can be tolled** (stopped) if a suspect flees the jurisdiction to avoid prosecution, it is possible for the statute to have run against one suspect but not another. A similar situation occurs when one suspect committed a felony and another person involved in the same crime spree only committed a misdemeanor that has a shorter statute of limitations. When either of these situations occur, the police may be interested in obtaining a statement from the suspect for whom the statute has expired in order to use the information against someone who can still be prosecuted. Under these circumstances, a suspect cannot refuse to talk on the grounds that it might incriminate him/her.

Immunity. A witness with immunity cannot be prosecuted for what he/she said, provided the confession is within the scope of the **immunity.** In most states, the prosecutor can grant immunity, but defense counsel does not have similar powers. Grand juries can also grant immunity. The formal documents filed with the court when immunity is granted specify the scope of the immunity. The most common types of immunity are use immunity (what is stated by the witness cannot be used against him/her) and transaction immunity (the witness cannot be prosecuted for the crimes specified; neither his/her statements nor evidence the police obtain independently can be used). A grant of immunity from federal prosecution carries with it immunity from state prosecution for the same offense, and vice versa.

If the witness is careless enough to tell about crimes not covered by immunity, charges can be filed. On the other hand, the immune witness cannot refuse to testify merely to protect a friend or save face. Refusal to testify is grounds for holding the witness in contempt of court. This type of contempt usually results in sending the witness to jail until he/she is willing to testify. Since the witness can be released as soon as the testimony is given, the witness is said to "hold the key" to the jail.

Double Jeopardy. **Double jeopardy** protects a person who has been either convicted or acquitted of a crime. The same crime, or lesser included charges, cannot be re-filed. The fact the jury convicted the defendant of a lesser included offense, when the more serious charge was filed, implies an acquittal on the more serious offense.

When there are multiple parties to the crime who are tried separately, the testimony of an accomplice who has already been tried and either convicted or acquitted can be very useful. Once again, there is no right to refuse to testify based on self-incrimination. As a practical matter, the prosecutor may delay using this approach until after the conviction has been affirmed on appeal. It is important to note that only convictions or acquittals activate this rule. Failing to file charges, winning suppression motions, or dismissing the case without prejudice do not qualify; neither does a trial ending in a "hung jury."

Examples of Situations Not Covered by Fifth Amendment

- Mary was charged with murder when she hired Harry, a "hit man" who killed her wealthy husband. At trial she convinced the jury of her innocence and was acquitted. If called to testify at Harry's trial, Mary cannot invoke the Fifth Amendment because double jeopardy will protect her from being prosecuted again for the murder.
- Sally stole sweaters from a department store. Shelby, a sales clerk, was charged with fraud for doctoring the sales records. The detective handling the case lost the file. When he found it 18 months later, charges could not be filed because the one-year statute of limitations had run on Sally's misdemeanor theft. If Sally were called to testify about the theft at Shelby's trial for felony fraud, she could not invoke the Fifth Amendment since she cannot be prosecuted for the theft because the statute of limitations has run.
- Ian was given "use immunity" when he agreed to testify against fellow gang members about a gang rape he had participated in. The week before the trial he received a letter threatening to kill him if he testified. At trial he was sworn in as a witness. When the prosecutor asked him a question about the rape, Ian claimed the Fifth Amendment. The judge instructed Ian that he could not claim the Fifth Amendment because he had immunity. Ian was told that he would be held in jail if he refused to testify.

14-1b How the Privilege against Self-incrimination Is Invoked

The appropriate way to invoke the privilege against **self-incrimination** varies with the stage of the criminal justice system where it is used. Prior to arrest and during field interviews, any person may refuse to answer questions, but the police have no duty to inform the suspect that he/she may do so. The suspect's use of the privilege at this stage depends on his/her prior knowledge of these rights. If the suspect wants to seek advice from an attorney at this phase of the investigation, it must be done at his/her own expense.

During custodial interrogations, the police must inform the suspect of his/her constitutional rights. In order to continue the questioning, a knowing, intelligent, and voluntary waiver must be obtained from the suspect. Coercion may not be used to persuade a suspect to talk. An indigent suspect has the right to have counsel appointed at government expense during custodial interrogation if he/she so desires.

At trial the proper procedure depends on who is invoking the Fifth Amendment privilege. If it is the defendant, the defense attorney indicates this indirectly by not calling him/her to the witness stand. While it is obvious to the jury that the defendant did not testify, the Supreme Court in *Griffin v. California* made it clear that no inference of guilt may be drawn from the invocation of this constitutional right.[1] The prosecutor may not ask the jury to infer that the only reason the defendant did not testify is that he/she is guilty. If the defendant makes a timely request, the judge must instruct the jurors that they may not draw this conclusion (*Carter v. Kentucky*).[2]

There is one exception to this procedure. If the defense counsel claims during the closing statement that the defendant never had an opportunity to explain his/her side of the case, the prosecution may inform the jury that the defendant had the right to testify but chose not to (*United States v. Robinson*).[3]

Other witnesses must take the stand, even if they have already said they refuse to testify. The privilege against self-incrimination is asserted in response to each question. In most cases the reason for invoking the privilege is obvious and no explanation is given in open court. If it appears there is no basis for invoking this privilege, the judge may ask the witness, outside the hearing of the jury and attorneys, to explain why the privilege applies.

Witnesses have the right to have their own attorneys present to give advice on how to answer questions. When a witness who does not have an attorney present starts to make an incriminating statement, the judge usually will stop the proceedings briefly to determine if the witness understands the gravity of what is happening. The judge, or the prosecutor at the judge's direction, frequently advises the witness of his/her right to remain silent by giving the *Miranda* warnings.

If the defendant takes the witness stand and lies under oath he/she can be punished. The obvious approach is to file charges for perjury. Another approach is to use the fact that the defendant committed perjury as an enhancement when calculating the sentence for the crime he/she was on trial for. The Supreme Court approved this practice but noted that an enhancement could not be imposed if it appeared the testimony was inaccurate due to confusion, mistake, or faulty memory. If the defendant objects to the enhancement there must be an independent finding by the judge that the testimony was a willful obstruction of justice, or an attempt to do so, that falls within the definition of perjury (*United States v. Dunnigan*).[4] This would occur at the sentencing hearing and does not necessitate a new trial.

Examples of How the Fifth Amendment Is Invoked
- Kevin was stopped about 100 yards from a building whose burglar alarm had just gone off. The police legally stopped him but did not arrest him. They questioned him without giving the *Miranda* warnings. Kevin knew he did not have to answer the questions, so he said, "Sorry, I refuse to answer your questions. Fifth Amendment." The police stopped the questioning.
- Lizzy was on trial for embezzlement. Her attorney told her that the Fifth Amendment gave her the right not to testify. She decided that was a good idea. During the defense case-in-chief, the defense attorney did not call Lizzy to testify.
- Martin had helped Lizzy alter the company books. He had not been arrested or charged with his part in the crime. The prosecutor called Martin as a witness. He answered the questions that he thought were safe. When the prosecutor asked an incriminating question, Martin asked to talk to his lawyer. After doing so, Martin told the judge that he refused to answer the question because of the Fifth Amendment.

14-1c Non-Testimonial Compulsion

The Supreme Court has repeatedly held that the Fifth Amendment privilege against self-incrimination applies only to **testimonial evidence.** Most commonly, this means statements that a person makes that are admissions or confessions. These may be either oral or written. The privilege does not apply to other incriminating evidence that may be obtained from a person.

Body Fluids. The results of blood, urine, or breath tests can be used in cases involving driving under the influence of alcohol. A variety of tests are done on blood and semen samples in sexual assault cases. DNA samples may be tested. Many other tests are used less frequently. All of these tests rest on the same basis as far as the Fifth Amendment is concerned. While the results may be very incriminating, no privilege can be asserted as grounds for refusing to take the tests because they are non-testimonial.[5]

Three other types of challenges can be used. If the arrest was illegal, usually due to lack of probable cause, body fluids can be excluded on the grounds of an illegal search and seizure. The Fruit of the Poison Tree Doctrine could then be used to exclude the laboratory tests. Due process could be asserted as a reason for excluding the test results if excessive force was used to obtain the samples. A variety of other rules of evidence can be invoked if the fluids were not handled in a manner that established the chain of custody, if the laboratory personnel were not adequately trained, or if the equipment used was not properly maintained.

Identifying Features. A person's appearance is also not testimonial evidence. The most commonly used identification procedure involves fingerprints. Due to the high scientific reliability of fingerprint identification, a match is very incriminating. Once again, the Fifth Amendment provides no protection because no testimony is required. The Fourth Amendment protects the suspect to the extent that the police may not take a suspect to the station for the purpose of obtaining fingerprints for comparison purposes unless there is consent or probable cause to make an arrest (*Hayes v. Florida*).[6] This does not prevent the police from rolling a set of prints at the scene where a legal field interview is conducted. The fingerprint cards made any time a person was legally arrested are very useful for the purpose of identifying fingerprints found at a crime scene. Print cards in government files for other purposes, such as applications for state licenses, can also be used.

Visual identification by victims and witnesses to the crime are treated in a similar manner. They are not testimonial (*United States v. Wade*).[7] The suspect cannot invoke the Fifth Amendment as a grounds for refusing to participate in a lineup or showup. The police do not violate the suspect's rights by showing mug shots or other photographs. Due process protects the suspect from unduly suggestive techniques used by the police. This will be discussed in more detail later in this chapter.

Exemplars. An exemplar is a sample. Handwriting exemplars and voice exemplars are frequently used for identification purposes. Neither is a testimonial (*United States v. Mara*).[8] The suspect is told what to write or say. For this reason the content of the exemplar is not an indication of guilt and cannot be incriminating. The visual or audio characteristics of the exemplar are incriminating, but these factors are not testimonial.

Sobriety Tests. Sobriety tests, whether conducted at the scene where a car is stopped on suspicion of drunk driving or later during booking, are not covered by the Fifth Amendment privilege. Actions in the sobriety test that indicate lack of muscle coordination, such as poor balance and slurred speech, are not testimonial. Questions that call for incriminating answers, such as "How many drinks did you have?" require *Miranda* warnings. Videotapes of the sobriety test are admissible in court but segments that would be considered interrogation must be excluded (*Pennsylvania v. Muniz*).[9]

Examples of Non-Testimonial Compulsion

- Erin was arrested on suspicion of driving under the influence of alcohol. The officer took her to the nearest emergency room and had a nurse draw a blood sample. The results of the blood test may be very incriminating but Erin cannot invoke the Fifth Amendment because blood is not testimonial evidence.

- Frank is a suspect in a rape case. The arresting officer used a swab to obtain a tissue sample from the inside of Frank's cheek. If the DNA test is positive, this tissue sample will be very incriminating but Frank cannot invoke the Fifth Amendment because tissue samples are not testimonial evidence.
- Robert was arrested for robbery. The police held a lineup using Robert and five other men. If the robbery victim picks Robert out of the lineup it will be very incriminating but Robert cannot invoke the Fifth Amendment because participation in a lineup is not testimonial evidence.
- Phyllis was arrested for forgery. She was given printed instructions and told to copy a paragraph using her own handwriting. If a questioned documents examiner determines that the handwriting exemplar indicates that Phyllis wrote the forged documents, it will be very incriminating but Phyllis cannot invoke the Fifth Amendment and refuse to make the exemplar because it is not testimonial evidence.

14-2 *Miranda* Warnings

Miranda v. Arizona[10] is one of the best known Supreme Court cases, yet there are many details surrounding the *Miranda* decision that still cause confusion. To help clear up some of these problems, four key areas will be addressed:

1. What are the *Miranda* warnings?
2. When must they be given?
3. How does a suspect waive his/her *Miranda* rights?
4. What rules apply to sequential interrogations?

14-2a Content of *Miranda* Warnings

Each officer must fully understand the **Miranda warnings** so he/she can explain them correctly to each suspect. The Supreme Court has permitted paraphrasing, but has been quite intolerant of misleading warnings. This includes answers to a suspect's questions about these rights. While the police would obviously feel it is best to make a full confession, it is the job of the defense attorney to decide the best tactic for the suspect to take. Police officers should not attempt to give legal advice.

Miranda **Warnings Defined**

Prior to custodial interrogation the suspect must be warned:

1. You have the right to remain silent.
2. Anything you say can and will be used against you in a court of law.

3. You have the right to have an attorney present during questioning.
4. If you cannot afford an attorney, one will be appointed at no charge to assist you during questioning.

The **right to remain silent** includes the right to refrain from making both oral and written statements. Nodding the head "yes" or "no" would also be covered. The suspect retains the right to refuse to answer questions at any time. Even though he/she agreed to talk at the beginning of the interview, the right to remain silent enables the suspect to stop the interrogation at any time.

Second, anything that the suspect says can be used against him/her in court. For emphasis, many departments warn the suspect that statements "can and will" be used against you in court. Statements that are not confessions can be used if they have any evidentiary value. Attempts to incriminate another person frequently are used to show guilty knowledge. Anything that is inconsistent with other statements made by this suspect can be used to impeach him/her at trial. Attempts to talk to the police "off the record" indicate that the suspect does not understand the warnings.

Third, the suspect has the **right to have an attorney present** during questioning. Law enforcement officers may not continue questioning a suspect after he/she has requested an attorney. The fact that an attorney will be appointed at arraignment is not enough. It should be noted, however, that this right is not a guarantee that an attorney will meet with the suspect immediately. The police have two alternatives—stop questioning or give the suspect an attorney. Since most attorneys routinely tell their clients not to make any statements to the police, it is not uncommon for the interrogation to be stopped when an attorney is requested. The suspect is returned to his/her cell but no attorney is called. This does not violate the suspect's rights.

Lastly, if the suspect cannot afford an attorney, one will be provided at no cost to the suspect. The purpose of this warning is to inform the **indigent suspect** that his/her lack of money will not prevent him/her from having an attorney present during questioning. It is not the duty of the police, however, to review the financial status of the suspect and give advice on whether he/she is eligible for a free attorney. The court usually makes this determination of eligibility at the arraignment. Neither is it appropriate for the police to tell the suspect that the court has the authority to order a person to repay the cost of the attorney. If the suspect requests an attorney, the police should proceed in the same manner regardless of the suspect's apparent wealth (or lack thereof): Questioning must stop.

Many law enforcement agencies have the *Miranda* warnings printed on pocket-size cards so officers can read them to each suspect. The purpose of the card is to insure that the warnings are given uniformly. But merely reciting the Court's language is not enough. The warnings must be given so that the suspect can understand them. The prosecution bears the burden of convincing the judge that the warnings were correctly explained to the suspect. This must be established by a preponderance of the evidence.

For juveniles, this means explaining the warnings in very simple terms. Similar problems may occur with illiterate and mentally impaired suspects. Intoxicated and mentally ill suspects also pose a challenge. If the suspect does not speak English fluently, an interpreter may be necessary. Care must be taken to make sure the interpreter and the suspect speak the same dialect. Subtle differences, if not clearly understood by the suspect, may make the warnings void.

Sample Dialogue to Give *Miranda* Warnings

Det. Dawson:	I have some questions for you, but before we begin I need to give you the *Miranda* warnings.
Johnny Johnson:	Oh, neat. I saw that on TV.
Det. Dawson:	I want you to pay close attention. This is not TV. You were arrested for a serious crime.
Johnny Johnson:	OK.
Det. Dawson:	Here is a *Miranda* card. I want you to read while I read it out loud. Item No. 1 says, "You have the right to remain silent." Do you know what that means?
Johnny Johnson:	Sure. It means I do not have to answer your questions.
Det. Dawson:	Good. Look at No. 2. It says "Anything you say can and will be used against you in a court of law." Do you know what that means?
Johnny Johnson:	I think it means that if I confess, you will tell about it when I go to trial.
Det. Dawson:	Well, that is part of it. But you need to understand that anything you say, not just a confession, can be used against you in court. Got that?
Johnny Johnson:	Yeah, I understand that.
Det. Dawson:	Now let's look at No. 3. It says, "You have the right to have an attorney present during questioning." Do you understand?
Johnny Johnson:	Well, yes and no. It says I have the right to have an attorney here while you question me. But I don't have an attorney so it doesn't apply to me.

Det. Dawson:	Yes, I know you don't have an attorney. But that is covered in No. 4. Look at it very closely. It says, "If you cannot afford an attorney, one will be appointed at no charge to assist you during questioning."
Johnny Johnson:	Oh, I see. I sure can't afford an attorney but if I want one I get one free. Right?
Det. Dawson:	Yes, that's right. All you have to do is ask.

14-2b When *Miranda* Warnings Are Required

The key to giving *Miranda* warnings is **custodial interrogation.** The suspect must be in custody at the time and the police must be interrogating him/her.

Custody, for the purposes of *Miranda,* is the equivalent of a custodial arrest (*Berkemer v. McCarty*).[11] It does not include traffic stops where citations are issued and the violator is released at the scene (*Pennsylvania v. Bruder*).[12] Brief field interviews based on reasonable suspicion are not covered. Neither does it apply to situations where the suspect is being questioned at the police station but is not under arrest (*Oregon v. Mathiason*).[13] Whether there is a custodial arrest is judged by an objective test; the subjective intent of the officer is not important.[14]

On the other hand, *Orozco v. Texas* held that it does not matter why the suspect is in custody.[15] Warnings are required if a suspect was arrested for one crime and questioned regarding a different one. Questioning by a different law enforcement agency also requires the warnings. *Miranda* warnings are even required if the suspect is questioned while in jail serving time on a totally unrelated offense.

In *Rhode Island v. Innis* and *Brewer v. Williams* the Supreme Court defined interrogation as the process of questioning, or its functional equivalent.[16] *Miranda* warnings are required prior to any interrogation that is done while the suspect is in custody. Asking questions about a crime is clearly interrogation. So is requesting a narrative statement. The Court has also included indirect attempts to obtain information. For example, if two officers engage in a conversation with the intent of being overheard and eliciting a response, this is the functional equivalent of interrogation. So is telling a suspect, "I want you to think about this ..." but never actually asking a specific question. Trial judges are left with the task of deciding which conversations were indirect questioning and which ones accidentally resulted in a response from the suspect.

As with the Fourth Amendment, the Fifth Amendment protections only apply to acts by government employees and their agents. If an accomplice who has decided to cooperate with the police questions the suspect the same rules apply as if the police had done it themselves. Questioning that the police did not authorize or condone that is done by a private person does not require *Miranda* warnings. Informants from the jail population can provide very useful information. They may report on anything they heard.

A 1990 Supreme Court case held that *Miranda* warnings are not required when an inmate is questioned by an undercover police officer. Voluntary statements made in this type of situation are admissible because none of the coercive elements of police interrogation are present when the inmate does not know he/she is being questioned by law enforcement personnel (*Illinois v. Perkins*).[17]

Miranda warnings may even be required prior to questioning by non-police personnel. The need for the warnings prior to a polygraph examination conducted by the police is fairly obvious. Warnings are not required if the defense requests the examination or the defendant consents to it, but it is still a good idea to give them. *Estelle v. Smith* held that psychiatric examinations conducted on behalf of the prosecution, or ordered by the court, also require *Miranda* warnings.[18]

Volunteered statements are admissible even though *Miranda* warnings were not given. They are also admissible if a suspect who refused to talk or requested an attorney later comes forward and volunteers information. As used in this context, volunteered means the suspect came forward on his/her own initiative and made a statement. The Supreme Court used the example of a person who came to the police station and immediately blurted out a confession to the desk officer. A suspect in a holding cell who bangs on the bars and wants to talk to an officer is another example. It is important to be aware, however, that any detailed questioning that follows the volunteered information is considered interrogation.

The courts recognize a minor exception to *Miranda* for the **booking** process. Questions related to name, address, person to notify in case of an emergency, date of birth, and a few other biographical facts are permitted without giving any warnings. No exception applies if questioning at booking is extended in order to obtain information needed for a criminal investigation.

Another exception recognized by the Supreme Court in *New York v. Quarles* is for **public safety.**[19] Brief questioning is permitted without giving *Miranda* warnings if it is done in order to obtain information that is needed immediately in order to protect others from harm. Asking where the suspect hid a gun would fit under this exception if the question was asked in order to prevent innocent people from being hurt by the gun.

Examples of When *Miranda* Warnings Are Required

- Police were questioning Adam at his home about a recent arson. Adam answered a few questions but when he realized he was the suspect in the case he said, "No more questions. I know my Fifth Amendment rights. If you want to talk to me again, call my attorney. Now leave my house."
- Bruce was stopped for speeding. The traffic officer asked, "Do you know how fast you were driving?" Bruce laughed and said, "Wait. Wait. You can't ask me questions unless you give me my *Miranda* warnings!" The officer replied, "Sorry, Mister. The D.A. says that we only have to give *Mirandas* after we arrest someone." Bruce groaned; the officer was right.
- Carl was caught trying to break into a house. He was arrested for attempted burglary. An officer handcuffed Carl and placed him in the backseat of the patrol car. During the drive to the station Carl said, "Hey, I'm going to win this case. You didn't give me the *Miranda* warnings." The officer replied, "Wrong! You only have the right to *Mirandas* if we question you after your arrest."
- Don was arrested for an assault that occurred the previous day. After arriving at the station the police decided to question him. Prior to starting questioning they gave him the *Miranda* warnings.
- Mike was arrested by an officer from City E Police Department. The day after the arrest officers from City M Police Department came to the jail and wanted to question Mike. The first thing they did after seating Mike in the interrogation room was give him the *Miranda* warnings. Mike asked, "Why did you do that?" An officer replied, "We have to give warnings any time we question someone who is in custody." Mike replied, "But you didn't arrest me." The officer replied, "It doesn't matter. If you are in custody and we question you, we have to give you the warnings."

14-2c Waiver of *Miranda* Rights

Once *Miranda* warnings have been correctly given to a suspect who is in custody, the police may try to obtain a waiver of the suspect's rights. This must be a **knowing, intelligent,** and **voluntary waiver.**

To have a knowing waiver, the suspect must have been correctly advised of his/her rights. The courts have uniformly required that the police show that they have done this. It is not presumed that anyone knows the *Miranda* warnings. Even though it may seem ridiculous for a police officer who arrests a prominent defense attorney or judge to advise him/her of the *Miranda* rights, it is still the best way to ensure that any statements obtained can be used in court.

"Intelligent," as used in this context, means that the person had the basic intelligence necessary to understand his/her rights. This may be an issue if a young juvenile is involved. It also comes up if the suspect is mentally impaired. Similar problems occur when the suspect is extremely intoxicated (either on alcoholic beverages or drugs). Only the most extreme cases qualify for suppression on the basis of lack of an intelligent waiver. This is especially so in intoxication cases—the courts generally admit confessions except when the suspects totally lack the ability to understand what is going on.

"Voluntary" is somewhat hard to define in this context. No coercion may be used to obtain a confession. The courts have taken a fairly rigid stance against coercion used to obtain a waiver of *Miranda* rights. During the interrogation that follows the waiver, police have been permitted more leeway in using deceptive tactics as long as the will of the suspect is not overborne.

Colorado v. Connelly limited the prohibition against coercion to acts of the police or their agents.[20] Factors outside the control of the police that are coercive will not cause a confession to be suppressed. For example, the fact that the suspect confessed after hearing "voices from heaven" ordering him/her to do so does not make the confession involuntary. On the other hand, a confession was held to be coerced when an informant, whom the police had asked to help them obtain a confession, told the suspect that he could protect the suspect from gang violence only if a full confession of past crimes was made.[21]

"Third degree" tactics offend due process. Physical force cannot be used to obtain a confession. Deprivation of food and/or sleep for long periods is not allowed. Neither are false promises of leniency, such as offers to drop charges or assurances that the suspect will get a light sentence if he/she confesses.

Absent one of these obviously coercive acts, the courts look at the totality of the circumstances. The key concept is that the police are not allowed to overbear the will of the suspect. This balances the acts of the police against the vulnerability of the defendant. What may be coercive when done to a naive teenager may be considered acceptable when applied to a streetwise ex-convict.

Lies and half-truths may be permitted. The police do not have to tell the suspect all of the crimes being investigated (*Colorado v. Spring*).[22] Neither do they have to inform him/her that someone has arranged for an attorney to come to the jail to provide counsel (*Moran v. Burbine*).[23]

The last issue involving the waiver of *Miranda* rights is the procedure used to obtain the waiver. The Supreme Court has not set a protocol. In fact, in *North Carolina v. Butler* the Court found a valid waiver based on the suspect's conduct.[24] The suspect had responded in the affirmative when asked if he understood his rights but did not reply when asked if he wished to waive them. The indication that he understood the warnings, coupled with the fact that he answered the questions asked by the police, was enough to convince the Court that a valid waiver had been obtained. In another case, the Court decided that the confession was admissible when the suspect gave an oral confession, even though his reply to the request for a waiver was that he refused to make a written confession (*Connecticut v. Barrett*).[25]

Despite these cases that condone less than explicit waivers, each officer should attempt to obtain as much evidence of a valid waiver as possible. Many agencies have the suspect sign a card that has the warnings printed on it. While the signature on the form is not conclusive (the suspect can still allege that he/she was forced to sign the card), it does provide an impressive exhibit that can be used at trial. Having the suspect initial each of the warnings on the *Miranda* card provides even stronger evidence of a waiver. Copious notes taken during the interrogation help. Tape recording the interrogation, including the process of giving *Miranda* warnings and requesting a waiver, is also useful.

Sample Dialogue to Obtain a Waiver of *Miranda* Rights

Det. Dawson:	OK, we've gone over all the warnings and you understand them. Is that correct?
Johnny Johnson:	Yeah, I understand them.
Det. Dawson:	Are you currently intoxicated or under the influence of any type of drugs?
Johnny Johnson:	No. I'm cold sober. I gave up doing drugs after I spent that time in detox.
Det. Dawson:	Do you read English well?
Johnny Johnson:	I do OK. I never finished high school but I was always good at reading.
Det. Dawson:	So you read the *Miranda* card and understand it.
Johnny Johnson:	Yeah, I read it. I didn't understand it all but I do now, after you explained it.
Det. Dawson:	I want to ask you some questions about why you were arrested. But I need to know if you think that I am forcing you to talk to me. Am I?
Johnny Johnson:	No. You aren't forcing me to talk. I'd shut up real fast if I thought you were trying to force me to talk.
Det. Dawson:	One last detail before I can ask you those questions. Look at the *Miranda* card, at the very bottom. There is a short paragraph there that says that you understand your rights and you are willing to talk to me. And that you are doing this voluntarily. All you need to do is sign it and then we can get on with the questions.
Johnny Johnson:	OK. I see it. Give me a pen and I'll sign it.

14-3 Sequential Interrogations

It is not uncommon for the police to interrogate a suspect more than once. The procedures that the police should follow at second (or later) interrogation sessions depend largely on what occurred previously.

14-3a Prior Interrogation without Valid *Miranda* Waiver

At one time, many courts held that none of the confessions following a statement obtained in violation of *Miranda* could be used to establish the prosecution's case. This was based on the "cat out of the bag" theory. Once the suspect had confessed, the courts believed the suspect was likely to confess again because he/she knew the police already knew he/she was guilty.

In 1985, the Supreme Court decided *Oregon v. Elstad,* which held that this theory did not apply.[26] If the first confession was involuntary, all subsequent confessions are inadmissible. On the other hand, if the first confession was voluntary but in violation of *Miranda,* a subsequent confession may be admissible if a new set of properly administered *Miranda* warnings were given and the suspect waived his/her rights. Each case is considered on its merits. *Miranda* warnings given only seconds after obtaining the inadmissible confession will not be viewed as effective. Using the first confession as the primary focus of the second interrogation session would likely trigger the Fruit of the Poison Tree Doctrine. A voluntary confession obtained several days after the suspect was released from custody will more than likely be admissible. The more scrupulous the police are in obtaining the second confession, the better chance they have of using it in court. No matter what the police do, the original confession obtained in violation of *Miranda* will remain inadmissible except for impeachment purposes.

Sample Dialogue to Start Interrogations When Prior Interrogation Was Conducted without Valid *Miranda* Waiver

Det. Dawson:	Johnny, have you been questioned since you were arrested yesterday?
Johnny Johnson:	Yes. Det. Smith asked me a bunch of questions right after they brought me here.
Det. Dawson:	OK. That was what I had heard. I want you to forget about talking to Det. Smith. Whatever you told him will not be used to convict you. I want you to just focus on the questions that I am going to ask. Can you do that?
Johnny Johnson:	I'll try.
Det. Dawson:	Now we just went over your *Miranda* rights. You understand them, right?

Johnny Johnson:	Yeah, I already told you that I do. I don't forget stuff that fast!
Det. Dawson:	And you are willing to answer my questions?
Johnny Johnson:	Yes. Just get on with it.

14-3b Prior Interrogation with Valid *Miranda* Waiver

If the first interrogation was conducted legally and the suspect agreed to talk, a subsequent interrogation can be conducted rather routinely. The Supreme Court has not required a new set of *Miranda* warnings every time questioning is resumed. The warnings are needed if the suspect is not likely to remember his/her rights. If there has been a lengthy delay between two interrogations, warnings should be administered again so the suspect cannot claim in court that he/she forgot his/her rights. It is also a good idea to give the warnings again if someone else gave them the first time. This serves as a guarantee that the warnings were given correctly.

Sample Dialogue to Start Interrogation When There Was a Prior Interrogation and a Valid *Miranda* Waiver

Det. Dawson:	Hi, Johnny. Did you have a good lunch?
Johnny Johnson:	It was OK, I guess. The food in here isn't great.
Det. Dawson:	Do you remember what we were talking about before lunch?
Johnny Johnson:	You talked a lot about my *Miranda* rights. Then you started asking questions about what I did yesterday.
Det. Dawson:	Why did we stop talking?
Johnny Johnson:	Because it was lunch time.
Det. Dawson:	I want to ask you some more questions. Is that OK?
Johnny Johnson:	Yeah, it's OK. This is taking too long.

14-3c Suspect Invoked Right to Remain Silent

Police must stop interrogation immediately if the suspect invokes the right to remain silent. This rule applies whether the suspect invoked the right to remain silent at the time the *Miranda* warnings were initially given or asserted the right after custodial interrogation was in progress. This does not mean, however, that the police may never try to resume questioning.

In *Michigan v. Mosley* the Supreme Court insisted that the suspect's rights be scrupulously honored.[27] Police may not badger the suspect with frequent attempts to get the suspect to talk, but after a reasonable time they may ask the suspect if he/she would like to continue the interrogation. A new waiver of the *Miranda* rights is mandatory at this point.

No specific guidelines have been established for renewing questioning after the suspect refused to talk. In the leading case, there was a two-hour gap between the interrogations; the second interview was conducted by different officers on a different floor of the police building and focused on a different crime. Each case will turn on its own facts. A reasonable time period must follow the request to remain silent. Tactics that appear to harass the suspect are not tolerated.

Sample Dialogue to Start Interrogation after the Suspect Invoked Right to Remain Silent

Det. Dawson:	Welcome back, Johnny. Have you thought about what you told me yesterday?
Johnny Johnson:	Yeah, I thought about it a lot last night.
Det. Dawson:	Yesterday you said you didn't want to talk to me anymore. Is that right?
Johnny Johnson:	Yeah, that's what I said.
Det. Dawson:	Would you like to talk to me now?
Johnny Johnson:	Yeah, I thought about it a lot and I have some things to say to you now.
Det Dawson:	I'm glad to hear that, but before we start I need to read the *Miranda* warnings to you again. When I finish you can sign the waiver form and we can talk. OK?
Johnny Johnson:	OK.

14-3d Suspect Invoked Right to Attorney

Edwards v. Arizona[28] establishes a rule that applies when a suspect who is in custody and being questioned requests an attorney: questioning must stop and can resume only if an attorney is present. This is a distinctly different rule than the one that applies if the suspect refuses to speak to officers: if the attorney was requested, the request cannot be revoked unless there is an attorney present; a lapse of time cannot be used to justify renewing questioning without an attorney present.

One of the biggest problems with the rule about requesting an attorney is determining when it applies. An unambiguous request for counsel automatically invokes it *(Smith v. Illinois).*[29] Unfortunately, suspects frequently make equivocal statements. In *Oregon v. Bradshaw*,[30] the Supreme Court found that the suspect's question: "Well, what is going to happen now?" permitted the officers to continue the interrogation. Each case will have to be decided on its own facts. It is important, however, that officers avoid the temptation to ignore a request for counsel and attempt to convince the suspect that he/she does not need or want an attorney.

Sample Dialogue to Determine If Suspect Has Invoked Right to an Attorney

Det. Dawson:	What did you just say?
Johnny Johnson:	I said, "Maybe I need an attorney."
Det. Dawson:	So, do you want an attorney?
Johnny Johnson:	Oh, gee, I'm not sure. You said I could have one. When you ask me all those questions I get scared. But I don't trust attorneys. It's so confusing. Maybe I should have one. What do you think?
Det. Dawson:	I just want to know if you want an attorney right now, at this minute. Give me a straight answer—yes or no.

If the officer determines that the suspect wants an attorney, the suspect must have an opportunity to speak with an attorney before questioning can continue; the attorney will also have to be present when a new waiver is sought. This rule applies in two situations: (1) the suspect asked for an attorney; and (2) the suspect refused to talk to the officer and requested an attorney. The time that elapses between interviews is no substitute for contact with an attorney. Questioning may resume only if the defendant has an attorney present (*Minnick v. Mississippi*).[31]

Sample Dialogue to Start Interrogation after Suspect Invoked Right to Attorney

Det. Dawson:	OK, Johnny. It's 4:00 P.M. When I was talking to you earlier you asked for an attorney. What happened after that?
Johnny Johnson:	You stopped talking to me and had some guy take me back to the holding cell.
Det. Dawson:	Have you had a chance to talk to an attorney?
Johnny Johnson:	Yes. I called the Public Defender's Office and talked to Mr. Brown.
Det. Dawson:	Is Mr. Brown an attorney?
Johnny Johnson.	Yes.
Det. Dawson:	Is Mr. Brown in this room right now?
Johnny Johnson:	Yes. He is sitting beside me. Sorry, I forgot to introduce you.
Det. Dawson:	Are you ready to talk to me now?
Johnny Johnson:	Mr. Brown doesn't want me to talk, but I need to tell you some stuff right away.
Det. Dawson:	OK. I'm giving you another *Miranda* card. Read it and sign it if you want to talk to me. Mr. Brown can stay here with you if you want.
Johnny Johnson:	Yeah, I know. You give me lots of those cards to sign.

In 1988, the Supreme Court made it clear in *Arizona v. Roberson* that the fact that the subsequent interrogation was about a different crime did not alter this rule.[32] The suspect had been arrested at the scene of a burglary. Immediately after the arresting officer gave the *Miranda* warnings, he demanded to see his lawyer. Three days later a different officer, who did not know the suspect had invoked his *Miranda* rights, questioned him about a different burglary. The confession was ruled inadmissible even though the second officer obtained a *Miranda* waiver before the suspect made an incriminating statement. The Supreme Court clearly stated that it intended to follow the bright line rule in *Edwards* without exceptions. This makes it imperative that officers communicate the request for an attorney to all potential interrogators. Noting it on the booking slip may be helpful.

Sample Dialogue to Interrogate Suspect Who Has Already Asked for an Attorney

Conversation between Det. Jones and Officer White who is in charge of the holding cells

Det. Jones:	I'm here to question Johnny Johnson. Please have him sent to Interrogation Room No. 3.
Officer White:	Let me check his file. Wait. There is a note that says he asked for an attorney when Det. Dawson interrogated him this morning.
Det. Jones:	Wow. I'm glad you told me that. If I'd gone ahead and questioned him the judge would have thrown it all out. Forget about sending him to the interrogation room.

14-4 Special Situations

Several situations require special attention: whether proper *Miranda* warnings are sufficient to make a confession admissible when the suspect was illegally arrested, procedures that should be modified when juveniles are questions, and the use of confessions for impeachment purposes. Complying with the normal *Miranda* procedures may not be enough in these situations.

14-4a Suspect Illegally Arrested

The Supreme Court refused to rule that all confessions made after a valid *Miranda* waiver are admissible. If the arrest was illegal, *Miranda* will not automatically make the confession admissible (*Lanier v. South Carolina;*

Brown v. Illinois; New York v. Harris; Kaupp v. Texas).[33] Instead of making all of these confessions admissible, the Court utilized the Fruit of the Poison Tree Doctrine. Confessions obtained after an illegal arrest are only admissible if the facts show that the taint of the unconstitutional act has dissipated. Each case must be reviewed on its own merits. Confessions obtained after the suspect has been released from custody are quite likely to be admissible. On the other hand, if any form of police brutality was present during the arrest the confession will be suppressed. Relevant considerations include observance of *Miranda*, the temporal proximity of the arrest and the confession, the presence of intervening circumstances, and particularly, the purpose and flagrancy of the official misconduct.[34]

Sample Dialogue to Start Interrogation after Suspect Was Illegally Arrested

Det. Dawson:	Good morning, Mr. Green.
Mr. Green:	Good morning.
Det. Dawson:	I've been reading your file. It looks like Officer Swenson arrested you last week but the D.A. refused to file charges. Some technicality about the arrest.
Mr. Green:	I don't know anything about technicalities. I just know they let me go home.
Det. Dawson:	What day did they let you go home?
Mr. Green:	Last Thursday. Four days ago.
Det. Dawson:	And why are you at the police station today?
Mr. Green:	You called me and said you wanted to talk to me and hear my side of it. It sounded like a good idea, so I came down.
Det. Dawson:	You are free to leave when you want to. Did you know that?
Mr. Green:	Yeah, sort of. Unless you arrest me first.
Det. Dawson:	That's right. So now, let's start talking.

NOTE: *Miranda* warnings are not required in this scenario because the suspect is not under arrest. Warnings are not required when the suspect is at the police station but not under arrest.

14-4b Interrogating Juvenile Suspects

All but very young juveniles are capable of waiving their *Miranda* rights. While the question of whether the suspect is in custody is the same for adults and juveniles,[35] the question of whether there was a valid waiver of the *Miranda* rights will be considered in the totality of the circumstances. The clarity of the warnings given is very important. Other factors include the age and intelligence of the juvenile. Prior contacts with the police and other evidence of sophistication related to the criminal justice system are relevant. Police tactics that intimidate or coerce are carefully scrutinized.

If juveniles ask to speak to their parents, the questioning must stop. The courts have treated this type of request as the equivalent of an adult demanding an attorney. *Fare v. Michael C.* held that requests to speak to a probation officer, on the other hand, have no conclusive effect.[36] It is important to take notice of any request the juvenile makes, however, because it may be considered as an indication that the suspect wants to terminate the questioning.

Sample Dialogue to Start Interrogation of Juvenile Suspect

Det. Dawson:	Hello, Michelle.
Michelle:	Hi.
Det. Dawson:	I'm here to talk to you about why you were arrested. Before I do that, I need to explain your rights to you. OK?
Michelle:	OK.
Det. Dawson:	How old are you, Michelle?
Michelle:	I'm 15. My birthday was last week.
Det. Dawson:	Do you go to school?
Michelle:	Yes. Wilson High.
Det. Dawson:	What grade are you in?
Michelle:	I'm a sophomore.
Det. Dawson:	What kind of grades do you get?
Michelle:	Mostly Cs and Ds. But they keep telling me I'm really smart and I could do better if I studied. School is so boring.
Det. Dawson:	Have you ever been in trouble with the law before?
Michelle:	Yeah. I was in Juvie last year.
Det. Dawson:	So you know about your rights.
Michelle:	Yeah. The Public Defender told me all about them when I was in Juvie waiting for my trial.
Det. Dawson:	OK. I'm going to go over your *Miranda* rights with you. I want you to listen real close because this is very important. OK?
Michelle:	OK. But don't use any big words. I get lost when people use too many big words.

14-4c Impeachment

Statements a suspect makes during an interrogation can be used to impeach his/her trial testimony as long as the statement was voluntary (*Harris v. New York*).[37] Coerced statements cannot be used in court, but any voluntary statement made during an interrogation that violated other aspects of *Miranda* can be used to impeach.

This rule is only activated if the person who was interrogated takes the witness stand and testifies in a manner that conflicts with the prior statements. It is important that the prosecutor be aware of any statements the police obtained even though they now realize that inappropriate procedures were followed.

Sample Court Dialogue to Introduce a Confession for Impeachment

Prosecutor:	The People call Det. Dawson.

Court clerk swears in Det. Dawson and he takes the witness stand.

Prosecutor:	Det. Dawson, did you interrogate Sean O'Neil on February 2, 2003?
Det. Dawson:	Yes, I did.
Prosecutor:	Did Sean O'Neil make any statements to you?
Defense Attorney:	Objection. Judge Wilson ruled that the statements Mr. O'Neil made to Det. Dawson are inadmissible because the *Miranda* warnings were not given correctly.
Prosecutor:	Your Honor, I am attempting to introduce Mr. O'Neil's statements for impeachment. The U.S. Supreme Court ruled in *Harris v. New York* that voluntary statements are admissible for impeachment purposes even if *Miranda* warnings were not given properly.
Judge:	Objection overruled. You may proceed, Mr. Prosecutor.
Prosecutor:	Det. Dawson, please answer the question.
Det. Dawson:	Yes, Sean O'Neil made several statements to me.
Prosecutor:	On direct examination, Sean stated that he was at his girlfriend's house between 8:00 P.M. and midnight on February 1, the night of the drive-by shooting. Is that what he told you on February 2?
Det. Dawson:	No. He told me that he was hanging out with some friends at a strip club. He claimed he arrived at 9:00 P.M. and stayed until it closed at 2:00 A.M. He never mentioned his girlfriend.

14-5 Post-Arraignment Confessions

The **right to counsel** attaches at the beginning of adversary court proceedings (*United States v. Gouveia*).[38] This is the arraignment unless some other proceeding, such as indictment by the grand jury, occurs first. From the time the right to counsel attaches, police may not interview a suspect without an attorney present unless there is a waiver of the right to counsel. It does not matter whether the interrogation takes place in a custodial setting.

Interrogation after Right to Counsel Attaches

Once formal court proceedings have begun, a suspect must waive the right to counsel prior to custodial or noncustodial interrogation. *Miranda* warnings may be used for this purpose.

The leading case is *Massiah v. United States*.[39] Massiah had been indicted by a federal grand jury for smuggling narcotics. He retained a lawyer, entered a "Not Guilty" plea, and was released on bail. Colson, his co-defendant, decided to cooperate with federal agents and allowed them to conceal a radio transmitter under the front seat of his car. While seated in Colson's car, Massiah and Colson discussed their upcoming trial and Massiah made several incriminating statements. The Supreme Court held that these statements were not admissible because they were obtained in violation of Massiah's right to counsel.

For interrogations that occur after arraignment or indictment, the key questions are: Was the accused made sufficiently aware of the right to have counsel present during questioning? Was he/she aware of the possible consequences of the decision to forgo the assistance of counsel? In *Illinois v. Patterson*, the Supreme Court said that a knowing, intelligent, and voluntary waiver of *Miranda* satisfies these criteria.[40] A similar problem arises if the defendant has been indicted prior to being arrested: statements that officers deliberately elicit anytime after the indictment without the suspect's attorney present are not admissible at trial.[41]

The Court refused to hold that the defendant must actually meet with an attorney prior to making this decision. If, on the other hand, the suspect demands to see an attorney or to have one present during questioning, interrogation must stop and cannot be resumed unless there is an attorney present.

For defendants who remain in custody, the rules that govern *Miranda* warnings apply whether or not an arraignment has occurred. Officers must be particularly alert, however, if the suspect has been arraigned but is currently not in custody. In these situations, even though there is no custodial interrogation, *Miranda* warnings or some other form of advice regarding the right to counsel must be given and a waiver obtained before discussing the case that has been filed. Table 14-1 compares the rights to counsel under *Miranda* and *Massiah*.

Since the right to counsel does not attach until the court proceedings begin, the normal *Miranda* rules apply to questioning conducted after the arraignment about charges that have not been filed. It may be difficult to determine which charges have been filed, particularly if the suspect has

T A B L E **14-1** Comparison of Right to Counsel under *Miranda* and *Massiah*

	Miranda	*Massiah*
When must suspect be advised of his/her rights?	Prior to custodial interrogation	Prior to interrogation that occurs after the first court appearance. Rule applies to suspects who are in custody and those that have been released but still have charges pending in court.
When does the suspect have the right to have an attorney present?	During any questioning by authorities that occurs after the suspect asks for an attorney.	At all interrogation sessions after the first court appearance.
What charges are covered?	Once the attorney is requested, there must be an attorney present during custodial interrogation about any crime.	Right to counsel applies to charges that have been filed in court. Right to have an attorney present during questioning on other crimes is governed by normal *Miranda* procedures.
Procedure for waiving right to counsel.	Valid waiver must be obtained with an attorney present.	Defendant can waive right to have attorney present on his/her own without an attorney present.
Warnings that must be given.	Police must give *Miranda* warnings and obtain a waiver in the presence of attorney.	Police must advise defendant of the right to have an attorney present and obtain a waiver. *Miranda* warnings may be used for this purpose but the Court has not specified that they are the only warnings that can be used. Attorney does not need to be present.

cases pending in several jurisdictions. Therefore, the safest practice is to give *Miranda* admonitions whenever talking to a suspect who has been arraigned.

Sample Dialogue to Start Interrogation to Obtain a Post-Arraignment Confession

Det Dawson: Good morning, Johnny. I haven't seen you for a long time.

Johnny Johnson: Yeah. That's because I've been in county jail for several months. But they finally let me out

Det. Dawson: Did you go to court while you were in jail?

Johnny Johnson: Yes. I had an arraignment in June and a preliminary hearing in July.

Det. Dawson:	Was this all about those burglaries I arrested you for last April?
Johnny Johnson:	Yes. They filed two counts of burglary. No other charges were filed, though. I guess I got lucky.
Det. Dawson:	Did they give you an attorney at the arraignment?
Johnny Johnson:	Yes. His name is Mr. Nelson. I have his card here in my wallet somewhere.
Det. Dawson:	OK. You are out of jail and you have an attorney. When you called I got the impression that you wanted to talk to me about your case. Is that true?
Johnny Johnson:	Yes. You always treated me fair.
Det. Dawson:	Before I can discuss anything, I need you to waive your right to have Mr. Nelson, your attorney, present. Or we can call him and ask him to come down here, if you prefer.
Johnny Johnson:	No, that's OK. The reason I called you was that I wanted to talk to you without him telling me what to do.
Det. Dawson:	The easiest way to handle this is to go over the *Miranda* warnings and then you can waive them, if you want to talk to me, that is.
Johnny Johnson:	Sure. I know my *Miranda*s by heart, you have given them to me so many times.
Det. Dawson:	Just the same, here is the *Miranda* card. Let's go over it to make sure we get everything right.

Summary

The Fifth Amendment privilege against self-incrimination only applies to statements that can be used against a person in a criminal trial. It does not apply if the statute of limitations has expired, the witness has immunity, or double jeopardy prevents refiling the charges.

Testimonial acts are covered: oral and written statements as well as assertive gestures. The following are not covered because they are not considered testimonial: body fluids (blood, urine, breath, etc.); identifying features (physical appearance and fingerprints); exemplars (handwriting and voice); DNA samples; and sobriety tests.

Miranda v. Arizona established that a suspect must be advised of his/her constitutional rights. These rights include the right to remain silent; the clear warning that anything said can be used against the suspect in court; the right to have an attorney present during questioning; and the right to have an attorney at public expense if the suspect is indigent.

Miranda rights need only be given prior to custodial interrogation, but it does not matter why the suspect is in custody. Interrogation includes both direct and indirect questions. To be valid, a waiver of *Miranda* must be knowing, intelligent, and voluntary. There is no required procedure that must be used to obtain the waiver. It may be oral, written, or inferred from the suspect's conduct.

Volunteered statements do not fall under *Miranda*. There is also an exception that permits biographical questions to be asked during booking. Another exception permits officers to ask urgent questions immediately following arrest in order to protect members of the public from danger.

If a suspect waives his/her *Miranda* rights, interrogation may be resumed at any time. An indication that the suspect wishes to remain silent must be scrupulously honored, but the police may ask for a new *Miranda* waiver at a later time. When the suspect requests a lawyer, the police may not attempt to question the suspect again unless there is a lawyer present.

Miranda warnings will not automatically make a confession admissible if the suspect was illegally arrested. Each case is considered on its facts.

Care should be taken when advising juveniles of their *Miranda* rights. A valid waiver can be obtained only if the juvenile fully understood the warnings. A juvenile's request to speak with parent(s) is considered the same as an adult's request for an attorney.

Statements made after incomplete *Miranda* warnings, or even when the warnings were not given, can be used to impeach. To be admissible for this purpose, the statements must have been made without coercion.

The right to counsel attaches at the first formal court appearance. This usually means arraignment or indictment. From that time on, the police may not question the suspect unless he/she has waived the right to have an attorney present. This rule applies to both custodial interrogation and questioning that occurs in non-custodial settings. *Miranda* warnings can be used to obtain a waiver of the right to counsel for this purpose.

Discussion Questions

1. Define the *privilege against self-incrimination,* and list three situations in which a suspect cannot invoke it.
2. List three types of evidence obtained from a suspect that are not considered testimonial.
3. State the *Miranda* warnings, and explain when they are required.
4. What is the standard for a valid *Miranda* waiver? Explain the acceptable procedures for obtaining a valid *Miranda* waiver.
5. Is it necessary to give a new set of *Miranda* warnings if the suspect has already waived his/her rights? Explain.
6. If the suspect invoked the right to remain silent, may officers attempt to interrogate him/her at a later time? Explain.
7. If the suspect asked for an attorney, may officers attempt to question him/her at a later time? Explain.
8. Can confessions be used in court if the suspect was illegally arrested prior to the interrogation? Explain.
9. Can a statement that was obtained in violation of *Miranda* be used in court? Explain.
10. What special procedures are required prior to interrogating a suspect who has been arraigned? Explain.

Endnotes

1. *Griffin v. California* 380 U.S. 609, 14 L.Ed. 2d 106, 85 S.Ct. 1229 (1965).
2. *Carter v. Kentucky* 450 U.S. 288, 67 L.Ed. 2d 241, 101 S.Ct. 1112 (1981).
3. *United States v. Robinson* 485 U.S. 25, 99 L.Ed. 2d 23, 108 S.Ct. 864 (1988).
4. *United States v. Dunnigan* 507 U.S. 87, 122 L.Ed. 2d 445, 113 S.Ct. 111 (1993).
5. *Schmerber v. California* 384 U.S. 757, 16 L.Ed. 2d 908, 86 S.Ct. 1826 (1966).
6. *Hayes v. Florida* 470 U.S. 811, 84 L.Ed. 2d 705, 105 S.Ct. 1643 (1985).
7. *United States v. Wade* 388 U.S. 218, 18 L.Ed. 2d 1149, 87 S.Ct. 1926 (1967).
8. *United States v. Mara* 410 U.S. 19, 35 L.Ed. 2d 99, 93 S.Ct. 774 (1973).
9. *Pennsylvania v. Muniz* 496 U.S. 582, 110 L.Ed. 2d 528, 110 S.Ct. 2638 (1990).
10. *Miranda v. Arizona* 384 U.S. 436, 16 L.Ed. 2d 694, 86 S.Ct. 1602 (1966).
11. *Berkemer v. McCarty* 468 U.S. 420, 82 L.Ed. 2d 317, 104 S.Ct. 3138 (1984).
12. *Pennsylvania v. Bruder* 488 U.S. 102, 102 L.Ed. 2d 172, 109 S.Ct. 205 (1988).
13. *Oregon v. Mathiason* 429 U.S. 492,, 50 L.Ed. 2d 714, 97 S.Ct. 711 (1977). See also, *California v. Beheler* 463 U.S. 1121, 77 L.Ed. 2d 1275, 103 S.Ct. 3517 (1983).
14. *Stansbury v. California* 511 U.S. 318, 128 L.Ed. 2d 293, 114 S.Ct. 1526 (1994).
15. *Orozco v. Texas* 394 U.S. 324, 22 L.Ed. 2d 311, 89 S.Ct. 1095 (1969).
16. *Rhode Island v. Innis* 446 U.S. 291, 64 L.Ed. 2d 297, 100 S.Ct. 1682(1980). See also, *Brewer v. Williams* 430 U.S. 387, 51 L.Ed. 2d 424, 97 S.Ct. 1232 (1977).
17. *Illinois v. Perkins* 496 U.S. 292, 110 L.Ed. 2d 243, 110 S.Ct. 2394 (1990).
18. *Estelle v. Smith* 451 U.S. 454, 68 L.Ed. 2d 359, 101 S.Ct. 1866 (1981).
19. *New York v. Quarles* 467 U.S. 649, 81 L.Ed. 2d 550, 104 S.Ct. 2626 (1984).
20. *Colorado v. Connelly* 479 U.S. 157, 93 L.Ed. 2d 473, 107 S.Ct. 515 (1986).
21. *Arizona v. Fulminante* 499 U.S. 279, 113 L.Ed. 2d 302, 111 S.Ct. 1246 (1991).
22. *Colorado v. Spring* 479 U.S. 364, 93 L.Ed. 2d 954, 107 S.Ct. 851 (1987).
23. *Moran v. Burbine* 475 U.S. 412, 89 L.Ed. 2d 410, 106 S.Ct. 1135 (1986).
24. *North Carolina v. Butler* 441 U.S. 369, 60 L.Ed. 2d 286, 99 S.Ct. 1755 (1979).
25. *Connecticut v. Barrett* 479 U.S. 523, 93 L.Ed. 2d 920, 107 S.Ct. 828 (1987).
26. *Oregon v. Elstad* 470 U.S. 298, 84 L.Ed. 2d 222, 105 S.Ct. 1285 (1985).
27. *Michigan v. Mosley* 423 U.S. 96, 46 L.Ed. 2d 313, 96 S.Ct. 321 (1975).
28. *Edwards v. Arizona* 451 U.S. 477, 68 L.Ed. 2d 378, 101 S.Ct. 1880 (1981).
29. *Smith v. Illinois* 469 U.S. 91, 83 L.Ed. 2d 488, 105 S.Ct. 490 (1984).
30. *Oregon v. Bradshaw* 462 U.S. 1039, 77 L.Ed. 2d 405, 103 S.Ct. 2830 (1983).
31. *Minnick v. Mississippi* 498 U.S. 146, 112 L.Ed. 2d 489, 111 S.Ct. 486 (1990).
32. *Arizona v. Roberson* 486 U.S. 675, 100 L.Ed. 2d 704, 108 S.Ct. 2093 (1988).
33. *Lanier v. South Carolina* 474 U.S. 25, 88 L.Ed. 2d 23, 106 S.Ct. 297 (1985); *Brown v. Illinois* 422 U.S. 590, 45 L.Ed. 2d 416, 95 S.Ct. 2254 (1975); *New York v. Harris* 495 U.S. 14, 109 L.Ed. 2d 13, 110 S.Ct. 1640 (1990); *Kaupp v. Texas* 538 U.S. 626, 155 L.Ed. 2d 814, 123 S.Ct. 1843 (2003).
34. *Kaupp v. Texas* 538 U.S. 626, 155 L.Ed. 2d 814, 123 S.Ct. 1843 (2003).
35. *Yarborough v. Alvardo* __U.S. __, 157 L.Ed. 2d __, 124 S.Ct. __ (June 1, 2004).
36. *Fare v. Michael C.* 422 U.S. 707, 61 L.Ed. 2d 197, 99 S.Ct. 2560 (1979).
37. *Harris v. New York* 401 U.S. 222, 28 L.Ed. 2d 1, 91 S.Ct. 643 (1971).
38. *United States v. Gouveia* 467 U.S. 180, 81 L.Ed. 2d 146, 104 S.Ct. 2292 (1984).
39. *Massiah v. United States* 377 U.S. 201, 12 L.Ed. 2d 246, 84 S.Ct. 1199 (1964).
40. *Illinois v. Patterson* 487 U.S. 285, 101 L.Ed. 2d 261, 108 S.Ct. 2389 (1988).
41. *Fellers v. United States* __ U.S. __, 157 L.Ed. 2d 1016, 124 S.Ct. 1019 (2004).

CHAPTER **15**

Identification Procedures

Outline

Key Terms

- Due process
- Lineup
- Photographic lineup
- Showup
- Unduly suggestive

After studying this chapter, you will be able to:

- Define and differentiate between lineup, showup, and photographic lineup.
- Explain Fourth Amendment rights applicable to identification procedures.
- Explain Fifth Amendment rights applicable to identification procedures.
- Explain Sixth Amendment rights applicable to identification procedures.
- Explain the due process guarantees that apply to identification procedures.

15-1 Definitions Used for Identification Procedures

Law enforcement officers use a variety of techniques to identify the perpetrators of crimes. In addition to conducting identification procedures in a manner that insures accurate identification of the suspect, Fourth, Fifth, Sixth, and Fourteenth Amendment rights must be protected.

There are three basic procedures used to allow victims or witnesses to identify the person who committed the crime:

- Lineups
- Showups
- Photographic lineups

These terms are defined for the purpose of this chapter to avoid confusion with other usages of the terms. Appropriate procedures for conducting these activities will be discussed later in this chapter.

15-1a Lineups

A **lineup** is a procedure where the victim or eyewitness is asked to view a group of people and select the one who committed the crime. Figure 15-1 shows an example of a lineup. Many police departments and jails have viewing rooms set aside for this purpose. These rooms may include marks on the wall to indicate height, special-effects lighting that can simulate whatever illumination existed at the crime scene, and one-way mirrors so the suspects cannot see the people making the identification. On the other hand, a lineup may also be done by merely having the group of people stand in front of the person who saw the crime being committed. Due to the need to assemble several people, lineups are rarely done in the field.

15-1b Showups

A **showup** is a much simpler procedure. One suspect is shown to the person who is to make the identification. This can be done in the field or at a police facility. Figure 15-2 shows an example of a showup.

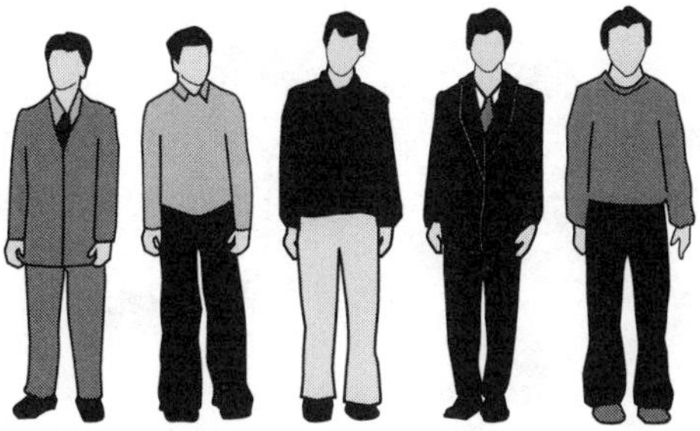

Figure 15-1
An Example of a Lineup

15-1c Photographic Lineups

Photographic lineups involve showing pictures. Figure 15-3 presents an example of a photographic lineup. The suspect does not need to be in custody when this is done. It may be done by handing the witness a few carefully selected photographs or by allowing him/her to look through mug books. High school yearbooks are also used if the suspect is a juvenile or young adult. While the photographs may be from any source, booking pictures are used most frequently because the police have easy access to them. If a tentative identification is made, the police may decide to hold a lineup.

15-2 Fourth Amendment Rights during Identification Procedures

The police do not have the authority to detain a suspect in order to conduct a lineup or showup unless the detention complies with the Fourth

Is this the person who hit you?

Figure 15-2
An Example of a Showup

Figure 15-3
An Example of a Photographic Lineup

Amendment. Random and "hunch" stops are not allowed. Neither may people be detained just because they fit a general description so that there will be enough people to make a valid lineup.

Fourth Amendment Rights during Identification Procedures Defined
Absent consent, there must be reasonable suspicion to stop a suspect in the field for a showup. If there is probable cause to arrest, the suspect may be transported to the police station for either a lineup or showup.

A suspect may be detained briefly based on reasonable suspicion. Identification procedures may be conducted at the scene of this detention, but the suspect may not be transported to the station during this type of detention.[1] Victims and witnesses can be transported to the location in order to conduct a showup.

Probable cause to arrest is necessary in order to transport the suspect to the police station. Once there, either a lineup or showup may be conducted. The identification procedures do not have to be related to the crime for which the suspect was arrested. For example, a suspect who was arrested for burglary can be put in a lineup by officers investigating a murder. It is also permissible to use inmates that are already in custody to provide an adequate number of people for a valid lineup.

The Fourth Amendment applies to detentions and arrests by the police. Photographic lineups are normally conducted using pictures that the police already have in their files. No one is detained in order to conduct this type of procedure. For this reason, Fourth Amendment rights do not apply to photographic lineups.

Examples of Fourth Amendment Rights during Identification Procedures

- A police officer arrived at a "robbery now" call. The suspect fled the scene as the police car approached. Melody, the victim, gave the officers a good description of the robber. Another officer patrolling about two blocks away saw a man running down the street who matched the description broadcast by the officer at the scene. The man was detained while the victim was transported to the scene. As soon as Melody saw the suspect she screamed, "That's him!"

- A traffic officer arrested James for drunk driving. After the blood test James was taken to the station for booking. An officer who walked through the booking area commented, "That guy over there looks just like the artist's drawing they are circulating in the serial rape case." James was placed in a lineup and the rape victims were asked to tell the officers if the rapist was in the lineup. Three women selected James; the others were not sure.

15-3 Fifth Amendment Rights during Identification Procedures

Being identified by an eyewitness is very incriminating. Unfortunately for the criminal, this is not enough to activate the Fifth Amendment. The privilege not to incriminate oneself only applies to testimonial communications.

Fifth Amendment Rights during Identification Procedures Defined

A suspect has no Fifth Amendment right to refuse to participate in a lineup or showup. He/she may not refuse to pose, wear appropriate clothing, or give voice exemplars.

In *United States v. Wade* and *Gilbert v. California,* the Supreme Court held that a legally arrested suspect had no Fifth Amendment right to refuse to participate in a lineup.[2] Neither may he/she refuse to put on clothing worn by the suspect when the crime was committed. The suspect can also be required to walk, take a particular stance, or make gestures observed during the commission of the crime.

Voice exemplars are not covered by the Fifth Amendment. Although they require the suspect to speak, he/she is told what to say. Therefore, the content of the speech is not incriminating. For this reason, the participants in a lineup or showup can be required to repeat what the victim claims the criminal said during the commission of the crime. For example, "Put the money in the bag," or "Scream and I'll kill you."

Distinctive features of the suspect may be re-created. Obviously, this cannot be done if it harms the people participating in the lineup or showup. If the crime was committed by a person with tape on his/her face, tape may be put on each participant's face. A make-up artist can create realistic scars, tattoos, etc. Realistic-looking wigs, toupees, and fake beards may be used.

While none of these procedures violates the Fifth Amendment, due process demands fundamental fairness. If special effects are used on one person in a lineup, similar techniques must be applied other participants if necessary to make them all have similar features.

Examples of Fifth Amendment Rights during Identification Procedures

- Jason was put in a lineup after his arrest for theft. He was very uncooperative and told the officers, "I know my Fifth Amendment rights. I demand to be taken back to my cell." The officers refused to comply with his demands because Jason does not have a Fifth Amendment right to refuse to participate in a lineup.
- Zoe was arrested for passing counterfeit bills. She was placed in a lineup and told to put on a jacket that was found at the crime scene. She refused and said, "My lawyer told me that I do not have to do this because I have a privilege not to incriminate myself." Officers told her she had to put the jacket on because wearing clothing found at the crime scene was not covered by the Fifth Amendment. She could refuse to make statements but she could not refuse to participate in the lineup.

15-4 Sixth Amendment Rights during Identification Procedures

The suspect has a right to counsel during a lineup only if adversary court proceedings have begun *(Kirby v. Illinois)*.[3] This usually occurs at an arraignment or indictment. While the Supreme Court has not explicitly addressed the right to counsel at a showup, it can be inferred that the suspect has the right to have an attorney present only if he/she has already been arraigned or indicted.

Sixth Amendment Rights during Identification Procedures Defined

A suspect who has been arraigned or indicted has the right to have an attorney present at a lineup or showup. There is no right to counsel at a photographic lineup if the suspect is not present.

Moore v. Illinois held that the defendant also has the right to have counsel present during in-court identifications procedures.[4] This applies when a witness is asked if the person who committed the crime is present in the courtroom. The same rule is used at arraignments, preliminary hearings, and trials. It also covers asking someone who is not on the witness stand to identify the suspect in the courtroom. It does not matter whether the identification is made before, during, or after the court hearing.

On the other hand, there is no right to counsel during an identification procedure if the suspect is not present. *United States v. Ash* held that photographic lineups do not activate the right to counsel.[5] The rule is the same whether the pictures are shown before or after arraignment. There is no right to counsel even if the prosecutor decides to show the witness pictures immediately before testifying at trial.

While there is a right to have an attorney present at some lineups and showups, the attorney does not have the right to run the show. Neither can he/she advise the suspect not to cooperate. The lawyer plays the role of an observer. In addition to not being allowed to tell the police how to conduct the lineup, the attorney does not have any duty to tell them to stop doing things that violate the suspect's rights. Whatever the attorney observes can be used in court to challenge the admissibility of identifications made at the lineup.

Examples of Sixth Amendment Rights during Identification Procedures

- Wendy was stopped when she attempted to flee the scene of a hit-and-run accident. A police officer transported a person who witnessed the accident to where Wendy was. Upon seeing the officer approach, she said "Wait a minute. I want my attorney here before that guy tries to put the blame on me." The officer who was detaining her said, "Sorry, but you do not have the right to have an attorney during showups that we do before your first court appearance."
- Steve was arrested for several burglaries and booked at the police station. The next day they held a lineup and asked eyewitnesses from several recent

burglaries to tell them if the person they saw commit the crime was present in the lineup. When being taken to the lineup room, Steve said "I demand an attorney." The officer replied, "You can have your attorney when you are arraigned tomorrow, but we do not have to provide one for a lineup held before the arraignment."

- About a week before trial was scheduled to start, the prosecutor decided that a lineup should be held to see if the eyewitness and victim could still remember what the attacker looked like. When Danny's attorney heard that the lineup was planned, he called the prosecutor and said, "What do you think you are doing? You know you can't hold a lineup now without me being there! He's already been arraigned!!" The prosecutor said, "You're right. I'd forgotten about that. The lineup is set for 2:00 P.M. tomorrow. Be there."

15-5 Due Process Rights during Identification Procedures

The purpose of the Fourteenth Amendment's due process clause is to insure that the justice systems in the 50 states are based on fundamental fairness. Similar Fifth Amendment protections apply to cases in federal courts. In the area of identification procedures, **due process** means that the police must not use unnecessarily suggestive techniques (*Foster v. California*).[6] Testimony about eyewitness identification will not be admissible in court if there is a substantial likelihood of mistaken identification.

15-5a Due Process Rights at Lineups and Photographic Lineups

Lineups and photographic lineups have many of the same problems. Nothing in the way these procedures are conducted may point to one individual. This usually involves two areas: how the participants are selected and how the witnesses are handled.

Due Process Rights during Identification Procedures Defined
Identification procedures must not be unduly suggestive. There must not be a substantial likelihood of mistaken identification.

One of the first rules is that there must be an adequate selection of individuals with similar characteristics. From five to seven individuals is adequate. The participants are usually drawn from the jail population and/or employees working near the viewing room. Each of them must match the general description of the perpetrator of the crime. For

Lineup that satisfies due process

Lineup that is unduly suggestive

The first lineup satisfies due process because there is nothing about it that suggests which suspect to select. Each person in the lineup has the same basic characteristics. The viewer must rely on memories of the event in question when making a choice. No one is singled out as the only possible match.

The second lineup does not satisfy due process because it is unduly suggestive. Only one suspect has all of the characteristics described by the person who gave a description of the person seen at the crime scene. A lineup would also be invalid if the eyewitnesses gave such vague descriptions that too many individuals could match the description given.

Figure 15-4
How Due Process Applies to Lineups

example, if the eyewitness said the crime was committed by an African-American male, no white males should be in the lineup. Obviously, it will not be possible to find five identical matches; in fact, using identical twins would defeat the purpose of a lineup. The goal is to have participants who are sufficiently similar so there is no clue as to which one is the suspect. Anything that makes the suspect stand out is prohibited because it is **unduly suggestive.** Figure 15-4 illustrates how due process is applied to lineups.

If any participant in the lineup has a particularly noticeable scar or tattoo, the lineup could be invalid unless something is done to either hide it or simulate the characteristic on all participants. Make-up artists can be used for this purpose. Similarity in hairstyles and facial hair is also necessary. Wigs and fake beards may be used for this provided they appear real.

Additional problems arise if the same witness views more than one lineup, photographic lineup, or showup. The fact that the witness sees one suspect twice may cause him/her to draw the inference that the person who was in both lineups is the one the police believe committed the crime. This is unduly suggestive because many people will conclude that if the police believe a person committed the crime, he/she must be the one who did it; they may distrust their memory and pick the person who was in multiple lineups. A better way to test the witness' memory is to place the suspect in one lineup and then conduct a "blank" lineup. The "blank" lineup contains people meeting the general description, but none of them is a suspect in the case. The witness, it is hoped, will not identify anyone in the "blank" lineup.

Care must be taken to prevent witnesses from drawing their conclusions based on the way the identification procedures were conducted rather than on their memory of the crime scene. Making an identification is not a committee assignment. Each witness must make an independent decision. It is best to separate witnesses, usually by allowing only one to be present in the viewing area at a time. Witnesses should not be allowed to tell each other which participant in the lineup is believed to be the criminal or even that the person seen committing the crime was (or was not) in the lineup.

The officers conducting the lineup or photographic lineup must be careful not to indicate which participant is believed to be the criminal. Each person in a lineup must be asked to do and say the same things. Equal time should be devoted to each participant. Avoid statements such as, "Look at No. 3 again," or "Don't you think No. 5 looks like the person who robbed you?" Police officers should also avoid making comments to each other that might be overheard by the observer.

A detailed report should be made on each identification procedure that was conducted. If at all possible, this should include a photograph taken while the lineup was in progress. All pictures used in a photographic lineup should be saved and attached to the report. The name and description of the person each witness identified must be included in the report. This is true whether or not the witness picked the "right" suspect.

Altering some of the pictures using a felt-tip pen is not permissible because it is obvious what has been done, but new computer scanners and

Figure 15-5
Showup That Satisfies Due Process

software now make it possible to add realistic looking beards, change hair-styles, etc. Pictures showing booking numbers are not recommended because the fact the person has been booked may unduly prejudice the viewer. Placing booking pictures in window envelopes that hide indications of their source is permissible. The lack of suitable pictures may make it impossible to have a photographic lineup in some cases.

15-5b Due Process Rights at Showups

Many of the protections against unduly suggestive lineups do not apply to showups because the witness usually views only one person. Some rules govern both types of identification procedures: Police should not coach the witnesses and witnesses must arrive at their conclusions independently. Figure 15-5 is an example of a showup that would satisfy due process.

Stovall v. Denno, the Supreme Court's first case about showups,[7] involved a murder case. Two people had been attacked: one was dead and the other in grave condition and being prepared for surgery. Doctors told the investigator that the patient had a very low chance of surviving the surgery. At that point the police brought the suspect to the hospital room and asked the patient if this was the person who attacked her and killed her husband. The Court's decision in the case appeared to restrict show-ups to emergencies, but *Neil v. Biggers* made it clear that the police can conduct showups when there is no emergency forcing them to do so. Instead, the due process analysis focuses on the reliability of the identification.[8] Factors the courts have considered include the following:

1. Opportunity of the witness to view the crime (including lighting and the length of time the witness was with the suspect).
2. Degree of attention the witness paid to the suspect while the crime was in progress.
3. Level of certainty of the witness.
4. Accuracy of the witness's prior description of the suspect.
5. Prior inaccurate identifications made by the witness.
6. Length of time between showup and crime.

The same approach was used in a case where only one photograph was shown for identification purposes (*Manson v. Brathwaite*).[9] While the Court criticized the police for using only one picture because it was suggestive, the conviction was upheld because the totality of the circumstances indicated that the witness was not swayed by it. The witness was a police officer who purchased heroin from the suspect while working undercover. Based on a general description, another officer left the suspect's picture on the undercover officer's desk. The justices concluded that the officer was not susceptible to the subtle inference that the person in the picture was the one the police believed committed the crime.

Example of Showup That Is Valid under Due Process

Veronica was the victim of a home invasion robbery. She called the police five minutes after the robbers left. When questioned by the police, she told them that she was held captive in the brightly lit bathroom for 30 minutes by the shorter suspect while the taller one ransacked the house. Neither robber wore a mask. She gave the following descriptions: one robber was a white male between 18 to 20 years old, between 5 feet 8 inches and 5 feet 10 inches tall, slender build, blond hair, and wearing a black sweatshirt and black denim pants; the other robber was an Hispanic male, about 25, between 5 feet 10 inches and 6 feet tall, black hair, muscular build, and wearing a navy blue hooded sweatshirt and navy blue sweat pants. The robbers left carrying several items of expensive jewelry in a black sock.

Several hours later the police stopped a car for speeding and became suspicious that the two males in the car were the men who robbed Veronica. Another patrol car picked Veronica up and brought her to the scene. She looked at the two men as they stood under a street light. After nearly a minute, Veronica said "I'm sure the short guy is the one that forced me into the bathroom and stayed there to make sure I didn't get out. I got a good look at him for a long time. The other guy is the right size, but I didn't get much chance to see his face, so I can't say for sure that he is the one."

15-6   Use of Identification Testimony at Trial

A witness may testify about any properly conducted identification procedure. While the prosecutor will ask about situations in which the witness correctly identified the suspect, the defense attorney will try to show as many misidentifications as possible. The ability of the witness to identify the witness may be challenged. This includes bad eyesight, poor memory, and a variety of other factors.

Some courts even allow psychologists to give expert testimony on the inherent problems with eyewitness identification. These problems include perception, memory, emotional state of the witness, and both conscious and unconscious motivation to identify someone as the perpetrator of the crime. The impact of stereotypes and prejudice may also be covered. Experts may be allowed to testify about the brain functions involved in memory and recall and explain why memory is not always accurate. Occasionally the results of psychological research on recall are also introduced into evidence.[10]

A hearing must be held if there is a question regarding the constitutional validity of the identification procedure *(Watkins v. Sowders).*[11] Testimony in the presence of the jury regarding lineups or showups that violate the right to counsel is grounds for automatic reversal of a conviction *(Gilbert v. California).*[12] The Harmless Error Rule applies to other violations. Fourth Amendment and due process errors result in reversals if there is a substantial chance that they influenced the outcome of the case.

The Fruit of the Poison Tree Doctrine has been applied to in-court identifications that followed improper pretrial procedures. If the in-court testimony is not influenced by the unconstitutional procedure, the witness may testify about the crime scene and make an in-court identification of the defendant. State courts frequently permit this type of testimony. The prosecutor may not ask questions about the improperly conducted lineup or other procedure, but the defense may ask about it on cross-examination.

United States v. Owens allowed testimony regarding a pretrial photographic lineup, even though the witness did not remember why he picked the defendant's picture.[13] He also did not remember seeing the defendant commit the crime. The victim's memory had been severely impaired due to the crime, which involved a beating with a metal pipe. The defense attorney introduced evidence that, while in the hospital, the victim had named another person as the assailant. The court held that the photographic lineup was admissible because there was no evidence that it was suggestive. The fact that the witness was available for cross-examination, even though he could not answer questions due to loss of memory, satisfied the Sixth Amendment's Confrontation Clause. The defense could not prevent the witness from taking the stand. Obviously, it could argue to the jury that the witness lacked credibility.

Sample Dialogues for Introducing Identification Testimony at Trial
Introducing Testimony about a Showup That Was Conducted Properly

Prosecutor:	Mrs. Worth, did the police ever ask you to identify the man that hit you?
Mrs. Worth:	Yes, they did. They called me at home one day and said they had someone they wanted me to look at. They wanted me to do that before they decided whether to file charges.
Prosecutor:	When was that?
Mrs. Worth:	Right after I got out of the hospital.
Prosecutor:	How long was that after he hit you?
Mrs. Worth:	A week.
Prosecutor:	Where did this identification procedure take place?
Mrs. Worth:	At the police station. I was sitting in what they said was an interview room when an officer brought in a man in jail clothing.
Prosecutor:	Who else was present?
Mrs. Worth.	Nobody. Just me, the officer, and the guy they brought in.
Prosecutor:	What did the officer say to you at the time?
Mrs. Worth:	She said "I want you to look at this man. Tell me if he is the person who hit you. Take your time and think about it. If you are sure that this is the man, tell me so. If you are not sure, tell me that, too. I don't want you guessing on this. This may be the right man but it might also not be the right one." Or something like that.
Prosecutor:	How long did it take you to make a decision?
Mrs. Worth:	My first impression was that it was him, but I spent a couple of minutes thinking back to the night of the attack and trying to remember exactly what he looked like.
Prosecutor:	And what did you finally tell Officer Bartlett?
Mrs. Worth:	I told her that the man standing there was the one who hit me. I was very sure it was him.
Prosecutor:	And is that man in the courtroom today?
Mrs. Worth:	Yes. [Points at defendant.] That is him sitting next to the defense attorney.

In-Court Identification of the Suspect by Witness Who Viewed a Lineup That Was Not Conducted Properly

Prosecutor:	Dr. Morgan, you have testified that your office was robbed. Did the police ever ask you to view a lineup and pick out the person who robbed you?
Dr. Morgan:	Yes, they had me attend a lineup.
Prosecutor:	Now, I know this will sound strange, but I want you to do your best to forget about what happened at that lineup. I want you to focus solely on what is occurring here in the courtroom today. OK?
Dr. Morgan:	OK. I will try.
Prosecutor:	Thinking about the day that you were robbed, did you get a good chance to see the person's face?
Dr. Morgan:	Yes. I looked up from my desk and he was standing there, staring at me. I must have looked at him for a full minute before he blindfolded me.
Prosecutor:	And could you identify that person today if you saw him?
Dr. Morgan:	Yes, I could. I'll never forget that face.
Prosecutor:	Now, using only the face you saw during the robbery as a guide, is the person who robbed you in the courtroom today?
Dr. Morgan:	Yes he is. He is right over there. [Pointing]
Prosecutor:	I need you to state for the record who you are pointing at.
Dr. Morgan:	I am pointing at the man in the blue shirt seated at the table with the sign that says "Defense."
Prosecutor:	Thank you, Dr. Morgan. That will be all.
Judge:	Defense, you can cross-examine the witness now.

Summary

The police frequently use three procedures to help eyewitnesses identify criminals: lineups, showups, and photographic lineups. Lineups involve showing the witness a group of possible suspects. Photographic lineups provide a selection of pictures of possible suspects for the witness to choose from. Showups are done by showing one suspect to the witness.

The Fourth Amendment prohibits stopping people without cause unless they consent. To detain someone for a showup in the field there must be at least a reasonable suspicion that this person committed a crime. Suspects may only be transported to a police station for identification procedures if there is probable cause to arrest them.

The Fifth Amendment protection against self-incrimination does not apply to identification procedures. The suspect may not refuse to participate in a lineup or showup. He/she can be required to speak, stand in a particular pose, or wear appropriate clothing.

Suspects can invoke the Sixth Amendment right to counsel during lineups and showups held after they have been arraigned or indicted. They have the right to have an attorney present, but the attorney only participates as an observer.

Due process requires identification procedures to be fundamentally fair. Anything the police do that suggests which person in a lineup or photographic lineup is the suspect violates due process. There should be enough people who are similar in appearance in the lineup to force the witness to demonstrate his/her memory and ability to observe. The police must not attempt to focus the viewer's attention on any one individual or coach the witness; no one else should be allowed to do so, not even other victims and witnesses from the same crime.

Showups are judged on the totality of the circumstances. Identifications are usually admissible if the witness had a good opportunity to observe the crime and could give a good description of the suspect. There does not have to be an emergency to justify the failure to conduct a full lineup.

Introduction of testimony at trial regarding identification procedures that violate the right to counsel is grounds for automatic reversal of a conviction. Other mistakes are judged by the Harmless Error Rule. The Confrontation Clause of the Sixth Amendment gives the defense the right to cross-examine witnesses who testify about lineups, showups, and photographic lineups.

Discussion Questions

1. Define *lineup,* and explain what constitutional rights apply.
2. Define a *showup,* and explain each applicable constitutional right.
3. Define *photographic lineup,* and explain what constitutional rights apply.
4. What types of errors in identification procedures will cause reversal of a conviction? Explain.
5. Assume that a person viewed an improperly conducted lineup. Will that person be allowed to testify in court? To make an in-court identification of the suspect? Explain.

Endnotes

1. *Hayes v. Florida* 470 U.S. 811, 84 L.Ed. 2d 705, 105 S.Ct. 1643 (1985); *Dunaway v. New York* 422 U.S. 200, 60 L.Ed. 2d 824, 99 S.Ct. 2248 (1979).

2. *United States v. Wade* 388 U.S. 218, 18 L.Ed. 2d 1149, 87 S.Ct. 1926 (1967); *Gilbert v. California* 388 U.S. 263, 18 L.Ed. 2d 1178, 87 S.Ct. 1951 (1967).

3. *Kirby v. Illinois* 406 U.S. 682, 32 L.Ed. 2d 411, 92 S.Ct. 1877 (1972). See also, *United States v. Wade*, supra.

4. *Moore v. Illinois* 434 U.S. 220, 54 L.Ed. 2d 424, 98 S.Ct. 458 (1977).

5. *United States v. Ash* 413 U.S. 300, 37 L.Ed. 2d 619, 93 S.Ct. 1568 (1973).

6. *Foster v. California* 394 U.S. 440, 22 L.Ed. 2d 402, 89 S.Ct. 1127 (1969).

7. *Stovall v. Denno* 388 U.S. 293, 18 L.Ed. 2d 1199, 87 S.Ct. 1967 (1967).

8. *Neil v. Biggers* 409 U.S. 188, 34 L.Ed. 2d 401, 93 S.Ct. 375 (1972).

9. *Manson v. Brathwaite* 432 U.S. 98, 53 L.Ed. 2d 140, 97 S.Ct. 2243 (1977).

10. *National Institute of Justice, Eyewitness Evidence: A Guide for Law Enforcemen.* (Washington, D.C.: U. S. Department of Justice, 1999); S. L. Sporer, R. S. Malpass, and G. Koehnken (eds.), *Psychological Issues in Eyewitness Identification* (Mahwah, NJ: Lawrence Erlbaum, 1996); B. L. Cutler and S. D. Penrod, *Mistaken Identification: The Eyewitness, Psychology, and the Law* (New York, NY: Cambridge University Press, 1995); M. Zalman and L. Siegel, "The Psychology of Perception, Eyewitness Identification, and the Lineup," *Criminal Law Bulletin* 27 (2): 159–176 (1991).

11. *Watkins v. Sowders* 449 U.S. 341, 66 L.Ed. 2d 549, 101 S.Ct. 654 (1981).

12. *Gilbert v. California*, supra.

13. *United States v. Owens* 484 U.S.554, 98 L.Ed. 2d 951, 108 S.Ct. 838 (1988).

Preparing the Case for Court

Outline

After studying this chapter, you will be able to:

- Describe how the prosecutor evaluates a case when deciding if it should be filed.
- List what precautions must be taken to insure that physical evidence will be admissible in court.
- Explain the process for subpoenaing witnesses.
- Identify the proper dress and demeanor of a peace officer in court.
- Describe what contacts an officer should have with lawyers, witnesses, and jurors.
- Explain how an officer should deal with the media.

16-1 Introduction

It is very important that a peace officer know the law of arrest, search and seizure, and confessions while working in the field. Proper techniques for preserving physical evidence at the crime scene are crucial. Understanding what is relevant and who is competent to testify are important in deciding to seek a criminal complaint.

Learning all of these things, however, may be wasted if the officer does not know how to prepare the case for trial. This is true even though many cases are plea bargained and never go to trial. If defense attorneys sense that the police cannot convince the jury that the defendant is guilty beyond a reasonable doubt, they usually will not persuade their clients to plea bargain. This chapter is designed to help police officers understand their duties in preparing the case for court.

16-2 Reviewing Facts of the Case

Police must have probable cause in order to make an arrest. The report prepared shortly after the arrest is made normally sets out the facts used to establish it. Supplemental reports usually detail what is discovered after the arrest. All of these reports must be reviewed in order to determine what charges should be sought.

Reviewing the case in preparation for presenting it to the prosecutor requires objectivity. Police sometimes make errors. Frequently these errors are caused by the stress of fast-breaking events. Constitutional rights may have been violated. Becoming defensive and denying the mistakes that were made will not delude an experienced prosecutor. Officers given the responsibility for presenting cases to the prosecutor must be able to review the case file and determine what evidence is admissible. Based on this, they should decide what charges to seek. This, of course, requires a good working knowledge of the penal code or other relevant statutes.

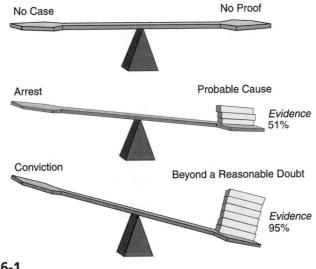

Figure 16-1
Likelihood of Conviction

Most prosecutors carry a heavy case load. Due to this and other factors, they usually do not want to file cases that they cannot win. Judges may also pressure prosecutors not to waste court time on weak or trivial cases. Prosecutors are more concerned with determining whether or not a jury will convict the defendant.

Probable cause to make an arrest is not a sufficient reason to file criminal charges. A conviction requires much stronger evidence than what is needed for a valid arrest. To arrest someone there must be probable cause, which means it is more likely than not that the person committed the crime. At a minimum, this equates to 51 percent certainty. To convict, there must be proof beyond a reasonable doubt. While the jurors do not need to feel 100 percent sure, the facts need to make them feel about 95 percent sure that the defendant is guilty. Figure 16-1 illustrates how the strength of evidence is related to the likelihood of getting a conviction.

The facts should be carefully assessed to determine if each element of each charge sought can be established beyond a reasonable doubt. If there is a doubt, lesser included offenses should be considered. For suspects that are on probation or parole, the potential sentence for the current offense should be weighed against the consequences of revoking probation/ parole. The person asking the prosecutor to file charges should be able to discuss the request in detail and provide the criminal history of the suspect. Habitually requesting charges that cannot be supported by the evidence only decreases the credibility of the police department in the eyes of the prosecutor.

| Case No. 04-1234 | Court File No. | SE 66-44-22 |
| Suspect: George Green | Charge: | Burglary |

Other cases pending against suspect: 04-1111 (murder)

Elements of Offense	Evidence	Comments
Entry	Pry marks on door.	Unable to match pry marks to items in evidence.
	Suspect's fingerprints found on drawer where cash was kept in house.	Suspect had access to house before forced entry occurred.
Structure	Home of John Smith 123 Broadway	
Intent	Theft of following items from the dwelling: Stereo, TV, and $500	No ID numbers on TV

Other facts: Burglary reported on 1/2/04. Victim had been out of town from 12/24/03 to 1/2/04. No eyewitnesses. John Smith has prior perjury conviction. Suspect was a friend of Smith until 12/20/03 when they had a violent argument. Suspect frequently visited Smith at his home while they were friends and may have left fingerprints prior to the date the crime occurred.

Figure 16-2
Sample Computer Screen for Outline of Charge

Outlining the charges is very helpful. A computer database is useful for this purpose. A convenient layout for reviewing the charges is a screen with three columns. Figure 16-2 shows a sample screen. In the first column, enter every element of each charge sought. In column two, opposite each element, note all evidence that can be used to establish it. The third column is used for comments related to strengths and/or weaknesses of the evidence. Any other important facts should also be noted. If a computerized system is not available, these comments can be made on 5 × 8 cards. The database or cards should be updated as new evidence develops in the case. By doing this, the case can easily be reviewed when it is time to prepare for trial.

Credibility of the witnesses is critical. The fact that the investigating officer believes the witness is not enough. The jury must also believe him/her. Objectively advising the prosecutor of factors that enhance or detract from the credibility of witnesses is important. Hiding weaknesses of the witnesses from the prosecutor will not help win the case. Defense attorneys specialize in demolishing the credibility of weak witnesses.

16-3 Working with the Prosecutor

In addition to investigating the case and asking the prosecutor to file the charges, the police are usually responsible for preservation of the physical evidence and serving subpoenas on witnesses. Both of these tasks have one thing in common—keeping track of the location of potential evidence.

16-3a Preparing Physical Evidence

In order to introduce physical evidence at trial, the prosecutor must know where the item has been, who has had access to it, and anything that has been done with it since it came into police custody. This will be needed to establish the "chain of custody" prior to admitting the item into evidence.

The prosecutor also needs to know the evidentiary significance of each piece of physical evidence. Probably the two most important facts will be where each item of evidence was found and what tests have been done on it. For example, the bullet was taken from the brain of the deceased during an autopsy and ballistic tests show it was fired from the gun found in the defendant's possession at the time of her arrest. Once again, it is very important to keep the prosecutor advised of all facts related to the physical evidence.

If the police tell the prosecutor about the positive tests conducted at the forensics laboratory but do not mention the negative tests, the prosecutor may falsely believe the case is very strong. Facts not known to the prosecutor may also give the defense an added edge during cross-examination. In fact, the prosecutor's lack of knowledge may even result in dismissal of the case if the defense can convince the judge that it was denied its constitutional right to discovery.

Physical evidence is prone to motions to suppress based on illegal search and seizure. For this reason the prosecutor needs to know all the facts on how each item was obtained.

Keeping track of all of the above details for each item of potential evidence is not easy, particularly when an item may be relevant to two or more crimes or there are multiple suspects. A computerized database is ideally suited for this task. Each time an event, such as a new court date or results of a laboratory test, is entered, every screen that uses that information will be updated. Figure 16-3 presents a sample screen. If a card system is used, the information will have to be posted to each card involved.

Case No. 04-1234   **Court File No.**   SE 66-44-22
Suspect: George Green   **Charge:**   Burglary

Other cases pending against suspect: 04-1111 (murder)

Evidence Tag No. 04-04   **Location:**   Bin 387

Description of item: RCA portable stereo model 345678X23.

Where obtained: In possession of George Green at time of his arrest.

Justification for seizure: Suspect stopped for running a red light. Record check
showed that suspect had outstanding warrant. Search of car incident to arrest
on warrant revealed RCA portable stereo listed above. Serial number run by
dispatcher and found to match item stolen during burglary reported by John
Smith on 1/2/04.

Chain of custody: Officer David A. Doe seized item on 1/2/04 at time of arrest
and ran serial number. He sealed item in plastic and stored in station evidence
locker bin 387. Officer Jane E. Jones removed item from evidence locker 1/4/04
and checked it for fingerprints. She sealed it in plastic and returned it to evidence
locker bin 387 on 1/4/04. Item taken to forensics laboratory on 1/8/04 by Officer
Sam Smith. Blood and tissue scrapings taken from item at forensics lab. Officer
Sam Smith sealed it in plastic and returned it to evidence locker bin 387 on
1/10/04.

Tests performed: Fingerprints on item do not match suspect's prints; unable
to identify fingerprints. Blood tests show the presence of human blood type O
positive. Tissue samples: inconclusive.

Comments: Suspect had several recent bruises at time of arrest and matched
description of person who was involved in a fight in the parking lot of Joe's Pool
Hall on 1/1/04. One person was shot during that altercation who had type O
positive blood. See Case No. 04-1111.

Figure 16-3
Sample Computer Screen for Physical Evidence

The database, whether electronic or paper, should contain sections for
the following:

1. Description of item
2. Where it was obtained
3. Facts justifying its seizure
4. Chain of custody
5. Tests that have been performed

Adequate space for other information that may be useful should also
be provided. If the computer database is kept current on each item of evidence, the officer should be able to answer any questions the prosecutor
may have.

16-3b Witnesses

Many prosecutors will ask the police for a list of witnesses. If time permits, a meeting may be set up to discuss which witnesses should be called. The prosecutor's office usually handles the paperwork for issuing subpoenas. The police frequently are asked to serve the subpoenas.

The prosecutor must be prepared for the impeachment of his/her witnesses. This requires a thorough knowledge of witnesses' backgrounds, including prior statements to police about the case, previous arrests, and convictions. Other problems, such as poor eyesight or hearing, must also be brought to the prosecutor's attention. A thoroughly prepared case includes notations about evidence that can be introduced to rehabilitate the witnesses. This obviously means that officers must be familiar with the rules for impeachment and rehabilitation.

Once again the police should keep accurate records on what a witness can testify about and where the witness can be located. The computer database, which already contains the outline of the charges and the description of the physical evidence, can also be used for this information. Figure 16-4 shows a sample screen. It should contain at least three things:

1. Current address of witness and other places witness might be found
2. Facts witness can testify about
3. Strengths and weaknesses of witness

It is quite possible that witnesses will move while the case is awaiting trial. If a key witness cannot be located, the case may have to be dismissed or result in an acquittal. This places one more burden on the police—keeping track of the witnesses. Addresses and telephone numbers must be kept current. Many courts now have victim-witness specialists who help with this, but the police cannot neglect these details if they hope to win the case.

Unfortunately, some witnesses become frustrated with the court proceedings and decide not to cooperate with the investigation. Frequent trips to the courthouse, particularly if they appear unnecessary because the defendant obtained a continuance, discourage witnesses. Once again, the burden falls on the police. Sometimes victim-witness assistance programs can help. Inconvenience to the victim should be reduced as much as possible. Positive attitudes are important. A witness who feels he/she is on trial or being unfairly treated by "the system" may testify unfavorably at trial.

Witnesses who cannot remember crucial events complicate the court proceedings. In major cases, it is good police procedure to talk with all witnesses a few days before trial or other court appearances in order to

```
Case No.          04-1111        Court File No.    SE 66-44-22
Defendant:        George Green    Charge:          Murder
Witness:          Suzie Q. Adams
Other cases involving witness:      none
Other cases pending against this suspect:    04-1234 (burglary)


Home address:                    Work address:
789 E. Main St.                  543 S. First St.
Anytown, CA                      Anytown, CA
(123) 456-7890                   (123) 987-6543
                                 Works 9-5 weekdays


Other places to locate witness:
Mother lives at 399 S. Tenth St., Anytown (123) 246-8102.
Witness frequents Joe's Pool Hall.


Testimony: Ms. Adams was a customer at Joe's Pool Hall on 1/1/04. She was
interviewed by the police 15 minutes after the shooting and described the assailant
as a 5'10" tall white male weighing 200 lbs., wearing a green turtleneck sweater and
blue jeans. She picked George Green out of a line-up held on 1/3/04.


Strengths and Weaknesses: Ms. Adams admitted having 4 drinks between 9:00
p.m. and midnight on 1/1/04. She is an LVN who works in a doctor's office and
routinely takes heights and weights of patients.
```

Figure 16-4
Sample Computer Screen for Witness

determine what they can recall. Attempts may be made to refresh their memories, but officers must never give the appearance of coaching the witness on what to say. Officers should have a working knowledge of both "present memory refreshed" and "past recollection recorded" when talking with these witnesses (see Sections 5-5 and 8-15). The prosecutor must be made aware of these potential problems so tactical decisions can be made on how to handle the case. Another type of problem is presented if the witness alters his/her testimony or refuses to testify. While a subpoena will give the court the power to force the witness to take the stand, the prosecutor needs to be aware of these problems in advance so a decision can be made on whether or not to risk calling the witness to the stand. Some states still follow the common law rule that you cannot impeach your own witness. Under this rule, the prosecutor could not try to show a prosecution witness is lying or has a poor memory. Even if the state will allow the prosecutor to impeach the witness, the extra time and testimony may not be worth the effort. There is always a hazard that the jury may believe the untruthful answer. It may also confuse the jury, or convince them that the case is weak.

If police officers suspect a witness plans to lie they can warn him/her of the penalty for perjury, but they cannot prevent the person from testifying if subpoenaed. Police protection and restraining orders can be sought if a witness is being harassed or intimidated. But the fact that the witness may be prosecuted for perjury or the defendant charged with intimidating the witness is not much help at this stage. The jury cannot be told of these possibilities.

16-4 Dress and Demeanor

During the investigation of the crime, officers focus on obtaining the facts. The prosecutor screens the case to determine if there is sufficient evidence to prove the crime beyond a reasonable doubt. Officers must not forget another important role of the jury—to assess the credibility of the witnesses. "Truth" does not always win if the jurors have a negative impression of the witness. This includes the officers who testify. For this reason it is important that each officer consider his/her own appearance and demeanor when preparing for court.

16-4a Appearance

"Dress for Success," the "Power Suit," and many other expressions reflect the importance of a person's physical appearance in business situations. The same is true in the courtroom. The jury's first impression of the witness will be based on physical appearance. For many jurors, this may be the single most important factor used to weigh the testimony. Good grooming is therefore crucial.

Officers who do not wear a uniform in their normal assignment, such as detectives, usually appear in court in civilian clothing. Opinions differ on whether patrol officers should testify in uniform. Some feel that the public respects law enforcement officers, and the uniform adds credibility to the witness. Others believe that a uniformed officer, especially one visibly wearing a gun, smacks of authoritarianism and has a negative impact on jurors. Community attitudes toward the police will have a lot to do with determining what an officer should wear. Formal or informal policies of the police department or prosecutor's office may provide guidance.

Whether the officer wears a uniform or civilian clothes, the clothing should be clean, neat, and fit appropriately. Jurors may infer that an officer who dresses in a sloppy manner is also sloppy in investigating the crime and handling the evidence.

If civilian clothing is worn, it is best to dress in conservative business attire. Flamboyant and gaudy clothing detracts from what the witness says. Officers must look professional. What is considered appropriate in a large, metropolitan area may be out of place in a rural farming community and vice versa.

The same rule applies to all aspects of the officer's appearance. Jewelry, cosmetics, and fragrances should be appropriate for a daytime business meeting. Hair, beards, and mustaches should be neatly styled in an appropriate manner. Even fingernails should be inspected to make sure they are clean and properly manicured.

16-4b Demeanor

The courtroom places high demands on the officer's professionalism. Each officer needs to remain polite and civil to everyone involved. The officer should be an unbiased pursuer of truth, not a persecutor of the defendant. This is not easy under cross-examination when the defense is trying to make painstaking detectives appear to be incompetent liars or "Keystone Cops."

Each officer must realize that the attorneys in the case are playing the roles assigned them by the criminal justice system. It is the duty of the defense attorney to impeach each witness if possible. During cross-examination the officer should try to remember that the defense is not attacking him/her personally although it may appear to be so at the time.

Good grammar is essential. Jurors may judge the intelligence of the witness by the grammar used. Vocabulary is also important. Each officer needs to select words that accurately answer the attorney's questions. A varied vocabulary also helps keep the jurors from being bored. Excessively technical language and police jargon ("cop talk") may confuse the jurors. Therefore, officers should avoid language that would not be understood by the average person.

While testifying, officers must make certain that they understand the question before answering it. If necessary, they should ask to have it repeated. Misinterpreting the question, or answering before the question has been completely stated, can result in testimony that confuses the jury. It can also make the officer look foolish and/or dishonest. Either of these impressions is damaging to credibility. A good witness pauses briefly after a question has been asked for three reasons: to allow time to think about the question; to give the jury the impression that the witness is thoughtfully deciding what to say; and to allow the attorneys time to make appropriate objections to the question before the answer is heard by the jury.

Most people, including jurors, dislike arrogance. Even though the officer firmly believes that he/she has conducted a perfect investigation and the defendant is obviously guilty, the officer must not appear smug while testifying. Care should also be taken to avoid letting the defense attorney lead the officer into stating that he/she never makes errors. This is a favorite tactic used to make small mistakes in the investigation look bigger.

Another trap officers fall into is appearing like "professional witnesses." Due to frequent court appearances, most veteran officers develop set patterns of speech while on the stand. Many appear to be almost testifying from rote memory. Some use short, clipped sentences spoken in a monotone. Defense attorneys like to infer that the testimony is less than honest because it appears to be memorized and used in case after case. This type of testimony may also cause jurors to become bored and unconsciously allow their attention to drift away from what is being said.

Any appearance of personal animosity toward the defendant or defense attorney should be avoided. It is the officer's duty to bring the guilty to justice, not to have a personal vendetta against criminal suspects. While most jurors have a general knowledge of the role of police in our society, they may favor the "underdog." If the "poor little defendant" is being picked on by the "mean policeman," the jurors may side with the defendant. Additionally, an officer who displays ill will toward the defendant is a prime candidate for impeachment on bias. The defense will strongly imply to the jury that the officer is either lying or exaggerating.

No one is expected to have total recall. "Present memory refreshed" was designed to help people recall things that had slipped from their memory. A witness should be ready to honestly admit refreshing his/her memory. The prosecutor should be prepared to ask relevant questions to show that this was legitimately done. Redirect can be used to show that the officer has not merely memorized an old police report or made up the testimony to conveniently fit the facts that have already been admitted into evidence. During closing arguments the prosecutor can emphasize the fact that any normal person forgets from time to time.

Example of Present Memory Refreshed

Prosecutor: Ms. Adams, do you clearly recall what happened on January 4, 2004?

Ms. Adams: Yes, I do.

Prosecutor: Have you done anything to help you remember the events that occurred that day?

Ms. Adams: Yes. I read the journal entries that I wrote that day, and the next day, too. Oh, I also read the newspaper clippings that I kept in the pocket of my journal.

Prosecutor:	Have you talked to anyone about the events in question?
Ms. Adams:	Yes, I talked to Det. Dawson.
Prosecutor:	I don't want you to repeat what the detective said, but can you tell us what you discussed with Det. Dawson?
Ms. Adams:	Well, he stopped by where I work. He asked if I remembered what happened. When I said I didn't remember it all, he let me read the police report.
Prosecutor:	So you refreshed your memory by reading your journal, the newspaper clippings, and the police report?
Ms. Adams:	Yes.
Prosecutor:	Did you talk to anyone else about it?
Ms. Adams:	No, just Det. Dawson.
Prosecutor:	And at this time, right now in court, you clearly recall what happened that day?
Ms. Adams:	Yes.

Demeanor off the witness stand is also important. Jurors frequently see the witnesses in the halls and elevators, and even the courthouse cafeteria and parking lot. If they observe horseplay, lewd remarks, and off-color jokes they may decide the officer is immature or prejudiced, and lose respect for the officer. Any negative impression may affect the weight given the officer's testimony. Care should be taken to make a favorable impression at all times.

16-5 Contacts with Lawyers, Witnesses, and Jurors

The police usually have more contact with the prosecutor than anyone else in the courtroom. Sometimes friction develops between them. Officers who have conducted a lengthy investigation may be upset to find that the prosecutor is not totally familiar with the case. Sometimes there is a difference of opinion on the tactics the prosecutor is using or anger about how the prosecutor's office has previously handled cases. No matter what type of problem arises, it is essential that it not come to the attention of the defense attorney or jurors.

It is a good idea, if possible, to talk about the case with the prosecutor before court begins. This should be done in a location where privacy is assured so that the case can be thoroughly discussed. During trial it may be necessary to write messages on a legal pad or pass notes to the prosecutor. This should be done in as unobtrusive a manner as possible. The jury's attention needs to remain focused on the witness and not on what is happening at the prosecutor's table.

Attorneys who come to the police station to talk with their clients may attempt to discuss the case with the officers. Once the defendant has been arraigned, however, the defense attorney should deal directly with the prosecutor. Police officers must direct any communications from the defense attorney or defendant to the prosecutor. Attempts by the prosecutor or police to contact the defendant directly are viewed as interfering with the attorney-client relationship. During this time period, if the police need to contact the defense attorney or defendant it is necessary to channel communications through the prosecutor's office. Figure 16-5 illustrates the flow of communication after arraignment between the people involved in a case.

Cordial relationships between officers and attorneys are necessary in court. Even though the defense attorney is obviously trying to defeat the case, officers must remain polite. There are two reasons for this. One is that those who work in the criminal justice system should respect each others' professionalism. The other is the jury. If jurors observe open hostility against the defense, they may decide the officers lack objectivity and their testimony is biased.

Impressions the jurors might receive also mandate avoiding excessive familiarity with the defense counsel and other courtroom personnel. Watching a group of good friends merely going through the motions of a trial may convince the jurors that the case is a sham or that it does not deserve to be taken seriously. Either of these opinions is bound to hurt the prosecution's case during jury deliberations.

Witnesses for both sides must be treated with common courtesy. This is important to maintain the dignity of the court proceeding as well as to avoid biasing the jury. On the other hand, constantly talking to the witnesses may convince the jurors that the police are setting up the testimony. This must be avoided.

Victims and witnesses frequently complain that they are forgotten by the criminal justice system. Keeping them informed of the progress of the case is important. Familiarizing witnesses with the court procedures before they are called to testify may help them better understand what is happening. It cannot be assumed that witnesses can learn the process by arriving early and watching the court proceedings; witnesses are usually excluded from the courtroom until they testify. Comfortable waiting rooms should be provided at the courthouse. All possible efforts should be made to avoid unnecessarily subpoenaing them. On-call subpoenas reduce the amount of time spent idly waiting in the courthouse or taking time off work to go to court only to find that the case has been continued.

Figure 16-5
Communication with Defendant after Arraignment

Whenever in the courthouse, officers must be alert to the presence of jurors. When not in the jury box, they may be almost anywhere. Jurors should only hear about the case from the witness stand. If they overhear conversations about the case, particularly relating to suppressed evidence, it may cause a mistrial. Jurors have been known to stop officers in the hall and ask about the evidence in the case. A polite explanation that the rules do not allow the officer to answer these types of questions must be given.

The officer must remember two things: never answer the out-of-court questions and never be rude to the jurors.

Example of Officer Contact with Juror

Juror: Officer! Officer!

Officer: Yes, Ma'am.

Juror: I have a question about what you said in court. Did you find anything when you searched that man?

Officer: I'm sorry, ma'am, but I can't answer any questions.

Juror: But this is important. What was in his pocket?

Officer: I can't answer anything outside of court. I know you would like to know that, but the jury is only allowed to consider the facts that are introduced in the trial. Jurors aren't allowed to ask witnesses questions outside of court. Please don't think I am being rude, but I must go now so there is no appearance of impropriety.

16-6 Press Coverage

The First Amendment governs freedom of the press. The Supreme Court has affirmed the media's right to cover almost all criminal court hearings but the media may be excluded in juvenile cases. A judge must give strong justification whenever part of a hearing is closed.

On the other hand, prejudicial pretrial publicity may endanger a conviction. The Supreme Court has allowed narrowly defined "gag" orders that prevent parties to the case, including attorneys and the police, from commenting to the media. Again, a strong justification is needed to make these orders. The Supreme Court has also upheld the constitutionality of state bar disciplinary rules that prohibit attorneys from making statements to the press that pose a substantial likelihood of prejudicing the case.

Most cases do not arouse sufficient media curiosity to be a problem. For this reason, many officers are unprepared for those cases that do. Each department needs guidelines on how to handle the media. Every officer must be familiar with them. Courtesy is required because an angry reporter can distort the facts and make the police appear incompetent, vindictive, or corrupt.

Care must also be taken to avoid "trying the case in the press." Statements given to reporters must be accurate, but the facts should be carefully reviewed to avoid inflammatory statements. It is usually wise to avoid disclosing the contents of confessions due to the sensationalism they may cause. Publication of a confession that is later held inadmissible runs a high likelihood of endangering the objectivity of the jury and causing a reversal of the conviction. This also applies to items that may have been seized illegally. Few juries are sequestered during the entire trial. Although the judge instructs the jurors to avoid listening to radio or television accounts of the case or reading about it in newspapers, the possibility of a juror finding out about the coverage of the case in the media must be considered. The police should avoid giving statements to the media during trial. A mistrial could be declared or a conviction reversed if a juror learned about these out-of-court statements before reaching a verdict.

Summary

Officers must carefully review the facts of the case prior to presenting it to the prosecutor for filing. They must be sure that there is evidence to establish probable cause for each element of the crime. The same is true when preparing for the trial—the prosecutor must consider the best way to use the available evidence to establish every element of the offense(s) beyond a reasonable doubt. Witnesses must be available to establish the chain of custody for each item of physical evidence. The evidentiary value of each item must be analyzed after considering all available information including the results of any laboratory tests that were performed.

All physical evidence must be reviewed and the chain of custody must be established for each item. Evidentiary value must also be determined after reviewing all relevant information including the results of forensic laboratory tests that were conducted.

Information must be maintained on each potential witness. It is important to know both what the witness is competent to testify about and where the witness can be located. It may also be necessary to interview each witness again to test his/her memory if there has been a lengthy delay between the occurrence of the crime and the trial.

Officers must appear neat and well groomed in court. Good grammar and vocabulary are important. Testimony must be in language the jurors can understand and not laced with police jargon. Overt hostility toward the defendant is unprofessional and may cause the jurors to become protective of the defendant.

Once a case has been filed there should be no direct communication between the police and the defense attorney or the defendant unless the prosecution has authorized it. Requests for discovery and other information must be channeled through the prosecutor.

Victims and witnesses should be afforded every professional courtesy. Subpoenaing them for court hearings should be restricted as much as possible in order to avoid causing them inconvenience. They should be kept informed on the progress of the case and their role in all court proceedings.

Officers must be cautious to avoid contact with jurors. While jurors must be treated courteously, they should not be given any opportunity to hear out-of-court conversations related to the case. Any request they have for additional information must be given to the judge—direct communications with the police are prohibited during trial.

The First Amendment gives the media the right to cover criminal trials, but the Sixth Amendment gives the defendant the right to an impartial jury. Prejudicial pretrial publicity must be avoided. Accurate descriptions of the crimes may be released to the media, but sensationalism may cause a mistrial. Any evidence that has a high potential for suppression because of the methods used to obtain it (*Miranda* violations, search and seizure problems, etc.) should not be disclosed. Any information to be released to the media should be funneled through press relations officers who are trained to deal with these situations.

Discussion Questions

1. Describe how an officer should evaluate the facts in a case prior to taking it to the prosecutor for filing.
2. What facts are necessary to establish the chain of custody for physical evidence? Explain.
3. What information does an officer need to maintain on potential witnesses in a case? How are subpoenas obtained for witnesses? Explain.
4. How should an officer dress and act in court? Explain.
5. List three things that may cause jurors to discredit the testimony of an officer.
6. Describe the relationship that should exist during trial between the defense attorney, the defendant, and the police.
7. Explain what can be done to help the witnesses prepare for trial.
8. How should an officer handle contacts with the jurors outside the courtroom? Explain.
9. Should the media have access to everything in the police department's files about the investigation of a crime? Explain.
10. Do members of the media have a constitutional right to be present during trial? Explain.

GLOSSARY

A

abandoned property Items that have been discarded and currently do not belong to anyone are referred to as abandoned property. The Fourth Amendment does not prevent searches of abandoned property; probable cause is not required to do this type of search.

administrative warrant An administrative warrant is required to conduct a non-criminal inspection unless consent has been given. The probable cause requirement is met by showing a reasonable legislative purpose for authorizing the inspection. Administrative warrants are used for inspections related to health and safety regulations, building and fire codes, and other non-criminal governmental functions. If the investigation is being done because there is suspicion that criminal activity is occurring on the premises, a regular search warrant is required.

Admissions Exception The Admissions Exception to the Hearsay Rule makes a statement admissible if: (1) it was made by a person who is a party to the lawsuit (in a criminal case, the defendant), and (2) the statement is used against the person who made it.

adoptive admission An adoptive admission (also called a tacit admission) refers to actions that indicate a person is adopting a statement made by someone else. This is usually done by remaining silent after being accused of wrongdoing under circumstances where an innocent person would be expected to deny the allegation. Adoptive admissions are admissible if they meet the criteria established in the Admissions Exception to the Hearsay Rule.

aerial searches Aerial searches involve observations made from helicopters and airplanes. As long as the flight is in public airspace and in compliance with FAA rules, there is no need to obtain a warrant or have probable cause to justify the intrusion. This rule applies even if the observed items were in the backyard of a residence surrounded by a high fence.

affidavit An affidavit is a written statement signed under oath or penalty of perjury. When officers seek arrest warrants and search warrants they must give the judge affidavits containing enough facts to establish probable cause.

ancient documents   Older documents may be admissible without calling witnesses to authenticate them if there are no indications that the document has been altered or tampered with. State law varies, but documents over 30 years old are usually referred to as "ancient documents." There is a separate exception to the Hearsay Rule that permits these documents to be admitted at trial. See Chapter 8 for detailed discussion of the requirements for admissibility under this exception.

Ancient Documents Exception   A document is admissible under the Ancient Documents Exception to the Hearsay Rule if it meets three criteria: (1) the document appears to be genuine; (2) people have acted as if it is genuine; and (3) it is at least as old as required by the legislature. State legislatures typically require that the document in question be at least 20 or 30 years old.

anonymous informant   A person who provides the police with information but does not give his/her name is called an anonymous informant.

apparent authority   When requesting permission to conduct a search, officers may rely on consent given by a person with apparent authority over the area. If it reasonably appears to the officers that the person has authority over the area, the search will be valid even though the person misleads the officers about his/her power to give consent.

arraignment   The arraignment is the first court appearance in a criminal case. At the arraignment the defendant is informed of the charges, a plea is entered, bail is set (if it is a bailable offense), the defendant is given the opportunity to obtain an attorney, and the next court date is set. The right to counsel "attaches" at arraignment—the defendant has the right to have counsel present during any meeting with police or prosecutor after arraignment as well as during all court appearances.

at issue   Something is "at issue" in a case if it is disputed. If the defendant pleads "not guilty" all facts necessary to establish the crime are "at issue." If the defense stipulates to facts, those facts are no longer "at issue." Example: in a rape case involving an attack by a stranger, the identity of the attacker is "at issue" and DNA tests can be introduced at trial to establish that semen recovered at the scene came from the defendant. In a "date rape" case where consent of the victim is at issue but the identity of the person who had sex with the victim is not, DNA tests would be inadmissible because their only purpose is to establish an issue that is not in contention.

attorney-client privilege   A client can prevent his/her attorney from testifying regarding information the client revealed in confidence. Key terms: (1) attorney: a person the client reasonably believes is licensed to practice law; (2) client: a person who consults with an attorney for the purpose of obtaining legal advice; (3) what is covered: confidential communications between attorney and client regarding the legal services sought; (4) who holds the privilege: client. Exceptions: consultation in preparation for future crimes is not privileged.

authentication   When discussing documentary evidence, authentication is showing that a writing is what it is claimed to be.

authorized admission An authorized admission is a statement made by a person who is authorized to speak on behalf of another person. Example: a statement by the CEO of Company X is admissible against Company X at trial. These statements are admissible if they meet the criteria established in the Admissions Exception to the Hearsay Rule.

B

ballistics expert A ballistics expert is a person with specialized training and experience in testing weapons and ammunition.

beyond a reasonable doubt Proof "beyond a reasonable doubt" is proof that leaves you firmly convinced. In criminal cases, the accused's guilt must be established "beyond a reasonable doubt."

blood alcohol Blood alcohol tests determine the percentage of alcohol in the blood. This test is frequently used to establish that a person was driving under the influence of alcohol but may be used in any case where intoxication is at issue. To be relevant, the blood sample must be taken in a medically approved manner as soon after the crime as possible.

body fluids Body fluids include blood, urine, semen, etc. A suspect cannot use the Fifth Amendment as a reason to refuse to provide samples of body fluids to be used for laboratory tests.

booking search The search done at the time a person is booked into the jail can include anything that could have been searched at the time of arrest. Any containers carried by the person being booked can be searched. Skin searches and body cavity searches are permitted based on U.S. Supreme Court decisions, but some states restrict searches of people booked solely on misdemeanor charges.

border search People and cargo entering the United States are subject to search. These searches can be done at the U.S. border or point of entry without suspicion that the person or item is entering the United States illegally. Searches are also done at checkpoints located within 100 miles of the U.S. border; the level of suspicion required to conduct these searches varies with the type of checkpoint involved.

burden of persuasion While the prosecution has the burden of proof in criminal cases on almost all issues, the defense has the burden of persuasion. The prosecution must prove the defendant's guilt. The defense does not have to prove that the defendant is innocent but it must persuade the jury that the prosecution has not established the defendant's guilt beyond a reasonable doubt. This can be done by discrediting prosecution witness and/or calling defense witnesses.

burden of proof The law assigns the burden of proof on an issue to one side or the other of a case. The side with the burden of proof must convince the jury that the fact exists. In a criminal case, the prosecution has the burden of proof on each element of every crime charged.

Business Records Exception A document is admissible under the Business Records Exception to the Hearsay Rule if it meets five criteria: (1) it was made at or near the time of the underlying event; (2) it was made by, or from information transmitted by, a person with firsthand knowledge acquired in the course of a regularly conducted business activity; (3) it was made and kept entirely in the course of a regularly conducted business activity; (4) it was made pursuant to a regular practice of that business activity; and (5) all the above are shown by the testimony of the custodian of the business records or other qualified witness.

C

canine searches Searches by reliable, trained dogs can be used to establish probable cause. If there is a reasonable suspicion that luggage contains drugs, it may be detained briefly to allow a narcotics-trained dog to sniff it.

case law Case law is the collection of appellate court opinions. Lawyers and judges study case law in order to find opinions that are relevant to the current case. Based on *stare decisis* these decisions are binding on lower courts until reversed, vacated, or overruled.

chain of custody The chain of custody (also called chain of possession or continuity of possession) accounts for everyone who has had possession of an item of real evidence from the time it came into police custody until it is introduced into court. It is used to show the judge and jury that the evidence has not been tampered with.

challenge for cause Used to remove a prospective juror from the jury on the grounds that he/she is unable to decide the case solely on the facts admitted at trial and the law the judge will give as jury instructions. Attorney's decision to use challenge for cause is based on juror's answers to questions during *voir dire;* and attorney must be able to convince the judge that the juror has formed opinions that will prevent him/her from deciding case on information presented at trial.

character Character describes what a person's moral traits really are. Since there is virtually no way to determine this, reputation is introduced at trial if relevant. "Character witnesses" actually testify about the person's reputation.

charge bargaining Charge bargaining is the process of working out an agreement between the prosecution and defense on what charges will be filed. Charge bargaining is similar to plea bargaining except that it occurs before the charges are filed.

circumstantial evidence Circumstantial evidence indirectly proves a fact. It requires the trier of the facts to use an inference or presumption in order to conclude that the fact exists.

citizen's arrest An arrest made by someone who is not a peace officer. Citizenship is not required. The person making the arrest must have observed the crime take place and must have probable cause to believe that the person arrested committed it. Citizen's arrests are most common in misdemeanors because police officers usually lack the authority to make arrests for misdemeanors that were not committed in their presence.

clergy-penitent privilege A penitent may prevent a member of the clergy from testifying about what the penitent revealed in confidence. Key terms: (1) clergy: priest, minister, or religious practitioner; (2) penitent: person who consults clergy for spiritual advice; (3) what is covered: confidential communications where the penitent sought spiritual guidance; (4) who holds the privilege: both the clergy person and penitent hold this privilege.

clerk's transcript The clerk's transcript is a copy of all documents filed with the court in the case, including the entries of the clerk during court days. It does not include a verbatim record of what occurred at each hearing.

closed container Any box, suitcase, or other container that can be securely closed and thereby hides the contents from view is considered a closed container.

competent witness A person is competent to be a witness if that person: (1) understands the duty to tell the truth; and (2) can narrate the events in question.

conclusive presumption A conclusive presumption mandates that the jury draw a specific inference if the basic fact has been established. The opposing side may try to disprove the basic fact but it is not allowed to introduce evidence to disprove the presumed fact when this type of presumption is used.

confidential communication As used in the law of privileges, any communication conducted under circumstances that protect the confidentiality of what is said or done is considered a confidential communication. The confidential nature of the communication is not violated if an attorney or doctor has necessary office staff present during the communication or staff does necessary work on the case. The communication is no longer confidential if the holder of the privilege voluntarily discloses the information to a person not covered by a privilege.

confidential informant A person who provides information for the police on the condition that the police will not disclose his/her identity is called a confidential informant.

consent search A consent search is a search based on permission from at least one person with apparent authority over the area. Consent must be given voluntarily but officers are not required to inform a person that they have the right to refuse consent. Officers do not need probable cause or any other legal justification for the search if they have consent.

contemporaneous declaration A statement is admissible under the Contemporaneous Declaration Exception to the Hearsay Rule if it meets two criteria: (1) it was made by the declarant to explain what he/she was doing; and (2) it was made at the time the declarant was performing the act that he/she was trying to explain.

Contemporaneous Objection Rule The Contemporaneous Objection Rule requires that attorneys state their objections to questions immediately after the question is asked. The purpose of the rule is to allow the judge to make a ruling on the question before the witness answers. This prevents the jury from hearing what might be prejudicial information. The Contemporaneous Objection Rule applies to both sides in all court proceedings.

controlled delivery A controlled delivery is the delivery of a package (or other object) while it is under surveillance by the police. The package usually has been legally seized prior to the delivery and the delivery is conducted in order to gain additional evidence and establish the identity of the intended receiver. Setting up a controlled delivery does not require a search warrant unless activities inside a home will be monitored.

corroborative evidence Corroborative evidence supports the prior testimony of another witness by providing additional evidence to confirm what the previous witness said without merely duplicating it. For example: if an eyewitness testified that he saw John at the scene of the crime, testimony by a police officer that John's fingerprints were found at the location would corroborate the eyewitness's testimony.

credibility of the witness The trier of the facts evaluates the credibility of the witness. After listening to the testimony, observing the witness's "body language," listening to the opposing side's attempts to impeach the witness, and considering the testimony of other witnesses, the jurors (or judge, in a trial without a jury) decide if the witness is telling the truth.

cumulative evidence Evidence is said to be cumulative if it merely restates what has already been admitted into evidence. The judge has discretion to limit the amount of cumulative evidence that can be admitted at a trial. Example: if there were 10 witnesses to a crime and all gave similar statements, the judge would probably rule that two or three witnesses could testify but not all 10 of them.

custodial interrogation Officers must give the *Miranda* warnings prior to custodial interrogation. Custody means the person is under arrest or otherwise deprived of his/her freedom. Interrogation is the process of questioning. Both direct and indirect questions require *Miranda* warnings. Temporary detention (field interviews) authorized by *Terry v. Ohio* (1968) does not require *Miranda* warnings. *Miranda* warnings are not required for questioning of an inmate by an undercover officer as long as the inmate does not know that he/she is being questioned by a law enforcement officer and the inmate has not been arraigned for the crime under discussion.

D

declarant As used in the Hearsay Rule, the declarant is the person who made the statement. When determining whether hearsay is admissible, the rules governing the exceptions to the Hearsay Rule are applied to the declarant—regardless of who is testifying about the statement at trial.

declarations against interest A statement is admissible under the Declarations against Interest Exception to the Hearsay Rule if it meets two criteria: (1) the person making the statement is not available to testify in court, and (2) the statement is against the interest of the person making the statement. A statement is considered to be against the interest of the person making it if it could result in criminal prosecution, monetary loss or impairment of an interest in real estate. See *state law* for complete list.

direct appeal A direct appeal is an appeal that is taken immediately after the conviction and is based solely on what happened at trial and other court hearings on the case. Transcripts of the original trial are used; no witnesses are called. No new evidence can be introduced during a direct appeal.

direct evidence Direct evidence proves a fact without the need for an inference or presumption. If direct evidence is believed by the jury, the fact it relates to is conclusively established.

direct examination Direct examination is the questioning of a witness by an attorney for the side that called the witness. During the prosecution's case in chief, the prosecutor conducts direct examination. This will be followed by cross-examination by the defense attorney.

discovery Discovery is the pre-trial process whereby one side is able to find out what evidence the other side has. Some states require each side to disclose nearly all evidence that it has in its possession (except material protected by the Fifth Amendment and other privileges) and give the opposing side copies of statements that have been made by witnesses. Lists of witnesses each side intends to call to testify at trial are also exchanged. The defense can not be required to disclose the defendant's statement or tell the prosecution in advance that the defendant will testify at trial.

documentary evidence Written and printed items are called documentary evidence; this is a subset of real evidence. Photographs, video and audiotapes, motion pictures, and computer-generated reports and graphics are also included in documentary evidence.

double hearsay Double hearsay refers to a hearsay statement that is contained in another hearsay statement. Example: in the statement "D said that E told her what F said," what F originally said is hearsay; when D attempts to repeat what F said it is double hearsay.

double jeopardy Being tried for the same crime twice is double jeopardy. This defense applies if the defendant has either been convicted (and the conviction upheld on appeal) or acquitted on the same charge or a lesser included offense. The view in the United States is that double jeopardy does not prevent re-filing charges and seeking a new conviction if the defendant's conviction is reversed on appeal.

due process Due process, as applied to lineups, showups, and photographic lineups, prohibits procedures that are unduly suggestive. Violations of due process result from disparities in height, weight, race, age, or other factors. Coaching or comments by the police or other people that are overheard by the person attempting to make an identification may be unduly suggestive if they influence the selection of the person who allegedly committed the crime.

dying declaration A statement is admissible under the Dying Declaration Exception to the Hearsay Rule if it meets four criteria: (1) at the time the statement was made the declarant had a sense that he/she would die very soon; (2) the declarant had firsthand knowledge of what he/she was saying; (3) the statement is about the cause and circumstances of the death; and (4) the declarant is now dead.

E

electronic surveillance Electronic surveillance involves the seizure (recording) of conversations by electronic transmitting devices and/or recording equipment. It may involve wiretaps or other types of listening devices. Title III of the Omnibus Crime Control and Safe Streets Act of 1968 allows federal judges to issue electronic surveillance warrants if there is a strong showing of need for this technique in the investigation of the serious federal felonies and organized crime activities listed in Title III. The warrant application must be screened by the U.S. Attorney General or his/her designee. An electronic surveillance warrant is valid for a maximum of 30 days but can be renewed based on a showing that probable cause still exists for the monitoring activity. Some states have electronic surveillance laws nearly identical to Title III; others are more restrictive. Unless specifically prohibited by the legislature, no warrant is required for a person to wear a transmitting or recording device or if someone has given permission to conceal these types of devices on their premises.

evidence Something that proves or disproves allegations and assertions. Evidence, in the legal sense, includes only what is introduced at trial. The testimony of witnesses, documents, and physical objects can all be evidence.

exception to *Miranda* for the booking process An officer or clerk who is filling out a booking slip may ask the suspect for name, address, and other necessary information without giving *Miranda* warnings. Extensive questioning would require *Miranda* warnings and a waiver.

excited utterance Excited utterances are also referred to as spontaneous declarations. A statement is admissible under the Spontaneous Statement Exception to the Hearsay Rule if it meets two criteria: (1) it tells about something the declarant observed with one of the five senses; and (2) it was made spontaneously while the declarant was still under the stress and excitement of the event.

Exclusionary Rule The Exclusionary Rule prohibits the use of unconstitutionally obtained evidence at trial. For example, if it is established that drugs were found by officers who conducted an illegal search, the drugs are suppressed (not allowed into court). The U.S. Supreme Court applied the Exclusionary Rule to the federal courts in the 1914 case of *Weeks v. United States,* and to state courts in the 1961 case of *Mapp v. Ohio.*

execution of a warrant A warrant is executed when peace officers act as directed by the warrant. A search warrant is executed when the search is conducted; an arrest warrant is executed when the arrest is made.

exemplars The most common exemplars used in the investigation of crimes are handwriting exemplars and voice exemplars. These samples, which the suspect is told how to prepare, are used for identification purposes. Example: if there was a demand note during a bank robbery, the suspect may be required to give a handwriting exemplar so a forensic document examiner can compare it to the ransom note and attempt to determine if the two documents were made by the same person.

experiment An experiment attempts to screen out all extraneous variables so that the experimenter can measure the impact of one factor. Only results of experiments that replicate all relevant conditions of the crime scene are admissible in court.

expert witness An expert witness is a person who is called to testify about a relevant event based on his/her special knowledge or training. Expert witnesses are only allowed if some evidence in the case is beyond the understanding of the average juror.

F

Federal Rules of Evidence The Federal Rules of Evidence were enacted by the U.S. Congress to govern the admission of evidence in federal court. Several states have adopted the Federal Rules.

field interview A field interview (also referred to as a temporary detention) is a brief detention for the purpose of determining whether a crime has occurred and the person detained should be arrested. Officers must have specific, articulable facts that lead them to believe that criminal activity is afoot. If there is reasonable suspicion that the person is armed, officers may frisk the person for weapons. *Terry v. Ohio* (1968) is the leading case.

fixed checkpoints Permanent Customs and Border Protection (CBP) stations on major highways near the United States border.

force An officer may use only reasonable force to detain a person. What force is reasonable will depend on the circumstances, but deadly force is only authorized if someone's life is in danger.

Foreign Intelligence Surveillance Act of 1978 Electronic surveillance on activities of foreign governments and their agents is controlled by the Foreign Intelligence Surveillance Act of 1978. It authorizes a small group of federal judges to issue warrants for wiretaps and other surveillance activities.

Forensic documents examiner A forensic documents examiner is involved in four main types of activities: (1) handwriting comparisons; (2) typewriter comparisons; (3) tests to determine if a document has been altered; and (4) paper and ink comparisons.

Former Testimony Exception A statement is admissible under the Former Testimony Exception to the Hearsay Rule if it meets three criteria: (1) the statement was recorded under oath at the prior court hearing; (2) the person whose testimony is introduced is not available to testify at the present court proceeding; and (3) the former testimony is either offered against a person who introduced the prior testimony or against a person who had the right and opportunity to cross-examine at the prior hearing.

frisk   Patting down the outer clothing for weapons is referred to as a frisk. A frisk is allowed during a temporary detention if the officers have reasonable suspicion that the suspect is armed.

Fruit of the Poison Tree Doctrine   Evidence derived from unconstitutionally obtained evidence is said to be the "fruit of the poison tree." It is inadmissible unless the taint of the illegal acts has dissipated. Example: officers failed to give *Miranda* warnings in a timely manner and the suspect told them where the murder weapon was hidden. Officers used this information to seize the murder weapon. The murder weapon will not be admissible in court because it is the fruit of an illegally obtained confession; the confession will also be inadmissible.

G

Good Faith Exception   Permits the use of unconstitutionally obtained evidence if officers were acting in good faith when seizing it. The Supreme Court has limited the Good Faith Exception to the Exclusionary Rule to situations where: there was reliance on a warrant that appeared to be valid on its face; arrests made under statutes that were later held unconstitutional; and arrests made after a records check revealed an outstanding warrant even if the fact that the warrant had been recalled had accidentally been omitted from the database.

H

habeas corpus   *Habeas corpus* proceedings are held in civil court when a person challenges the legality of his/her confinement. These proceedings may be filed only if the petitioner is currently being held in custody illegally. Examples: denial of reasonable bail, failure to release an inmate at the expiration of a sentence, a conviction obtained when the defendant was denied the right to counsel, confinement in a mental hospital after the person has regained mental competence, etc.

Harmless Error Rule   The Harmless Error Rule states that an error will not cause a case to be reversed on appeal unless the appellate court believes the error was likely to affect the outcome of the case.

Hearsay Rule   The Hearsay Rule makes hearsay declarations inadmissible at trial. There are many exceptions to the Hearsay Rule. An attorney who wishes to introduce hearsay at trial must be able to state which exception to the Hearsay Rule is applicable to the statement.

hold the defendant to answer   If the judge at the preliminary hearing is convinced that there is enough evidence that the crime was committed and the defendant is the perpetrator, the defendant will be "held to answer" on the charge. This means that the judge authorizes the prosecution to proceed to trial with the case.

husband-wife privileges   There are two husband-wife privileges: **Privilege for confidential communications:** A husband or wife may prevent the other from testifying about communications made in confidence during their marriage. Key terms: (1) husband and wife: valid marriage is required (in states recognizing common law marriages, common law marriages are covered); (2) what is covered: confidential communications made during the marriage; (3) who holds the privilege: either spouse; and (4) exceptions to the privilege in criminal cases: crimes committed by one spouse against the other spouse; crimes committed by one spouse against the children of either spouse; failure to support a spouse or child; and bigamy. **Privilege not to testify:** Depending on state law, either the defendant's spouse has the right to refuse to take the witness stand and testify against his/her spouse or the defendant has the right to prevent his/her spouse from taking the witness stand. Key terms: (1) husband and wife: valid marriage is required (in states recognizing common law marriages, valid common law marriages are covered); (2) what is covered: testifying in court during the time the marriage exists; (3) who holds the privilege: usually the person being called to testify (consult law in your state); and (4) exceptions in criminal cases: crimes committed by one spouse against the other spouse; crimes committed by one spouse against the children of either spouse; failure to support a spouse or child; and bigamy.

hypothetical question   A hypothetical question states a group of facts and asks an expert witness to draw conclusions based on the facts given in the question. All of the facts in the hypothetical question must have been introduced into evidence in the case. It is not necessary for the expert witness to have personally examined the evidence mentioned in the hypothetical question.

I

identifying features   Identifying features include how a person looks (in person or a photograph) as well as other distinctive things used for identification such as fingerprints. The Fifth Amendment does not protect the suspect from use of identifying features.

immunity   When a person is granted immunity he/she is guaranteed that no criminal charges will be filed. Immunity is formally granted by the prosecutor. Transaction immunity protects the person from prosecution for specific crimes no matter how the evidence is obtained. Use immunity prevents the prosecution from using the immune statements against the person who made them, but does not prevent the prosecutor from filing charges and obtaining a conviction if evidence is available from other sources.

impeachment   Impeachment is the process of showing that the judge and jury should not believe what a witness has said while testifying. The main grounds for impeachment are: bias or prejudice; prior felony convictions; immoral acts and uncharged crimes; prior inconsistent statements; inability to observe; and reputation.

Independent Source Exception   To admit evidence under the Independent Source Exception to the Exclusionary Rule, the prosecution must be able to convince the judge that the police discovered the evidence without relying on unconstitutional procedures.

indictment   An indictment is the formal document stating the charges the grand jury has decided the defendant should face at trial.

indigent suspect   An indigent suspect, as used when considering *Miranda* rights, is a suspect who cannot afford to hire an attorney.

Inevitable Discovery Exception   The U.S. Supreme Court recognizes an exception to the Exclusionary Rule that allows unconstitutionally seized evidence to be admitted in court if the judge is convinced that it was inevitable that the evidence would have been found legally.

inference   An inference is a conclusion that is drawn from the facts. When circumstantial evidence is used, the jury must infer that a fact exists based on other evidence that logically causes the jury to draw that conclusion.

information   The document filed by the prosecution after the preliminary hearing is called the information. It is similar in format to the criminal complaint but only contains charges that the defendant was "held to answer" on at the end of the preliminary hearing.

J

jail searches   Officer may search an inmate or any place in the jail or prison if there is an administrative reason for the search. Probable cause is not required. The need to maintain security and stop the flow of contraband justifies nearly all searches in custodial facilities. Only slight suspicion is needed to conduct body cavity searches of inmates.

judicial discretion   When applying the law to fact situations and making appropriate rulings there is a great deal of judicial discretion. This means that the judge has the authority to consider the facts and make a ruling for a specific case. Examples: the Sixth Amendment gives the defense the right to cross-examine witnesses, but if the judge determines that the right is being abused he/she may limit cross-examination; when a judge sentences a criminal defendant, the judge usually has discretion in setting the length of the sentence, granting probation, etc.

judicial notice   Judicial notice is usually limited to facts that are public knowledge, commonly known scientific facts, and federal, local, and international laws. When a judge utilizes his/her authority to take judicial notice of a fact, the jurors are instructed that they must conclude that that fact exists. No evidence is introduced at trial to prove the fact.

K

knock-and-announce procedure   Prior to entering a house officers are required to comply with the knock-and-announce procedure. They must knock or otherwise announce their presence, state who they are, and state why they are there. The notice requirements do not apply if the facts indicate an immediate threat to the officer's safety, strong likelihood of immediate destruction of evidence, or imminent escape of the suspect. The Supreme Court has refused to authorize exceptions based solely on the nature of the crime under investigation. If officers are in the process of complying with knock and announce and any of the above situations develop, the "substantial compliance" rule allows them to proceed without completing the warnings.

L

latent prints The term latent prints refers to fingerprints that are recovered at the crime scene or from other items of evidence. They are compared to fingerprints that are on file in order to determine the identity of the person who left the latent prints.

lay witness A lay witness is a person who observed an event that is relevant to the case on trial. Lay witnesses are allowed to testify about any relevant event that was observed with one or more of the five senses (sight, hearing, smell, touch, or taste). Lay witnesses are not allowed to give opinions.

laying the foundation Laying the foundation is the process of establishing the preliminary facts that are required before certain types of evidence can be admitted. Example: before a gun found at a homicide scene can be admitted, it must be established that this is the same weapon found at the crime scene, it is in the same condition that it was at the time it was found, and that no one has had an opportunity to tamper with it.

leading question Leading questions are questions that suggest the desired answer. Leading questions are permitted during cross-examination. During the prosecution's case in chief, the defense attorney is allowed to ask leading questions when cross-examining the prosecution witnesses.

limited admissibility Limited admissibility describes the situation where evidence is introduced at trial but the jury is instructed that it may use this evidence for one purpose but not any other. For example, evidence may be introduced to show that a witness lied. This can be used to attack the credibility of the witness but may not be used to prove that the defendant is guilty of the crime.

lineup A lineup involves showing a victim or eyewitness a group of people to see if he/she can identify the person who allegedly committed the crime. There must be a sufficient number of people in the lineup to give a valid opportunity to make an identification. The people placed in the lineup should be of similar physical appearance and dressed so that no one stands out as the suspect. The suspect has the right to have an attorney present at a lineup if the lineup is held after the suspect has been arraigned or indicted.

M

material evidence   Evidence is considered material if it is relevant to some fact that is at issue in the case and it has more than just a remote connection to the fact.

matter of law   Legal issues are decided by the judge; such decisions are sometimes referred to as a "matter of law." They include rulings on the law, such as the admissibility of evidence, application of the Hearsay Rule, privileges, etc. They also include facts that are admitted into evidence by the use of stipulations and judicial notice. When a fact becomes a "matter of law," the judge instructs the jury that they must conclude that the fact has been proven.

Miranda **booking exception**   Police are not required to obtain a waiver of the *Miranda* rights when asking routine booking questions.

Miranda **public safety exception**   At the time of arrest, officers are allowed to ask a few pointed questions without obtaining a *Miranda* waiver if this is necessary to protect the public from imminent harm. This exception is most likely to arise when a weapon is believed to be at the scene or a kidnap victim has not been found.

Miranda **waiver**   Any waiver of *Miranda* rights must be knowing, intelligent, and voluntary. The person making the waiver must know his/her constitutional rights, have sufficient intelligence to understand them, and waive them without coercion.

Miranda **warnings**   The U.S. Supreme Court in the case of *Miranda v. Arizona* (1966) ruled that prior to custodial interrogation the suspect must be given the following warnings: "You have the right to remain silent; anything you say can and will be used against you in a court of law; you have the right to have an attorney present during questioning; if you cannot afford an attorney, one will be provided free." A knowing, intelligent, and voluntary waiver of these rights must be obtained before questioning in order to make any statements the suspect makes admissible in court.

Misplaced Reliance Doctrine   No warrant is required to obtain conversations that can be overheard by the police or their agents based on the misplaced reliance of the suspect. Each person bears the burden of restricting his/her conversations to people who will not reveal them to the authorities.

models   The most common models used at trial are maps and diagrams. To be admissible, they must be to scale and accurately depict the location in question.

modus operandi   *Modus operandi* literally means the method of operation. Many criminals become creatures of habit and commit the same crimes in the same way. This distinctive method of committing a crime is referred to as a *modus operandi*. When the suspect has a known *modus operandi*, the prosecutor may be allowed to introduce testimony about other crimes the defendant is known to have committed. If distinctive features of the prior

crimes match those of the crime for which the defendant is on trial, the jury
may infer that the defendant committed the present crime.

N

negative hearsay Negative hearsay is the use of the fact that no record of an
event was found to show that the event did not occur. Example: the fact that
John's time card was punched on Monday is hearsay that can be used to show
that John was at work on Monday; the fact that John's time card was not
punched on Thursday can be used as negative hearsay to show that he did not
go to work on Thursday.

news media privilege Many states give members of the news media protection
from being cited for contempt of court if they refuse to reveal confidential
sources of information gathered while working on a news story. Key terms:
(1) reporter: person employed by the media to investigate stories and report
on them (media includes print media as well as radio and television);
(2) what is covered: reporter's notes and identity of informants; (3) who holds
privilege: reporter; and (4) exceptions in criminal cases: some states make an
exception in the prosecution of serious crimes if it can be shown that there is
no other source for the information requested.

O

Open Fields Doctrine The Open Fields Doctrine adopted by the U.S. Supreme
Court allows law enforcement officers to search open areas not associated
with residences. This applies even if the field is fenced and/or posted with
"no trespassing" signs.

Opinion Rule The Opinion Rule states that opinions of the witnesses are not
admissible because it is the function of the trier of the facts to draw their own
conclusions (inferences). Lay witnesses may not give opinions but expert
witnesses are allowed to give professional opinions.

P

parol evidence Parol evidence refers to testimony that is introduced to establish
the contents of a document. The Best Evidence Rule requires that the original
or duplicate of a document be produced rather than relying on parol
evidence. If a satisfactory explanation can be provided for the absence of the
original and duplicates, the judge may allow parol evidence.

past recollection recorded Past recollection recorded refers to a statement by
the witness that was made near the time of the event. It can be in writing or
on tape. When the witness has unsuccessfully tried to refresh his/her memory,
the previously recorded statement may be admissible at trial under an
exception to the Hearsay Rule. See *Past Recollection Recorded Exception* for the
list of requirements that must be met in order to introduce the statement.

Past Recollection Recorded Exception A document is admissible under the Past
Recollection Recorded Exception to the Hearsay Rule if it meets six criteria:

(1) the statement would be admissible if the declarant testified at the current trial; (2) the witness currently has insufficient present recollection to testify fully and accurately; (3) the report was made at a time when the facts were fresh in the memory of the witness; (4) the report was made by the witness, someone under his/her direction, or by another person for the purpose of recording the witness's statement; (5) the witness can testify that the report was a true statement of the facts; and (6) the report is authenticated.

peremptory challenges Peremptory challenges are used to remove prospective jurors from the jury on the basis of the prosecutor or defense attorney's subjective opinions. The attorneys are not required to state why they use peremptory challenges. Peremptory challenges may not be used to exclude jurors based on race or gender. The number of peremptory challenges that can be used in a case is set by state law.

photographic lineup A photographic lineup involves showing a victim or eyewitness pictures of potential suspects and asking him/her to indicate whether a picture of the person who allegedly committed the crime is in the group viewed. A sufficient variety of pictures should be used to permit valid identification. The persons in the pictures should be sufficiently similar in appearance to avoid being unduly suggestive. There is no right to have an attorney present at a photographic lineup no matter when it is conducted.

physician-patient privilege A patient has the right to prevent his/her physician from testifying regarding confidential communications made while the patient was seeking diagnosis or treatment. Key terms: (1) physician: person reasonably believed by the patient to be licensed to practice medicine; (2) patient: person who consulted physician for purposes of diagnosis or treatment; (3) what is covered: information obtained by the physician for the purpose of diagnosing or treating the patient; (4) who holds the privilege: patient; (5) exceptions in criminal cases: advice sought on how to plan or conceal a crime; and information the physician is required by law to report to authorities. Many states do not allow the defendant to use this privilege in criminal cases.

plain feel When an officer is conducting a pat down based on reasonable suspicion that a person is armed, the officer may seize an item if he/she can tell by the distinctive feel of the object that it is contraband. This rule applies even though the item in question does not feel like a weapon. Officers are not allowed to manipulate or squeeze the item to determine if it is contraband.

Plain View Doctrine It is not a search for officers to observe items that were left where the officers can see them while the officers are legally on the premises. The Plain View Doctrine requires that the officer be legally at the spot where the observation was made; it does not allow the officer to pick up or examine an item to determine whether it is contraband, stolen, etc. An officer must have probable cause in order to seize items found in plain view.

plea bargaining Plea bargaining is the process whereby the prosecution and defense work out an agreement for the defendant to plead guilty to one or more charge(s) without a trial if the prosecutor will drop some of the original charges or support a lighter sentence.

point of entry For the purpose of border searches, a point of entry is a facility, such as an airport, that is the first place that a traveler lands in the United States. International airports are points of entry and can be located anywhere in the United States.

police informant privilege The police have a privilege not to disclose the identity of their confidential informants unless the identity of the informant is crucial to the defendant's case. Key terms: (1) police: applies to all law enforcement agencies; (2) informant: person who supplies information to police in confidence; (3) what is covered: name and address of the informant; (4) who holds the privilege: law enforcement agency; and (5) exceptions: identity of informant must be disclosed if it is important in the defendant's case.

police personnel files Police and other governmental agencies have a privilege not to disclose the contents of their personnel files unless the information is relevant to the defendant's case. Key terms: (1) personnel files: permanent personnel records of an employee (police personnel files include investigations of an officer conducted by internal affairs); (2) what is covered: records concerning performance of officer and investigations of his/her conduct; (3) who holds the privilege: law enforcement agency; (4) exceptions: must disclose information relevant to the defense.

polling the jury Polling the jury is the process of asking each juror if he/she agrees with the verdict that has just been read. The jurors are polled in the courtroom after the verdict for each charge is read and then they are dismissed.

posed picture (photograph) A posed picture is a photograph that was made to illustrate a fact in the case. It may come from a re-enactment of the crime. Posed pictures are usually admissible if they accurately depict the facts of the case. The jury will be told that they are posed and were not taken during the crime.

preliminary hearing (also called preliminary examination) Held before a judge to determine if there is sufficient admissible evidence to justify making the defendant face a criminal trial on the charges. If it is determined that sufficient evidence has been presented, the defendant will be "held to answer" on the charges. In most states a preliminary hearing is not held if the case has been presented to a grand jury or if all charges are misdemeanors.

present memory refreshed Present memory refreshed refers to the process of refreshing the memory of a witness, either before or during trial. After the memory has been refreshed, the witness can testify based on his/her memory of the events. The witness is subject to cross-examination about what was done to refresh his/her memory.

Present Memory Refreshed Rule   The basic rule is that anything can be used to refresh memory. Witnesses must, however, be able to testify from memory and not merely repeat what was used to refresh their memory.

present sense impression   A statement is admissible under the Contemporaneous Declaration (also called a present sense impression) Exception to the Hearsay Rule if: (1) it was made by the declarant to explain what he/she was doing AND (2) it was made at the time the declarant was performing the act he/she was trying to explain.

presumption   A presumption is a conclusion that the law requires the jury to draw from one or more facts that have been established by the evidence introduced at trial.

prima facie   The prosecution has established a *prima facie* case if it has introduced sufficient evidence to convince the judge that it is more probable than not that the defendant committed the crime charged. The prosecution must establish a *prima facie* case at the preliminary hearing. It is a lower burden of proof than what will be required at trial.

primary evidence   Under the Best Evidence Rule, primary evidence refers to an original document or a duplicate.

prior consistent statements   A statement is admissible under this exception to the hearsay rule if: (1) the witness has been impeached on the basis of prior inconsistent statements (a consistent statement that was made before the alleged inconsistent statement may be admissible to rehabilitate the witness); (2) cross-examiner has alleged that the witness recently changed his/her testimony (prior consistent statement made before the alleged change may be used to rebut this allegation); or (3) cross-examiner has alleged that the witness altered his/her testimony due to bias or other bad motive (prior consistent statement made before the alleged bias/motive arose can be introduced).

prior identification   A statement is admissible under the Prior Identification Exception to the Hearsay Rule if it meets three criteria: (1) the witness has testified that he/she accurately identified the person who committed the crime; (2) the witness identified the defendant or another person as the person who committed the crime; and (3) the identification was made when the crime was fresh in the witness's memory.

prior inconsistent statements   A statement is admissible under the Prior Inconsistent Statements Exception to the Hearsay Rule if it meets two criteria: (1) the statement is inconsistent with testimony given on the witness stand by the person who made the prior statement; and (2) the witness was asked about the inconsistent statement and given a chance to explain.

probable cause   Sufficient facts to convince a reasonable person that it is more likely than not that an event occurred.

probative force   Probative force means that an item of evidence tends to prove a fact that is in issue in the case. Various pieces of evidence will have different amounts of probative force. Examples: in a rape case, DNA tests matching semen stains left at the scene with the defendant's DNA have great probative force; the testimony of a witness who identified the rapist based on a fleeting glance under poor lighting conditions will have much less probative force than the DNA test results.

probative value A fact has probative value if it tends to prove (or disprove) the existence (or non-existence) of something that is at issue in the case.

protective sweep A "protective sweep" is a search of the premises for the safety of the officer. It is limited to a visual inspection of places in which a person might be hiding. A protective sweep is limited to the immediate adjoining area unless there is reasonable suspicion that someone is hiding in a more remote spot.

Public Records Exception A document is admissible under the Public Records Exception to the Hearsay Rule if it meets three criteria: (1) a public employee made the document within his/her scope of duty; (2) the document was made at or near the time the event occurred; and (3) the sources of the information and method and time of preparation indicate the record is trustworthy. Records of vital statistics (births, deaths, marriages, etc.) are admissible if: (1) the maker of the record is required by law to report the event to a governmental agency; and (2) the report was made and filed as required by law.

Public Safety Exception The U.S. Supreme Court recognizes an exception to the Exclusionary Rule and allows unconstitutionally obtained evidence to be admitted in court if there was brief questioning or searching at the time of arrest for the purpose of protecting the public or rescuing the victim. This exception has been used to locate weapons the suspect hid and to help find kidnap victims. Detailed questions are not allowed without *Miranda* warnings.

R

real evidence Anything that can be perceived with the five senses (except testimonial evidence) that tends to prove a fact at issue is called real evidence. Another name frequently used for real evidence is physical evidence.

reasonable force An officer may use only reasonable force to detain a person. What force is reasonable will depend on the circumstances, but deadly force is only authorized if someone's life is in danger.

reasonable suspicion An officer may detain someone briefly for questioning based on reasonable suspicion. Police must have specific, articulable facts that indicate that criminal activity is afoot.

rebuttable presumption A rebuttable presumption is not conclusive. Once the side relying on a rebuttable presumption introduces evidence to establish the presumed fact, the opposing side may introduce evidence to either disprove the basic fact or disprove the presumed fact.

rebuttal   Rebuttal is the part of the trial where the prosecution calls witness in an attempt to disprove what the defense witnesses said during the defense's case in chief.

rehabilitation   Rehabilitation is the process of trying to prove to judge and jury that a witness should be believed even though the witness has already been impeached.

rejoinder   Rejoinder is the part of the trial when the defense is allowed to call witnesses and attempt to cast doubt on what prosecution witnesses testified about during rebuttal.

relevant evidence   Any evidence that tends to prove or disprove any disputed fact in the case is relevant evidence. An item merely needs to show that it is more probable that the fact exists than it appeared before the evidence was introduced. No single piece of evidence has to make a fact appear more probable than not.

reporter's transcript   The reporter's transcript is a verbatim record of what occurred in court. It is made from notes taken by the court reporter.

reputation   A person's reputation is what other people believe about that person's character. It may or may not be an accurate reflection of character. If reputation is relevant, "character witnesses" may be called to testify about the person's reputation for traits that are relevant to the case such as honesty, brutality, etc.

Reputation Exception   A statement is admissible under the Reputation Exception to the Hearsay Rule if it is about the reputation of a person among his/her associates or in the community. Some states also allow the witness to testify regarding his/her personal opinion about the person whose reputation is in issue.

return (of search warrant)   A return is a document, usually printed on the back of a search warrant, where the police state when the warrant was executed. An itemized inventory of what was seized is also included.

right to counsel   The right to counsel attaches at the first court appearance. After that time, officers must obtain a waiver of the right to counsel prior to interrogation. This rule applies to custodial and non-custodial interrogation after the arraignment or indictment.

right to have an attorney present   A suspect has the right to have an attorney present during custodial interrogation. If he/she requests an attorney, questioning must stop and may only resume if there is an attorney present. If questioning is stopped for this reason the police do not have to call an attorney unless they intend to resume questioning. If the suspect has already been arraigned or indicted, he/she has the right to have an attorney present at lineups, showups and during questioning regarding the charges that have already been filed (whether or not the suspect is in custody at the time of this interrogation).

right to inventory a vehicle   Whenever a vehicle is legally impounded the authorities have the right to inventory its contents. This results in an itemized list of all items present in the vehicle at that time. Inventories are allowed regardless of the reason the vehicle was impounded.

right to remain silent   A suspect has the right to remain silent during custodial interrogation. Even if a suspect waives his/her *Miranda* rights, the suspect retains the right to refuse to answer specific questions or to stop the interrogation at any time. If a suspect invokes the right to remain silent officers must stop questioning but may request a new *Miranda* waiver after waiting long enough to indicate to the suspect that his/her rights will be scrupulously honored.

roadblock   A roadblock involves the stopping of all vehicles traveling on a street or highway. Officers may stop all vehicles or stop a percentage of the cars (such as every fourth car). The U.S. Supreme Court has approved the use of roadblocks to check for drunk drivers but has refused to authorize stopping vehicles to check for drugs. Roadblocks may be established to hand out wanted flyers for recent crimes and request the public's help in finding the suspect.

roving checkpoint   A roving checkpoint is a checkpoint set up for temporary use by Customs and Border Protection (CBP) agents. It usually consists of a few cars, several officers, and portable barriers. There are no permanent buildings at the location intended to be used as a checkpoint.

S

school searches   School officials may search students if there is reasonable suspicion that the student has broken the law or violated a school rule. This search is not confined to a pat down for weapons. Purses and other personal items may be searched.

search   An examination of a person, his/her house, personal property, or other locations when conducted by a law enforcement officer for the purpose of finding evidence of a crime.

search incident to arrest   Contemporaneous with an arrest, officers may search the person arrested and the area under his/her immediate control. This search may be as thorough as necessary. It is not restricted to looking for weapons or evidence of the crime for which the person was arrested.

secondary evidence   Under the Best Evidence Rule, secondary evidence refers to all types of evidence used to establish the contents of a document when neither the original document nor a duplicate is available. This would include rough drafts as well as testimony about what the document said.

seizure   The act of taking possession of a person or property.

self-authenticating   Self-authenticating documents can be introduced into evidence without calling witnesses to authenticate them. Examples: documents bearing the government seal, notarized documents, and official publications.

self-incrimination   The making of a statement (oral or written) that can result in criminal liability for the person who made it. The privilege against self-incrimination comes from the Fifth Amendment of the U.S. Constitution. It does not cover physical evidence such as fingerprints, blood samples, DNA, or handwriting exemplars; it also does not apply if it is not possible to prosecute the person making the statement due to double jeopardy, expiration of statute of limitations, or granting of immunity.

sequestered A jury is sequestered when it is kept away from people who are not on the jury. In high-publicity cases, the jury may be housed in a local hotel for the duration of the trial. It is more common to sequester the jurors while they are deliberating on the verdict. Many juries are not sequestered at all.

showup A showup involves having a victim or eyewitness view one person in order to make an identification of the person who allegedly committed the crime. The suspect has the right to have an attorney present at a showup if the showup is held after the suspect has been arraigned or indicted.

sobriety tests Sobriety tests are frequently given to determine if a person is intoxicated. The most commonly used ones involve breath, blood, and urine. The U.S. Supreme Court has ruled that a suspected drunk driver cannot claim the Fifth Amendment as grounds to refuse to participate in a sobriety test.

spontaneous statements A statement is admissible under the Spontaneous Statement Exception to the Hearsay Rule if it meets two criteria: (1) it tells about something the declarant observed with one of the five senses; and (2) it was made spontaneously while the declarant was still under the stress and excitement of the event. Spontaneous declarations are also referred to as "excited utterances."

stare decisis In our common-law system, prior decisions of appellate courts are considered binding on lower courts (until reversed, vacated, or overruled). This is called *stare decisis.*

statement As used in the Hearsay Rule, a statement refers to all types of communications: oral, written, those recorded on audio- or videotape or on computer disks, and non-verbal gestures.

statute of limitations The statute of limitations is established by the legislature. It sets the time limits on when criminal charges can be filed. For example, in most states misdemeanor charges must be filed with the court clerk within one year of the day the crime was committed; for felonies the period is longer (frequently 3 to 6 years) and for some crimes, such as murder, there is no statute of limitations and the charges can be filed at any time. If the period specified in the statue of limitations has expired, the person who committed the crime cannot claim the Fifth Amendment as a reason not to answer questions about the crime, therefore *Miranda* warnings are not required. (See also *tolling statute of limitations.*)

stipulation A stipulation is an agreement between all sides to a lawsuit to allow the jury to conclude that a fact exists. Once a stipulation is made, no evidence will be introduced to prove the stipulated fact. The judge will instruct the jurors that they must conclude that the stipulated fact exists.

substantial compliance Substantial compliance with knock-and-announce procedures prior to entering a house is sufficient if, while the required procedures are being conducted, officers hear or see something that indicates further delay would result in physical harm to the officers, destruction of evidence, or escape by the suspect.

suppression hearing The suppression hearing is a court hearing, usually held prior to the trial, for the purpose of deciding whether evidence may be used at trial. Evidence that the judge rules may not be used is suppressed. This is a common proceeding if there are questions about whether the police complied with search and seizure rules and/or properly obtained a confession.

T

tacit admission As used in the hearsay rule, a tacit admission occurs when a statement is made by someone else and then a person adopts it as his/her own statement. This is usually done by remaining silent when accused of wrongdoing under circumstances where an innocent person would be expected to deny the allegation. Tacit admissions are also referred to as "adoptive admissions."

temporary detention Temporary detentions are also referred to as field interviews. A person may be detained temporarily if there is reasonable suspicion that he/she is involved in criminal activity. If there is reasonable suspicion that the person is armed, officers may frisk the person for weapons.

testimonial evidence 1. Testimony of a competent witness, testifying under oath or affirmation in a court proceeding, is called testimonial evidence. Affidavits and depositions are frequently included in testimonial evidence. 2. Testimonial evidence, as the term is used when discussing the *Miranda* warnings, means oral and written statements that a suspect makes in response to questions. It does not apply to handwriting and voice exemplars because others dictate what the suspect should say or write.

tolling statute of limitations The statute of limitations establishes a deadline for filing charges; for example, in many states misdemeanor charges must be filed within one year of the date the crime occurred. Some events "stop the clock" on the statute of limitations; this is referred to as tolling the statute of limitations. Many states toll the statute of limitations if a person leaves the state in order to avoid apprehension and/or arrest.

trier of the facts The role of the trier of the facts is to evaluate the evidence and decide which facts have been sufficiently proven. In a jury trial, the jurors are the triers of the facts. In a trial held without a jury, the judge is both the trier of the facts and the trier of the law.

trier of the law The role of the trier of the law is to decide what law applies to a given case. This includes giving the jury instructions on the definitions of the crimes(s) charged, ruling on objections made at trial (such as hearsay), and deciding whether *Miranda* and search and seizure rules were correctly followed by the police. In a trial, the trier of the law is the judge.

U

unduly suggestive   A lineup or photographic lineup is unduly suggestive if it points out one person as the suspected criminal. This could be caused by disparities in height, weight, race, age, or other factors. Comments and coaching by the police or other people viewing the identification procedure that indicate which person is believed to have committed the crime would also be unduly suggestive. Unduly suggestive lineups and photographic lineups violate due process.

V

valid on its face   A statute or warrant is valid on its face if it appears to be constitutional. Officers may act in reliance on these statutes and warrants until they learn that they are unconstitutional. If it can be determined by the wording that a warrant or statute is defective, police are not authorized to act pursuant to it at all.

voir dire   *Voir dire* is the process of asking questions in order to determine if someone is qualified. During *voir dire* of the jury the prospective jurors are asked questions in order to determine if they have formed opinions about the defendant's guilt and other relevant issues. Information obtained during *voir dire* is used by prosecution and defense attorneys when exercising challenges for cause and peremptory challenges.

W

weight of each piece of evidence   The trier of the facts determines the weight to be given to each piece of evidence. One of the key factors influencing this decision is the credibility of the witness(es) who testified about the item. The jurors (or judge, in a trial without a jury) can disregard evidence even if there is no other evidence presented on the issue if they believe the witness is not telling the truth. Based on their own common sense, jurors also decide how much weight to give each piece of evidence—one item might be conclusive, another so trivial that they disregard it.

INDEX

Note: Page numbers in italics identify an illustration. An italic *t* next to a page number (e.g., 177*t*) indicates information that appears in a table.